IN THE AGORA:
THE PUBLIC FACE OF CANADIAN PHILOSOPHY

Mark Kingwell, John Ralston Saul, Jan Zwicky, Thomas Hurka, Will Kymlicka, Graeme Hunter, Paul and Patricia Churchland, Michel Seymour, Arthur Schafer, Charles Taylor – the list of Canadian philosophers who have made important contributions to public debate is a long one. Here, in a single volume we find their views on topics ranging from free speech to free trade, from science to citizenship, from terrorism to tyranny, and from ethics to the environment.

In the Agora celebrates the unique perspectives, distinctive voices, and important contributions of Canadian philosophers, bringing them together to speak candidly on issues of popular public debate. Following a foreword by John Ralston Saul, editors Andrew D. Irvine and John S. Russell have carefully collected over a hundred essays into an accessible, controversial, and lively book that delves into a wide number of significant issues.

A spirited and engaging read, *In the Agora* effectively illustrates how Canadian philosophers have contributed to public discourse and enriched our world. It is a collection that is sure to prompt both interest and debate.

ANDREW D. IRVINE is a professor in the Department of Philosophy at the University of British Columbia.

JOHN S. RUSSELL is an instructor in the Department of Philosophy at Langara College.

Edited by Andrew D. Irvine and John S. Russell
with a Foreword by John Ralston Saul

In the Agora

The Public Face of
Canadian Philosophy

UNIVERSITY OF TORONTO PRESS
Toronto Buffalo London

© University of Toronto Press Incorporated 2006
Toronto Buffalo London
Printed in Canada

ISBN 0-8020-3895-6 (cloth)
ISBN 0-8020-3817-4 (paper)

∞

Printed on acid-free paper

Library and Archives Canada Cataloguing in Publication

In the agora : the public face of Canadian philosophy / edited with an
introduction by Andrew D. Irvine and John S. Russell.

Includes index.
ISBN 0-8020-3895-6 (bound)
ISBN 0-8020-3817-4 (pbk.)

1. Applied philosophy – Canada.   I. Irvine, A.D.   II. Russell, John, 1956–

AC5.I5 2006   191   C2005-907489-2

University of Toronto Press acknowledges the financial assistance to
its publishing program of the Canada Council for the Arts and the
Ontario Arts Council.

University of Toronto Press acknowledges the financial support for
its publishing activities of the Government of Canada through the
Book Publishing Industry Development Program (BPIDP).

Contents

IV The Contemporary World

V Authority and the Individual

IX National Unity

Foreword

There are two obsessions that negate the idea of philosophy. The first is having the answer. Being right. The second follows neatly. It involves believing in the primary importance of agreement.

It may just be possible to establish that something is absolutely wrong, but even that is a dubious intellectual position. It is also possible to believe that disagreement is the nature of a Manichean world. But that again mistakes a battle between truths for the messy reality of thought. Finally, it is possible to mistake the concept of thought and discussion for relativism – to conclude that in the absence of absolute answers there are no ethical signposts on the darkling plain.

This book is about thinking, not agreeing. And it is about thinking in public. I don't mean by that popularized ideas, as if more serious stuff was being dealt with at some inaccessible level. This book is filled with a wide sweep of thinkers who reject the idea of closed shops for intellectual specialists. They are all, in their own way, used to working in public.

This doesn't mean these thinkers only have public moments. As the editors point out, there are also "abstract and often technical issues, issues of interest only to the specialist." What history tells us is that these more obscure moments are the equivalent of technical matters in any profession. They are essential but they are not the essential nature of the subject. Only a nuclear scientist may understand the technique of building a nuclear bomb or a nuclear reactor. But the essential question is whether we want one or the other, in what form or circumstance we might want them, in what conditions we might use them.

What follows are discussions about the essential nature of our condition. They are naturally and unavoidably central to public thought and debate.

JOHN RALSTON SAUL

Acknowledgments

This collection would not have been possible were it not for the generosity of its many contributors. Not only have they added greatly to public debate in Canada over the years, it has been both a pleasure and a privilege to work with them on this project.

Although a few of the essays in this volume are available in other anthologies, almost all are being reprinted here for the first time. By bringing them together in a single volume, we hope readers will gain an appreciation for the breadth of writing done by Canadian philosophers. Most essays appear in their original form; others have been shortened or slightly revised especially for this collection; yet others are appearing here for the first time.

For their help in selecting, editing, and translating these essays, we are indebted to the following people: Vincent Bergeron, Steven Davis, Bryn Dharmaratne, David Gauthier, Joan Irvine, Katherine Irvine, Jenn Neilson, Joy Russell, Roger Seamon, Michel Seymour, and John Woods. We are also grateful to two anonymous referees whose detailed comments have improved the collection greatly.

Finally, we want to thank Len Husband, Frances Mundy, Matthew Kudelka, and the production staff at the University of Toronto Press, both for their encouragement and for expertly seeing this book through to publication. If readers obtain even half as much pleasure from reading this collection as we had in assembling it, clearly it will have achieved its goal.

Contributors

Paul Bartha received his BSc in mathematics from the University of Toronto and his PhD in philosophy from the University of Pittsburgh. He is an associate professor of philosophy at the University of British Columbia and an expert on issues in probability, decision theory, and modal logic.

Grant Brown received his DPhil in philosophy from Oxford University and his LLB from the University of Alberta. He currently practises law in Edmonton and has published extensively on affirmative action, bias in the legal system, and related issues.

James Robert Brown is a professor of philosophy at the University of Toronto. His most recent books include *Philosophy of Mathematics: An Introduction to the World of Proofs and Pictures*, published by Routledge, and *Who Rules in Science? An Opinionated Guide to the Wars*, published by Harvard University Press.

Alister Browne received his PhD in philosophy from the University of British Columbia. He is a clinical associate professor and ethics theme director in the Faculty of Medicine at the University of British Columbia.

Katharine Browne received her BA from the University of Toronto and her MA from the University of British Columbia. She is currently a doctoral student in philosophy at the University of Toronto, where she is researching topics relating to rationality and ethics.

Leslie Burkholder received his PhD in philosophy from MIT and teaches in the Department of Philosophy at the University of British Columbia. He is editor of *Philosophy and the Computer*, published by Westview Press.

Patricia Smith Churchland has degrees from the University of British Columbia and Oxford University and is the University of California President's Professor of Philosophy at the University of California, San Diego. Her books include *The Computational Brain* (together with Paul Churchland and T.J. Sejnowski), *On the Contrary* (with Paul Churchland), and *Neurophilosophy* and *Brain-Wise*, all published by MIT Press.

Paul M. Churchland has degrees from the University of British Columbia and the University of Pittsburgh and holds the Valtz Chair of Philosophy at the University of California, San Diego. His books include *Matter and Consciousness*, *A Neurocomputational Perspective*, *On the Contrary*, and *The Engine of Reason, The Seat of The Soul*, all published by MIT Press; *Images of Science*, published by the University of Chicago Press; and *Scientific Realism and the Plasticity of Mind*, published by Cambridge University Press.

Steven Davis is a professor of philosophy and director of the Centre on Values and Ethics at Carleton University in Ottawa. He is the author of *Philosophy and Language*, published by Bobbs-Merrill, and together with Philip Bryden and John Russell, co-editor of *Protecting Rights and Freedoms*, published by the University of Toronto Press. His latest book is an edited collection of essays with Brendon Gillon titled *Semantics: A Reader*, published by Oxford University Press.

Thomas De Koninck is a professor of philosophy at Laval University and has taught at Université de Bourgogne, the Institut d'Études Politiques in Paris, and the University of Notre Dame. A Rhodes Scholar, he is a member of the Order of Canada and the Royal Society of Canada as well as a past president of the Canadian Philosophical Association. His books include *De la dignité humaine*, which was awarded the La Bruyère prize by the French Academy in 1996, *La nouvelle ignorance et le problème de la culture*, and *Philosophie de l'éducation: Essai sur le devenir humain*, all published by Presses universitaires de France.

John Dixon received his PhD in philosophy from the University of British Columbia and his LLD (honoris causa) from Simon Fraser University. He currently teaches at Capilano College in North Vancouver. From 1991 to 1993 he served as senior advisor to Canada's Deputy Minister of Justice and then as special advisor to the Minister of National Defence. With Stan Persky, he is the co-author of *On Kiddie Porn: Sexual Representation, Free Speech and the Robin Sharpe Case*, the winner of a 2001 Donner Foundation Prize for Best Book on Canadian Public Policy. He is also the author of *Catastrophic Rights: Experimental Drugs and AIDS*. Both books were published by New Star Books.

Jeffrey Foss is a professor of Philosophy at the University of Victoria. He is the author of *Science and the Riddle of Consciousness: A Solution*, published by Kluwer Academic Publishers, and *Science and Philosophy: The Broad Spectrum of Issues*, forthcoming.

David Gauthier has degrees from the University of Toronto, Harvard University, and Oxford University. Before retirement, he taught philosophy at the University of Toronto and the University of Pittsburgh. He has been a fellow of the Royal Society of Canada since 1979. His books include *Moral Dealing: Contract, Ethics and Reason*, published by Cornell University Press, and *Practical Reasoning*, *The Logic of Leviathan*, and *Morals by Agreement*, all published by Oxford University Press.

Trudy Govier received her PhD in philosophy from the University of Waterloo and has taught philosophy at Trent University and the University of Winnipeg. Her books include *Forgiveness and Revenge*, published by Routledge, *A Delicate Balance: What Philosophy Can Tell Us about Terrorism*, published by Westview Press, and *A Practical Study of Argument*, published by Wadsworth. She is a member of the department of philosophy at the University of Lethbridge.

Leo Groarke received his PhD in philosophy from the University of Western Ontario and is dean of the Brantford Campus of Wilfrid Laurier University. He is the editor of *The Ethics of the New Economy*, published by Wilfrid Laurier University Press, and the author of *Greek Scepticism*, published by McGill-Queen's University Press. With Christopher Tindale, he is the co-author of *Good Reasoning Matters!* published by Oxford University Press.

Paul Groarke received his PhD in philosophy from the University of Waterloo and has taught in the department of criminology at St Thomas University. He is also a lawyer and a member of the Canadian Human Rights Tribunal. He is the author of *Dividing the State: Legitimacy, Secession and the Doctrine of Oppression*, published by Ashgate.

Ian Hacking holds the Chair of Philosophy and History of Scientific Concepts at the Collège de France and is University Professor of Philosophy Emeritus at the University of Toronto. He is also a Companion of the Order of Canada. His books include *The Emergence of Probability*, published by Cambridge University Press, *The Social Construction of What?* published by Harvard University Press, and *Rewriting the Soul*, published by Princeton University Press. His book *The Taming of Chance*, published by Cambridge University Press, was included in the Modern Library's 'List of the 100 Most Important Non-fiction Books Published in English during the Twentieth Century.'

William Hare teaches the philosophy of education at Mount Saint Vincent University where he is a professor of education. He obtained his PhD from the University of Toronto. His books include *In Defence of Open-Mindedness* and *Open-Mindedness and Education*, both published by McGill–Queen's University Press, and *What Makes a Good Teacher*, published by Althouse Press.

Graeme Hunter is a professor of philosophy at the University of Ottawa. He is co-editor of *The Leibniz Lexicon*, published by Georg Olms Verlag, editor of *Spinoza: The Enduring Questions*, published by University of Toronto Press, and author of *Radical Protestantism in Spinoza's Thought*, published by Ashgate.

Thomas Hurka is Chancellor Henry N.R. Jackman Distinguished Professor of Philosophical Studies at the University of Toronto. He is the author of *Virtue, Vice, and Value*, published by Oxford University Press, *Perfectionism*, also published by Oxford, and *Principles: Short Essays on Ethics*, published by Harcourt Brace.

Andrew Irvine received his PhD from Sydney University and is a professor of philosophy at the University of British Columbia. His books include *Argument*, written with John Woods and Douglas Walton and published by Prentice Hall Canada, and *Bertrand Russell: Critical*

Assessments, edited in four volumes and published by Routledge. He is a Canadian Commonwealth Fellow, a Killam Fellow, a past president of the B.C. Civil Liberties Association, and a member of the Board of Governors of the University of British Columbia.

Ray Jennings is a professor of philosophy and director of the Laboratory for Logic and Experimental Philosophy at Simon Fraser University. He obtained his PhD from the University of London and is the author of *The Genealogy of Disjunction*, published by Oxford University Press.

Mark Kingwell is a professor of philosophy at the University of Toronto and a contributing editor of *Harper's Magazine*. His books include *Better Living* and *The World We Want*, both published by Viking, *Dreams of Millennium*, published by Faber and Faber, *Practical Judgments*, published by University of Toronto Press, and *A Civil Tongue*, published by Pennsylvania State University Press, which won the Spitz Prize for political theory. Kingwell has also won the National Magazine Award for essay writing. His most recent book, a study of the Empire State Building, will appear with Yale University Press in 2006.

Eike-Henner W. Kluge is a professor of philosophy at the University of Victoria. He was the first expert witness in medical ethics recognized by Canadian courts and has served in that capacity in Alberta, British Columbia, and Ontario. He was the founding director of the Canadian Medical Association's Department of Ethics and Legal Affairs. His books include *The Metaphysics of Gottlob Frege*, published by Nijhoff, *The Practice of Death*, published by Yale University Press, *The Ethics of Deliberate Death*, published by Kennikat Press, *The Ethics of Electronic Patient Records*, published by Peter Lang, *A Handbook of Ethics for Health Informatics Professionals*, published by the British Computer Society and endorsed by the International Medical Informatics Association, and *Biomedical Ethics in a Canadian Context* and *Readings in Biomedical Ethics*, both published by Prentice Hall Canada.

Will Kymlicka received his DPhil in philosophy from Oxford University and is Canada Research Chair in Political Philosophy at Queen's University, Kingston. His books include *Contemporary Political Philosophy, Politics in the Vernacular, Finding Our Way, Multicultural Citizenship*, and *Liberalism, Community and Culture*, all published by Oxford University Press.

Peter Loptson received his PhD in philosophy from the University of Pittsburgh and is a professor of philosophy at the University of Guelph. His books include *Theories of Human Nature*, published by Broadview Press, *Philosophy, History, and Myth*, published by the University Press of America, and *Reality: Fundamental Topics in Metaphysics*, published by University of Toronto Press.

Lou Marinoff received his PhD in philosophy from University College, London. He is an associate professor and former Chair of Philosophy at The City College of New York, and founding president of the American Philosophical Practitioners Association (APPA). His books include *Plato Not Prozac: Applying Philosophy to Everyday Problems*, published by HarperCollins and translated in twenty-five languages, *Philosophical Practice*, published by the Academic Press, and *The Big Questions*, published by Bloomsbury.

Jan Narveson is Professor Emeritus in the Department of Philosophy at the University of Waterloo. His books include *Morality and Utility*, published by Johns Hopkins Press, *The Libertarian Idea* and *Moral Matters*, both published by Broadview Press, and *Political Correctness – For and Against, For and Against the State*, and *Respecting Persons in Theory and Practice*, all published by Rowman and Littlefield.

Stan Persky teaches philosophy at Capilano College in North Vancouver, British Columbia. He is the author of *Then We Take Berlin*, published by Knopf, and *Autobiography of a Tattoo*, published by New Star Books. He is also co-author (with John Dixon) of *On Kiddie Porn: Sexual Representation, Free Speech and the Robin Sharpe Case*, also published by New Star Books, which won a 2001 Donner Foundation Prize for Best Book on Canadian Public Policy.

John Russell received his PhD from Cornell University and teaches philosophy at Langara College in Vancouver. He is ethics advisor to the University of British Columbia Clinical Research Ethics Board and a past president of the B.C. Civil Liberties Association. He is editor of *Liberties*, published by New Star Books, and co-editor (with Philip Bryden and Steven Davis) of *Protecting Rights and Freedoms*, published by University of Toronto Press.

John Ralston Saul received his PhD from King's College, University of London, and is a Companion in the Order of Canada as well as a Chevalier in the Ordre des Arts et des Lettres de France. His books include *Voltaire's Bastards: The Dictatorship of Reason in the West*, *The Doubter's Companion: A Dictionary of Aggressive Common Sense*, his Massey Lectures, *The Unconscious Civilization*, which won the 1996 Governor General's Literary Award for Non-Fiction, and, most recently, *The Collapse of Globalism*. He is also the author of five novels and the only Canadian to receive the Pablo Neruda Medal, presented by the Chilean government to one hundred intellectuals and artists around the world to celebrate the hundredth anniversary of the birth of Pablo Neruda.

Arthur Schafer is a professor of philosophy and director of the Centre for Professional and Applied Ethics at the University of Manitoba. He is a Canadian Commonwealth Fellow, an Honorary Woodrow Wilson Scholar, a Canada Council Fellow, and the author of *The Buck Stops Here: Reflections on Moral Responsibility, Democratic Accountability and Military Values*, prepared for the Canadian Commission of Inquiry into the Deployment of Canadian Forces to Somalia.

Michel Seymour received his PhD in philosophy from the Université du Québec à Trois-Rivières and is a professor of philosophy at Université de Montréal. He is the author of *L'institution du langage*, published by Les Presses de l'Université de Montréal, *La nation en question* and *Le pari de la démesure: L'intransigeance du Canada face au Québec*, both published by l'Hexagone, and *Pensée, langage et communauté*, published by Bellarmin.

Susan Sherwin is University Research Professor of Philosophy at Dalhousie University and a Fellow in the Royal Society of Canada. She is the author of *The Politics of Women's Health*, written with the Feminist Health Care Ethics Research Network, and *No Longer Patient: Feminist Ethics and Health Care*, both published by Temple University Press. She is also co-editor of *Health Care Ethics in Canada*, published by Thomson Nelson.

Charles Taylor is Professor Emeritus at McGill University. His books include *The Malaise of Modernity*, based on his 1991 Massey Lectures and published by Anansi, *Multiculturalism and the Politics of Recognition*, published by Princeton University Press, *Reconciling the Solitudes: Essays on Canadian Federalism and Nationalism*, published by McGill-Queen's University Press, and *Philosophical Arguments*, published by Harvard University Press.

John Woods is Charles S. Peirce Professor of Logic at King's College, London, and director of the Abductive Systems Group at the University of British Columbia. His most recent books include *Paradox and Paraconsistency*, published by Cambridge University Press, and *Argument*, co-authored with Andrew Irvine and Douglas Walton and published by Prentice Hall Canada. He is a former president of Academy II within the Royal Society of Canada and a former President of the University of Lethbridge.

Jan Zwicky received her PhD from the University of Toronto and is an associate professor of philosophy at the University of Victoria. She is the author of *Lyric Philosophy*, published by University of Toronto Press, and *Wisdom and Metaphor*, published by Gaspereau Press. She has also published six collections of poetry, including *Songs for Relinquishing the Earth*, which won the Governor General's Literary Award for Poetry in 1999.

IN THE AGORA

Introduction: The Public Face of Canadian Philosophy

ANDREW IRVINE AND JOHN RUSSELL

Legend has it that in the morning the Greek philosopher Aristotle lectured to his students as they strolled together in his garden. Then, in the evening, he gave a second set of lectures specially designed for members of the general public. In the morning he spoke on topics of interest only to his students, but later in the day he threw open the gates to his school, the Lyceum, letting in anyone who wanted to enter. Topics of discussion included current politics, the importance of education, how to distinguish between plants and animals of various kinds, proposed changes to the law, how best to organize one's family, or the city-state, or the Olympics – anything and everything that was of interest to ordinary Athenians.

Thus were born the two faces of Western philosophy. On the one hand, philosophy concerns itself with abstract and often technical issues, issues of interest only to the specialist. On the other hand, philosophy also discusses a broad range of questions that are of interest to almost everyone.

For example, are there rules to tell us how we should live our lives? Or are all values subjective? Do we have an obligation to be as honest with strangers as we are with our friends? Or do different ethical standards apply in different circumstances? How should we raise our children? If abortion is permissible, why isn't infanticide? Are some sources of information more reliable than others? How can we be sure what the government tells us is true? Should we go to war? What does it mean to say we have a right to something? How much control should the government have over us? How much control should we have over the government?

Questions like these are of interest to even the most practical people.

They are also the kinds of questions that can be investigated carefully and systematically – or, as we might also say, philosophically. In fact, the very meaning of the word 'philosophy,' coming as it does from the two Greek words *philia* (meaning love) and *sophia* (meaning wisdom), tells us that anyone who is a 'lover of wisdom' is in some sense a philosopher. The same word also explains why philosophers are interested in almost every kind of knowledge.

Philosophers are also known for their habit of challenging intellectual complacency. Perhaps this is why they have regularly been at the forefront of social change throughout history. In fact, it is not much of an exaggeration to say that many of the guiding principles of Western culture have been philosophical inventions from start to finish: Aristotle's hypothesis that man is a rational animal, Aquinas' attempt to reconcile faith with reason, Locke's claim that no government can be legitimate unless it has the consent of the people it governs, Hume's arguments in favour of atheism, Smith's observation that self-interest works invisibly to provide benefits to everyone, Wollstonecraft's arguments in favour of the equality of women and men, Mill's arguments in favour of individual liberty – all have influenced our lives to such an extent that they often strike the contemporary reader as little more than common sense. Yet nothing could be further from the truth. Each of these authors gave voice to ideas that originally appeared revolutionary. Only over time did they begin to sweep the world.

A generation before Aristotle, another famous philosopher also spent much of his time debating in public, although with less happy results. While sitting in the agora, Athens' central marketplace, and while exercising in the gymnasium, Socrates engaged in conversation with anyone who would join him. Soon many of his ideas about knowledge and justice began to be discussed throughout the city. However, not everyone believed Socrates' influence was for the good. Not long after he turned seventy in 399 BCE, an Athenian jury sentenced him to death.

Exactly why Socrates was executed remains a matter of controversy even today. According to some accounts, he refused to honour the state gods. According to others, his constant arguing in public was corrupting the young. Some of Socrates' students may even have been involved in an attempt to overthrow the government. At his trial, Socrates treated the charges with good-natured contempt. The unfortunate result was that the jury sentenced him to death.

Whatever the actual reason for his execution, Socrates' story underscores the importance of philosophy, not just for the Greeks, but for all of us today. As Aristotle and Socrates both recognized, public discourse has the power to change society. Simply put, ideas matter. Public disagreement is thus not something to be avoided, difficult though it may be to embrace.

Philosophers understand this better than most. They are a constitutionally argumentative lot – and for good reason. Disagreements challenge us to develop carefully weighed conclusions about any number of issues. They challenge us to exercise judgment. This is no small task. Indeed, it takes heart and purpose, as well as skill at reasoning, as perhaps will be apparent in the pages that follow.

Canadian philosophers have long participated in public debate. Arthur Schafer, Mark Kingwell, Jan Zwicky, Graeme Hunter, John Ralston Saul, Thomas Hurka, Trudy Govier, Will Kymlicka, David Gauthier, Paul and Patricia Churchland, Charles Taylor, and others – in one way or another, all of these people have helped set this country's social and intellectual agendas. If not quite household names, they are all writers whose work is widely read by Canada's leading opinion makers and editorial-page writers.

Whether on free speech or free trade, terrorism or tyranny, the environment or national unity – all topics addressed in this book – Canadian philosophers have played an important role in establishing our country's political, cultural, and scientific priorities. In contrast to the narrow technician cloistered within the academy, these people understand that it is part of their duty to speak out on the major issues of their day and to participate in public discourse on a wide variety of topics.

Sitting outside the cobbler's shop in the centre of the Athenian agora, Socrates showed his fellow Athenians how reasoned argument might influence their daily lives. He also showed them what a demanding and necessary – and at times frustrating – task this could be. It was because of this that the Roman senator, Cicero, said that Socrates 'brought philosophy from heaven down to earth.'

Cicero's metaphor remains a welcome one today. For whether it is Aristotle lecturing in his garden, Socrates engaging passersby in the agora, or Mark Kingwell or John Dixon or John Ralston Saul commenting on the nightly ·news, philosophers have had a long tradition of participating in public debate. We hope this book will serve as a record of their continued contribution to matters that affect us all.

PART I

Science and the Environment

1 Expanding Our Perspective

PAUL M. CHURCHLAND

The weight of today's evidence indicates that conscious intelligence is a wholly natural phenomenon. According to a broad and growing consensus among philosophers and scientists, conscious intelligence is the activity of suitably organized matter, and the sophisticated organization responsible for it is, on this planet at least, the outcome of billions of years of chemical, biological, and neurophysiological evolution.

If intelligence develops naturally, as the universe unfolds, then might it not have developed, or be developing, at many places throughout the universe? The answer is clearly yes, unless the planet Earth is utterly unique in possessing the required physical constitution, or the required energetic circumstances. Is it unique in the relevant respects? Let us examine the evolutionary process, as we now understand it, and see what the process requires.

Basically, it requires a system of physical elements (such as atoms) capable of many different combinations, and a flow of energy (such as sunlight) through the system of elements. This describes the situation on the prebiological earth, some four billion years ago, during the period of purely chemical evolution. The flow or flux of energy, into the system and then out again, is absolutely crucial. In a system *closed* to the entry and exit of external energy, the energy-rich combinations will gradually break up and distribute their energy among the energy-poor elements until the level of energy is everywhere the same throughout the system – this is the *equilibrium* state. Like water, one might say, energy seeks its own level; it tends to flow 'downhill' until the level is everywhere the same.

'If intelligence develops naturally, as the universe unfolds, then might it not have developed, or be developing, at many places throughout the universe?'

This humble analogy expresses the essential content of a fundamental physical law called the Second Law of Thermodynamics. In a closed system not already in equilibrium, any energy exchanges tend ruthlessly to move the system toward equilibrium. And once a system has reached this lowest or equilibrium state, it tends to remain there forever – a uniform, undifferentiated murk. The formation of complex, interesting, and energy-rich structures is then profoundly unlikely, since that would require that some of the system's internal energy flow back 'uphill' again. It would require that a significant energy *im*balance spontaneously appear within the system. And this is what the Second Law effectively prohibits. Evidently, the evolution of complex structures is not to be found in a closed system.

If a system is open to a continuous flux of energy, however, then the situation is completely transformed. For a schematic illustration, consider a glass box, full of water, with a constant heat source (a fire, say) at one end, and a constant heat sink (something to absorb heat energy) at the other. Dissolved in the water is some nitrogen and some carbon dioxide. One end of the box will grow quite hot, but as fast as the fire pours energy into this end of the system, it is conducted away towards the cooler end and out again. The average temperature inside the box is therefore a constant.

Consider the effect this will have on the thin soup inside the box. At the hot end of the box, the high-energy end, the molecules and atoms absorb this extra energy and are raised to excited states. As they drift around the system, these energized parts are free to form high-energy chemical bonds with one another, bonds that would have been statistically impossible with the system in global equilibrium. A variety of complex chemical compounds is therefore likely to form and to collect towards the cool end of the system, compounds of greater variety and greater complexity than could have been formed without the continuous flux of heat energy. Collectively, carbon, hydrogen, oxygen, and nitrogen are capable of literally millions of different chemical combinations. With the heat flux turned on, this partially open or *semiclosed* system starts vigorously to explore these combinatorial possibilities.

It is easy to see that a kind of competition is then taking place inside the box. Some types of molecules are not very stable, and will tend to fall apart soon after formation. Other types will be made of sterner stuff, and will tend to hang around for a while. Other types, though very unstable, may be formed very frequently, and so there will be quite a few of them in the system at any given time. Some types catalyse the formation of their own building blocks, thus enhancing further formation. Other types engage in mutually beneficial catalytic cycles, and form a symbiotic pair of prosperous types. In these ways, and others, the various types of molecules *compete* for dominance of the liquid environment. Those types with high stability and/or high formation rates will form the largest populations.

The typical result of such a process is that the system soon displays a great many instances of a fairly small variety of distinct types of complex, energy-storing molecules. (Which types, from the millions of types possible, actually come to dominate the system is dependent on, and highly sensitive to, the initial make-up of the soup, and to the flux level.) The system displays an order, and a complexity, and an unbalanced energy distribution that would be unthinkable without the flux of energy through the system. The flux pumps the system. It forces the system away from its initial chaos, and toward the many forms of order and complexity of which it is capable. What was improbable has become inevitable.

The preceding experiment is schematic, concocted to illustrate a general principle, but instances of it have actually been performed. In a now famous experiment, Urey and Miller, in 1953, re-created the earth's prebiotic atmosphere (hydrogen, methane, ammonia, and water) and subjected a flask full of it to a steady electrical discharge. After several days of this energy flux, examination of the flask's contents showed that many complex organic compounds had formed, including a number of different amino acids, the units from which protein molecules are constructed. Other versions of the experiment tried different energy sources (ultraviolet light, heat, shock waves), and all displayed the same pattern: an energy flux induces order and complexification within a semiclosed system.

Nature has also performed this experiment – with the entire earth, and with billions of other planets. For the earth as a whole is also a semiclosed system, with the sun as the energy source, and the black void surrounding us as the low-temperature energy sink. Solar energy has been flowing through this gigantic system for well over four thousand million years, patiently exploring the endless possibilities for order, structure, and complexity inherent in the matter it contains. Small wonder it has outperformed the artificial systems described.

From this perspective it is apparent that any planet will support a rich evolutionary process, if it possesses a rich variety of elements in some liquid solution, and enjoys a suitable energy flux from a nearby star. Roughly how many planets, in our own Milky Way galaxy, meet these conditions?

There are roughly 100 billion, or 10^{11}, stars in our galaxy. How many of them possess planets? Theories of stellar formation, spectrographic studies of stellar rotation, and telescopic studies of the dynamic effects of dark companions agree in indicating that effectively all stars except the super-hot giants possess a planetary system of some kind. The super-hot giants are but a small percentage of the stellar population, so their deletion still leaves us close to 10^{11} planetary systems in the galaxy.

How many of these will contain a planet suitably constituted and suitably placed? Suitable constitution suggests that we should consider only second-generation systems, formed from the debris of earlier stellar explosions, since these are the main source of the elements beyond hydrogen and helium. This leaves us rather less than half the available systems, so we are down to about 10^{10}. In these remaining systems, planets with an acceptable constitution promise to be fairly common. In our system alone, Earth, Mars, and two of Jupiter's moons show significant water, if we demand water as our evolutionary solvent. Jupiter's moons have an extra significance, since giant Jupiter and its twelve-plus satellites almost constitute a miniature solar system in their own right, the only other example available for close study. Interestingly, Jupiter's second and third satellites, Europa and Ganymede, each contain about as much water as the entire Earth: though smaller in area, their oceans are very much deeper than ours. If we may generalize from these two systems, then, water planets will be found across a wide range of stellar systems, and some systems will boast two or more.

Nor do water planets exhaust the possibilities. Liquid ammonia and liquid methane are common solvents also, and they are entirely capable of sustaining evolutionary processes. Such oceans occur on much colder planets, and would sustain the exploration of chemical bonds of much lower energy than characterize the biochemistry of Earth. Those bracing environments constitute an alternative evolutionary niche. Altogether, suitable constitution seems not to be a problem. So let us stick with an estimate of at least 10^{10} planets suitably constituted for significant chemical evolution.

How many of these will be suitably placed, relative to the energy-supplying star? A planet's orbit must be within its star's 'life zone' – far enough from the star to avoid boiling its solvent away, yet close enough to keep it from freezing solid. For water that zone is fairly wide, and there is a better than even chance that some planetary orbit will fall inside it. We need a *water* planet inside it, however, and these are perhaps only one in every ten planets. Let us estimate, conservatively, that only one in a hundred of our remaining systems contains a suitably placed water planet. Suitably placed ammonia and methane planets are also to be expected, but the same considerations yield a similar estimate for them, so we are left with an estimate of roughly 10^8 planets that are both suitably placed and suitably constituted.

This estimate assumes a star like our sun. But while the sun is already a smallish and undistinguished star, most stars are smaller still, and cooler, and will thus have smaller life zones. This could reduce the chances of suitable placement by another one or two factors of ten. Even so, sun-sized stars make up roughly 10 per cent of the relevant population, and their consideration alone would leave us with at least 10^7 blue-ribbon planets.

Our conservative estimate, therefore, is that the evolutionary process is chugging briskly away, at some stage or other, on at least ten million planets within this galaxy alone.

What is significant about this number is that it is large. The kind of process that produced us is apparently common throughout the universe. This conclusion is exciting, but the real question here remains unanswered: In how many of these cases has the evolutionary process articulated matter to the level of actual *life*, and in how many of these has it produced *conscious intelligence*?

These fractions are impossible to estimate with any confidence, since that would require an understanding of the *rates* at which evolutionary development takes place, and of the alternative paths it can pursue. So far, we have insufficient grasp of evolution's volatile dynamics to unravel these matters. We are reduced to exploring relevant considerations, but these can still be informative. Let us start with the common conception, hinted at in the preceding paragraph, that evolution has two large and discontinuous gaps to bridge: the gap between non-life and life, and the gap between unconsciousness and consciousness. Both of these distinctions, so entrenched in common sense, embody a degree of misconception. In fact, neither distinction corresponds to any well-defined or unbridgeable discontinuity in nature.

Consider the notion of life. If we take the capacity for self-replication as its essential feature, then its emergence need represent no discontinuity. Molecules that catalyse the formation of their own building blocks represent a lower position on the same spectrum. One need only imagine a series of progressively more efficient and fast-acting molecules of this kind, and we can culminate smoothly in a molecule that catalyses its building blocks in a sequence so they may hook up as fast as they are produced – a self-replicating molecule. There is no discontinuity here, no gulf to be bridged. The *environment* may display discontinuities, as the efficiency of a certain replicator passes a critical point relative to its competition, but this is a discontinuity in the consequences of self-replication, not in the mechanisms that produce it.

On the other hand, mere self-replication may be too simple a conception of life. There are some grounds for rejecting it. We can imagine some very simple molecules that, in a suitably artificial and contrived chemical environment, would replicate themselves. But this alone need not tempt us to count them as alive. In any case, there is a more penetrating characterization of life at hand, which we can illustrate with the cell – the smallest unit of life, according to some accounts. A cell is itself a tiny, semiclosed, self-organizing system, within the larger semiclosed system of the earth's biosphere. The energy flowing through a cell serves to maintain, and to increase, the order internal to the cell. In most cells the energy flux is chemical – they ingest energy-rich molecules and pirate the energy they release – but cells capable of photosynthesis make direct use of the solar flux to pump their metabolic processes. All of this suggests that we define a living thing as any semiclosed physical system that exploits the order it already possesses, and the energy flux through it, in such a way as to maintain and/or increase its internal order.

This characterization does capture something deeply important about the things we commonly count as alive, and it embraces comfortably the multicelled organisms, for a plant or animal is also a semiclosed system composed of tiny semiclosed systems: a vast conspiracy of cells rather than (just) a vast conspiracy of molecules. Even so, the definition has some mildly surprising consequences. If we accept it, a beehive counts as a living thing. So does a termite colony. And so does a human city. In fact, the entire biosphere counts as a living thing. For all of these things meet the definition proposed.

At the other end of the spectrum – and this returns us to the discontinuity issue – some very simple systems can lay claim to life. Consider the glowing teardrop of a candle flame. This too is a semiclosed system, and though its internal order is small and its self-maintenance feeble, it may just barely meet the conditions of the definition proposed. Other borderline systems will present similar problems. Should we reject the definition, then? No. The wiser lesson is that living systems are distinguished from non-living systems only by degrees. There is no metaphysical gap to be bridged: only a smooth slope to be scaled, a slope measured in degrees of order and in degrees of self-regulation.

The same lesson emerges when we consider conscious intelligence.

Consciousness and intelligence come in different grades, spread over a broad spectrum. Certainly intelligence is not unique to humans: millions of other species display it in some degree. If we define intelligence, crudely, as the possession of a complex set of appropriate responses to the changing environment, then even the humble potato displays a certain low cunning. No metaphysical discontinuities emerge here.

But that definition is too crude. It leaves out the developmental or creative aspect of intelligence. Consider then the following, more penetrating definition. A system has intelligence just in case it exploits the *information* it already contains, and the energy flux through it (this includes the energy flux through its sense organs), in such a way as to *increase* the information it contains. Such a system can *learn*, and that seems to be the central element of intelligence.

This improved characterization does capture something deeply important about the things we commonly count as intelligent. And I hope the reader is already struck by the close parallels between this definition of intelligence, and our earlier definition of life as the exploitation of contained order, and energy flux, to get more order. These parallels are important for the following reason. If the possession of information can be understood as the possession of some internal physical order that bears some systematic relation to the environment, then the operations of intelligence, abstractly conceived, turn out to be just a high-grade version of the operations characteristic of life, save that they are even more intricately coupled to the environment.

This hypothesis is consistent with the brain's use of energy. The production of large amounts of specific kinds of order requires a very substantial energy flux. And while the brain constitutes only 2 per cent of the body's mass, it consumes, when highly active, over 20 per cent of the resting body's energy budget. The brain too is a semiclosed system, a curiously high-intensity one, whose ever-changing microscopic order reflects the world in impressive detail. Here again, intelligence represents no discontinuity. Intelligent life is just life, with a high thermodynamic intensity and an especially close coupling between internal order and external circumstance.

What all this means is that, given energy enough, and time, the phenomena of both life *and* intelligence are to be expected as among the natural products of planetary evolution. Energy enough, and planets, there are. Has there been time? On Earth, there has been time enough, but what of the other 10^7 candidates? Our uncertainty here is very great.

A priori, the probability is vanishingly *small* that we are the very first planet to develop intelligent life: no better than one chance in 10^7. And the probability shrinks further when we consider that stars had already been pumping planets with energy for at least ten billion years when our solar system first condensed into being, some four-and-a-half billion years ago. If anything, we entered the evolutionary race with a long handicap. On the other hand, evolutionary rates may be highly volatile, varying by orders of magnitude as a function of subtle planetary variables. That would render our time handicap insignificant, and we might yet be the first planet in our galaxy to develop intelligence.

No decision made here can command confidence, but a forced decision, made under the preceding uncertain assumptions, would have to guess that something on the order of half of the relevant candidates are behind us, and half are ahead. This 'best guess' entails that something like 10^6 planets in this galaxy alone have *already* produced highly intelligent life.

Does this mean that we should expect little green men in flying saucers to frequent our atmosphere? It does not. Not even if we accept the 'best guess.' The reasons are important, and there are three of them. The first reason is the spatial scattering of the 10^6 planets. Our galaxy has a volume of over 10^{14} cubic light years (that is, the distance covered in a year's time when moving at the speed of light – 186,000 miles per second × 1 year, which is nearly six trillion miles), and 10^6 planets scattered throughout this volume will have an average distance between them of over five hundred light years. That is a most inconvenient distance for casual visits.

The second and perhaps more important reason is temporal scatter. We cannot assume that all of these 10^6 planets will develop intelligent life simultaneously. Nor can we be certain that, once developed, intelligent life lasts for very long. Accidents happen, degeneration sets in, self-destruction occurs. Suppose, for illustration, that the average lifetime of intelligence on any planet is 100 million years (this is the interval between the appearance of the early mammals and the nuclear holocaust that might destroy us within the century). If these intelligent stretches are scattered uniformly in time, then any planet with intelligence is likely to have only 10^4 concurrently intelligent planets for company, with an average distance between them of 2,500 light years. Moreover, nothing guarantees that those other cradles of intelligence concurrently boast anything more intelligent than field mice, or sheep. Our own planet has surpassed that level only recently. And highly intelligent, high-technology civilizations may last on average only 1,000 years, by reason of some inherent instabilities. In that case they will almost always be utterly and tragically alone in the galaxy. The case for highly intelligent company is starting to look rather thin.

And so it is, if we assign suicidal tendencies to all potential company. If we do not, then we may return to a more optimistic estimate of current company. If we assume an average duration for intelligent life of between one and five billion years, then temporal scatter will still leave us with 10^5 planets concurrently abreast or ahead of us in evolutionary development. This may seem finally to hold promise for some little green men and some edifying communication, if only by radio telescope. But it does not, for the third and most important reason of all: the potentially endless variation in the different *forms* that life and intelligence can take.

Our biosphere has been articulated into individual units of independent life: cells and multicelled organisms. None of this is strictly necessary. Some biospheres may have evolved into a single, unified, massively complex and highly intelligent 'cell' that girdles the entire planet. Others may have synthesized their cells, or multicelled elements, into a similarly unified singular planetary individual. For one of us to try to communicate with such an entity might be like a single bacterial cell in the local swamp attempting to communicate with a human by emitting a few chemicals. The larger entity is simply not 'interested.'

Even with more familiar creatures, a different environment can demand different sense organs, and different sense organs can mean very different brains. (Generally speaking, brains must evolve from the sensory periphery inward, developing in ways that serve the modalities available.) Creatures that navigate by felt electric fields, hunt by direction finders in the far infrared, guide close manipulation by stereoaudition in the 50-kilohertz range, and communicate by fugues of aromatic hydrocarbons are unlikely to think in the same grooves as a human.

Strange sense organs aside, the particular cluster of cognitive talents found in us need not characterize an alien species. For example, it is possible to be highly intelligent and yet lack all capacity for manipulating numbers, even the ability to count past five. It is equally possible to be highly intelligent and yet lack any capacity for understanding or manipulating language. Such isolated deficits occasionally occur in humans of otherwise exemplary mental talents. The first is a rare but familiar syndrome called *acalculia*. The second, more common affliction is called *global aphasia*. We must not expect, therefore, that a highly intelligent alien species must inevitably know the laws of arithmetic, or be able to learn a system like language, or have any inkling that these things even exist. These reflections suggest further that there may be fundamental cognitive abilities of whose existence *we* are totally unaware!

Finally, we must not expect that the goals or concerns of an alien intelligent species will resemble our own, or even be intelligible to us. The consuming aim of an entire species might be to finish composing the indefinitely long magnetic symphony begun by their prehistoric ancestors, a symphony where the young are socialized by learning to sing its earlier movements. A different species might have a singular devotion to the pursuit of higher mathematics, and their activities might make as much sense to us as the activities of a university mathematics department would make to a Neanderthal. Equally important, racial goals themselves undergo evolutionary change, either genetic or cultural. The dominant goals of our own species, five thousand years hence, may bear no relation to our current concerns. All of which means that we cannot expect an intelligent alien species to share the enthusiasms and concerns that characterize our own fleeting culture.

The point of the preceding discussion has been to put questions about the nature of intelligence into a broader perspective than they usually enjoy, and to emphasize the extremely general or abstract nature of this natural phenomenon. Current human intelligence is but one variation on a highly general theme. Even if, as does seem likely, intelligence is fairly widespread within our galaxy, we can infer almost nothing about what those other intelligent species must be doing, or about what form their intelligence takes. If the theoretical definition of intelligence given earlier is correct, then we may infer that they must be using *energy* (perhaps in copious quantities) and creating *order*, and that at least some of the order created has something to do with sustaining fruitful interactions with their environment. Beyond that, everything is possible. For us, as well as for them.

2 Is It Time for a New Space Race?

ANDREW IRVINE

The summer of 2004 marked the thirty-fifth anniversary of Neil Armstrong's first steps on the surface of the moon. After blasting off from Cape Canaveral on 16 July 1969, the Apollo 11 lunar module set down in the Sea of Tranquility four days later to the cheering of scientists and schoolchildren alike.

As anyone who lived through that moon landing knows, it was a magical time, full of amazement and promise. If we could reach the moon, we told one another, we could achieve anything. And we were right.

But looking back over the past several decades, we have to ask ourselves why we have never gone back. Why have we never again ventured beyond the edge of the earth's tiny envelope? Between 1969 and 1972 twelve men walked on the surface of the moon. Since then we have been content to do little more than tinker at the edge of space. Where have all our big dreams gone?

Reaching Mars is the obvious next step. Unlike the moon, Mars is rich in the elements necessary for life. Our nearest planetary neighbour is capable of hosting a self-sustaining human and robot colony in a way that the moon is not. But to establish even a robot colony will require an initial human presence. As with so many opportunities, placing a man or woman on the surface of Mars is just a matter of time.

The only question is this: Will it be our generation that takes this step? Or will we be content to leave this challenge to our children or grandchildren? Will we be remembered as the generation that had the vision and ability to walk and work on the surface of the Red Planet? Or will this be left to someone else?

Just as importantly, when we go to Mars will it be, as everyone assumes, under an American flag? Or is there any reason why the history books should not record that it was a Canadian who first set foot on the surface of the only other habitable planet in our solar system?

This idea is not as far-fetched as it might seem, and it is an opportunity that does not come along very often. Canadians today are closer to being prepared to land on Mars than the Americans were in 1961 when President John F. Kennedy gave his famous speech declaring America's intention to land a man on the surface of the moon and return him safely to earth. At that time, the Americans certainly were not leading the space race. All the technological and scientific advantages were with the Soviets. Had the British or the French or the Germans made the political decision to reach the moon first, they might have succeeded, and the history of the late twentieth century could have turned out quite differently.

Today it is clear that the Americans are better prepared to reach Mars than we are. But without the political will, any advantages in hardware mean nothing. The desire to be there first is just as essential as rocket fuel and computer software. Without it, the Americans may never even leave the ground.

This is not to minimize the challenges of such a mission. It will be a long trip. But such a trip would be no longer than many of the sea voyages that were made to explore the New World during the sixteenth and seventeenth centuries. Of course it will be risky but, again, far less risky than it was for many of those same explorers who sailed the surface of the earth with little more than an astrolabe and a compass.

'When we go to Mars will it be, as everyone assumes, under an American flag? Or is there any reason why the history books should not record that it was a Canadian who first set foot on the surface of the only other habitable planet in our solar system?'

And it will be expensive. But once again, the cost of such a mission is not beyond reach. The price tag for the ill-fated Apollo 13 moon mission was not much more than the cost of the Hollywood movie of the same name. Today, the cost of an average shuttle mission is less than that of many other major government initiatives.

And this takes us to the real point. If money is a measure of our priorities, why should we prefer to spend our tax dollars subsidizing our failing fisheries rather than supporting our young scientists? If we are willing to pay $10 to see *Star Wars* and its innumerable sequels and prequels two or three times a year for a decade, why wouldn't we be willing to pay the same amount to see the real thing?

For whichever nation reaches Mars first, the scientific and technological returns will be immense. Even more important will be the reawakening of the promise and imagination that were present during the Apollo years. This goal is less tangible, but equally real. And it is clearly something to strive for.

Although everyone remembers Neil Armstrong's name, few people remember the name of the second man to walk on the surface of the moon, lunar module pilot Edwin 'Buzz' Aldrin. Even fewer people remember the name of the command-module pilot, Michael Collins, who stayed in orbit around the moon while Armstrong and Aldrin explored its dusty surface.

Being first counts for a lot. And landing the first robot on the surface of Mars doesn't count. Today almost no one remembers that it was the Soviets, and not the Americans, who were first to land an unmanned spacecraft successfully on the surface of the moon. But compared to Neil Armstrong's footprint, the Soviet effort is a pale second best.

The first human step on the surface of Mars will be made only once. Why shouldn't it be a Canadian?

3 Should We Implant Life on Mars?

THOMAS HURKA

Sometimes to understand where you are, you have to go a long way away and look back. So it is in ethics: it can help us decide what's moral here and now to think about remote possibilities. That's one reason to ask: Should we implant life on Mars?

This question has been posed by NASA scientist C.P. McKay and York University biologist Robert Haynes. Mars can't support life now – it's far too cold – but it was warmer before and could be made warmer again by planetary engineering. This might involve reducing the reflectivity of the polar ice caps on Mars and injecting small amounts of greenhouse gases into the Martian atmosphere.

'In dealing with the environment we have to use our own values, that is, our own ideas about what is good. These values need not be human centred. They can agree with 'deep ecology' that there is intrinsic worth in ecosystems and other non-human aspects of the environment. But they must be our values, and they can sometimes justify acting against natural forces.'

If life existed on Mars before, warming the planet might unfreeze this life. If not, we could implant micro-organisms selected (or genetically engineered) to fit the new Martian environment. It might take two hundred years to implant a microbial ecosystem, which could then be left to evolve on its own.

If this becomes possible, should we do it? (It would be enormously expensive, but ignore that.) The question pulls apart two ideas that are run together in contemporary thinking about the environment.

One idea is that humans should respect nature as it is, not interfering with natural processes or trying to impose our values on them. The other is that we should value nature for its vitality, richness, and delicate balancing of life forms.

These ideas lead to the same conclusions about many contemporary environmental issues, for example, about preserving the tropical rainforest. There nature as it is, is vital and diverse; nature as it would be after human intervention is barren and shorn of unique species.

But the ideas come apart when we think of implanting life on Mars. The first idea says this would be wrong, a violation of Mars's integrity as a dead planet. The second says that if diversity is good on earth, it is good everywhere; we should enliven Mars, not for our sake, but to give it a more valuable environment.

The first idea isn't philosophically defensible. Just because something exists doesn't by itself show that it's right or good. (This is the fallacy in all moral arguments about what's 'natural' or 'unnatural.') Nor is there any reason to believe that natural processes always produce what is, by independent criteria, best. This must often happen; the very flourishing of life shows that. But there are exceptions.

In the very long run, the sun will heat up and destroy all life on earth. If Harvard paleontologist Stephen Jay Gould is right, the trend of evolution has been to reduce genetic diversity: there are fewer kinds of life now than 550 million years ago. At particular times, floods or ice ages can destroy ecosystems; if we could prevent this by technology, we'd be right to do so.

Yet the first idea lingers in environmental thinking. Many people who cite the preservation of species as one reason to halt deforestation or global warming would oppose genetic engineering to create new species. But if genetic diversity is worth preserving, isn't it also worth increasing? (Since artificial life could be dangerous, we'd need to be cautious. But natural mutations can also be dangerous.)

Or think about global warming. Though its overall environmental effect would be bad, some regions would benefit. The Arctic, for example, would be able to support more varieties of plant and animal life, as it did years ago. Yet how many environmentalists regret that if we avoid warming, this won't happen?

In dealing with the environment we have to use our own values, that is, our own ideas about what is good. These values need not be human centred. They can agree with 'deep ecology' that there is intrinsic worth in ecosystems and other non-human aspects of the environment. But they must be our values, and they can sometimes justify acting against natural forces.

This creates an exciting prospect for the future. If we can ever solve our problems on earth we can turn our attention beyond it, spreading what's environmentally valuable on our planet to places that would otherwise be barren. We can implant life on Mars and then on other bodies throughout the universe.

4 Wilderness and Agriculture

JAN ZWICKY

When the wildlife control officer from the county came, he confirmed we had a problem: 'They'll take every tree within two hundred yards either side.' He was eager to set the dynamite and watch the dams go up but, having grown up hunting north of the Sault, he didn't like the part of his job that required him to kill the beavers: 'Don't shoot what you can't eat.' But there was no point blowing the dams, he said, if you didn't kill the beavers, too – they'd just rebuild, usually overnight. He told me, trying to reassure me I think, that they weren't particularly 'nice' critters: he'd seen them use traps, with the bodies of their dead kin still inside, to repair dynamited dams. Thinking about it later that evening, I couldn't decide if that made them sinners, or saints.

There was no question I could get the county to do the work. Our fords had been destroyed, the banks were being seriously destabilized, we were losing fences and, arguably, the whole horse pasture might eventually be cut off – all of which meant your tax dollars could be spent on our farm, to control beavers in the name of 'conservation.' And while it was nice to be invited to think of myself as a responsible eco-citizen making hard choices for the greater environmental good, it was pretty clear that accepting that invitation was just a way of simplifying and obscuring the real issues.

In the first place, there was my hopeless prejudice in favour of the trees: trees are so beautiful. Think of what they do with light and wind, think of their patience, their vulnerability. And these particular trees – mostly poplars – their slimness and whiteness, the exquisite lisp of the aspens, the perfume of the balsams in late spring. Their presence along the riverbank, and the colonies in the east pasture and on Baldy (the oxymoronically named hummock in our south field), defined the visual presence of the farm. They constituted its margins, which, as Wendell Berry has observed, are not only ecologically important, but essential to a certain sort of rhythmic pleasure humans take in landscape. (This is not to say landscape without obvious margins can't give us aesthetic pleasure, but that it gives us pleasure of a different, or sometimes more subtle, sort.) Anyway, there was no question that without the trees our farm would not be as easy on the eye. Nor would it look 'the way it had always looked' – that is, exist visually as a symbol of historical permanence, of my present's continuity with my past.

So it was very convenient for me that the course of 'conservation' turned out to be the path of least resistance. I could tell I wanted to be beguiled – but precisely because I could tell that, it wasn't happening. So what was wrong with wanting to save trees? Why was the coincidence of private desire and public policy making me uneasy?

Once I'd put the question in those terms, the answer seemed pretty obvious: both were serving the interests of a certain *way* of appreciating nature, a way that was arguably opposed to the interests of nature itself. Or to put it another way: the trees stood at the interface between wilderness and agriculture – me on one side, the beavers on the other – and my unease stemmed neither from private scruple nor ecological complexity, but simply from the fraught, puzzling nature of that interface itself. Western Europeans and their postcolonial descendents have, in the last hundred years, discovered that it won't work to proceed as if agriculture had *no* relation to wilderness; but we still have very little idea what that relation should be.

One of my friends once remarked, as though it constituted a reductio ad absurdum of environmentalists' views, 'Why, they're even against agriculture!' Er, but – when you stop to think about it, what's so crazy about that? The suggestion that humans require agriculture – or at least the current North American version of it – to survive as a species is patently false; while the suggestion that it has been responsible for massive environmental damage both on this continent and elsewhere is indisputably true. 'Well,' my sceptical friend might continue, 'that's not a problem with *agriculture*, it's a problem with the way it's practised, with its scale.' But this begs the question of what other scale it might be practised on. European, colonial, and postcolonial agriculture are not phenomena independent of patterns of settlement and exchange, economies and trade, population densities and, nowadays, corporate profit. To change the style and scale of agriculture would be to change culture itself. What my friend wants is what we've got, with maybe the odd design modification. What environmentalists have seen is that that desire is not sustainable in the long run. In a way, my friend is right, it *is* the scale, not the fact of some human culturing relation to land, that's the problem; but to change the scale significantly would be to change everything else about the way we live.

What is wilderness? Typically, we think of it as 'unsullied' nature, nature in her 'natural' state. But push on this a little and two further assumptions emerge: that there are (or have been) portions of the earth completely unaffected by human activity; and that human activity is, by definition, 'unnatural.' I'm not so sure about either of these claims. I agree that a great deal of what my own culture does and advocates in relation to non-humans is wrong, unhealthy, and disruptive of relatively stable cycles of growth and decline. I agree that its practices themselves fail to exhibit the complexity, rhythm, and balance that are hallmarks of 'natural' processes. But none of this has to do with what is essentially *human*: it has to do with a particular ideological inheritance.

And, although I agree with Bill McKibben that because of my culture's insensitivity we are now, globally, confronting 'the end of nature' – PCBs concentrating in the Arctic, the plastic loops from six-packs washing up on remote atolls in the South Pacific – I don't see how the ecological truths underlying its demise weren't ever thus. What members of my culture are coming to realize is that the planet constitutes an astonishingly complex whole, composed of many disparate but interacting subsystems, themselves composed of smaller subsystems. But this fact has not been *created* by environmental crisis: it is something that environmental crisis merely makes more visible. As long as there have been humans on the earth, their activities, like those of all other beings, have in more

'I want to argue that wilderness depends, not on the absence of human interaction with the land, but rather on its quantity and style. Wilderness exists, I'll suggest, in greater or lesser degrees wherever we allow communities of non-humans to shape us at least as much as or more than we shape them.'

and less subtle ways affected the smaller and larger ecologies in which they have occurred. Because PCBs are poisonous, and especially because my culture has produced a lot of them, we are now *aware* of 'human presence' where we were not aware of it before. But the atmosphere has always dispersed, carried, and concentrated various human by-products. If human activity is 'unnatural,' and therefore defiling of the wild, there hasn't been any true wilderness for at least 200,000 years.

'Wait a minute,' someone might say, 'you're missing the point. Nobody's going to deny humans have always been mixed up in their environment. But there's something different in kind about the abominations introduced by twentieth-century European warfare and industrial capitalism. Of course "wilderness" doesn't mean "no campfires" – but it does mean "no strontium 90."' Does it, though? Is it the bare presence or absence of certain substances – however minuscule their quantities, and however produced – that determines the presence or absence of wilderness? (Suppose lightning, striking some dust gathered for ceremonial purposes, produces a molecule or two of strontium 90 ...) Well, no: quantity *is* a factor – and, it would appear, so is motive.

These observations, taken together with the inevitability of ecological interaction between humans and their environments, are why I want to argue that wilderness depends, not on the absence of human interaction with the land, but rather on its quantity and style. Wilderness exists, I'll suggest, in greater or lesser degrees wherever we allow communities of non-humans to shape us at least as much as or more than we shape them. (Of course, if you think no such openness presently occurs anywhere, and has no possibility of occurring in the future, you'll want to cast that last sentence irrevocably in the past tense.)

Trevor Herriot, in his searching and perceptive chronicle of the Qu'Appelle, *River in a Dry Land*, comes at the same issue from the other side:

> Most of our problems began when we hammered our hunting spears into ploughshares. From that point on, it has been one valley after another – Euphrates, Nile, Ganges, Rhine, Seine, St Lawrence, Mississippi, Hudson – evicting the local hunter-gatherers and pastoralists, replacing them with farmers who soon multiply, filling the valley with a civilization that venerates the tiller's short-term residency, calling this 'settlement,' while dismissing the hunter's long-term residency, several thousand years of seasonal migration and ecological congruency as mere 'nomadism.'

It is not, in other words, human culturing that destroys wilderness: it is the manner of that culturing and the attitude behind it. Many human societies have negotiated – and in places, I'd argue, their remnants continue to negotiate – the border with the non-human world in a way that has permitted and permits both sides to flourish: thinning and weeding, aerating and fertilizing, burning and irrigating, all with the aim of increasing the health and complexity of various plant communities and thereby their own harvests. What they have tended not to do is break the sod, or clear-cut, or fish with dragnets; they have not, in general, aimed to eliminate whole communities of native species in order to promote dependence on non-native cultivars. Above all, their populations have stayed relatively low in relation to the populations of the wild species they live, and lived, among.

Viewed from this perspective, *wilderness* and *agriculture* are not dichotomously opposed terms that, between them, exhaust the possibilities. Rather, it begins to look as though *agriculture* is a term that mediates between the non-human and its exploitation – a.k.a. industrial logging, corporate fisheries, or, more generally, agribiz. The Greek word we usually translate as 'wild' is *agrios*, which means literally 'of the field'; but it is formed from the word *agros*, field, which is the root of our word *agriculture*. In this etymology the wild and the cultivated come from the same place, the field that accommodates and sustains them both. Agribiz, by contrast, sees the field only as the arena of short-term capital profit. In such a field, there is no room for wilderness, nor, for that matter, culture in its broader sense.

But what does this mean for our farm? Surely we're not engaged in agribiz? We've got less than half a section under cultivation, low till, no pesticides, herbicides, or chemical fertilizers, we use small equipment ... Yes, but there wouldn't be a beaver 'problem' on SW32-57-08-W5 if the land those numbers designated weren't 'in production,' if the poplars and spruce and willow hadn't been cleared from everything *except* the banks, hummocks, and steep hillsides. The beavers could take as much as they wanted and the course of the river wouldn't be 'destabilized' if the place were still wild. There'd be plenty of balsam and aspen left for the occasional human, passing through, to enthuse over.

Is this, then, the direction of the solution: to campaign for a reduction in human population, a return to a more nomadic way of life, and in the meantime to put the farm back down to trees and leave the beavers be? Perhaps. But even this proposal – maybe I'm just kidding myself? – seems to bear the stamp of insufficient subtlety and complexity. It forgets that individuals, too, are ecologies of history and desire, as much as cultures. While my planetary thinking head recognizes the ecological wisdom of the suggestion, my locally acting heart isn't sure it's up to it. My grandfather *homesteaded* this place. Neither my mother nor my grandmother could imagine putting it back to trees; I can barely imagine it. And I don't just mean the landscape. I mean all that labour, the struggle it represented, the hopes that fed it, the violence it required – there's something fantastic about thinking it might all have been a mistake. More difficult, I find, than wondering if the species itself might be an evolutionary dead end. It's more like trying to think through whether you yourself should have been born.

And here's something else. I can't think of a 'nomadic,' non-agribizcious society that, as a female, I'd be willing to choose over the one I already belong to. This could easily be because I haven't read enough, or it could be because what I've read has been filtered through English-speaking patriarchy. I know there's a wing of feminist analysis that locates women's oppression in the advent of private property, which itself seems to have begun with ownership of herd animals. But if what I've read about the sexual division of labour in many Palaeolithic cultures is correct, or about the political privileges of women, even in societies that trace descent matrilineally, I am not at all sure that reversion to such a way of life – even if it were possible – represents an ideal I could aspire to. There's a link between the Enlightenment's vision of science used to better the human lot and the rate at which, as a culture, we've exploited the wild; there's also a link between that vision and a more genuinely democratic human politics.

What then should I do? How to balance personal loyalty, ecological common sense, political realism, aesthetic inclination, cultural guilt, and leave room for the play of all those things I know I don't know enough about, possibilities I can't yet imagine? I don't know. If wilderness is not chaos, but complex, living pattern, it can, at least to some extent, be understood. But if it is complex, living pattern and not a dissociated array of raw materials, then that understanding will consist of more than a set of facts about the bottom line. Coming to it will be a bit like learning how to dance. It will require musicality, patience, social courage, attention to the other, and, above all, time.

We might even say that the acquisition of such virtues – the coordinated wisdom of *agros* and *agrios* that we must allow the non-human to teach us – is what culture is about. But time is not a virtue. Time, as Anaximander suggested several centuries ago, is the judge of virtue, that which assesses the justice or injustice of all coming-to-be and passing-away. Time is what neither I nor the poplars, neither the farm nor the beavers, have on our side. In its absence, we must choose without discernment, and any principled action we might take will carry the taint of imposed, rather than responsive, order. In its absence we will fail to enact an agricultural relation even to the complex, living patterns of our own lives.

5 Murdering Trees?

TRUDY GOVIER

I once took a small boy to a museum displaying the stump of a five-hundred-year-old tree. When I offered a cheery commentary explaining how scientists knew the tree was five hundred years old, he exclaimed with horror, 'They cut it down?' As a jaded adult, I had simply assumed that some huge old trees are cut down and have their stumps displayed in museums. Not being grown up, he was shocked. With childhood innocence and a capacity for wonder, he saw the old tree as a being meriting special awe. It was not an object for human use, even if that human use was to be in a museum.

I was reminded of that response while reading *Carmanah*, a book published by the Western Canada Wilderness Committee as part of a campaign to preserve old forest on Vancouver Island. The Carmanah Valley contains Sitka spruce ten to sixteen feet in diameter, towering to heights of three hundred feet, aging to five or six hundred years. There are some red cedar estimated to be nearly a thousand years old. This is a Canadian rainforest. Pictures of it move people to tears. Being there is unforgettably wonderful and overwhelming.

What is so special about huge old trees? They are immensely tall and beautiful. They remind us of a remote and pristine history, a lost time when the land was green and the rivers blue. Carmanah trees stood when oceans teemed with whales, seals, and fish; when native peoples quietly walked the woods and paddled the waters; when there were no roads, cars, planes, malls, or computers. When I see these trees, I feel moved, dwarfed and subdued by these beings so much older and grander than I. They have survived for hundreds of years.

Those giant trees are irreplaceable. If we destroy them, future generations can never know the beauty and imaginative inspiration that we experience. To cut down a tree that has taken five hundred years to grow and use it for our trivial contemporary needs seems arrogant to the point of blasphemy. Centuries of growth and grandeur for musical instruments, books, houses, or furniture? Worse yet, for disposable diapers or toilet paper?

Still, I am not one to regard the killing of a tree as murder, any more than I think of it as murder to pull a carrot from the ground or consume a cabbage or a head of lettuce. Many products central to human life come from trees and other growing things. Like other life, human life entails the destruction of some other living beings. I have no evidence that trees have souls aspiring for a longer life or that they feel pain when cut down by loggers. Still, very old trees seem to me to be something special. They stand like wise elders, silent witnesses to a peaceful past. They strike me as grand old creatures which merit respect.

It is partly their size that makes these trees inspiring – their immense grandness and dwarfing height. But still more, it is their age that marks the trees of old-growth forests. If a tree could grow to three hundred feet in a decade, we would not feel the same about felling it, for its size would not mark centuries of endurance and it could readily be replaced. The giants of old-growth forests have endured for centuries; that is why we should feel respect for them. They are survivors. If we cut them down, to use them purely as resources for human artifacts and consumption, we are in effect saying that our transitory needs are

> 'To think that animals and plants, rocks, streams, and hills exist only in order to fulfil human desires and needs is arrogance indeed. We human beings are not as special as we think: we live within nature, not above it.'

more significant than centuries of life in the wind and the sun. Such exaltation of ourselves, such disproportionate emphasis on our transitory wishes, signifies human arrogance and lack of respect.

As the size of these trees dwarfs us, their age should dwarf our projects. Being survivors in nature – striking and unusual survivors – they merit a certain respect. And many people seem naturally to feel this kind of respect for old trees. It's a little like the case of Lanny the Lobster. Lanny, a huge old lobster, was shipped from Nova Scotia to a restaurant in Kitchener, Ontario. When the restaurant owner discovered that Lanny weighed a full twenty pounds, he was so impressed with his size and likely age that he was unwilling to use the giant lobster for food. Feeling that Lanny had improbably survived decades in the cold North Atlantic, he decided that death in the kitchen's boiling water would be an inappropriate end. This man, we may note, did not feel it was wrong to kill smaller, younger, and more normal lobsters for human consumption. Quite the contrary: his business depended on it. But Lanny was special.

Lanny was huge, old, and, as such, deserving of respect – a grand old tree of lobsters. The Kitchener man shipped him back to Nova Scotia. Fishermen, encircled by news reporters, applauded his arrival. With the approval of all assembled, frogmen lowered Lanny to the ocean floor. There he soon died – no doubt in shock after his travails and travels. Lanny did not die in a distant restaurant but was granted a more fitting death, a death with dignity on the ocean floor where he belonged. Witnesses recognized that his long life was more significant than an urban dinner in Kitchener.

Such attitudes of respect for survival in nature are by no means universal, which is one reason why logging in old forests is such a controversial matter. Proponents of old-growth logging typically see all of nature, including its largest lobsters and oldest trees, purely and simply as *resources* for human use. Where trees are concerned, a compact expression of this attitude can be gleaned from a brief study of the *Oxford Encyclopedia of Trees*, which describes cedar and spruce with reference to their potential usefulness in construction and manufacturing. One pro-logging advocate called Canada's West Coast rainforest 'a cellulose cemetery.' Trees provide cellulose, something people want and need; that's what trees do; they are a resource for people. From this point of view, people and their needs are at the centre of the world. It is their lives that count; animals and plants exist only to serve their purposes. It is we human beings who must and will make decisions about what to do with the earth's resources, how many to use now, how many to save for later. Nature is our *resource*. And it is pure emotionalism to think that beings like trees and lobsters can merit respect.

Whether plants and animals are *merely* a resource raises the whole issue of humanity's place in nature. It is human beings who construct religious, ethical, and legal systems, write works about values and economics, and make policy decisions in corporate and government structures about what is going to happen on this earth. In reflecting on life and nature, we human beings tend to make ourselves the heroes of history. We see the world through our own eyes and put our own interests first. From one point of view, this stance is only realistic; it is based on recognition of the plain fact that we human beings – not grizzly bears, spotted owls, lobsters, or giant spruce – are the ones who will devise policies and undertake actions in this world. But from another standpoint, that of deep ecologists, this human-centred thinking amounts to unparalleled arrogance.

Deep ecologists reject the assumption that ethics and policy must be human-centred. They insist that nature and natural objects have value *in themselves*, and not just for us. According to deep ecologists, trees and other natural beings are vital entities in their own right. Their value is as great as that of human beings, and they would have that value even if human beings did not exist. To think that animals and plants, rocks, streams, and hills exist only in order to fulfil human desires and needs is arrogance indeed. We human beings are not as special as we think: we live within nature, not above it. We have no entitlement from God or elsewhere to reign over nature and settle its fate. For all our science and technology, we are still vulnerable creatures of nature, and we deceive ourselves if we think we can control it. Because our decisions and frighteningly powerful technologies can be drastically damaging to the natural order, we should be humble and careful. We are not superior beings in charge of the earth.

Deep ecologists see all things in the biosphere as having 'an equal right to live and blossom.' When they say 'all,' they really mean *all*. The cactus, the human, the elephant, the old cedar – all have equal intrinsic worth. So too the ant, the bee, the maggot, and the AIDS virus. Deep ecologists are stronger on metaphysics and empathy than on policy advice. They urge that, with no exceptions – not even for scorpions and bacteria – we should kill other living beings only with respect and regret, and only to meet our 'vital needs.' We should never kill without sufficient reason.

Working out a practical ethic and politics based on deep ecology would be a challenge, to put it mildly. Which of our human needs are vital needs? And what reasons will count as sufficient reasons? When it comes to practical administration and policy decisions, deep ecology seems deeply impractical.

Deep ecology makes no distinction among biological creatures: it is a doctrine of biological egalitarianism. All living creatures are equal: the cactus, the virus, and the ant; the human being, the elephant, and the mouse; the dandelion, the young tree, and the grand old cedar. From the standpoint of this egalitarian doctrine, it would be just as offensive to cut down a small tree in a reforested area as to cut down a five-hundred-year-old tree in the Carmanah. Rather ironically, this aspect of deep ecology does nothing to solve the problem of grand old trees.

Fortunately, there are other approaches to the problem. Ecologically, forests provide habitat for insects, birds, and animals; prevent soil erosion due to wind and water; fertilize surrounding soil; and act as lungs for the earth in balancing carbon dioxide and oxygen. Emotionally and artistically, they provide solace, inspiration, and respite – as is so obvious from the *Carmanah* pictures. The special case for huge old trees can be argued in purely practical terms. They provide unique habitat, extraordinary tourist regions, and special emotional inspiration.

Is it a crime, morally equivalent to murder, to cut down a grand old tree? Struggling with the conundrum, I cannot say I think so. It shows a terrible arrogance and lack of respect and imagination. It is short-sighted ecologically and unfair to future generations of human beings and thus, in all probability, wrong. But not in the way that murder is wrong. A convincing case for preserving old trees can be made without recourse to deep ecology. We and other beings need these trees – and for more than cellulose.

6 The Environmentalist Faith

JEFFREY FOSS

Do environmentalists ever go too far? It must seem like they do to the quail that used to nest in the park near my home in Victoria. The local nature sanctuary society has decreed that Scotch broom, a local shrub that grows in the park, must be destroyed since it is an invasive foreign species. It was introduced by European colonists, hence it is not native, hence it does not deserve to live.

During the last two winters, teams of young people have been paid to cut down the broom. One result is that the quail have returned to their nesting grounds only to find them in ruins. The broom used to provide them cover, a place to raise their families, but environmentalists have destroyed it. The quail perch sadly on the stumps and stacks of dead broom, while overhead the local hawks soar and pick them off.

'Does it seem odd to you that environmentalists should be busy killing plants and animals? If so, you simply aren't up to speed on environmentalist doctrine.'

South of the border in the United States, where going too far achieves degrees of perfection not often attained in Canada, Montana wildlife managers propose to poison seventy miles of Cherry Creek to eradicate non-native rainbow and brook trout to make way for native westslope trout.

Does it seem odd to you that environmentalists should be busy killing plants and animals? If so, you simply aren't up to speed on environmentalist doctrine. Invasive species, it is written, drive out native species and thus reduce *biodiversity*. Never mind that every single species in Canada invaded it since the last ice age – we are supposed to be in a biodiversity *crisis*. But this isn't the only crisis. The atmosphere, oceans, soil, mountains, plains, forests, jungles – *all* of nature – is said to be in a state of crisis.

So environmentalists go too far in what they say. They repeatedly and incessantly warn us that environmental disaster is just around the corner. Approaching disaster calls for desperate action, but desperate action is not often highly intelligent.

So we spend hundreds of dollars to wash out and recycle every tonne of old tin cans, at greater cost to ourselves and the environment than producing that tonne of iron from the ore. British Columbia has pledged to build a sewage treatment plant for Victoria, though science shows there is no pollution problem, and treatment plants simply convert sewage into greenhouse gases and sludge. Protesters defy the law to save a few trees in Vancouver and prevent the widening of roads, while fires *naturally* caused by lightning destroy, on average, nearly two million hectares of trees in Canada each year. Genetically modified foods are condemned by environmentalists, though without them we must place more land under cultivation and use more pesticides and fertilizers to feed ourselves. The litany of folly goes on and on.

It's time to wake up and realize that the sky is not falling. Unbiased scientific investigation reveals that our effects on the environment are more modest than we have been taught to believe by environmentalists, while the changes wrought by Mother Nature herself can be huge. Fortunately, there is still time to take a deep breath, calm down, and assess the situation more realistically.

Why is it that it is so hard to view environmental issues calmly and realistically? It is because, I suggest, environmentalism has become a new and zealous religion. Our environmental errors are not mere mistakes, but are seen as moral failures, as sin, and to make matters worse, none of us is completely innocent. We are, brothers and sisters, sinners against the environment, creator of us all. Or so the environmentalist tells us. Unless we mend our ways, there will be hell to pay. The globe will overheat, the oceans will rise to drown us, radiation will stream through the holes in the ozone to burn flesh and foliage, the fragile web of life will be torn, and we will be put utterly asunder. Environmental apocalypse steadily draws near, and it is our fault – our fault for farming the land, for fishing the seas, for driving our cars, for using our refrigerators and air conditioners. Verily alone among creation, we humans are the destroyers of the environment. Our farms, fisheries, highways, and fridges are merely the tools of our greed, laziness, and low technological cunning. At root our sin is pride and disrespect for Mother Nature, who holds our very lives in Her hands. We must cast off our arrogance, return to the old days and simpler ways, when we lived in harmony with nature, before we ate of the tree of the knowledge of science and technology.

The religiosity of these ideas is, I trust, too obvious to bear elaboration. Moreover, for most people in most countries and cultures environmental doctrines garner immediate resonance and credence. Their scientific credibility is scarcely questioned. The rank-and-file environmentalist, like the population in general, has but a modest knowledge of science, and even less love for it. They partly blame science, with its engines, electricity, vaccinations, and designer vegetables, for perceived environmental degradation. They leave the scientific credibility of their beliefs in the hands of environmentalists who do have scientific credentials, like the famous Dr Suzuki.

Inspired by their leaders, the soldiers of the faith disrupt fishing, blow up oil wells, chain themselves to trees, and blockade mining roads, among numberless other good works. They are not interested in the finer points of the science which they are told justifies and requires their actions. Soldiers and theoreticians have always been disparate lots.

But we must never confuse environmentalism with environmental science, no matter how popular it may be to do so. Environmental science is the enterprise of discovering the facts about the whole natural system around us. Environmentalism adds to this science prophecy (usually apocalyptic), policy, and ethics.

Whereas environmentalism has its certainties, environmental science is exploratory, disputatious, and *amazingly difficult*. The established sciences have earned their reputations applying analytic methods to limited phenomena like planetary motion, polio, and photosynthesis, breaking them down into smaller and smaller pieces, spawning specialties and specialists along the way. Unfortunately, the environment is a far more complex system than anything science has yet explained. It can be understood, not by analysis, but rather by putting all the pieces back together again. Environmental science is *essentially* holistic. Environmental scientists must, uncharacteristically, be generalists rather than specialists, working not in the lab, but (like humanists) in the library, consuming the research of specialists in an attempt to synthesize global theories that make sense of countless pieces.

The scholarly publications of environmental scientists are suffused with questions, puzzles, mysteries, and confessions of ignorance – not just about the details, but about the central processes themselves. It is thought that weather, population cycles, and other ecosystemic parameters are 'chaotic' (that is, deterministic but unpredictable). The environment is a disequilibrium system given to abrupt, massive, and unpredictable change. Given the accident that all of human civilization and recorded history has occurred during this brief interglacial thaw we now enjoy, we have just realized Mother Nature's inconstancy.

Undeterred by this noisy background of whimsically fractal temperature swings, environmentalist doctrine states that *the* cause of the current warming trend is human production of greenhouse gases through
forestry, farming, and fossil-fueling. Capitalizing on guilt, and writing
off their own hubris, environmentalists say *we* are to blame, despite the
fact that global warming – and cooling – has an antiquity that dwarfs
human civilization, the tropical rainforests, and the current environmental status quo. The new enemy has, nevertheless, an oddly familiar
face: the capitalist, whose vice is traditional greed, and whose anti-deity
is good old profit.

Environmental science is younger, less conservative, less self-assured.
Our records of temperature are relatively recent, fragmentary, and predominantly taken in the temperature-distorting environments of cities.
Satellite data indicate global cooling, not warming. Global temperatures apparently were higher in 1400 than they are now, and then fell
during the 'little ice age,' *despite* the concurrent increase in carbon
dioxide levels. In 1900 temperatures began to recover, but most of the
warming (three-quarters of the 1-degree rise) occurred prior to 1940,
while most of the carbon dioxide increase (two-thirds of the 65 parts per
million increase) came after 1940, during the global cooling trend from
1940 to 1975.

But so what? Scientifically sophisticated climatological Cassandras
can always find some datum within the meteorological noise in favour
of their prophecies. In the 1970s, we were warned of the coming ice
age – and it is true that temperatures have risen approximately to the
levels where previous reversals into ice ages have occurred. Fire or ice –
take your pick.

Prophecy aside, climatologists generally realize it is the absorption
and transport of heat by the oceans, not the atmosphere, that is the main
engine of climate change. Given the last *El Niño*, this realization may
hopefully become more widespread. It is, moreover, elementary that
there is fifty times as much water vapour in the atmosphere as there is
carbon dioxide, and water is an excellent greenhouse gas. Happily,
water also corrects overheating by forming reflective cloud cover. This
also makes it difficult to model, and so it is usually left out of computer
models of the atmosphere.

Speaking of computer models, those used by the Intergovernmental
Panel on Climate Change (or IPCC) to predict an *anthropogenic* heating
of 1.9 to 2.3 degrees by 2040 had an *average* error of 3 degrees in
predicting past climate changes. In the teeth of such uncertainties, IPCC

confidence about what will happen and how, when, and why is marvellous. But marvels sometimes sustain scientific explanation. One scientist, a former member of the IPCC, reports that the IPCC automatically neglects hypotheses that do not accord with its favoured doctrine.

Similar sloughs of uncertainty are found behind the storefront clarity of environmental doctrines on chlorofluorocarbons, the so-called ozone hole, the reduction of biodiversity, the fragmentation of grizzly terrain, the safety of fish farming, and so on.

Not that I claim to know all about the environment – far from it! Nobody does. Environmental scientists are just beginning their investigations. But during the process of discovery, let's all lighten up a little. The environment is not on its last gasp in intensive care. It has survived cometary impacts and global freezes, beside which our influence pales to insignificance. One day, our species may gain the knowledge and understanding needed to take control of the environment. But who knows? Perhaps then we will decide to arrest the next ice age and create the mythical Garden of Eden that has never yet existed. Until then, be of good cheer.

7 Creating the Phenomena

IAN HACKING

By legend and perhaps by nature philosophers are more accustomed to the armchair than the workbench. So it is not so surprising that we have gone overboard for theory at the expense of experiment. Yet we have not always been so insulated. Leibniz has been described as the greatest pure intellect the world has ever known. He thought about everything. Although he was less successful in building windmills for mining silver than he was in co-inventing the differential calculus, the remarks of that hyperintellectual about the role of experiment are undoubtedly more faithful to scientific practice, then and now, than much of what occurs in modern textbooks of philosophy. Philosophers such as Bacon and Leibniz show we don't have to be antiexperimental.

One role of experiments is so neglected that we lack a name for it. I call it the creation of phenomena. Traditionally, scientists are said to explain phenomena that they discover in nature. I say that often they create the phenomena, which then become the centrepieces of theory.

The word 'phenomenon' has a long philosophical history. In the Renaissance some astronomers tried to 'save the phenomena,' that is, produce a system of calculation that would fit known regularities. Not everyone admired that. Who will beat Francis Bacon's scorn when he writes, in a 1625 essay, *Superstition*: 'They are like astronomers, who did feign eccentrics and epicycles, and such engines or orbs, to save the phenomena; though they knew, there were no such things.'

> '*As a paradoxical generalization, one can say that most experiments don't work most of the time. To ignore this fact is to forget what experimentation is doing.*'

Yet the great French historian and philosopher of science, the eminent antirealist Pierre Duhem, would admiringly take the same tag to name one of his books, *To Save the Phenomena*. Bas van Fraassen recycles it for a chapter title in his book, *The Scientific Image*. Such authors teach that a theory provides a formalism to embed the phenomena within a coherent order, but the theory, where it extends beyond the phenomena, indicates no reality. They take for granted that the phenomena are discovered by the observer and the experimenter. How then can I say that a chief role for experiment is the creation of phenomena? Do I propound some sort of ultimate idealism in which *we* make the phenomena that even Duhem counts as 'given'? On the contrary, the creation of phenomena more strongly favours a hard-headed scientific realism.

There is no more familiar dictum than that experimental results must be repeatable. On my view, that works out as something of a tautology. Experiment is the creation of phenomena; phenomena must have discernible regularities – so an experiment that is not repeatable has failed to create a phenomenon.

Undergraduates and high-school students know different. There is no more common comment on 'teaching evaluations' of courses with a laboratory component than that the experiments do not work, the numbers have to be cooked, the reaction doesn't react, the phage does not grow. The laboratory just has to be improved!

Nor is this problem peculiar to the years of preapprenticeship. Here is another familiar story. My university has a very complex and expensive device, X, of which there are few in the world; perhaps only ours works very well. It is the sort of device for which you book a year in advance, and are refereed by endless panels, before you are allowed to have two days working on X. Young hotshot A at our institution is obtaining some very striking results with X. Established figure B, in the same field, arrives for his two days and leaves frustrated. He even suggests we take a long hard look at A's work. Is A really getting what he claims to get? Or is he cheating? (This is a true story based on a tenure case that I reviewed.)

Now of course some laboratory courses are just awful. Sometimes old B has lost the knack or young A really is cheating. But as a paradoxical generalization, one can say that most experiments don't work most of the time. To ignore this fact is to forget what experimentation is doing.

To experiment is to create, produce, refine, and stabilize phenomena. If phenomena were plentiful in nature, summer blackberries there just for the picking, it would be remarkable if experiments didn't work. But phenomena are hard to produce in any stable way. That is why I spoke of creating and not merely discovering phenomena. That is a long, hard task.

Or rather there are endless different tasks. There is designing an experiment that might work. There is learning how to make the experiment work. But perhaps the real knack is getting to know when the experiment is working. That is one reason why observation, in the philosophy-of-science usage of the term, plays a relatively small role in experimental science. Noting and reporting readings of dials – Oxford philosophy's picture of experiment – is nothing. Another kind of observation is what counts: the uncanny ability to pick out what is odd, wrong, instructive, or distorted in the antics of one's equipment. The experimenter is not the 'observer' of traditional philosophy of science, but rather the alert and observant person. Only when one has got the equipment running right is one in a position to make and record observations. That is a picnic.

The preapprentice in the school laboratory is mostly about acquiring or failing to acquire the ability to know when the experiment is working. All the thinking has been done, all the designing, all the implementation, but something is still missing. The ability to know when the experiment is working includes, of course, having sufficient sense of how this artifice works in order to know how to put it right. A laboratory course in which all the experiments worked would be fine technology but would teach nothing at all about experimentation. At the opposite end of the scale, it is not surprising that young hotshot A gets results and distinguished visitor B does not. A has had the opportunity to know the apparatus better; he has made part of it and suffered through its failures. That is an integral part of knowing how to create phenomena.

8 Science Rules

JAMES ROBERT BROWN

Like Wordsworth, 'My heart leaps up when I behold a rainbow in the sky.' There is much to be said about rainbows that isn't part of the usual domain of science. Rainbows were explained by Descartes long ago and his account has largely stood up. It has to do with the refraction of light in drops of water. There are lots of other accounts of rainbows that are just plain wrong. Among the false accounts is the one that says rainbows are a sign from God that he won't flood the earth again. Rainbows aren't that, but they are beautiful.

We often hear that there are many ways to understand reality, and that science is just one of these – none should be thought better or worse than others. To the liberal-minded, this view can be appealing. If the view means only that rainbows are as Descartes says *and* that they are beautiful, then who could object? But claiming more than this is rubbish, if it also means that rainbows are something else entirely. It's one thing for a cultural group to have its own political goals, but quite another for it to have its own version of science.

In saying this, there is a great worry – dogmatism. Science is fallible and Descartes' theory might be wrong, but that does not mean that all perspectives are correct. It only means that some other theory – so far undiscovered – is the true one.

Much recent work in the history, philosophy, and sociology of science has been right to conclude that there are loads of social factors at work in science; but this same work has been wrong to the extent that it thinks that reason and evidence are not playing a dominant role. Scientific objectivity is both possible and actual. Values and objectivity can and do coexist. Thus, of all the things that could be called the science wars – those points of conflict between science and culture – the relationship between epistemology and politics is arguably the most central and most important to understand.

There are other issues, too, and some of them involve politics. For example, one concerns religion and science. Religious and social conservatives are more often than not happy with science and technology so long as it has no bearing on cherished beliefs about religion and morals. Darwin, of course, is a lightning rod. There are endless battles over evolution, especially in the United States. Anti-evolutionists are often in high places. While he was president, Ronald Reagan said that evolution is 'only a theory.' His intent was to cast doubt on Darwin, but among scientists, it only cast doubt on Reagan's sanity. The religious Right has had remarkably little impact on science itself: its real threat is to science education. American school boards seem bent on making American children as poorly educated as possible.

Another concern that forms part of the science wars is environmentalism. It is hard to imagine the environmental movement without standard science. Standard science discovered the hole in the ozone layer over the Antarctic and its connection to the increase in skin cancer. Standard science detected the presence of toxins in drinking water and the adverse effects they have on our health. Standard science created a multitude of models of the weather, each indicating potentially harmful global warming. The environmental movement is most effective when it acts on the information provided by standard science. Without that information, any action would be unmotivated. Yet some environmentalists have an ambivalent attitude towards science.

'Science is the single most important institution in our lives. That claim ought to make us sit up and take notice – but it doesn't.'

Perhaps the picture of nature that the contemporary sciences give us is fundamentally flawed. Much of their success is tied to a reductionist and mechanistic attitude. This outlook leads us to think that nature can be divided into isolated parts which can be manipulated without consequence for the rest. Such an attitude, these critics contend, can lead us into thinking we can introduce a particular new crop in some part of the world without ramifications for other vegetation or for preferred ways of life.

Despite all this, science is the single most important institution in our lives. That claim ought to make us sit up and take notice – but it doesn't. We've become complacent. Coming to understand how science works and how it can be made to serve us better is surely – along with the elimination of poverty, to which it is connected – the first task for us all.

9 Is Scientific Progress Inevitable?

ANDREW IRVINE

When my daughter was nine, I took her to see an aboriginal medicine wheel in rural Saskatchewan. Built between 1,500 and 4,500 years ago, some 150 of these stone structures are still scattered throughout the Canadian prairies and the American Midwest. Most are found within 200 kilometres of the confluence of the Red Deer and South Saskatchewan Rivers. Many have spokes like a wagon wheel. Others have series of concentric circles. Some are in the shape of turtles or people.

The medicine wheel we visited rests atop the rolling Moose Mountains, a two-and-a-half-hour drive southeast of Regina. Constructed by the Plains Indians, it consists of a central stone cairn and five stone spokes laid out at various angles from the cairn. At the end of each spoke is a smaller cairn. An elliptical ring of stones, approximately sixty-two by fifty feet, surrounds the central cairn.

It is difficult to take children much younger than nine or ten to this wheel since they need to be able to control a horse to reach it. You also need permission from the Pheasant Rump Reserve and a guide to show you the way.

Once you reach the site, it's easy to be impressed. For one thing, the view is tremendous. As everyone knows, Saskatchewan is flat. This means that from a good rise of land there is nothing between you and the horizon. Just as on the ocean, on a clear day the only thing blocking your view is the curvature of the earth.

Also it's a rare thing in North America to come face to face with any man-made object as old as England's Stonehenge or Egypt's pyramids. The mere fact that some of these structures have stood undisturbed for thousands of years is enough to remind you of the shortness of your own life and the fragility of human existence.

Another thing of which we are reminded is the fragility of science. We often think of science as something inescapably linked to progress, and of progress as continually marching forward. We assume that there is something inevitable about the increase of knowledge and the benefits this knowledge brings. Yet nothing could be further from the truth. The advancement of knowledge in general – and of scientific knowledge in particular – is much more like a Saskatchewan wheat field than a solid rock structure: without appropriate care and nurturing, it could very easily shrivel up and die.

This point was brought home as we looked at the Moose Mountain medicine wheel. It is likely that there is no single explanation as to why these stone structures were built. Some may have been built to commemorate the dead; others as ceremonial sites to help communities observe important occasions; and yet others simply as landmarks on an otherwise barren prairie. Whatever their original purpose, there is no denying that all of the sites have had important spiritual connections to Native communities, both past and present.

'We often think of science as something inescapably linked to progress, and of progress as continually marching forward. We assume that there is something inevitable about the increase of knowledge and the benefits this knowledge brings. Yet nothing could be further from the truth.'

But some of the wheels may also have been built with a more scientific purpose in mind. Two structures in particular, the Moose Mountain medicine wheel and the larger but similar Bighorn wheel in Wyoming more than 700 kilometres away, have spokes marking several important astronomical sightings. The two wheels have so many similarities that one archeologist has commented that they could have been built from the same set of plans.

Perhaps most striking, the longest spoke in both wheels lines up directly with the point of sunrise at the summer solstice. As every ancient people could observe throughout the year, sunrise and sunset shift along the horizon. As spring comes closer, the sunrise moves farther north each morning. This continues until 21 June, the summer solstice, when the sun's northern motion stops. Six months later the winter solstice marks the end of the sun's opposite motion southward along the horizon. Other small cairns mark the positions of three of the northern hemisphere's brightest stars: Aldebaran in the constellation Taurus, Rigel in Orion, and Sirius in Canis Major.

Today, the alignments between the cairns and these various astronomical sightings are off by a few degrees, but if corrections are made for how the stars have shifted over the centuries since the cairns were built, the alignments become nearly perfect.

The importance of the astronomical sciences to many ancient cultures has been well documented. It's not at all improbable that this knowledge would also have been important to the Plains Indians. Whenever we speak of a 'blue moon' or the 'dog days of summer,' we are reflecting the significance the night sky had to ancient cultures. On the prairies, the summer solstice was marked by important ceremonies such as the sun dance; it would also have helped regulate the nomadic movements of a people with no written calendar. It is also interesting that many medicine wheels have spokes or cairns that point to other, similar structures fifteen, thirty, even seventy kilometres away.

Today, the astronomical knowledge underlying these structures has been all but lost to the original inhabitants of the plains. Even so, this knowledge was once of great importance to aboriginal communities, as evidenced by the fact that even today they recognize and celebrate these monuments as sacred sites.

Just as importantly, these monuments remind us that scientific knowledge is not inevitable, that it can just as easily decline as advance. They tell us that scientific progress is linked in complex, unpredictable ways to social progress, and vice versa.

When I think about these issues, I'm reminded of the words of the philosopher Sidney Hook. As he neared the end of his life, having witnessed the social and political turbulence of almost the entire twentieth century, he was convinced that nothing about human existence is inevitable. As he put it,

> Looking back on a life longer than I ever expected ... I am confident that one of my strongest beliefs will remain unaltered. This is the overwhelming conviction that what has happened need not necessarily have happened. The great events of our time, or of any time, good or bad, victories or disasters, need not have occurred. I am not saying that anything could have happened at any time. We do not live in a magical world or one of absolute chance. ... Yet the more closely we explore the tangled web of causation of any historical event, the more likely it is that we will conclude that it didn't have to be.

In other words, there is no guarantee that social progress will continue unabated or that scientific knowledge will continue to increase. Unless we continue to nurture what is important, to look for ways to improve what we already have, life has no guarantees.

We know that science has the potential to alleviate hunger, disease, and even war. But without the will to protect these accomplishments and the desire to improve on them, life will remain unpredictable. Scientific knowledge remains a rare and valuable commodity in the history of the world, and this is as true today as it was thousands of years ago.

PART II

Mind, Intelligence, and the New Technologies

1 From Descartes to Neural Networks

PATRICIA SMITH CHURCHLAND

Reflex behaviour, Descartes reasoned, could be explained in terms of the physical connections of nerves and muscles. But for non-reflexive behaviour, behaviour produced by intelligence and planning, he could not imagine a physical explanation. In his famous summation 'I think, therefore I am,' the 'I' was considered a non-physical thing, a soul existing independently of the physical brain but in some kind of causal interaction with it. The Cartesian idea of two very different substances – the mental and the physical – has enduring appeal. The subjective phenomena of which we see or think seem to be entirely different from the physical activity of brain cells.

'Descartes was a seventeenth-century visionary, pre-Darwin, pre-Turing, and pre-neuroscience. Informed by neuroscience and computer science, we can modernize his vision and begin to discern the shape of a new theory about the nature of the mind – of what it is for the physical brain to see, learn, and understand itself; of what it is to be a human being.'

Yet how things seem is often not how science discovers them to be. The earth does in fact move even though it seems not to; 'solid' matter is in fact mostly empty space; living things were not created, but evolved from simpler structures. Descartes and introspection notwithstanding, those of us who are physicalists expect that by discovering the nature of the brain and the principles governing how it works, we can understand perception, learning, and other 'mental' functions in neurobiological terms.

How fares the physicalist program? In recent decades progress in neuroscience has been spectacular, and a great deal is now known about the properties of neurons and about the complex molecules that affect the responses of neurons. Over the same time, experimental psychology and clinical neurology have yielded behavioural data that reveal much about the scope and character of psychological capacities such as visual perception and memory. These data are essential if neuroscientists are to know exactly what the functions are for which they are seeking mechanisms.

If we already understand much about the nature of cells and about the general character of psychological capacities, is that not sufficient to explain how we learn, see, or talk? No: necessary these data surely are, but sufficient, alas, they cannot be. The reason is that the brain is a kind of computer, and to understand how the brain works we need also to understand the computational principles that nervous systems employ. To be sure, neurons are the basic units, but they interconnect to form networks and systems. If we are to understand how the brain enables us to see and learn, we must understand how networks of cells interact to represent, transform, and store information.

The hard part is to figure out what kind of computer the brain is. The problem would be easier if the brain resembled the familiar von Neumann computers, with their serial, digital architecture, unmodifiable connections, and memory banks. The resemblance is very feeble, however; the brain seems to be a computer with a radically different style. For example, the brain changes as it learns, it appears to store and process information in the same places, its elements are analog rather than digital, and it is comparatively fault-tolerant. Most obviously, the brain is a parallel machine, in which many interactions occur at the same time in many different channels. Moreover, natural selection being what it is, there is a premium on solutions that are fast and approximate rather than slow but exact.

The dramatic conceptual breakthrough has been the invention of computer models that to a first approximation are brain-like. Neural network models (also called connectionist models or parallel distributed-processing models) attempt to capture, at some appropriate level of abstraction, the computational principles governing networks of neurons in nervous systems. Typically the models have neuron-like units, axon-like lines connecting the units, and modifiable synapse-like weights on the connection lines.

A major discovery has been that these model networks can learn. Rather like organisms with a nervous system, they can extract commonalities from examples and generalize to new cases. The key to their learning is that their synapse-like weights can be modified incrementally so that the answer the network gives to a question over time gets closer and closer to the correct answer. How do the weights know in what direction and by how much to change? Various algorithms have been devised to adjust the weights of synapses – as a function of error on the previous input–output trial, for example.

By means of such algorithms a network can be trained – as opposed to being simply programmed – to perform surprisingly complex tasks. For example, it can be trained to distinguish the sonar echoes of rocks from those of metal objects. It is technologically important that simple network systems can thus learn to solve problems of such complexity; the finding is also illuminating theoretically, because real nervous systems too must learn by using various strategies for modifying synapses. Just what algorithms the brain actually uses for synapse modification is not known; the hope is that convergent research from neuroscience and from network modelling will be able to discover them.

Other seminal ideas emerging from neural network modelling have provided insight into what the brain could be doing. The general problem of the nature of computations and representations in nervous systems is now more approachable because cognitive representations in model networks simply *are* patterns of activity across a large population of units; computations from one pattern to another. All of this means that representations must typically be distributed across large neuronal populations rather than being assigned to individual 'grandmother' cells. Motor control is likewise distributed rather than emanating from 'command' neurons.

Although the modelling of nervous systems is still in its infancy and we do not yet have any model that exactly explains how we see or learn, there is a gathering conviction that current lines of research, like the network models themselves, are converging on answers. Progress so far does provoke educated speculation about the neurobiological basis of our mental lives. Descartes was a seventeenth-century visionary, pre-Darwin, pre-Turing, and pre-neuroscience. Informed by neuroscience and computer science, we can modernize his vision and begin to discern the shape of a new theory about the nature of the mind – of what it is for the physical brain to see, learn, and understand itself; of what it is to be a human being.

2 How Do Neurons Know?

PATRICIA SMITH CHURCHLAND

My knowing *anything* depends on my neurons – the cells of my brain. More precisely, what I know depends on the specific configuration of connections among my trillion neurons, on the neurochemical interactions between connected neurons, and on the response portfolios of different neuron types. All this is what makes me *me*.

The range of things I know is as diverse as the range of stuff at a yard sale. Some is knowledge how, some knowledge that, some a bit of both, and some not exactly either. Some is fleeting, some enduring. Some I can articulate, such as the instructions for changing a tire; some, such as how I construct a logical argument, I cannot.

Some learning is conscious, some not. To learn some things, such as how to ride a bicycle, I have to try over and over; in contrast, learning to avoid eating oysters if they made me vomit the last time just happens. Knowing how to change a tire depends on cultural artifacts, but knowing how to clap does not.

And *neurons* are at the bottom of it all. How did it come to pass that we know *anything*?

Early in the history of living things, evolution stumbled onto the advantages accruing to animals whose nervous systems could make predictions based on past correlations. Unlike plants, which have to take what comes, animals are movers, and having a brain that can learn confers a competitive advantage in finding food, mates, and shelter and in avoiding dangers. Nervous systems earn their keep in the service of prediction and, to that end, map the *me-relevant* parts of the world – its spatial relations, social relations, dangers, and so on. And, of course, brains map their worlds in varying degrees of complexity and relative to the needs, equipment, and lifestyle of the organisms they inhabit. Thus humans, dogs, and frogs will represent the same pond quite differently. The human, for example, may be interested in the pond's water source, the potability of the water, or the potential for irrigation. The dog may be interested in a cool swim and a good drink, the frog in a good place to lay eggs, find flies, bask in the sun, or hide.

Boiled down to essentials, the main problems for the neuroscience of knowledge are these: How do structural arrangements in neural tissue embody knowledge (the problem of representation)? How, as a result of the animal's experience, do neurons undergo changes in their structural features such that these changes constitute knowing something new (the problem of learning)? How is the genome organized so that the nervous system it builds is able to learn what it needs to learn?

The spectacular progress over the past three or four decades in genetics, psychology, neuroethology, neuroembryology, and neurobiology has given the problems of how brains represent and learn and get built an entirely new look. In the process, many revered paradigms have taken a pounding. From the ashes of the old verities, a very different framework is arising for thinking about ourselves and how our brains make sense of the world.

Historically, philosophers have debated how much of what we know is based on instinct, and how much on experience. At one extreme, the rationalists argued that essentially all knowledge was innate. At the other, radical empiricists, impressed by infant modifiability and by the impact of culture, argued that all knowledge was acquired.

Knowledge displayed at birth is obviously likely to be innate. A normal neonate rat scrambles to the warmest place, latches its mouth onto a nipple, and begins to suck. A kitten thrown into the air rights itself and lands on its feet. A human neonate will imitate a facial expression, such as an out-stuck tongue. But other knowledge, such as how to weave or make a fire, is obviously learned postnatally.

Such contrasts have seemed to imply that everything we know is either caused by genes or caused by experience and that these categories are exclusive and exhaustive. But recent discoveries in molecular biology, neuroembryology, and neurobiology have demolished this sharp distinction between nature and nurture. One such discovery is that normal development, right from the earliest stages, relies on both genes and epigenetic conditions. For example, a female (XX) fetus developing in a uterine environment that is unusually high in androgens may be born with male-looking genitalia and may have a masculinized area in the hypothalamus, a sexually dimorphic brain region. In mice, the gender of adjacent siblings on the placental fetus line in the uterus will affect such things as the male/female ratio of a given mouse's subsequent offspring, and even the longevity of those offspring.

On the other hand, paradigmatic instances of long-term learning, such as memorizing a route through a forest, rely on genes to produce changes in cells that embody that learning. If you experience a new kind of sensorimotor event during the day – say, for example, you learn to cast a fishing line – and your brain rehearses that event during your deep sleep cycle, then the gene *zif*-268 will be up-regulated. Improvement in casting the next day will depend on the resulting gene products and their role in neuronal function.

Indeed, important recent discoveries have made it increasingly clear just how interrelated 'nature' and 'nurture' are and, consequently, how inadequate the old distinction is. Hitherto, it was assumed that brain centres – modules dedicated to a specific task – were wired up at birth. The idea was that we were able to see because dedicated 'visual modules' in the cortex were wired for vision, that we could feel because dedicated modules in the cortex were wired for touch, and so on.

The truth turns out to be much more puzzling.

For example, the visual cortex of a blind subject is recruited during the reading of Braille, a distinctly non-visual, tactile skill – whether the subject has acquired or congenital blindness. It turns out, moreover, that stimulating the subject's visual cortex with a magnet-induced current will temporarily impede his or her Braille performance. Even more remarkably, activity in the visual cortex occurs in normal seeing subjects who are blindfolded for a few days while learning to read Braille. So long as the blindfold remains firmly in place to prevent any light from falling on the retina, performance of Braille reading steadily improves. The blindfold is essential, for normal visual stimuli that activate the visual cortex in the normal way impede acquisition of the tactile skill. For example, if after five days the blindfold is removed, even briefly while the subject watches a television program before going to sleep, the Braille performance under blindfold the next days falls from its previous level. If the visual cortex can be recruited in the processing of non-visual signals, what sense can we make of the notion of the dedicated-vision module, and of the dedicated-modules hypothesis more generally?

> 'Historically, philosophers have debated how much of what we know is based on instinct, and how much on experience ... But recent discoveries in molecular biology, neuroembryology, and neurobiology have demolished this sharp distinction between nature and nurture.'

What is clear is that the nature versus nurture dichotomy is more of a liability than an asset in framing the inquiry into the origin of plasticity in human brains. Its inadequacy is rather like the inadequacy of 'good versus evil' as a framework for understanding the complexity of political life in human societies. It is not that there is nothing to it; but it is like using a grub hoe to remove a splinter.

An appealing idea is that if you learn something, such as how to tie a trucker's knot, then that information will be stored in one particular location in the brain, along with related knowledge – say, of the difference between reef knots and half-hitches. That is, after all, a good method for storing tools and paper files – in a particular drawer, at a particular location. But this is not the brain's way, as Karl Lashley first demonstrated in the 1920s.

Lashley reasoned that if a rat learned something, such as a route through a certain maze, and if that information was stored in a single, punctate location, then you should be able to extract it by lesioning the rat's brain in the right place. Lashley trained twenty rats on his maze. Next he removed a different area of cortex from each animal, and allowed the rats time to recover. He then retested each one to see which lesion removed knowledge of the maze. Lashley discovered that a rat's knowledge could not be localized to any single region; it appeared that all of the rats were somewhat impaired and yet somewhat competent – although more extensive tissue removal produced more serious memory deficit.

As improved experimental protocols later showed, Lashley's non-localization conclusion was essentially correct. There is no such thing as a dedicated memory organ in the brain; information is not stored on the filing cabinet model at all, but distributed across neurons.

A general understanding of what it means for information to be distributed over neurons in a network has emerged from computer models. The basic idea is that artificial neurons in a network, by virtue of their connections to other artificial neurons and the variable strengths of those connections, can produce a pattern that represents something – such as a male face or a female face, or the face of Churchill. The connection strengths vary as the artificial network goes through a training phase, during which it gets feedback about the adequacy of its representations given its input. But many details of how actual neural nets – as opposed to computer-simulated ones – store and distribute information have not yet been pinned down, so computer models and neural experiments are co-evolving. Many surprises – and even a revolution or two – are undoubtedly in store.

Even so, neuroscience, psychology, embryology, and molecular biology are together teaching us about ourselves as *knowers* – about what it is to know, learn, remember, and forget. But not all philosophers embrace these developments as progress. I take it as a sign of the backwardness of academic philosophy that one of its most esteemed living practitioners, Jerry Fodor, is widely supported for the following conviction: 'If you want to know about the mind, study the mind – not the brain, and certainly not the genes' (*Times Literary Supplement*, 16 May 2003, 1–2). If philosophy is to have a future, it will have to do better than that.

Some other philosophers believe that what we call external reality is naught but an idea created in a non-physical mind, a mind that can be understood through introspection and reflection. To these philosophers, developments in cognitive neuroscience seem, at best, irrelevant.

The element of truth in the approach taken by these philosophers is their hunch that the mind is not just a passive canvas on which reality paints. Indeed, we know that brains are continually organizing, structuring, extracting, and creating. As a central part of their predictive functions, nervous systems are rigged to make a coherent story of whatever input they get. 'Coherencing,' as I call it, sometimes entails seeing a fragment as a whole, or a contour where none exists; sometimes it involves predicting the imminent perception of an object as yet unperceived. As a result of learning, brains come to recognize a stimulus as indicating the onset of meningitis in a child, or an eclipse of the sun by the earth's shadow. Such knowledge depends on stacks upon stacks of neural networks. There is no apprehending the nature of reality except via brains, and via the theories and artefacts that brains devise and interpret.

From this it does not follow, however, that reality is *only* a mind-created idea. It means, rather, that our brains have to keep plugging along, trying to devise hypotheses that more accurately map the causal structure of reality. We build the next generation of theories upon the scaffolding – or the ruins – of the last. How do we know whether our hypotheses are increasingly adequate? Only by their relative success in predicting and explaining.

But does all this mean that there is a kind of fatal circularity in neuroscience – that the brain necessarily uses itself to study itself? Not if you think about it. The brain I study is seldom my own, but that of other animals or humans, and I can reliably generalize to my own case. Neuroepistemology involves many brains – correcting one another, testing one another, and building models that can be rated as better or worse in characterizing the neural world.

Is there anything left for the philosopher to do? For the neuro-philosopher, at least, questions abound: about the integration of distinct memory systems, the nature of representation, the nature of reasoning and rationality, how information is used to make decisions, what nervous systems interpret as information, and so on. These are questions with deep roots reaching back to the ancient Greeks, with ramifying branches extending throughout the history and philosophy of Western thought. They are questions where experiment and theoretical insight must jointly conspire, where creativity in experimental design and creativity in theoretical speculation must egg each other on to unforeseen discoveries.

3 The Role of Logic

RAY JENNINGS

Reasoning about even the most mundane things can be tricky. For example, most of us believe that we're not infallible. Being people of reasonable humility, we accept that at least some of our beliefs must be false. But which ones? The fact that we have accepted the beliefs we have means that we think they are all true. But if so, how can we also accept the belief that some of them are false? One might hope that it is the job of logic to help resolve this kind of puzzle. But if so, how?

Logicians have traditionally distinguished between factual claims and logical claims. The claim that Russell has a brother is a factual claim. In contrast, the claim that 'Russell has a sibling' follows from 'Russell has a brother' is a logical claim. It has long been thought that factual claims are the kinds of things capable of being learned by experience. Logical claims, in contrast, have been thought to be learned by reason alone. False beliefs may turn out to be either factual or logical in nature. If you mistakenly think that Russell has no brothers, this is a mistaken belief about the world. If you think that Russell has no siblings even though he has a brother, this is not so much a mistake about the world, as about which sentences *follow from* others. In short, the former is a factual pickle; the second is a logical one.

To put the matter a little differently, in some cases we are mistaken about *the truth of a factual claim*. In other cases, we are mistaken about the *preservation of truth within an inference*. Or to use yet other words, sometimes confidence in a belief comes directly through observation; sometimes it comes indirectly because it is *inherited* from other sentences. Confidence that comes directly from experience begets confidence that does not. The same is true of other properties such as reasonableness and believableness. On the other hand, misgivings need not be inherited. Just because I might have misgivings that Russell has a brother, it need not follow that I also have misgivings that he has a sibling.

Direct experience bestows a status upon some sentences that it does not bestow upon others. It bestows confidence, say, that Russell has a brother. That confidence is then inherited by other perhaps originally unforeseen sentences, just as citizenship that is bestowed with ceremony upon members of one generation will be inherited without ceremony by offspring not yet conceived. The revoking of citizenship, in contrast, need not affect the status of one's children.

This simile provides a key to understanding the science of logic. Just as in a political community where some goods will be inherited between generations and some will not, some 'goods' will be inherited between 'generations of sentences' while others will not. Logic thus becomes an experimental branch of 'property law' for 'communities of sentences.' Which logical claims are true will not be discovered by reason alone, since many of logic's most fundamental questions will be capable of being answered only within context-specific circumstances. For example, within a given system of sentences and a given context, what constitutes a good? And under what conditions will such goods be inherited?

Traditional property law evolved from tribal practices in which perhaps only land and livestock and their derivative products originally were considered to be goods. Today, logic is evolving in a similar way. Just as property law evolved as cooperative societies created new goods, logic is extricating itself from an archaic custom in which truth was considered the only sentential good. Nowadays governments are charging work groups with anticipating legislative challenges that may well arise from the many ways that technol-

'Logic has a fundamental role to play in data exploitation, not as a tribunal, and certainly not as a judge issuing forth necessities, but as a laboratory of imaginative experimentation and as a source of insight into possibilities.'

ogy can force a broadening of the conception of social goods. But technology and theoretical science also enrich human language – something we have learned as new philosophical methods better enable us to understand language in general. With these changes comes a new flexibility in our conception of what is of value in sentences; and this conception evolves as our 'communities of sentences' evolve.

We can find out whether 'the golf clubs are in the closet' is true or false by looking in the closet, but there is no guarantee that every sentence a new theory throws up will have these properties rather than some others. For example, 'the neuroptron has inverse angularity' may turn out to be neither true nor false in the physics of quasi-bleptonal curvatures; instead, that neuroptron will be either alpha-closed or alpha-open or alpha-clopen. Such new sentences of new languages may defy classification within the hoary old categories of truth and falsity. In bleptoplanar logic, for example, it is the property of alpha-clopenness, not the property of truth, that is inherited under blepto-implication. (Sadly, for further information about the fascinating world of bleptonal surface physics, and prolapsive physics more generally, the reader must wait until the subject is invented.) Here is a second example: if we are convinced that it is both blowing and either snowing or raining we can readily convince ourselves that it is either blowing and snowing or blowing and raining. But what holds universally for meteorological phenomena need not hold universally for quantum phenomena. The quantum physicist, confident in some degree that state A holds and that state B or C holds, can remain uncommitted as to whether either state A and B holds or state A and C holds.

As governments charge committees of legal theorists with thinking about various goods and their transfer, so universities and industry charge logical theorists with discovering and thinking about preservation-worthy properties of sentences specific to particular domains, whether it be the domain of quantum objects or pop-up toasters or the surface geometry of an airfoil. The language in which such properties are expressed is by no means fixed, and therefore neither is the range of values to which its sentences are susceptible.

This relegation of truth to informal conversational uses should not be surprising. In moments when we are as frank as Pontius Pilate, we realize that we haven't much of an idea what truth is. In introductory philosophy classes, instructors canvass a few classical theories of truth, but soon let the subject drop, and no one worries when the vocabulary recurs, as it does throughout their professional life and writings, without the matter ever having been settled. For the logician, in contrast, the language of truth and falsity provides a *reading* for two values that are often labelled 1 and 0; but all the logician needs to know for his purposes is that the two values are distinct. Which of the two is designated for preservation is a matter of convenience and tradition. Moreover, the use of numerals signals a readiness to add more values (1/2 or 2, say, or all the real numbers in the unit interval) for greater diversity, accordingly as an application requires it or as an experimental fancy takes him; and for a logician nothing dictates an interpretation of these values except convenience or application. If you have an appliance that boasts fuzzy logic, you can be sure that whatever logic is genuinely embodied in its design, it has more than just two values.

And one last point about truth, before we move along. Since we don't know what it is, we don't know whether it is a completely simple property with no properties of its own or a relatively complex one. If it's complex, then we might expect there to be closely related subspecies of truth, which we are perhaps as yet unable to distinguish. In this case, we might want not just to preserve truth, but to preserve particular types of truth. In this case, we will need some way, perhaps numerical, of marking the distinctions. So here again is opportunity for experimental logic, as we ask which combinations of logical principles reliably preserve which kinds of truth.

This point also invites us to think about logic as experimental property law. In more primitive times, goods were items within the disposition of an individual. We have said already that the variety of such items has been vastly increased. But we must also recognize that the class of items regarded as capable of having goods has also become a good deal more complex, so that it now includes political entities such as cities, districts, provinces, states, and nations, as well as civil entities such as partnerships, corporations, foundations, universities, and so on. Such entities can possess many of the goods that individuals can, but the creation of such political and civil fictions has also created new kinds of goods disposable only derivatively by component individuals.

A similar kind of development has occurred within the study of logic. Logicians have long realized that even on no more than their non-committal understanding of truth, questions can arise about its preservation from one body of data to another. Two avenues of investigation have thus traditionally corresponded to two obvious generalizations of inheritance. First, what system of logical principles would guarantee that if all of the sentences in one body of data are true, then all of the sentences in the other one are too? And second, what system would guarantee that if all of one body are true, then at least one sentence of the other body is true?

More recently, a third question has led to an intriguing variety of theories with much more general applications in data management and automated reasoning. This is the question of which properties are preserved when a body of data is augmented one sentence at a time. This of course takes us back to the beginning. Suppose that you have a body of beliefs all gained directly from experience, and all individually true. This gives a derivative but specifically 'corporate' property to the set of beliefs – namely, that all of its members are true. Now we can ask: Which additional, unobserved sentences inherit truth from this set of beliefs? If we can distinguish those sentences that do from those that do not, we can then add sentences of the former sort one by one to the original body of beliefs such that each resulting body of beliefs will inherit the corporate property of its predecessor set – namely, that all of its members are true. Standard logic performs this role adequately, even superbly in some circumstances. Even if there are many sentences that inherit truth from the set but standard logic does not let us infer, we know that any sentences that it does pick out can be added to the set without loss of corporate property.

Understanding logic in this way gives us a partial answer to our earlier question of what constitutes a good. For a body of data, *a good must at least be a property that merely random enlargements cannot be relied upon to preserve*. The application of logic must then allow us to distinguish enlargements that inherit the good from enlargements that do not. What's more, a good logic cannot be distinguished from a bad one independently of the specification of a good to be preserved. As we have remarked, if the good to be preserved is that all data in the body are true, then standard logic will normally be adequate if not sufficient. But if not all of the data are true, then standard logic becomes inadequate because the only property it preserves is not present to be preserved. Moreover, if we distinguish only the conditions *all true* and *not all true*, the remaining property is not a good, since it is inherited by any random enlargement of the body of data. Since in real life most bodies of data are not all true – and in some cases, such as the totality of one's beliefs, *cannot* be all true – practical applications have demanded that a wider range of corporate goods be identified, and enlargements regulated in such a way as to preserve those goods that the applications require to be inherited.

Recent logical theorists have occupied themselves with identifying corporate goods that even inconsistent bodies of data can possess, and articulating the principles that ensure their inheritance. Take, for example, the set of beliefs of an intellectually humble person. Surely this will be an inconsistent set, but if the sole inconsistency is a consequence of humility (believing that some of one's beliefs must be false when in fact this is one's only false belief), then the inconsistency is, as we might say, *maximally dilute*, since it requires the whole body of beliefs to reveal itself. At the other extreme, imagine believing a genuine contradiction such as '3 + 3 = 6 and 3 + 3 ≠ 6.' This would be a *maximally concentrated* contradiction, since it reveals itself in a single belief. Between the two extremes, it is easy to see that all of the intermediate dilutions are possible, and that the more dilute the better, since the less likely we are to reason from an inconsistent subset. In fact any dilution sufficient to defeat our capacity to consider beliefs jointly should keep the inconsistency below the radar of conscious thought. So a system of inference that permitted no augmentation that increased concentration of inconsistency would ensure that its dilution was preserved.

One other illustration will bring our discussion to a close. We should observe that if a body of data has no single inconsistent sentence – that is, if it has less than maximally concentrated inconsistency – then other identifiable properties may assume importance as corporate goods. Imagine that you are collecting data from, say, five independent sources, or that a robot is collecting data from five different senses, each of which is able to ensure the consistency of its submissions. You, on the receiving end of the data, might nevertheless be faced with inconsistencies between submissions. In the worst case, you might find that no pair of submissions could consistently be merged. Even in this dire circumstance, the data you have received might have features worth preserving. For example, you might not want to augment the data by adding inferences that required the total data to be parcelled into six consistent batches, where before it required only five. You might add no more than the data common to all five sources. This ultraconservative strategy would take unanimity as a good, and preserve that. A less conservative strategy would aim to preserve what could be called *the level of inconsistency* of the data – that is, the least number of consistent bundles into which the data could be separated. One still conservative strategy that achieves this aim would be to regard yourself as forced to add only those data that could be standardly inferred from at least one bundle on every such separation. The task of the applied logician is to devise a system of inferential rules that permit us to infer all and only those sentences that can be added without increasing the level of incoherence.

Now, however difficult it may have been to accept that inconsistent data can have any assets worth preserving, we have to admit that there are different kinds of inconsistency, and that we can see that the nature of the inconsistency of a particular body of data may be (economically, strategically, politically) important information. Understood by analogy with the law of properties, logic has a fundamental role to play in data exploitation, not as a tribunal, and certainly not as a judge issuing forth necessities, but as a laboratory of imaginative experimentation and as a source of insight into possibilities.

4 Paradox and Probability

PAUL BARTHA

What does it mean to be rational?

One famous answer comes from the eighteenth-century Church of England bishop, Joseph Butler. In his book *The Analogy of Religion*, Butler tells us that 'probability is the very guide of life.' Butler's idea was that being rational means weighing whatever evidence we can find and then giving it no more and no less influence over our lives than it deserves.

Butler's doctrine was actually invented and put to spectacular use a century earlier, by the French thinker Blaise Pascal. Pascal showed that when it comes to making rational decisions, probability is but half the story. 'Reason cannot decide' whether or not God exists, he wrote, but reason can nevertheless compel us to gamble that He does. Pascal's Wager is the argument that the prospect of an infinite reward for religious belief, even if discounted by allowing only a tiny probability that God exists, swamps any finite expectation that can be derived from mere worldly pleasures.

Pascal's argument was the earliest application of what has become the fundamental rule of rational decision-making for most economists and philosophers: choose the action that maximizes expected value (or expected utility). To make use of the principle, of course, we need to have well-defined probabilities and well-defined values (that is, structured preferences).

Is this principle prescriptive or descriptive? In 1738, Daniel Bernoulli employed expected-utility reasoning to explain why it makes more sense for the poor to purchase insurance than for the rich: the utility of an increment of wealth (and the disutility of loss) is much greater for the former than for the latter. In Bernoulli's essay, the principle is mainly prescriptive – it tells us how we ought to act – but it is also taken to describe the behaviour of any reasonable agent.

Is it irrational, then, to make choices that don't maximize expected value? Many recent studies of human behaviour show that we display a shocking disrespect for the principles of decision theory. We start smoking, knowing it to be harmful and addictive. We are willing to drive across town to save $10 on a $15 oil change for our car, but not to save $10 on a $750 television. We tend to prefer a 'sure thing' (a guaranteed win) even when some alternative action appears to have higher expected value. Our preferences may vary depending on how a situation is described. We may even assign a higher probability to the proposition that a woman is a feminist bank teller than to the proposition that she is a bank teller, in violation of the most basic principles of probability theory.

In none of these cases, though, is it obvious that we are guilty of acting or thinking in an irrational manner. Two American psychologists, Daniel Kahneman and Amos Tversky, spent thirty years studying these kinds of actions and inferences. In 2002, their work was recognized when Kahneman won the Nobel Prize for Economics. (Unfortunately, by then Tversky had died, so his name wasn't included on the prize list.) Kahneman drew a sharp contrast between intuitive and deliberative choices. Deliberative choices conform to the norms of decision theory. Intuitive choices, largely shaped by evolutionary pressures, are guided by simple heuristics and frequently diverge from the recommendations of expected-utility reasoning. In his Nobel Prize speech, Kahneman stated: 'Most behaviour is intuitive, skilled, unproblematic, and successful.' Heuristic principles that are appropriate for rapid decision-making and largely successful are not obviously irrational.

In the research of many economists, we find that if we set out to explain these or other anomalous-looking patterns of behaviour, we can often construct a model that restores their rationality. In fact, we frequently can do this without having to sacrifice the principle of maximizing expected value. For instance, we can introduce the cost of complex deliberation as part of the decision process. Inability to find a model may be taken as a sign of failure on the part of the social scientist, rather than as proof that ordinary folks are acting irrationally!

What is the upshot? The principle of maximizing expected value can still be upheld as a fundamental criterion of rationality, but on a somewhat different basis than we might initially have expected. First, it is almost always fruitful to investigate stable and widespread patterns of human behaviour under the charitable assumption that they are (in some respect) rational. To label such behaviour patterns irrational is effectively to locate them beyond the bounds of inquiry. Second, given this predisposition to be charitable, the equation of rationality with maximization of expected value amounts to no more than a commitment to a paradigm of explaining behaviour in terms of maximization.

A very different set of puzzles – of interest mainly to philosophers – arises when we consider how the principles of decision-making apply to *super-beings*. Pascal's Wager can serve as an illustration. Many have dismissed Pascal's argument by suggesting that the notion of infinite value is meaningless for finite human beings. But whether or not that is the case, we can still consider whether the wager would be compelling to a rational being who could experience infinite happiness.

Bringing infinity into the picture generates many amusing paradoxes about rational decision-making. Consider a being that lives forever and is trying to decide when to open a bottle of Everbetter wine. The wine improves every day, so it is always rational to wait another day; but is it rational to wait forever? Clearly not. So what's an immortal being to do? Or, put yourself in the position of a deity contemplating the creation of a world containing infinitely many creatures, each just slightly better off alive than dead. Does this world contain infinite goodness? Is it better than a world with finitely many much happier creatures? Or, going back to Pascal's argument, suppose that we are faced with a choice between many different deities, each promising an infinite reward to his or her believers. In such a case, we might well argue that the injunction to maximize expected value provides no guidance.

This second class of puzzles, though not motivated by the observation of human behaviour, may sometimes be useful in understanding it. Maybe some people who perform great acts of self-sacrifice are gambling on a Pascalian wager. The same goes for terrorists willing to fly airplanes into buildings. In both cases, perhaps, certain goals are taken as being infinitely more valuable than anything else, including human life. The same sort of preference structures might be needed to understand the 'rationality' of acts of great heroism and fanatical evil. Even apart from whether such philosophical puzzles contribute direct insight into human behaviour, they are valuable if our objective is to understand what it means to be rational in general.

Both for human beings and for super-beings, expected-utility reasoning sometimes appears to fail. But what unites philosophers meditating on abstract puzzles and economists modelling perverse human behaviour is the directive to seek, at least initially, a solution that characterizes rational decision-making in terms of maximization.

5 Could a Machine Think?

PAUL M. CHURCHLAND AND
PATRICIA SMITH CHURCHLAND

Artificial-intelligence research is undergoing a revolution. To explain how and why, we first need a flashback.

By the early 1950s the old, vague question, 'Could a machine think?' had been replaced by the more approachable question, 'Could a machine that manipulated physical symbols according to structure-sensitive rules think?' This question was an improvement because formal logic and computational theory had seen major developments in the preceding half-century. Theorists had come to appreciate the enormous power of abstract systems of symbols that undergo rule-governed transformations. If those systems could just be automated, then their abstract computational power, it seemed, would be displayed in a real physical system. This insight spawned a well-defined research program with deep theoretical underpinnings.

Could a machine think? There were many reasons for saying yes. One of the earliest and deepest reasons lay in two important results in computational theory. The first was Church's thesis, which states that every effectively computable function is recursively computable. 'Effectively computable' means that there is a 'rote' procedure for determining, in finite time, the output of the function for a given input. 'Recursively computable' means, more specifically, that there is a finite set of operations that can be applied to a given input, and then applied again and again to the successive results of such applications, to yield the function's output in finite time. The notion of a rote procedure is non-formal and intuitive; thus, Church's thesis does not admit of a formal proof, but it does go to the heart of what it is to compute, and many lines of evidence converge in supporting it.

The second important result was Alan M. Turing's demonstration that any recursively computable function can be computed in finite time by a maximally simple sort of symbol-manipulating machine that has come to be called a universal Turing machine. This machine is guided by a set of recursively applicable rules that are sensitive to the identity, order, and arrangement of the elementary symbols it encounters as input.

These two results entail something remarkable – namely, that a standard digital computer, given only the right program, a large enough memory, and sufficient time, can compute *any* rule-governed input–output function. That is, it can display any systematic pattern of responses to the environment whatsoever.

More specifically, these results imply that a suitably programmed symbol-manipulating machine (hereafter, SM machine) should be able to pass the Turing test for conscious intelligence. The Turing test is a purely behavioural test for conscious intelligence, but it is a very demanding test even so. (Whether it is a fair test will be addressed below, where we also encounter a second and quite different 'test' for conscious intelligence.) In the original version of the Turing test, the inputs to the SM machine are conversational questions and remarks typed into a console by you or me, and the outputs are typewritten responses from the SM machine. The machine passes this test for conscious intelligence if its responses cannot be discriminated from the typewritten responses of a real, intelligent person. Of course, at present no one knows the function that would produce the output behaviour of a conscious person. But the Church and Turing results assure us that, whatever that (presumably effective) function might be, a suitable SM machine could compute it.

This is a significant conclusion, especially since Turing's portrayal of a purely teletyped interaction is an unnecessary restriction. The same conclusion follows even if the SM machine interacts with the world in more complex ways: by direct vision, real speech, and so forth. After all, a more complex recursive function is still Turing-computable. The only remaining problem is to identify the undoubtedly complex function that governs the human pattern of response to the environment and then write the program (the set of recursively applicable rules) by which the SM machine will compute it. These goals form the fundamental research program of classical AI.

Initial results were positive. SM machines with clever programs performed a variety of ostensibly cognitive activities. They responded to complex instructions, solved complex arithmetic, algebraic, and tactical problems, played checkers and chess, proved theorems, and engaged in simple dialogues. Performance continued to improve with the appearance of larger memories and faster machines and with the use of longer and more cunning programs. Classical, or 'program-writing,' AI was a vigorous and successful research effort from almost every perspective. Occasional denials that an SM machine might eventually think seemed uninformed and ill motivated. The case for a positive answer to our title question was overwhelming.

There were a few puzzles, of course. For one thing, SM machines were admittedly not very brain-like. Even here, however, the classical approach had a convincing answer. First, the physical material of any SM machine has nothing essential to do with what function it computes. That is fixed by its program. Second, the engineering details of any machine's functional architecture are also irrelevant, since different architectures running quite different programs can still be computing the same input–output function.

Accordingly, AI sought to find the input–output *function* characteristic of intelligence and the most efficient of the many possible programs for computing it. The idiosyncratic way in which the brain computes the function just doesn't matter, it was said. This completes the rationale for classical AI and for a positive answer to our title question.

Could a machine think? There were also some arguments for saying no. Through the 1960s, interesting negative arguments were relatively rare. The objection was occasionally made that thinking was a non-physical process in an immaterial soul. But such dualistic resistance was neither evolutionarily nor explanatorily plausible. It had a negligible impact on AI research.

A quite different line of objection was more successful in gaining the AI community's attention. In 1972, Hubert L. Dreyfus published a book that was highly critical of the parade-case simulations of cognitive activity. He argued for their inadequacy as simulations of genuine cognition, and he pointed to a pattern of failure in these attempts. What they were missing, he suggested, was the vast store of inarticulate background knowledge every person possesses and the common-sense capacity for drawing on relevant aspects of that knowledge as changing circumstance demands. Dreyfus did not deny the possibility that an artificial physical system of some kind might think, but he was highly critical of the idea that this could be achieved solely by symbol manipulation at the hands of recursively applicable rules.

Dreyfus's complaints were broadly perceived within the AI community – and within the discipline of philosophy as well – as shortsighted and unsympathetic, as harping on the inevitable simplifications of a research effort still in its youth. These deficits might be real, but surely they were temporary. Bigger machines and better programs should repair them in due course. Time, it was felt, was on AI's side. Here again the impact on research was negligible.

Time was on Dreyfus's side as well: the rate of cognitive return on increasing speed and memory began to slacken in the late 1970s and early 1980s. The simulation of object recognition in the visual system, for example, proved computationally intensive to an unexpected degree. Realistic results required longer and longer periods of computer time, periods far in excess of what a real visual system requires. This relative slowness of the simulations was darkly curious; signal propagation in a computer is roughly a million times faster than in the brain, and the clock frequency of a computer's central processor is greater than any frequency found in the brain by a similarly dramatic margin. Yet on realistic problems, the tortoise easily outran the hare.

Furthermore, realistic performance required that the computer program have access to an extremely large knowledge base. Constructing the relevant knowledge base was problem enough, and this was compounded by the problem of how to access just the contextually relevant parts of that knowledge base in real time. As the knowledge base got bigger and better, the access problem got worse. Exhaustive searches took too much time, and heuristics for relevance did poorly. Worries of the sort Dreyfus had raised finally began to take hold here and there even among AI researchers.

At about this time (1980), John Searle authored a new and quite different criticism aimed at the most basic assumption of the classical research program: the idea that the appropriate manipulation of structured symbols through the recursive application of structure-sensitive rules could constitute conscious intelligence.

Searle's argument is based on a thought experiment that displays two crucial features. First, he describes an SM machine that realizes, we are to suppose, an input–output function adequate to sustain a successful Turing test conversation conducted entirely in Chinese. Second, the internal structure of the machine is such that, however it behaves, an observer remains certain that neither the machine nor any part of it understands Chinese. All it contains is a monolingual English speaker following a written set of instructions for manipulating the Chinese symbols that arrive and leave through a mail slot. In short, the system is supposed to pass the Turing test, while the system itself lacks any genuine understanding of Chinese or real Chinese semantic content.

The general lesson drawn is that any system that merely manipulates physical symbols in accordance with structure-sensitive rules will be at best a hollow mock-up of real conscious intelligence, because it is impossible to generate 'real semantics' merely by cranking away on 'empty syntax.' Here, we should point out, Searle is imposing a non-behavioural test for consciousness: the elements of conscious intelligence must possess real semantic content. In sum,

The Chinese Room

Axiom 1   Computer programs are formal (syntactic).
Axiom 2   Human minds have mental contents (semantics).
Axiom 3   Syntax by itself is neither constitutive of nor sufficient for semantics.
Conclusion   Programs are neither constitutive of nor sufficient for minds.

One is tempted to complain that Searle's thought experiment is unfair because his Rube Goldberg system will compute with absurd slowness. Searle insists, however, that speed is strictly irrelevant here. A slow thinker should still be a real thinker. Everything essential to the duplication of thought, as per classical AI, is said to be present in the Chinese room.

Searle's paper provoked a lively reaction from AI researchers, psychologists, and philosophers alike. On the whole, however, he was met with an even more hostile reception than Dreyfus had experienced. In his writings, Searle forthrightly lists a number of these critical responses. We think many of them are reasonable, especially those that 'bite the bullet' by insisting that, although it is appallingly slow, the overall system of the room-plus-contents does understand Chinese.

We think those are good responses, but not because we think the room understands Chinese. We agree with Searle that it does not. Rather, they are good responses because they reflect a refusal to accept the crucial third axiom of Searle's argument: '*Syntax by itself is neither constitutive of nor sufficient for semantics.*' Perhaps this axiom is true, but Searle cannot rightly pretend to know that it is. Moreover, to assume its truth is tantamount to begging the question against the research program of classical AI, for that program is predicated on the very interesting assumption that if one can just set in motion an appropriately structured internal dance of syntactic elements, appropriately connected to inputs and outputs, the same cognitive states and achievements can be produced as are found in human beings.

The question-begging character of Searle's axiom 3 becomes clear when it is compared directly with his conclusion: '*Programs are neither constitutive of nor sufficient for minds.'* Plainly, his third axiom is already carrying 90 per cent of the weight of this almost identical conclusion. That is why Searle's thought experiment is devoted to shoring up Axiom 3 specifically. That is the point of the Chinese room.

Although the story of the Chinese room makes axiom 3 tempting to the unwary, we do not think it succeeds in establishing axiom 3, and we offer a parallel argument in illustration of its failure. A single transparently fallacious instance of a disputed argument often provides far more insight than a book full of logic chopping.

Searle's style of scepticism has ample precedent in the history of science. The eighteenth-century Irish bishop George Berkeley found it unintelligible that compression waves in the air, by themselves, could constitute or be sufficient for objective sound. The English poet and artist William Blake and the German poet and naturalist Johann W. von Goethe found it inconceivable that small particles by themselves could constitute or be sufficient for the objective phenomenon of light. Even in the twentieth century, some people have found it beyond imagining that inanimate matter by itself, and however organized, could ever constitute or be sufficient for life. Plainly, what people can or cannot imagine often has nothing to do with what is or is not the case, even where the people involved are highly intelligent.

To see how this lesson applies to Searle's case, consider a deliberately manufactured parallel to his argument and its supporting thought experiment:

The Luminous Room

Axiom 1	Electricity and magnetism are forces.
Axiom 2	The essential property of light is luminance.
Axiom 3	Forces by themselves are neither constitutive of nor sufficient for luminance.
Conclusion	Electricity and magnetism are neither constitutive of nor sufficient for light.

Imagine this argument raised shortly after James Clerk Maxwell's 1864 suggestion that light and electromagnetic waves are identical, but before the world's full appreciation of the systematic parallels between the properties of light and the properties of electromagnetic waves. This argument could have served as a compelling objection to Maxwell's imaginative hypothesis, especially if accompanied by the following commentary in support of axiom 3:

> Consider a dark room containing a man holding a bar magnet or charged object. If the man pumps the magnet up and down, then, according to Maxwell's theory of artificial luminance (AL), it will initiate a spreading circle of electromagnetic waves and will thus be luminous. But as all of us who have toyed with magnets or charged balls well know, their forces (or any other forces for that matter), even when set in motion, produce no luminance at all. It is inconceivable that you might constitute real luminance just by moving forces around!

How should Maxwell respond to this challenge? He might begin by insisting that the 'luminous room' experiment is a misleading display of the phenomenon of luminance because the frequency of oscillation of the magnet is absurdly low, too low by a factor of 10^{15}. This might well elicit the impatient response that frequency has nothing to do with it, that the room with the bobbing magnet already contains everything essential to light, according to Maxwell's own theory. In response, Maxwell might bite the bullet and claim, quite correctly, that the room really is bathed in luminance, albeit a grade or quality too feeble to appreciate. (Given the low frequency with which the man can oscillate the magnet, the wavelength of the electromagnetic waves produced is far too long and their intensity is much too weak for human retinas to respond to them.) But in the climate of understanding here contemplated – the 1860s – this tactic is likely to elicit laughter and hoots of derision. 'Luminous room, my foot, Mr Maxwell. It's pitch-black in there!'

Alas, poor Maxwell has no easy route out of this predicament. All he can do is insist on the following three points. First, axiom 3 of the above argument is false. Indeed, it begs the question despite its intuitive plausibility. Second, the luminous room experiment demonstrates nothing of interest one way or the other about the nature of light. And third, what is needed to settle the problem of light and the possibility of artificial luminance is an ongoing research program to determine whether, under the appropriate conditions, the behaviour of electromagnetic waves does indeed mirror perfectly the behaviour of light.

This is also the response that classical AI should give to Searle's argument. Even though Searle's Chinese room may appear to be 'semantically dark,' he is in no position to insist, on the strength of this appearance, that rule-governed symbol manipulation can never constitute semantic phenomena, especially when people have only an uninformed common-sense understanding of the semantic and cognitive phenomena that need to be explained. Instead of exploiting one's understanding of these things, Searle's argument freely exploits one's ignorance of them.

With these criticisms of Searle's argument in place, we return to the question of whether the research program of classical AI has a realistic chance of solving the problem of conscious intelligence and of producing a machine that thinks. We believe the prospects are poor, but we rest this opinion on reasons very different from Searle's. Our reasons derive from the specific performance failures of the classical research program in AI, and from a variety of lessons learned from the biological brain and a new class of computational models inspired by its structure. We have already indicated some of the failures of classical AI regarding tasks the brain performs swiftly and efficiently. The emerging consensus on these failures is that the functional architecture of classical SM machines is simply the wrong architecture for the very demanding jobs required.

What we need to know is this: How does the brain achieve cognition? Reverse engineering is a common practice in industry. When a new piece of technology comes on the market, competitors find out how it works by taking it apart and divining its structural rationale. In the case of the brain, this strategy presents an unusually stiff challenge, for the brain is the most complicated and sophisticated thing on the planet. Even so, the neurosciences have revealed much about the brain on a wide variety of structural levels. Three anatomic points will provide a basic contrast with the architecture of conventional electronic computers.

First, nervous systems are parallel machines, in the sense that signals are processed in millions of different pathways simultaneously. The retina, for example, presents its complex input to the brain not in chunks of eight, sixteen, or thirty-two elements, as in a desktop computer, but rather in the form of almost a million distinct signal elements arriving simultaneously at the target of the optic nerve (the lateral geniculate nucleus), there to be processed collectively, simultaneously, and in one fell swoop. Second, the brain's basic processing unit, the neuron, is comparatively simple. Furthermore, its response to incoming signals is analog, not digital, inasmuch as its output spiking frequency varies continuously with its input signals. Third, in the brain, axons projecting from one neuronal population to another are often matched by axons returning from their target population. These descending or recurrent projections allow the brain to modulate the character of its sensory processing. More important still, their existence makes the brain a genuine dynamical system whose continuing behaviour is both highly complex and to some degree independent of its peripheral stimuli.

Highly simplified model networks have been useful in suggesting how real neural networks might work and in revealing the computational properties of parallel architectures. For example, consider a three-layer model consisting of neuron-like units fully connected by axon-like connections to the units at the next layer. An input stimulus produces some activation level in a given input unit, which conveys a signal of proportional strength along its 'axon' to its many 'synaptic' connections to the hidden units. The global effect is that a pattern of activations across the set of input units produces a distinct pattern of activations across the set of hidden units.

The same story applies to the output units. As before, an activation pattern across the hidden units produces a distinct activation pattern across the output units. All told, this network is a device for transforming any one of a great many possible input vectors (activation patterns) into a uniquely corresponding output vector. It is a device for computing a specific function. Exactly which function it computes is fixed by the global configuration of its synaptic weights.

There are various procedures for adjusting the weights so as to yield a network that computes almost any function – that is, any vector-to-vector transformation – that one might desire. In fact, one can even impose on the network a function one is unable to specify, so long as one can supply a set of examples of the desired input–output pairs. This process, called 'training up the network,' proceeds by successive adjustment of the network's weights until it performs the input–output transformations desired.

Although this model network vastly oversimplifies the structure of the brain, it does illustrate several important ideas. First, a parallel architecture provides a dramatic speed advantage over a conventional computer, for the many synapses at each level perform many small computations simultaneously instead of in laborious sequence. This advantage grows larger as the number of neurons increases at each layer. Strikingly, the speed of processing is entirely independent of both the number of units involved in each layer and the complexity of the function they are computing. Each layer could have four units or a hundred million; its configuration of synaptic weights could be computing simple one-digit sums or second-order differential equations. It would make no difference. The computation time would be exactly the same.

Second, massive parallelism means that the system is fault-tolerant and functionally persistent; the loss of a few connections, even quite a few, has a negligible effect on the character of the overall transformation performed by the surviving network.

Third, a parallel system stores large amounts of information in a distributed fashion, and any part of it can be accessed in milliseconds. That information is stored in the specific configuration of synaptic connection strengths, as shaped by past learning. Relevant information is 'released' as the input vector passes through – and is transformed by – that configuration of connections.

Parallel processing is not ideal for all types of computation. On tasks that require only a small input vector but many millions of swiftly iterated recursive computations, the brain performs very badly, whereas classical SM machines excel. This class of computations is very large and important, so classical machines will always be useful, indeed, vital. There is, however, an equally large class of computations for which the brain's architecture is the superior technology. These are the computations that typically confront living creatures: recognizing a predator's outline in a noisy environment; re-

'*Could science construct an artificial intelligence by exploiting what is known about the nervous system? We see no principled reason why not.*'

calling instantly how to avoid its gaze, flee its approach, or fend off its attack; distinguishing food from non-food and mates from non-mates; navigating through a complex and ever-changing physical/social environment; and so on.

Finally, it is important to note that the parallel system described is not manipulating symbols according to structure-sensitive rules. Rather, symbol manipulation appears to be just one of many cognitive skills that a network may or may not learn to display. Rule-governed symbol manipulation is not its basic mode of operation. Searle's argument is directed against rule-governed SM machines; vector transformers of the kind we describe are therefore not threatened by his Chinese room argument even if it were sound, which we have found independent reason to doubt.

Searle is aware of parallel processors but thinks they too will be devoid of real semantic content. To illustrate their inevitable failure, he outlines a second thought experiment, the Chinese gym, which has a gymnasium full of people organized into a parallel network. From there his argument proceeds as in the Chinese room.

We find this second story far less responsive and compelling than his first. For one thing, it is irrelevant that no unit in his system understands Chinese, since the same is true of nervous systems: no neuron in my brain understands English, although my whole brain does. For another, Searle neglects to mention that his simulation (using one person per neuron, plus a fleet-footed child for each synaptic connection) would require at least 10^{14} people, since the human brain has 10^{11} neurons, each of which averages more than 10^3 connections. His system would require the entire human populations of over 10,000 earths. One gymnasium would not begin to hold a fair simulation.

On the other hand, if such a system were to be assembled on a suitably cosmic scale, with all its pathways faithfully modelled on the human case, we might then have a large, slow, oddly made but still functional brain on our hands. In that case, the default assumption is surely that, given proper inputs, it *would* think, not that it couldn't. There is no guarantee that its activity would constitute real thought, because the vector-processing theory sketched above may not be the correct theory of how brains work. But neither is there any a priori guarantee that it could not be thinking. Searle is once more mistaking the limits on his (or the reader's) current imagination for the limits on objective reality.

The brain is a kind of computer, although most of its properties remain to be discovered. Characterizing the brain as a kind of computer is neither trivial nor frivolous. The brain does compute functions, functions of great complexity, but not in the classical AI fashion. When brains are said to be computers, it should not be implied that they are serial, digital computers, that they are programmed, that they exhibit the distinction between hardware and software, or that they must be symbol manipulators or rule followers. Brains are computers in a radically different style.

How the brain manages meaning is still unknown, but it is clear that the problem reaches beyond language use and beyond humans. A small mound of fresh dirt signifies to a person, and also to coyotes, that a gopher is around; an echo with a certain spectral character signifies to a bat the presence of a moth. To develop a theory of meaning, more must be known about how neurons code and transform sensory signals, about the neural basis of memory, learning, and emotion, and about the interaction of these capacities and the motor system. A neurally grounded theory of meaning may require revision of the very intuitions that now seem so secure and that are so freely exploited in Searle's arguments. Such revisions are common in the history of science.

Could science construct an artificial intelligence by exploiting what is known about the nervous system? We see no principled reason why not. Searle appears to agree, although he qualifies his claim by saying that 'any other system capable of causing minds would have to have causal powers (at least) equivalent to those of brains.' We close by addressing this claim. We presume that Searle is not claiming that a successful artificial mind must have *all* the causal powers of the brain, such as the power to smell bad when rotting, to harbour slow viruses such as kuru, to stain yellow with horseradish peroxidase, and so forth. Requiring perfect parity would be like requiring that an artificial flying device lay eggs.

Presumably he means only to require of an artificial mind all of the causal powers relevant, as he says, to conscious intelligence. But which exactly are they? We are back to quarrelling about what is and is not relevant. This is an entirely reasonable place for a disagreement, but it is an empirical matter, to be tried and tested. Because so little is known about what goes into the process of cognition and semantics, it is premature to be very confident about what features are essential. Searle hints at various points that every level, including the biochemical, must be represented in any machine that is a candidate for artificial intelligence. This claim is almost surely too strong. An artificial brain might use something other than biochemicals to achieve the same ends.

This possibility is illustrated by Carver A. Mead's research at the California Institute of Technology. Mead and his colleagues have used analog VLSI techniques to build an artificial retina and an artificial cochlea. (In animals the retina and cochlea are not mere transducers: both systems embody a complex processing network.) These are not mere simulations in a minicomputer of the kind that Searle derides; they are real information-processing units responding in real time to real light, in the case of the artificial retina, and to real sound, in the case of the artificial cochlea. Their circuitry is based on the known anatomy and physiology of the cat retina and the barn owl cochlea, and their output is dramatically similar to the known output of the organs at issue.

These chips do not use any neurochemicals, so neurochemicals are clearly not necessary to achieve the evident results. Of course, the artificial retina cannot be said to see anything, because its output does not have an artificial thalamus or cortex to go to. Whether Mead's program could be sustained to build an entire artificial brain remains to be seen, but there is no evidence now that the absence of biochemicals renders it quixotic.

We, and Searle, reject the Turing test as a sufficient condition for conscious intelligence. At one level our reasons for doing so are similar: we agree that it is also very important how the input–output function is achieved; it is important that the right sorts of things be going on inside the artificial machine. At another level, our reasons are quite different. Searle bases his position on common-sense intuitions about the presence or absence of semantic content. We base ours on the specific behavioural failures of the classical SM machines and on the specific virtues of machines with a more brain-like architecture. These contrasts show that certain computational strategies have vast and decisive advantages over others where typical cognitive tasks are concerned – advantages that are empirically inescapable. Clearly, the brain is making systematic use of these computational advantages. But it need not be the only physical system capable of doing so. Artificial intelligence, in a non-biological but massively parallel machine, remains a compelling and discernible prospect.

6 I Checkmate, Therefore I Am

MARK KINGWELL

A familiar ambivalence surfaced a few years ago when chess grand-master Gary Kasparov attempted to face down his non-human opponent, the computer Deep Junior.

On the one hand, many of us root for Mr Kasparov. He represents the hope that creative human intelligence is superior to the algorithm crunching of even the biggest, fastest computer. On the other hand, some of us root for Junior. Why? Because, somewhere in there, we harbour a little fear that defeat of a supercomputer might mean – as events so often prove – that all technology is fallible.

It's an old conundrum, and one on display in far more serious ways elsewhere. In the aftermath of the Columbia space shuttle disaster, investigators gathered clues, sought reasons, reconstructed events. What went wrong? Did a system fail or malfunction? Or was there human error? A faulty decision, a moment of panic or confusion?

It used to be a truism in the air crash investigation business that, in the end, the answer was almost always 'pilot error,' a judgment that was final if harsh – and, in essence, biblical. If you seek the roots of disaster, look no further than the imperfection of man. But that answer is too easy, since it assumes the very premise it should be questioning, namely, our shaky but necessary faith in the machines we build and fly.

'It used to be a truism in the air crash investigation business that, in the end, the answer was almost always "pilot error," a judgment that was final if harsh – and, in essence, biblical. If you seek the roots of disaster, look no further than the imperfection of man.'

You see the problem. If we start distrusting machines, it's only a few short steps to the neo-Luddites and the Unabomber. Less wildly, we might start to wonder if those smart bombs and fly-by-wire F-16s are really so great after all. We assign agency (and so blame) only to Maj. Harry Schmidt, not the bomb he dropped on helpless Canadian soldiers; but surely part of that awful chain of events was the absolute accuracy of the weapon, which magnified the adrenaline-fuelled mistake of the man. Where does the line get drawn?

Distrust breeds distrust, largely because fear highlights dependence. We tend to blame ourselves rather than the machines because we *must* believe in them: they control so much of our lives. And when we don't blame ourselves, we most often blame that great black box, chance. In the case of Columbia, the space odyssey ended up being deadly, not because a computer ran amok, but just because things went wrong, the tragic accumulation of probabilities. Misfortune, not murder. But that does not solve the problem of our complex, sometimes hostile dependence on machines.

Which brings us back to Mr Kasparov and Deep Junior. These chess matches are no longer the big news they once were, in part because Mr Kasparov, acknowledged as the greatest player in the world, has already been defeated by a machine. In 1997, he was edged 3.5 points to 2.5 by the IBM machine Deep Blue, Deep Junior's 'father,' in a loss invariably referred to as 'humiliating.'

Nor does chess grip the popular imagination the way it did when legendary paranoiac Bobby Fischer challenged Boris Spassky in the Cold War of the mind, in Reykjavik in 1972. I remember following that series move for move through articles in *Time* magazine – a fact that now seems not just quaint but incredible. Chess crazies still challenge passersby in the famous southwest corner of Washington Square Park, a place where you can score coke and a rook-led victory steps from each other, but searching for Bobby Fischer is, these days, more a metaphor for nurturing your child than a celebration of chess.

The result is that man–machine matches are now small-time news. Facing a computer six years after his original 1997 match, Mr Kasparov played six games against Junior, a machine built by the Israeli scientists Amir Baran and Shay Bushinsky. The two opponents were tied after four games, with a win each and two draws.

In these games the human grandmaster employed a version of the strategy he attempted against Deep Blue, what insiders call 'going off book.' The computer's advantage over a human is its massive processing power, which allows it to scan millions of possible move combinations, but also its precise knowledge of every recorded game its opponent has played. So Mr Kasparov tried mixing it up with Deep Blue in 1997, changing his style and inventing new gambits. The program caught on and adjusted, eventually winning.

In his rematch, Mr Kasparov attempted even more radical jukes and openings against Deep Junior, hoping to throw the computer off with unorthodox combinations like quick-step deployment of a king in front of his queen. In other words, the best strategy against a presumptively rational opponent is creative irrationality.

'I think I made a brilliant move to get Deep Junior out of the book and make it think on its own,' Mr Kasparov explained. 'If you play aggressive chess and throw in a little twist you can get great positions against the strongest computer programs.'

If it works, the Krazy Kasparov strategy will no doubt be chalked up as a victory of human spontaneity over machine literalness. It's the same dodge routinely used to mock Mr Data, the stiff android on *Star Trek: The Next Generation*, or the crude computers on the original *Star Trek*, thick-witted logic-bashers whose circuits could be fried by the merest hint of paradox. We'll all breathe a sigh of relief and think, 'You can't beat a little animal creativity! Way to go, humans!'

But consider the downside. Computers as powerful as Deep Junior are self-revising. They accommodate subtleties and nuances; they can modify their behaviour to meet a human's instrumental aggression. In many senses of the word, they think and create.

It follows that they can, like any human, learn to make deadly miscalculations as well as brilliant moves. When we defeat our machines, we merely bring them down to our imperfect, irrational level. We only win for losing. How very human.

7 The Credible-Computer Conundrum

JOHN RUSSELL AND ANDREW IRVINE

Can computers be trusted?

We aren't yet at the stage where a computer like HAL in *2001: A Space Odyssey* dictates our every move, but we do rely on computers to assist us with the development of everything from airline schedules to precision medical instruments. And even relatively simple errors can cause serious difficulties.

In addition, the complexity of many computer programs is now mind-boggling. Some are hundreds of thousands of lines long. Many are so complicated that no human mind will ever be able to check them. In many cases we now rely on computers to check their own reliability. Does this make sense?

Especially in high-risk situations, we like to think that we have more than simple empirical evidence from experimental trials that a computer is reliable. For example, before relying on a computer program designed to assist air traffic controllers, we want to be sure that it won't lead to accidents under conditions in which it hasn't yet been explicitly tested.

But if we use computers to test their own reliability, isn't this just like arguing in a circle? Unless we are sure of a computer's reliability to begin with, what good is a computer proof that a computer program is reliable?

Although worrisome, this problem is not new to science. It is a variant of something called the Experimenter's Regress. This regress arises as follows:

Q: How do we know a particular phenomenon occurs? For example, how do we know we have a pure sample of a particular substance? Or how do we know whether a given drug will have a desired consequence?

A: By constructing an experiment.

Q: But how do we know the scientist constructing the experiment has acquired the skill to design and operate the experiment reliably?

A: By whether or not the experiment yields the correct result.

Q: But how do we know the experiment yields the correct result?

A: This depends on whether the phenomenon is in fact there to detect.

Q: But how do we know the phenomenon is in fact there to detect?

A: By constructing an experiment ...

And so on.

In many cases the only way to determine whether someone has the skill necessary to design and operate an experiment is to see whether the experiment yields the appropriate results. But if so, it will always be possible to reject the results of an experiment, especially when they lead to controversial claims.

Some social scientists, including H.M. Collins, the man who gave the Experimenter's Regress its name, conclude that this shows that science, at bottom, is a subjective, social enterprise.

As one social scientist puts it, 'Experiments alone seldom resolve controversies. Often the regress can be broken only by appeals to other factors or combinations of factors, whether it be the power of theory, institutional prestige, or rhetoric.' If experiments alone do not decide these types of issues, perhaps it is social factors – such as how famous or highly respected a scientist is – that ultimately prove decisive.

In the case of computers, a similar regress arises. Although it is comparatively easy to check a computer's reliability for tasks such as balancing a bank statement, consider those cases in which a computer is used to prove complex mathematical theorems.

For example, the proof of the Four-Colour Theorem – the claim that any map can be coloured using a maximum of four colours in such a way that no two adjoining countries share the same colour – is one that turns out to be so long and complicated that no human mind will ever be able to understand it completely. How can we ever know whether the 'proof' is in fact reliable?

Once again we are faced with a regress:

Q: How do we know a particular theorem is true? For example, how do we know that the Four-Colour Theorem is true?

A: By constructing a computer program to prove or disprove it.

Q: But how do we know the computer program is reliable?

A: By whether or not it produces the correct result.

Q: But how do we know it produces the correct result?

A: This depends on whether the theorem is in fact true.

Q: But how do we know the theorem is in fact true?

A: By constructing a computer program to prove or disprove it ...

And so on.

Here again, it may turn out that we can never know the fact of the matter. This is not only a worry if we want to understand the Four-Colour Theorem. It is also disturbing if we are trying to establish the reliability of air traffic control systems, or medical diagnostic systems, or even programs designed to help us do our income tax.

Just as with the Experimenter's Regress, the Computer Regress appears to show that the only way to determine whether a computer program is in fact reliable is by seeing whether it produces the correct result. But if so, whenever we are uncertain about what that result should be, it will always be possible to conclude that the computer is in error. It seems that accepting the result depends on whether we trust computers, or on whether we trust those people who tell us we can trust computers.

Once again, if Collins is correct, social convention, as much as scientific fact, will be what influences our decision to accept or reject these types of results. Is Collins correct?

In answer to this question, many scientists and philosophers point out that, just like other factors, social factors can always be 'filtered out' using good scientific method. Just as we can devise experiments to control for the influence of other corrupting variables, we can also control for the influence of social biases. And if this is right, it is difficult to believe that, at bottom, science is primarily a matter of rhetoric or social standing.

'Checking for the existence of social factors is something science does well. Double-blind experiments, blind peer reviews, openness about research methodology, and the demand that results be replicated are just a few of the many filtering methods that scientists, philosophers, and statisticians have devised to check for social and other experimental biases.'

In fact, checking for the existence of social factors is something science does well. Double-blind experiments, blind peer reviews, openness about research methodology, and the demand that results be replicated are just a few of the many filtering methods that scientists, philosophers, and statisticians have devised to check for social and other experimental biases. Indeed, the need for such filters has been recognized from the earliest days of modern science.

For example, before allowing the Venetian Doge, Leonardo Donà, to view the moon through his newly invented telescope, Galileo first showed him how a distant church could be made to appear as if it were much nearer. Galileo knew that controversy would arise if he and others claimed that the moon was marked by craters and mountains. Such observations would show that the moon was not a perfect sphere, as foretold by the theology of his day. By first allowing the Doge to gain confidence in his telescope as a magnifying instrument, Galileo made it more difficult for theologians to claim it was the instrument that was at fault when it showed the moon's imperfections.

To us, and to many in Galileo's time, this sort of test represents a compelling basis for identifying and setting aside certain social ideologies. Even so, ultimately Galileo was forced to recant his views in front of the Inquisition. Despite this, the general point remains. Just as it is important to discover ways of independently testing each physical factor within an experiment, social factors also can – and must – be examined to discover how they affect the advancement of knowledge. Our knowledge of phenomena is thus intimately linked to our knowledge of experimental method.

Much the same point can be made about today's computers. Prior to their use in crucial experiments, individual components of even the most complicated computer hardware and software can be tested in a variety of contexts, including those in which we already know what the outcome should be. If the testing is done properly, corrupting factors can be anticipated and properly accounted for.

Such testing will always be fallible. But to the extent that we are willing to bring foresight, imagination, and a fair and open mind to the development of diagnostic software, even the most complex computers will turn out to be just as reliable as any other highly reliable scientific instrument.

8 The Future of Intimacy

MARK KINGWELL

There is a quality of early morning light in Vancouver that you don't find in the rest of the country, a Turneresque wash of greys and blues that suffuses English Bay in romantic obscurity and makes the nearby Coastal Range look like a pod of humpback whales moving out to sea with infinitesimal slowness. It feels like the birthplace of the world except for the foreground: blocks of half-completed buildings, piles of concrete rubble, and the lurking silhouettes of high-load cranes. The joggers and rollerbladers, inevitable and ubiquitous even at six a.m., pick their way nimbly through all this ambiguous evidence of Pacific Rim optimism. If there has been a downturn in the local economy – twenty thousand jobs lost in one month alone, an 11 per cent decline in house prices, a 40 per cent drop in volume – you wouldn't know it from the building sites or the packed restaurant patios. Vancouver really is the every-city of *The X-Files*, a generic urban location of hustle and intrigue, and it seems to represent the future – a future confident, multiracial, physically fit, comfortable with technology, and happily, even ecstatically, capitalistic.

Is it also a likely future? The economic doomsayers would have us believe that all the pan-Asian and Pacific revivalism is just empty currency-driven puffery. And perhaps they are right: there is quite enough evidence to suggest that the reality of globalization is not the liberalizing dream of modern economics, but instead a nightmare of emergent class conflict, tribal hatreds, and technological imperialism.

Neal Stephenson's 1992 novel *Snow Crash*, a cult phenomenon of cyberpunk action and inventively dystopian speculation, fills in the details of this not-so-rosy picture. The book, set in a near-future California of gated communities (or 'Burbclaves'), private freeways, and quasi-governmental companies known as 'franchulates,' has become an underground best-seller, one of those defining documents of the culture that never quite show up on the radar screens of network television or mainstream newspapers. The central action concerns the efforts of L. Bob Rife, a global media magnate, to resurrect an ancient religion – also an ancient computer virus – to reprogram the brains of the world's population. His point of entry is The Raft, a floating country of refugees, displaced persons, and pirates, which is moving towards the vulnerable west coast of North America, whose distracted, drug-addled, materialistic, and self-interested inhabitants are powerless to resist. The U.S. federal government has been reduced to Fedland, a bureaucratic nonentity with a glad-handing president who can't get anyone to take him seriously.

It might seem capricious to consider a science fiction novel significant in shaping the future, but as the American philosopher Richard Rorty noted recently in his careful assessment of *Snow Crash,* visions of the future can have an unusually powerful bearing on the present. Rorty chided the 'pessimism' of Stephenson's vision and lamented its tendency to induce a sense of impotence. How we imagine the future dictates, in larger part than we know, the kind of future we will actually create.

Any simple dichotomy of optimism and pessimism is too crude to capture the nuances of the issue, however. Advocates would have us believe that the question of life a hundred years hence is one either of utopia or dystopia, wondrous emancipation or dank enslavement – a form of bipolar thinking that is particularly prevalent at cultural limit-times like the much-discussed, entirely arbitrary, and yet immensely compelling millennium. Both options sport hidden dangers.

The trouble with utopian visions is that they hide the realities of the messy transition – think of the blithe elimination of poverty and hunger in the *Star Trek* series. They can also become a platform for intolerant, occasionally violent social change: witness the dominant political movements of the past bloody century. Not least, utopias run the risk of making any actual, step-wise reform look paltry and therefore somehow contemptible. It is in this sense that, as the saying goes, the perfect is the enemy of the good.

Similarly, dystopian visions are often an invitation to gloomy inaction rather than a needed wake-up call. They stunt feelings of hope that might translate into political action. They feed on our fears and anxieties, working them up into fully formed bad dreams of a dark future. They make us feel powerless or overwhelmed: instead of acting, we quiver in a depressed stasis.

There is good evidence that such cultural pessimism has been widespread throughout history, but there is also something that must be acknowledged as unique to our times. In *Amusing Ourselves to Death,* the media critic Neil Postman discusses what he calls the problem of 'the information-action ratio' – the structure of human responsiveness that determines how much information, and what sort, is usefully assimilable. Our current mass-information media offer virtually limitless information. This triggers a kind of overpowering ennui that steals upon us when we think of how many impossible demands there are for action.

It is essential that we bring all issues tangled in the ball of thread we call the future – technology, globalization, environmental changes – down to a level where we can think about them productively.

Consider a small example. Anyone who knows me personally is aware that my favorite techno-toy is a cordless headset phone. This little machine has changed my life more than almost any other piece of technology, in large part because it facilitates the interplay of work and leisure. Using the headset, I can glimpse a future in which we all achieve, on demand, what computer programmers like to call seamless ubiquity: the ability to access a communications or computation system from any point. I am now able to carry on phone conversations from every corner of my apartment, and I can do so with my hands free. I can talk to a friend while signing for a parcel delivery, or do a radio interview while chopping vegetables.

Sometimes, in moments of self-indulgent adolescent vanity, I even imagine I look pretty cool with the headset on. This is surely part of its appeal, at least for men of my generation, raised as we were on Gerry Anderson's Supermarionettes, and Captain Scarlet and the Thunderbirds, as well as more recent echoes in John Cusack's well-equipped professional killer in *Grosse Point Blank* – not to mention Pierce Brosnan as James Bond, or Madonna and Bobby Brown on stage during a concert tour. Of course, it's entirely possible that I just look geeky, not so much savvy gadget king as stock-control boy at The Gap.

The headset is only a minor piece of technology, but it hints at the real issues in thinking about the future. We have spent a lot of time lately either decrying or celebrating technology, with the hype-masters of *Wired* magazine squaring off against various neo-Luddites and advocates of media fasting. But most of us, in thoughtful moments, realize that technology is entirely devoid of interest unless it makes some aspect of daily life easier or more interesting – or if it, in rare cases, increases the degree of justice in our world.

The base-level facts of existence – that we must rise and face each day, and that at some point this circadian cycle will cease for each one of us – will not be altered by the passage of a century. Whatever changes, these will remain the same. And they cast any technological, economic, and social changes in their only worthwhile light. What happens to the people around the globe – what happens in their daily lives of seeking security, love, and happiness – as we pass into the new era of the twenty-first century?

What particularly fascinates me in this attempt to bring the future down to a human scale is the concept of intimacy, the phenomenon of closeness, one person to another. How is it that we are able to form and maintain relationships, to carry on conversations that build up a web of interpersonal connections so vast and complicated they can only be captured by the nearly banal phrase 'human civilization'?

This daily miracle, which we rarely pause to acknowledge, let alone celebrate, is the key to thinking about the imaginable future. It is unlikely that the next hundred years will change one of the key features of human life – namely, that consciousness is irreducibly inward, forcing us to find our connections to others by outward means. Intimacy will continue to play its joyful, vexing, complex role in our lives, and the subtle dialectic of private and public will continue to dominate our institutions, occupations, entertainments, and, most of all, our sense of ourselves.

Our machines will always change, often in ways that technological cheerleaders will choose to call progress, but beneath the faster and better wiring, our longing for connection will remain the same.

I have been away from home a lot lately, travelling from city to city across this country and south of the border. On a recent Sunday, I had breakfast with my wife in Boston, lunch with a friend in Toronto, and dinner with a colleague in Ottawa. I started writing this essay in Montreal, worked on it in Vancouver, Edmonton, and Calgary, fiddled with the first few paragraphs in Winnipeg, fleshed out some other parts in upstate New York, and then finished it in Toronto.

> '*Our machines will always change, often in ways that technological cheerleaders will choose to call progress, but beneath the faster and better wiring, our longing for connection will remain the same.*'

Covering all those miles, trundling in and out of departure lounges and putting in hours in rental cars, gives you an appreciation for the vastness and variety of Canada: the way provincial politics dominates Edmonton in a way it doesn't in Winnipeg; the way Vancouver has, like Paris, apparently cornered the regional market on beautiful people; the way the smog and the driving habits get worse every year in Toronto.

This kind of travel also forces an awareness of technology's gifts. Many of us now board transcontinental planes with all the excitement of commuters entering a subway car, and I boot up my laptop absent-mindedly in a hotel restaurant, the way I might open a door. These are the small miracles of modern life, incredible privileges, ones within the grasp of less than one-fifth of the planet's inhabitants. And there are many more on the way, things that will alter the details of daily life in ways we can hardly guess at.

What matters to me, or anyone else, in all this? That I could have dinner with my parents and brothers in Vancouver last month, the first time in four years that we had all been together, with my mother passing around old snapshots of her and my father when they were first together – wonderful black-and-white portraits, my father with his lanky good looks and Harry Connick haircut, my mother sprightly at nineteen, the sweet little messages she wrote to him on the back of each photo. That I can check my e-mail in Calgary and read a welcome message from a friend in England, saying that he has a new son. That I can, finally, come home again and find the restful, familiar comfort of my little apartment, the reassuring and human routine of doing the laundry, watering the plants, shopping for food, and cooking a meal for myself.

We all realize that as humans we find much of our deepest happiness in intimacy, in the sharing of ourselves with one another. This communion is the texture of life, the cross-hatching beneath our fingers as we run them over the passage of time. There is a mystery here, a deeply human thing that must be acknowledged before we can move on into the future, a future that is coming whether we like it or not. The critic Walter Benjamin once said that we don't move into the future facing forward so much as we back into it, gazing out over the past. It might be even more accurate to say that we back into it, gazing fixedly down at our feet.

The word 'intimate' contains an illuminating contradiction that is worth dwelling on before we take our next backward steps. As an adjective, 'intimate' means personal: the intimate details of your life that only you can know. It comes from the Latin word *intimus*, which means 'inmost.' In this sense, 'intimate' captures the strange opacity of individual consciousness, that irreducible first-personal character of identity which at some level is impenetrable by anyone outside.

To be intimate in this sense is to be inward. But the adjective is also used, more commonly, to describe the act of sharing that inwardness with another: an intimate conversation, an intimate friendship. This hints at the ambiguity in the word, and in the concept. Considered as a verb now, 'intimate' also means to declare, to communicate, to set out a message. In English we change the pronunciation to distinguish the two uses of the word, and the verb form derives more proximately from the Latin verb *intimare,* meaning to announce. But the deep connection is clear: to intimate is to share a message, though not always an inward one; to be intimate is to be inward, though not always in a way that can be shared.

This play of closeness and distance, of inside and outside, is at the centre of human life. Trapped, of necessity, inside our own minds, we try, with the crude but wonderful tools of language and touch and expression, to bridge the unbridgeable gap between one person and another. We intimate things and hope, thereby, to become intimate: to join our private lives together in the public space that lies between us, where meaning resides. It doesn't always work: our words are misconstrued, our intentions twisted, our messages changed in the telling like the comical distortions of the telephone game. But we go on trying because otherwise we are nothing, our stories fall untold and therefore, somehow, unlived.

We also hear intimations from elsewhere. Intimations of immortality, as Wordsworth said, where life and experience hint at the transcendent possibilities buried in our limited selves: the way we can go beyond ourselves, can feel a sense of purpose or belonging that is not illusory because we sense our connection to a scheme of things. We may also hear intimations of mortality, those whispers of the shade that throw life suddenly into high relief and, if we are listening closely enough, may clarify the possibilities of happiness in this life.

Finding our way into the future is not a matter of deciding which big picture is most likely. It is not, perhaps, a matter of big pictures at all. Like Socrates' basic question – 'What is the life worth living?' – the question of the future is one that must start with a thousand smaller ones. What are you going to do today? Tomorrow? Next month? The future is constructed of the infinite number of present moments passing through our hands. With each one we have an opportunity to make our inwardness responsive to the needs of others.

We need ideals to guide us in that responsiveness: justice, primarily, and the respect for other entities on which it is ultimately based. Indeed, we can no longer restrict our pursuit of these connections to other members of our race, our nationality, even our species. Nor can we allow the triumph of private life and private goods that has been wrought in these past three centuries of modernity to atrophy the public life and public good that alone makes a society, or a civilization, worthwhile.

We therefore have to countenance the possibility that some of the private luxuries we have enjoyed – ones which are too rapacious of resources, too disproportionate in their distribution – will no longer be tolerable as time goes on. Our intimate lives may change in ways we do not always like because we can no longer ignore the voices in our ears – and in our hearts – that intimate we must share even more.

The problem is that if we let the question spin off into trying to imagine the future as such, the result can only be an overwhelming set of demands that will, paradoxically, have the effect of deadening our responsiveness. People defect from responsibility then, hiding in gated communities and surrounding their property with private police forces. Taxpayers begin to see themselves more as clients than as citizens, able to take their purchasing power for social services elsewhere than to inefficient or redistributive governments.

That revolt is rooted in anxiety, in perceived external threats to our security and comfort. We all feel that anxiety now and then, and because it comes from within, it may even seem perfectly justifiable. After all, it is a dangerous world. However, no retreat into isolation will protect our intimate connections if we lack a common destiny to support them and give them purpose. The challenge is to get on with the hard business of making the world a slightly better place, one step at a time, ignoring the increasingly strident prophets of both boom and doom. The truth about the future is, as always, both less spectacular and more demanding – like everyday life itself.

PART III

Education and Culture

1 Broad Subjects Free Us from Narrow Minds

ANDREW IRVINE

'Only the educated are free,' says the Stoic philosopher Epictetus. By this he means that education has the potential to free us from the constraints of class, culture, and nation. Education is what gives us the ability to go beyond our own experience, to see unexpected alternatives, to think outside the box.

For example, by reading Anne Frank's *Diary* we are transported across time and space to experience what it was like to live in hiding during the Nazi purges. By learning about the discoveries of Gregor Mendel and Isaac Newton, we find it easier to face new scientific and medical challenges with optimism. By reading about the fall of the Holy Roman Empire, we discover how to protect our own society from decay and decline.

Another famous Greek philosopher had a different view. 'If you ask what is the good of education in general,' wrote Plato, 'the answer is easy: that education makes good men, and that good men act nobly.'

On this view, choosing the right action and leading a good life require that we learn all we can about the world, human nature, and ethics. Just as becoming a good carpenter requires that we learn about the practice of carpentry, becoming a good person requires that we learn about the nature of the good.

In the modern period there is yet a third value attached to education. This is that we must all be able to read and think about a wide variety of topics for democracy to flourish. Since laws and institutions ultimately find their foundation in the sovereign will of a country's citizens, it is only through an educated citizenry that democracy can prevail.

These three suggestions about the value of education are no doubt interconnected, and if we accept them, we must also acknowledge that they require us to be exposed to something more than narrow, technical training. All three suggestions rely crucially on the so-called 'impractical' disciplines of the humanities. They emphasize what is often called a liberal education.

Yet far from being the centre of the modern university, as these

arguments envisage, humanities departments might rightly be characterized as the ghettos of today's university. Like a once prosperous city
centre that has been abandoned in the rush to the suburbs, humanities
departments are among the least prosperous sectors of the university.

The gap between federal funding for the humanities and for the pure
sciences serves as an example. Although the Social Sciences and
Humanities Research Council (SSHRC) represents 55 per cent of all
students and researchers in Canada, it funds just 5 per cent of these
students and 15 per cent of these researchers.

In contrast, although the Natural Sciences and Engineering Research
Council (NSERC) represents only 30 per cent of all students and researchers, it has a budget much larger than that of SSHRC. As a result, it
is able to fund 20 per cent of the students and 60 per cent of the
researchers it represents.

Collectively, it appears that we have decided that the task of maintaining the humanities is simply not worth the money.

As if to emphasize this point, one premier recently suggested that
universities might consider abandoning degrees in the humanities. In
this, he was suggesting another view of education, one that also has a
long tradition. This is the view that, unlike the sciences, the humanities
fail to help us improve the human condition.

Through science we are able to harness the elements, conquer disease, and master nature. It is through science that we are able to learn
about everything from earthquakes to penicillin. In doing so, we improve our quality of life. In the words of the eighteenth-century Enlightenment thinker Paul-Henri d'Holbach, 'Man is unhappy because he is
ignorant of nature.'

However, we do ourselves and our children a disservice when we
abandon the goals of a liberal education in favour of those of the
sciences and the professions. The current decline in funding to humanities departments across Canada will not only affect adversely the goals
of Epictetus and Plato, it will also ultimately diminish our understanding of nature. Science and the humanities are just too closely linked in
practice for this not to occur. The same connections also hold between
the humanities and the professional faculties such as business, law, and
medicine.

Essential to the development of such practical disciplines are so-
called transferable skills – basic reading and writing skills, critical thinking skills, and general knowledge. All of these skills come primarily
from the humanities. For the practical-minded it is also worth empha-

sizing that these are the skills that help distinguish Canada's highly educated employees from those in many competing labour markets, including Mexico's.

Furthermore, in an economically integrated yet culturally plural world, such skills are essential if we are to understand and communicate with people whose backgrounds and views are different from our own. Living together successfully in the global village requires an informed understanding of different languages, cultures, and ways of life. A liberal education helps us meet these challenges. Epictetus, a Roman slave, clearly understood this. For him, education was a precondition of responsible world citizenship, an idea that he and his followers introduced.

'What distinguishes classical literature, history, music, art, and philosophy from other subjects is their intrinsic value. These subjects are important and universal simply because they have the potential to speak to all people and all generations. They teach us, as much as anything can, about our shared humanity.'

There is another perspective on the humanities that is also worth emphasizing: they should be studied, not for any instrumental reason, but simply for their own sake. Enjoying good literature, understanding history, studying philosophy, and appreciating music and art all serve as ends in themselves.

At a time when so many people find their lives unfulfilling, it is odd that we have decided as a society to devalue those very pursuits that are of value purely for their own sake. What distinguishes classical literature, history, music, art, and philosophy from other subjects is their intrinsic value. These subjects are important and universal simply because they have the potential to speak to all people and all generations. They teach us, as much as anything can, about our shared humanity.

Today there is wide agreement that each generation has a duty to preserve its natural environment for future generations. It is a pity that there is not equally wide agreement about our duty to preserve those intellectual achievements that make up our non-physical environment. As humanities departments face greater and greater pressures to prove their relevance to specific vocational outcomes, it's worth emphasizing that we have an obligation to study and teach those disciplines that have formed the backbone of our common culture for the past three thousand years, regardless of their short-term consequences.

Today we are able to read the works of Epictetus and Plato only because earlier generations, despite every hardship over the centuries, had the foresight to preserve them for us. What will future generations say of us if, given our unquestioned prosperity, we fail to do the same for them?

2 The Young and the Jobless

GRAEME HUNTER

Not long ago the University of Ottawa student newspaper published a letter in its end-of-term edition in which an English student lamented the 'futility' of her education.

'Don't get me wrong,' she wrote. 'Some of it was pleasant. Some of my professors were knowledgeable, insightful individuals. Even so, being taught something that is utterly inapplicable to today's job market has doomed me to an endless chain of McJobs, no matter how affable my teachers were.' She then continued as follows:

> I always did well in English, I always loved writing, and I thought my skills might get me somewhere. I suppose it serves me right for ignoring the warnings of my parents – 'You know what a B.A. means ... Barely Anything!'
>
> It's four years and $30,000 later, and I still don't have enough knowledge to land myself a well-paying job ...
>
> I'm not alone in my plight either. A lot of my friends in anthropology, history, philosophy and sociology are in the same boat as me.
>
> So my question is, what exactly was the point of the past four years? Quite frankly, it seems like an exercise in futility.

I would like to try to answer her final question, but first it would help to consider what former Ontario premier Mike Harris would say. He would agree with the student's parents: 'This is not about any particular university,' he would tell her. 'You are a lamentable illustration of what is wrong with the public university as such. University today is out of touch with students' needs and that is precisely what we need to change.'

Students have been outspoken in their opposition to Mike Harris's proposals, but here is one student, surely, who ought to find herself in basic agreement with the Harris agenda. She at least would have to say, 'Yes, Mr Harris, I wish I had had the wisdom to study computer science, or engineering, or business administration, so that I could be leaving the university with a real prospect of employment. It is true that I would then likely know nothing of Shakespeare, Blake or Eliot; it is true that I would probably be incapable of drafting the forceful letter I sent to the student newspaper, or even of coming to so clear an understanding of my own position, but I would have that all-important job waiting for me at the end of the line.'

I do not know the author of that letter personally. But I doubt that she would respond so to Mr Harris, if she spoke from her heart. Her letter is proof that she has something to offer the labour market that a more practical course of study would not have given her. She has the sort of articulate clarity that is perennially in demand. Can it be that the weakness she complains of in her education is really its strength? Humanities education was never meant to be vocational and therefore it cannot be criticized for not delivering some particular job at the end of the line.

'University fulfils its purpose whenever it enables students to read the best writers with understanding and to articulate their own best thoughts. At their best, the humanities know no better equipment for life and work than this and, as CEOs of large companies continue to affirm, neither do they.'

University fulfils its purpose whenever it enables students to read the best writers with understanding and to articulate their own best thoughts. At their best, the humanities know no better equipment for life and work than this and, as CEOs of large companies continue to affirm, neither do they.

A couple of years ago I asked a large class in 'critical thinking' to read and discuss an essay that took a lofty view of university's purpose. In the middle of the discussion, a sharp, high achiever grew so exasperated that he stood up to deliver his point. 'I know exactly what you're saying,' he said, 'and I'm prepared to learn all these high-minded opinions just to pass this course. But I want you to know what all of us are thinking. We know that when we walk out the door, we are confronted with a different world where getting ahead is what counts.'

Before I could reply, a middle-aged student jumped in with a more effective rejoinder than I could have made. 'You shouldn't assume you are speaking for all of us,' she told the student. 'I left a six-figure income to come back to university and this is the kind of discussion I came back for. I was single and well enough off to afford to come back. But I would like you to know that there is not one of my six-figure-income friends who doesn't envy me, even if they're not able to follow my example.'

The silence that greeted her remark may not have been six-figured, but it was golden.

3 How to Get to the Top

THOMAS HURKA

How should Canada educate students to compete successfully in the business world? Some provincial governments think it is by teaching them business. For example, the Alberta government recently announced plans for an 'unprecedented' expansion of business education at its three universities.

However, recent evidence suggests that this approach is mistaken. We will produce better managers if we educate them first in traditional subjects in the arts and sciences. We may do best of all if we educate them in philosophy.

Each year, thousands of undergraduates write admissions tests for prestigious graduate programs. There's the Law School Admission Test (LSAT), the Graduate Management Admission Test (GMAT) for business study, and the Graduate Record Examination (GRE) for other fields. One study done for the U.S. Department of Education compared tests of students from different disciplines, with surprising results.

Consider the GMAT, used for admission to MBA programs and, ultimately, to the highest levels of management. Undergraduate business students, whom you'd think would be especially well prepared for this test, do badly on it, scoring below the average for all test takers. The best results are by math students, followed by philosophy students and engineers.

This is typical. Business students score below average on almost all the tests, as do – excepting engineers – all other students in applied or occupational fields. The best results come from students in the natural sciences and humanities. The study concludes that on tests measuring aptitude for advanced professional study, 'undergraduates who major in professional and occupational fields consistently *under perform* those who major in traditional arts and science fields.'

The most consistent performers are philosophy students. They are first out of twenty-eight disciplines on one test, second on another, and third on a third. On their weakest test they are still 4.6 per cent above the average, the best performance on a weakest test of any group.

Though the data here are less consistent, the superior performance of arts and science students continues after university. According to sociologist Michael Useem, they have more difficulty finding beginning managerial jobs than those with business or professional degrees because they lack specific skills in finance or engineering. When they are hired, it is usually lower in the company hierarchy. Once hired, however, they advance more rapidly than their colleagues.

On average, arts and science graduates end their careers level with business and engineering graduates, having closed the gap between them. In some companies with less of an engineering or MBA 'culture,' they pass them. An AT&T study showed that after twenty years with the company, 43 per cent of liberal arts graduates had reached upper-middle management, compared to 32 per cent of business majors and 23 per cent of engineers. The Chase Manhattan Bank found that 60 per cent of its worst managers had MBAs while 60 per cent of its best managers had BAs. At IBM, nine of the company's top thirteen executives had liberal arts degrees.

What explains the success of arts and science students? Many arguments for liberal education cite a contemporary cliché – that we live in a time of unprecedented change. If the world is in flux, an applied education will soon be out of date. Better the breadth and flexibility given by general studies.

A better explanation points to what cannot change: the basic elements of reasoning and problem solving. The study of admissions tests found that students do best 'who major in a field characterized by formal thought, structural relationships, abstract models, symbolic languages, and deductive reasoning.' The more abstract a subject, the more it develops pure reasoning skills; and the stronger a person's reasoning skills, the better she'll do in any applied field.

This fits the data from business. Corporations report that although technical skills are most important in low-level managerial jobs, they become less so in middle and top jobs, where the key traits include communications skills, the ability to formulate problems, and reasoning skills. Liberal arts education may be weak in the prerequisites for beginning managerial jobs but it provides just what's needed for success at the top.

This doesn't mean there's no place for business education. Canadian industry needs specialized business skills, and our universities should supply them. But in the increasingly competitive world economy there will be a premium on vision, creativity, and analytical power – traits better fostered by liberal education.

This points to the recommendation now heard most from chief executive officers: first an arts and science degree in a field like English, physics, or philosophy, then an MBA. First some general intellectual skills, then the specific knowledge needed to apply those skills in business.

So to train successful business leaders, Canada should strengthen education in the arts and sciences. And this will have another effect. Students educated in the liberal arts will be more rounded individuals, knowing more about the natural world and the history of their culture. They will also be better at reasoning about morality and politics. At the very least, this will be a nice side effect.

4 The Case for a Liberal Education

JOHN WOODS

The notion of a liberal education is not well understood these days. Possibly the most prevalent misinterpretation is that an education is liberal only to the extent that its curriculum is free of 'structure' – that is, free of required courses and prerequisites, and perhaps, too, of mandatory assignments and obligatory examinations. Not far behind is the view that what makes an education liberal is its 'freedom' from useful consequences. On this understanding, a liberal education can have at most intrinsic value and lies open only to whatever justification attends intrinsic value in a tough and pragmatic world. *Ars gratia artis.* Still another misconception is that a liberal education is one free to all and, hence, because of its ambitions for universality, that it alone discharges the true meaning of the university – *universitas.*

We do not here meet logically exclusive interpretations; indeed, they have a way of being jointly promulgated and, in some quarters, jointly despaired of. But they are, all of them, quite wrong. It is true that a liberal education implies certain freedoms, but freedom from structure or standards is not one of them, and still less is freedom from work. No, the basic freedoms from are these: freedom from religious dogma and political control of the curriculum. Nor is an education liberal to the extent that it honours the 'true meaning of the university' – the education of everyone

> *'Literacy and articulateness, acumen and discernment, sensitivity and judgment and exposure to the best that has been written and thought. These are the socially essential "by-products" of a good liberal education.'*

whomsoever. *Universitas* does not mean that. It means 'all of us' in the sense of a community for learning, a *Studium Generale*, in which idea there are no implications of exhaustive enfranchisement.

There is, however, something to the position that a liberal education is bereft of career linkages. A liberal education is not a vocational education. Who these days will forbear to wonder what its justification is, apart from its intrinsic value? What is its purpose?

The term 'liberal education' has etymological connection with the Latin *liberi*, for freemen, to whom alone, in classical Rome, an education was available. Here was an education that fixed its attention on a simple truth, which served as its rationale: no matter what occupation a citizen may choose, he is called upon to take part in, and to pass judgments on, decisions of public policy. It is, therefore, but a step to the consequence that the education of a free citizen must be sufficiently broad and rich to equip him to judge wisely. Here is the kernel of the deeper truth and greater importance, for our time, of a liberal education: it is required for the health of democracies. A state is democratic only to the extent that its principal actions are either reasonably direct functions of decisions by all the citizenry, or are open to their fairly direct intervention. Unless we are so naïve as to suppose that such decisions and interventions need not be informed ones and need not be scrutinized for consistency and soundness of purpose, it is unavoidable that we ask: 'What is the education that best serves the citizen in his judgments of the actions of policies of his democracy?'

Some years ago it could be claimed without pause that a command of reading, writing and speech is the *sine qua non* of a liberal education. The evident collapse of literacy among today's schooled young gives rise to a painful dilemma. Either illiteracy is no bar to a life of intellectual and political freedom, or the schools have become an unwitting impediment to democracy. Perhaps there are subtle and hidden factors that lessen the severity of the problem; if they exist, I am not aware of them. I am only left to scramble over one horn of the dilemma by reaffirming the necessity of the basic literacies raised as high as we know how. The other horn I leave for us all to be ashamed and sad about, and very, very angry.

These days, citizens of Canada must be ready with opinions (not by any means final opinions) about overpopulation, poverty, and ecological stresses in general; about ideological strife, racial discord, and separatism; about a national energy policy, tax reform, and the shape of the nation's economy; about the very structure of contemporary government itself; about life and death as devices of social policy; and about much else besides.

These are broadly political issues of considerable complexity. Their final and uniquely correct determination (should there ever be such a thing) is certainly beyond the powers of most of us. But in a democracy this is not, and never has been, an appropriate basis for withholding one's views, or for abandoning one's obligation to figure things out as best one can; to muddle through if necessary, but not necessarily to muddle through.

Genuine and *useful* understanding waits upon a command of the salient facts, but also upon the capacity for critical evaluation. Who is not moved to great (if not always sympathetic) sadness by the spectacle of a person who is awash in facts that he cannot organize, manage, or understand and who does not have the means of sorting premise from conclusion and assumption from proof?

It cannot seriously be denied that a rightful ideal of a democracy is to make its decisions and to prosecute its aims with wisdom. He who is wise is a good judge of value, is ready with a distinction between cost and worth. Such a person possesses, to the extent that he is wise, discernment and horse sense. Wisdom endows us with intellectual perspective, equips us to probe and to take the measure of fundamental principles. Wise people, Aristotle would say, possess 'intellectual virtue,' by which they may resist the artful rhetorical flourish designed to shake confidence in matters about which non-confidence is undeserved, or to tilt perspective and blunt judgment.

Literacy and articulateness, acumen and discernment, sensitivity and judgment and exposure to the best that has been written and thought. These are the socially essential 'by-products' of a good liberal education. Yet some would say that a liberal education is incompatible with vocational and professional training and that there is too little time for either or both. I say, 'Rubbish!'

Year after year, more and more of our citizens are allowed (and encouraged) to postpone economic self-sufficiency until quite the better part of their first quarter-century. If in what was well over half the lifetime of a man or woman of the Renaissance, one cannot achieve both a liberal and vocational preparation for (the rest of one's) life, it is folly to look to so forbidding a notion as *impossibility* to know the reason why. In all events, one fact in particular stands out, daring us to take note of it. This is that 'there is a paradox connected with (merely) vocational training. The more vocational it is, the narrower it is; the narrower it is, the less likely it is to serve usefully in earning a living.' Sidney Hook goes on to say that 'there is no reason – except unfamiliarity, with the idea – why vocational education should not be liberalized to include the study of social, economic, historical, and ethical questions.'

So here we stand. An essential component of a healthy, functional democracy is missing – and (paradoxically) growingly *caused* to be missing – because of policies of *etatiste* liberal democratic governments whose vision of the maximum social good is almost single-mindedly economic (more paradox still). Without that essential component, as we may have unhappy occasion to see, life will grow solitary, poor, nasty, brutish, and *long*, oh so very long.

5 Why Intellectuals Care about the Flintstones

THOMAS HURKA

In an SCTV sketch called 'Philosophy Today,' a group of academics sit around a TV studio waiting for their discussion show to begin. As the cameras roll, the moderator announces the topic for the day: 'Were the Flintstones a rip-off of the Honeymooners?' A heated discussion ensues.

The sketch is hilarious, but also deeply insightful. A real intellectual would want to know, would be excited to learn, that the Flintstones *were* a rip-off of the Honeymooners.

What is an intellectual? Some people think intellectuals are distinguished by their interest in certain highbrow subjects. Intellectuals like poetry, painting, and architecture. They talk about international and national (though never local) politics. They consider no dinner party complete without some discussion of opera, and they get annoyed when you interrupt to ask whether they don't think Fred Flintstone was modelled on Ralph Cramden and Barney on Ed Norton.

'Intellectuals want to unify information. They know that the greatest scientific advances occur when what appeared to be distinct phenomena are seen to follow from the same laws, as when Newton gave the same explanation for the motions of heavenly bodies as for the motions of objects on earth.'

These aren't intellectuals, just highbrows. Real intellectuals differ, not in the subjects they follow, but in the approach they take to any subject. They want to know or understand everything. They care about poetry and architecture, but they also look at the ordinary world around them.

Understanding means knowing generalizations, and real intellectuals look for generalizations on all subjects. They try to spot trends in advertising and popular television. They wonder whether any unifying characteristics distinguish American sports from those popular in other countries. They debate the hypothesis that as you mount through the social classes, the writing on 'legible clothing' (clothing with words on it) gets progressively smaller and eventually disappears.

Intellectuals want to unify information. They know that the greatest scientific advances occur when what appeared to be distinct phenomena are seen to follow from the same laws, as when Newton gave the same explanation for the motions of heavenly bodies as for the motions of objects on earth. Something similar happens when you see the parallels between Wilma's relationship to Fred and Alice's to Ralph: smarter than, exasperated by, but always lovey-dovey and forgiving at the end of the show.

Intellectuals follow popular culture, but in its social context. They find it curious that in the 1950s, when TV was a luxury of the well-to-do, many popular programs featured working-class characters, whereas in the 1960s, when TV ownership became universal, the subjects were almost exclusively middle class.

This is reflected in the Flintstones and the Honeymooners. Like Ralph and Ed, Fred and Barney are working men with ordinary jobs and interests. But where Ralph and Ed live in apartments, Fred and Barney, in a concession to the 1960s, have detached houses in the suburbs.

Even when they discuss the same subjects, highbrows and real intellectuals do so differently. Highbrows think discussing, say, politics intellectually means making lots of references to various Great Dead Political Thinkers. They are demons of quotesmanship. In their writings, 'Spinoza said' follows 'de Tocqueville remarked' follows 'Burke pointed out.'

Real intellectuals don't do this. They've read the great philosophers, but they don't need to advertise this fact. And they don't like to bludgeon people with famous names. They know that what made the great thinkers great was not their snappy remarks, but their extended arguments, and that what you need to persuade someone honestly is also an argument – perhaps extended, perhaps complex, but in straightforward language and without needless references.

Once again, it is content versus style. Highbrows think being intellectual means knowing certain facts. For real intellectuals it means thinking logically, precisely, and with an eye to important generalizations.

A persistent hawker of highbrowism is Woody Allen. In his movies a woman is often transformed into an intellectual by a man – in *Annie Hall* by Mr Allen himself, in *Hannah and Her Sisters* by that awful sculptor. In each case the process is the same: the man recommends some books, the woman reads them and, presto, she's a thinker. At the end she gives full credit for her transformation to her (now ex-) lover.

There's no hint in these movies that reading big books isn't enough. Mr Allen doesn't consider that you have to challenge the arguments you read, and that if you do, the credit for what you learn goes to you, not to whoever compiled your book list.

Highbrows want big reforms in education. They want students to stop listening to rock 'n' roll and read a series of set Great Books, works approached with reverence as stores of useful quotations and eternal truths. Real intellectuals also want students to read great books, but in the way their authors wanted: as presenting arguments that need to be probed as carefully for weaknesses as for insights, not accepted on faith.

Highbrowism is dangerous, because it erects unnecessary barriers. It discourages would-be intellectuals from addressing ordinary people and creates resentment of the intellectuals' airs. Highbrows want nothing to do with Fred Flintstone and Ralph Cramden, and Fred and Ralph would want nothing to do with them. But real intellectuals care as much about life in Bedrock and at the bus company as about anything they can appreciatively understand.

6 The Ideal of Open-Mindedness

WILLIAM HARE

It is tempting to smile at those who saw no need to peer into Galileo's telescope since the nature of heavenly bodies was already known to them. As they knew, scripture plainly recorded (in Joshua 10:13) that the sun on one occasion stood still in the middle of the sky and, consequently, heliocentrism could not be true. If absolute certainty is already at hand, what need is there to inquire and investigate? Yet the history of science is littered with similar certainties that turned out to be illusory – the impossibility of airships, X-rays, and continental drift, for example. But hindsight is not available when we need it most. The difficult task is to recognize that a new idea deserves consideration, and to be willing to entertain it seriously, at the moment when we ourselves are strongly inclined to favour a view with which it conflicts.

If we are honest with ourselves, our own reactions when faced with rethinking a belief we have long accepted are often not dissimilar to those of Galileo's contemporaries. When we are inclined to be contemptuous of those who would not see what was before their eyes, it is worth returning to our own day and our own inclinations. Congressman John Lewis from Georgia remarks, with respect to reactions to a 2001 exhibit showing James Allen's collection of photographs of lynchings in the United States, that 'many people today, despite the evidence, will not believe – don't want to believe – that such atrocities happened in America not so very long ago.' The examples will vary, but a similar point could no doubt be made in every society. The evidence is there, if we will only consider it, but open-mindedness is defeated by deep-seated assumptions that make it too painful to recognize the truth.

Open-mindedness is an intellectual virtue properly ascribed when an individual or a community is disposed to take into account all that is relevant to forming a sound judgment, and likewise disposed to reconsider judgments already made, or in formation, in the light of emerging difficulties, especially when it is tempting to avoid acting in these ways. In any absolute sense it is unattainable, and even relative success can be elusive. Those who try to be open-minded must steer clear of bias, prejudice, doctrinaire beliefs, hasty conclusions, fear of the truth, and pressure to conform, all of which undermine attempts to examine evidence seriously. To echo René Descartes' observation with respect to good sense, everyone fondly imagines that open-mindedness is part of his or her own outlook, however rare it may be in other people; but this very tendency is itself yet another obstacle to becoming open-minded. Not being ready to recognize the possibility of such a fault in ourselves, we are not sufficiently alive to the forces that bring about closed-mindedness.

The challenge to entertain new possibilities is accompanied by the danger of being taken in by attractive but foolish nonsense. We must be receptive and welcoming to theories and discoveries that conflict with existing beliefs; but the history of science also tells us that this disposition can lead to credulity. Reflection on the Galileo story, reminding us of stubborn resistance, may even encourage untoward hospitality. Scientists in the early twentieth century were too ready to welcome Piltdown Man; and more recently, some have been ready to embrace cold fusion, psychokinesis, facilitated communication, and other embarrassments. A willingness to

> 'To echo René Descartes' observation with respect to good sense, everyone fondly imagines that open-mindedness is part of his or her own outlook, however rare it may be in other people; but this very tendency is itself yet another obstacle to becoming open-minded.'

believe in these ideas only reveals how easily scientists can, in Martin Gardiner's inimitable words, 'be hornswoggled.' Before we point to the credulity of others, however, hands up all those who are quite sure they would not have been among that panic-stricken radio audience listening to 'The War of the Worlds' in 1938.

Open-mindedness surely deserves a central place in any philosophical account of education that is to prove satisfying. If we take seriously the notion of genuine inquiry, together with such related ideas as considering all sides to a question, paying attention to counter-evidence, viewing one's conclusions as provisional, learning from one's mistakes, and trying to rid oneself of bias, then the attitude of open-mindedness immediately presents itself as having fundamental significance. To be open-minded is, after all, to be critically receptive to alternative possibilities, to be willing to think again despite having formulated a view, and to be concerned to defuse any factors that constrain one's thinking in predetermined ways. Without such dispositions that make for open-mindedness, inquiry degenerates into nothing more than the attempt to find whatever reasons will support the particular conclusions that one desires and that have been accepted in advance. As C.S. Peirce remarks, the conclusion determines what the reasoning will be – a process he rightly labels 'sham reasoning.'

Genuine inquiry, in contrast, involves struggling against preconceived ideas, hasty conclusions, and other factors that distort and undermine our efforts, in a determined effort to arrive at whatever beliefs, interpretations, explanations, theories, policies, or value judgments seem warranted as a result of attending to the widest range of considerations that can be adduced, always mindful that further experience, reflection, imagination, and exchange of ideas may lead to these tentative views being overturned or modified. By its very nature, such inquiry is open-minded; and open-minded inquiry, both as a way of learning and as the desired outcome itself, is an indispensable feature of education if education is to mean more than simply reinforcing prejudices or receiving beliefs uncritically. A view of education emerges in which inquiry and reflection constitute ongoing and fallible processes framed by such regulative ideals as understanding, judgment, appreciation, sound interpretation, and knowledge. These ideals are always beyond our reach, of course, but they operate as goals we may hope to approach wherever the passion to learn, as Peirce puts it, is not contaminated by having an axe to grind.

7 Human Destiny

THOMAS DE KONINCK

This is an immense theme. Our conception of it depends on no less than our understanding of the meaning – or absence of meaning – of the human condition, of human knowledge, of art, of science, of ethics and politics. And it depends on our understanding of the task of education, which has always been acknowledged as one of the key challenges facing the human condition.

Kant thought education to be 'the greatest and the most difficult problem which can be posed to man. For discernment depends on education, and education, in turn, depends on discernment.' The formation of persons is the result of *culture*. This excellent word refers us at once, not to some artificial, external model, but rather to the only adequate model, that of the living organism, which as Goethe pointed out cannot be measured by means of something outside it, but 'must itself provide the gauge' for this measure. It suggests the continuity of growth proper to life, as well as autonomy; but also fragility and dependence on the environment. The fundamental meaning of 'culture' is the one offered by Cicero: *cultura animi*, that is, the growth and bloom, not of a mere plant, but of the human spirit itself – heart and mind – to its highest potential. In other words, the very life of a human being as such: 'A field, however fertile, will not be productive without cultivation, nor will the soul without teaching.' Nature and nurture need each other and each is impotent without the other. And as Cicero concludes: 'the cultivation of the spirit is philosophy.'

We are speaking, in fact, of the education to be free. The full, effective exercise of liberty requires discipline, and enough discernment or critical sense to enable one to integrate the panoply of knowledge usefully – all of which can only be acquired through culture. The quality of life for persons and societies alike is a matter of culture – indeed, it depends on culture.

In Shakespeare's words,

> He that made us with such large discourse,
> Looking before and after, gave us not
> That capability and god-like reason
> To fust in us unus'd.

Thanks to the power of speech, man is able to set forth the advantageous and the harmful, the just and the unjust. Any human association is really one for living beings who have this sense of good and evil, of justice and injustice, who share it by means of language, and who secure the corresponding realities by the same token. As a classic of contemporary philosophy proclaims, we '*do* things with words.' One often underestimates the extraordinary power of words – a most beneficial power, of course, when used for good intent; but equally harmful, too, when used for the opposite intent. You may utterly destroy a man's reputation, and thus his entire range of action for a lifetime, by simply whispering a word or two in a neighbour's ear. How can a few harmless vocal sounds be invested with such power? Conversely, the common good can best be served by the human power of speech: public institutions serving justice are founded on it – indeed, so is the whole political order.

This large discourse with which we are made does not stop at this service, however. We may use it to pour out to one another our innermost concerns or the wonderful, infinite scope of thought itself. We may use it also to transform the world for better or for worse. Words (*logoi*) derive their power from that of the thoughts (*logoi* again) they are meant to signify. They reveal and mirror the mind (*logos*) and humans themselves.

Shakespeare was right: god-like reason, god-like *logos*, should not fust in us unused. Recent history (Auschwitz and its successors, for example) has shown that man is apt to use that reason to become the most degraded of all living things. But it has also shown us that he can be the noblest of them as well. What such observations invariably bring out is the most fundamental question of all: How can humans become, in Pindar's words, what they are? How can they achieve goodness and felicity? How can they be brought to perfection? That is the challenge of human virtue, or of human excellence, and the ultimate raison d'être of politics.

What is really at stake when we raise such questions is the very dignity of man in the ethical sense, in the sense of the whole extent of human activity, of man's freedom. It is tantamount to asking: How can we really be free? And this is really what culture is all about, in the spirit of the Socratic adage that 'an unexamined life is not worth living.' For that is what is entailed when we take culture in the fullest and most pregnant sense of the word, as meaning the cultivation of the best in humans: to bring people's marvellous potential to full bloom so that they become worthy of what their great nature calls for. The alternative is 'an unweeded garden that goes to seed.'

To cultivate man's spirit is to cultivate his freedom, to lead to maturity his ability to be *causa sui*, or one's own cause, controlled by nothing and none other than himself, enjoying, in Pascal's words, 'the dignity of causality.' The opposite of freedom is servitude, slavery, alienation in one form or another. Whatever enslaves us we acknowledge to be, as such, contrary to freedom. In order to be able to order our whole lives, we need immunity from external coercion, and we also need psychological freedom. But the heart of the matter is inner coercion: what is most apt to enslave us is within ourselves.

For man confronts a contrariety between his desires and his reason – a contrariety, in other words, between his perceptions of the immediate, the product of his sensory knowledge, and his apprehension of the future, which his intellect enables him to foresee. Our minds press us to resist, in view of the future, even while our desires impel us to obey the attractions of those goods that excite our senses, be they external (such as touch) or internal (such as imagination). Is this apparent, immediate good, the real good? How can the attraction of the apparent good ever coincide with that of the real good? Human life can be described as a struggle to achieve the coincidence of these two opposites. Yet it would be utopian to expect that discernment between the real and the apparent could ever become unnecessary. The reason why liberty is such an unbearable burden to some is thus not far to seek.

Another way to put all of this is to say, 'There are two in us.' Thus Aquinas: 'In homine duo sunt, scilicet natura spiritualis, et natura corporalis.' And Goethe's Faust:

Zwei Seelen wohnen, ach, in meiner Brust,
Die eine will sich von der andern trennen.

'Though our outward humanity is in decay, yet day by day we are inwardly renewed,' writes St Paul. As Coomaraswamy has illustrated so well, the fount of human wisdom provides us with assertions to the same effect from 'our whole metaphysical tradition, Christian and other,' including 'the Vedanta, Buddhism, Islam, and in China.' The clearest statement is probably St Paul's to the Romans: 'I discover this principle, then: that when I want to do the right, only the wrong is within my reach. In my inmost self I delight in the law of God, but I perceive that there is in my bodily members a different law, fighting against the law that my reason approves and making me a prisoner under the law that is in my members, the law of sin.'

Only insofar as he can overcome the yoke of contrariety can man direct himself toward goodness. Freedom means liberation from contrariety, and these words point the way: 'luô, eleutheroô, liberare.' The *Bhagavad Gita* says: 'liberated from the two contraries,' 'released from the pairs of opposites ... he is easily released from bondage.' If the human mind were not itself above contrariety, we would never be able to direct ourselves to one or the other opposite, to choose knowingly and freely. This is why Dante is right to say that all intelligent beings, and they alone, have been endowed with freedom: 'The greatest gift which God in his bounty bestowed in creating, and the most conformed to his own goodness and that which he most prizes, was the freedom of the will, with which the creatures that have intelligence, they all and they alone, were and are endowed.'

Authentic freedom thus implies a spontaneous choice of what is good. The motion must proceed from myself, originate in my true self; it must be directed towards the real good – that is, the true, objective good. But the objective good cannot be known as such by my sensory powers left to themselves. If you are hungry, your senses will not help you see the fruit as something not to be eaten. What they perceive is for them something of an absolute. Your genuine good can be seen and chosen only thanks to powers transcending contrariety. The mind, the will, and human love are such powers.

How can I aim at the best choice attainable to me? By being as much in command, as autonomous, as is humanly possible, by being a slave to no one, not even to myself. To pursue the simile of shooting, the hand must be experienced, the movements of the body spontaneous and quite unhindered; most of all, the eyes must be clear, far-sighted, trained to focus quickly and as precisely as possible on the target. Similarly, unless my mind, which is as the 'eye of the soul,' has been trained to aim well, it will always be difficult for me to attain the truth, be it theoretical or practical. Yet until I see for myself, I am as the blind – dependent on others and to that extent not free. The other parts of me likewise need much training, of course, and they all have a vital function; but for actions to proceed from myself, to originate in my true self (as we said) and above all to be right, sight in the mind – the ability to aim well – comes first and foremost.

Consider a classic example of perception. A stick or an oar in water invariably appears bent. Never will your eye be able to make the line of the oar in water appear straight, try as you might; yet not only do you know it *is* straight – and your hand will confirm it – but you know, of course, that this is only an *appearance*, since the oar is in *reality* straight. The relativity of sensory perception, and the opposition between the apparent oar (in your eye) and the real oar (with which you row) is grasped as a matter of fact. Another way of putting this is to say that your mind seeks objective truth, beyond appearances, while taking the latter into account. The discernment between bent and straight implies a simultaneous grasp of both these opposites. But there is another pair of contraries involved in our example that is much more vital to us: I mean illusion and reality, falsity and truth. This is where our intellect manifests itself most characteristically. This apparent gold is really false gold; the true nature of this apparent friend is that of a foe.

If I were then to ask myself which is my true self, I should be obliged to concede that it is not the mere empirical man, the perceiver of apparently bent sticks in water, but much more so the one who seeks to know the true nature, not only of the stick, but also even of himself. The question of what is man's true nature as opposed to mere empirical man is itself only possible owing to intellect. The very denial of this, just as, for that matter, the denial that there could be any more than empirical man – the claim, in other words, that man is no more than what he appears to sense – is itself a pretence of truth and a product of mind.

Thus we see we cannot do without truth, without constantly trying to adapt our minds to *what* things are – that is, to the true essence and the true being of things – and this of course includes our own essence and our own being, the search for identity, for authenticity. 'He who orders "Know thyself" bids us know the soul,' says Socrates: if a man were content with body or with empirical man, this would be to know 'the things that are his but not himself.'

Our experience tells us, then, that by the intellect we mean this power whereby we may read into the heart of things that they are of this and not of that nature, even should appearances be to the contrary. And we know, too, that through the range of that experience, we find no peace until we have found the *true* answer, or the *right* practical solution. 'The whole of science is nothing more than a refinement of everyday thinking,' wrote Einstein.

Indeed, one great contemporary manifestation of this very human inclination is provided by experimental science. With a truly philosophical sense of wonder, Einstein added, a page or two later:

The very fact that the totality of our sense experiences is such that by means of thinking ... it can be put in order, this fact is one which leaves us in awe ... One may say 'the eternal mystery of the world is its comprehensibility.' It is one of the great realizations of Immanuel Kant that the setting up of a real external world would be senseless without this comprehensibility.

There is a wealth of ideas contained in these reflections; to none of them can we possibly do justice here. We must be content to note in passing the insistence on the fact that reality is somehow essentially connected with thought; and on the fact, to which Einstein returns, that this is manifest through order: 'the production of some sort of order among sense impressions.'

But most deserving of admiration, in fact, is the presence of some order in the *totality* of our experience, that not only should the world be *comprehensible*, but that humans should themselves be able in some way to comprehend it thanks to thought. To be comprehended, things must evidently somehow *be* in us, but the nature of truth implies much more still: their real – as opposed to their merely apparent, outward, superficial – being must be present in us, and our very awareness of such a fact is part of the fact itself, as is obvious in the experience of certainty. To fall back on our previous example, when I claim to *know* for certain that the oar *is* straight, I declare full awareness of it as it *is*, as well as of the exclusion of its contrary in reality, for I mean that the oar *is not* bent *and* that what appeared to be the case *is not* so. Affirmation and negation obstinately keep recurring in human language because the human intellect never tires of discerning between *the real* and the *not real*, pronouncing the true and the false. This is tantamount to saying, therefore, that reality openly reveals itself, as it truly is, in your intellect and mine, and more precisely in one's awareness of one's activity.

As we just saw, Einstein is further drawing our attention to the comprehensibility of the whole universe, the *totality*, thus echoing Pascal's similar remarks: 'Through space the universe grasps me and swallows me up like a speck; through thought I grasp it'; 'But even if the universe were to crush him, man could still be nobler than his slayer, because he knows that he is dying and the advantage the universe has over him. The universe knows none of this. Thus all our dignity consists in thought.' The same contrast between mind and body is brought out differently, but with no less felicity, by Chesterton in his remarkable essay on humour: laughter is due, he writes, to

a purely human realization of the contrast between man's spiritual immensity within and his littleness and restriction without; for it is itself a joke that a house should be larger inside than out. According to such a view, the very incompatibility between the sense of human dignity and the perpetual possibility of incidental indignities produces the primary or archetypal joke of the old gentleman sitting down suddenly on the ice. We do not laugh thus when a tree or a rock tumbles down, because we do not know the sense of self-esteem or serious importance within.

The best minds of ancient Greece had from the outset likewise been struck by this 'contrast between man's spiritual immensity within and his littleness and restriction without.' When in *De Anima* Aristotle makes the famous statement that 'the soul is in a way all existing things,' he is not only summing up again what he has repeated elsewhere, but also is reiterating the close affinity between intellectual natures and the totality of being, emphasized so consistently and so profoundly by most of the pre-Socratics, notably by Heraclitus, Parmenides, and Anaxagoras: *logos* and *nous* aim at *panta*, 'all things.'

Is one, though, suggesting that we do in effect, according to such views, hold in our minds all existing things? On this score, suffice it to quote Aristotle eight lines lower: 'These must be either the things themselves or their forms. Not the things themselves; for it is not the stone which is in the soul, but its form. Hence the soul is as the hand is; for the hand is a tool of tools, and the intellect is a form of forms and sense a form of objects of perception.'

All these converging views attest to the scope of human knowledge, unlimited in its potentiality. It is easy to see that there is no limit to what your intellect can come to know, as even knowledge of, say, an infinite name already makes plain: non-horse somehow contains everything except horse; should one doubt it, let him or her tell us what else it does not cover. When I pretend I know nothing, I claim to be ignorant of everything. Yet how can I know that I know nothing unless I apprehend, in some fashion, however inadequate, everything? As Sartre reminds us, 'nothingness' implies 'being,' and so 'everything.' However differently, 'being' is said of all things and found in all things; so that the concept of 'being' enables us, however inadequately and remotely, to reach out to every being and non-being. One can perhaps best verify such infinity and universality within the human mind by considering concepts of the most perfect beings, or primary causes. Even while wondering whether God exists, my intellect investigates whether there exists an ultimate cause of all beings, or some supreme Being, or an Absolute – an inquiry that cannot take place without some ever clearer notion of totality. But one need not seek so far: the most familiar concepts – time, say, or the human person – are complex enough! Each universal is already a totality, a unity within many. Einstein was right: we are brought back to everyday thinking, where universals and totalities are commonplace. Witness ordinary language.

'Love is not love which alters when it alteration finds.' Upon what values does genuine, lasting love or friendship rest? It has to rest on the goods of the soul, since all others alter. It has to rest chiefly, in fact, on the goods of the mind, those that may confer to it that trained eyesight which we have just contended human beings need in order to be free. In a word, genuine friendship itself can only be attained through 'culture'; the very nature of authentic friendship requires culture in the sense explained above. The values of the spirit are what friends share and exchange above all: they are the life and soul of friendship. Furthermore, those are the goods that lend themselves most easily and most delightfully to communication. They are the most common and fundamental human concern, whether conscious or not. The quest for freedom, for meaning, is present in everyday human life. Even if daily conversation does not always couch it under the loftiest guises, it is there for everyone to see, as ordinary language and the arts constantly illustrate.

'What is really at stake ... is the very dignity of man in the ethical sense, the whole extent of human activity, of man's freedom. It is tantamount to asking: How can we really be free? And this is really what culture is all about.'

When probed – albeit under various guises – every kind of strong human attachment reveals an indomitable desire for the immortal happiness of the beloved. There are glimpses of eternity in our lives at least in that form. One example is a mother's true affection for her child: her desire for its continued well-being at all costs to herself, even when it entails her sacrificing her life for it and never being able to see or to take part in that well-being herself. We find here the element of intended permanence and, especially, that of wanting the good of the other. The reason one tends to draw one's examples preferably from *eros*, however, when speaking of love, may be that it provides the most obvious instances of being carried out of the here and now and out of oneself. *Eros* means of course love in the sense of passion (passivity is indeed the key to its whole nature, which all its meanings in some way retain), evident first in sexual love. But as Plato so forcefully emphasized, and as a long tradition of theological and mystical literature has repeatedly brought to the fore, it must also be understood to mean the yearning and the ravishment provoked by beauty in all its manifestations, visible not merely to the eye of the body, but to the eye of the soul as well, or to that of the heart, meaning of course intellectual enlightenment, moral beauty, and ultimately the cause of all beauty and all authentic love whom many believe to be God.

8 Taming *The Tempest*

GRAEME HUNTER

The idea of education is only one motif in Shakespeare's *The Tempest* and yet almost every line of the play is fragrant with it. Most of what I have learned in a lifelong love affair with education I find reflected there.

Like a proper education, *The Tempest*'s redemptive tale matures over many years. Though the dramatic action takes place in a single afternoon, the audience is made aware of twelve crucial years of dramatic time, background history without which that afternoon's events would be unintelligible. At the close of the afternoon, all that history is redeemed, and the play, like a graduation exercise, points forward in anticipation of a better future. We must acquaint ourselves briefly with *The Tempest*'s strange chronicle before we can understand its educational significance.

The central character of *The Tempest* is Prospero, Duke of Milan. Twelve years prior to the play's events, Prospero deputized his brother Antonio to govern Milan in his stead. His reasons for entrusting the government to his brother were selfish though not otherwise ignoble: he wanted to devote himself entirely to the occult arts, to white magic, with which, like many of his Renaissance contemporaries, he was fascinated. His brother Antonio was a Renaissance man of quite another stamp, in the image of the infamous philosopher Machiavelli, whose book, *The Prince*, constituted a guidebook for despotic rulers.

Antonio was interested only in power, and posssessing it intoxicated him. He therefore conceived a plan for betraying and supplanting his brother, and at a burdensome cost to the free duchy of Milan, he enlisted the military help of King Alonzo of Naples in carrying it out. Milan agreed to pay tribute to Naples forever after. At that steep price, Antonio secured Alonzo's cooperation, and Prospero, the rightful duke, was overthrown.

The conspirators dared not kill Prospero and his infant daughter, Miranda, for fear of causing a popular uprising. So, they charged a trusted Neapolitan counsellor, Gonzalo, with the task of disposing of the duke and his daughter. Gonzalo, as it turns out, was both merciful and wise. Although he carried out his charge of banishing the former

Duke of Milan, he did so with more humanity than they had intended. He put the exiles in the unseaworthy boat that had been provided for them, but he did not leave them in the full destitution that had been planned. Instead, he gave them sufficient clothing and food to make survival possible and, most important of all, he provided Prospero with the magic books for which he had sacrificed his dukedom. Helped by providence, their boat drifted to an enchanted Mediterranean island.

Prospero there encountered and subdued by magic certain good spirits, the chief of them being Ariel, and an evil monster called Caliban. At first, Prospero befriended the monster and tried to educate him, but after Caliban attempted to rape Miranda, he was treated as a slave. During his twelve years as master of the island, Prospero has devoted his time to magic and to the education of Miranda, who is fifteen years old and a paragon of innocent beauty.

Meanwhile, in the great world of Europe, Claribel, the daughter of Alonzo, became engaged to the king of Tunis. A royal party sailed from Naples to attend her wedding to the African king. On the return voyage, the ship carrying Alonzo, Antonio, and their entourage passed close to Prospero's island, and the sorcerer, discovering this fact by his magic art, caused a storm to sweep the ship off course and wreck itself on the island's reef. With this tempest, the action of the play begins.

The occupants of the ship reach shore in different places, each individual or group assuming the others drowned. In the course of his adventures on the island, each man is given an opportunity to reveal his true nature. Evil men are shown to be prisoners of their character, moving inexorably towards greater degradation. Good men are able to grow in goodness through self-denial and discipline. In particular, King Alonzo's son, Ferdinand, is purified by the discipline that Prospero imposes on him and so becomes fit for betrothal to Miranda at the play's end.

But in addition to such natural developments of character, Prospero, by his magic art, is able to intervene secretly and effectively in the cause of good, with the result that no evil event on the island is exactly what it seems. Actions that are evil in intent are turned to good effect and, in the end, reconciliation and forgiveness are exchanged among all (except, perhaps, Caliban). When harmony has been restored, Prospero gives up his occult powers so as to sail back with the others to Milan, resuming the political responsibilities he ought never to have let go.

Like all of Shakespeare's great plays, this one means nothing less than everything. Do not look in it for coded messages about Shakespeare's life or prejudices: any you find will be just your own inventions. *The Tempest* advocates no ideology; it pursues no social or political agenda. It is great art and therefore (*pace* postmodern criticism) nothing but a mirror in which are reflected truths about the world and about ourselves. Shakespearean art is an enchanted mirror, for it reflects things not as they try to appear, but as they really are.

No doubt *The Tempest* never sets out to discuss education. It is about education only because it examines so tenderly and so profoundly the development of a young girl. Prospero is the great teacher, Miranda the ideal pupil. The island is their school, and like every school it is also a theatre in which a dramatic struggle is enacted between benign forces (like Ariel) and forces of darkness (symbolized by Caliban). Light and dark, good and evil, edification and destruction, all vie for supremacy on the island as they do in the hearts of the characters; meanwhile the teacher, Prospero, like a gardener seeks to cultivate the good and suppress the bad. *The Tempest* was likely Shakespeare's final play. It contains a mature vision of how teaching and learning ought to be adjusted to each other and to the difficult environment of a fallen world. When I look into the play's polished mirror, I see six deep truths about education.

You Can't Win Them All: Caliban

One of the big questions in education today concerns who ought to get it. The code word is *accessibility*. Should schooling be for everyone? To say that there are people who cannot profit from school is thought by many to be undemocratic. They call it 'elitism.' School is a universal right, we are all supposed to believe.

But Caliban is uneducable. Prospero calls him 'a devil, a born devil, *on whose nature nurture can never stick;* on whom my pains, humanely taken all, all lost, quite lost.' And Miranda calls him an 'abhorred slave, *which any print of goodness will not take,* being capable of all ill.'

Miranda and Prospero agree, then, that an individual can be evil in a way that places him beyond the redemptive power of education. Are they right about this? If so, what makes it so? It is certainly not stupidity. Caliban knows what is expected of him. His defect lies elsewhere – in the will. What makes some people uneducable is that they hate what is good, including what Dante called 'the good of the intellect.' Caliban betrays his real nature when Miranda reminds him of how she once taught him to speak. 'I endowed thy purposes with words that made them known,' she says. But Caliban replies:

You taught me language; and my profit on't
Is, I know how to curse. The red plague rid you
For learning me your language!

One of the greatest ornaments of a good education is that one learns proper speech, but Caliban despises it. And in his contempt for language he shows that one can become so comfortable with what is ugly, mean, and low that it becomes one's standard. Education is an invitation to climb a mountain. There are only two possible responses. You must either begin climbing or declare that the valley in which you were born is just as good. The implication is obvious: a good education can only be acquired by people who are seeking goodness. The only things bad people are capable of getting are *diplomas* and *degrees.*

Not that many people with PhDs in education might not argue on Caliban's side. They might say, for example, that English grammar is nothing but an imposition by the upper classes on the lower classes, or by white folks on folks of other races, or by natives on immigrants, and so on. Having no eye for beauty or no sense of propriety, they think that education is only a question of power. Whatever calls for discipline must therefore be some form of repression. Such people often have degrees, but they lack education. The good of the intellect has eluded them.

Is education therefore undemocratic? Not a bit. Whoever will may come, but wise educators recognize that there are some who will not come. Caliban represents something shiftless, self-regarding, and malignant that is part of each of us, though it is dominant in only a few. And educators like Prospero will find their 'pains, humanely taken all, all lost, quite lost,' if they try to educate Caliban. Classical education, therefore, is not for all, since not all will accept its universal invitation.

Discipline Is a Universal Need: Miranda

Another image represented on the burnished surface of the play is that of a beautiful and innocent-seeming girl, Miranda. Her name means 'she who must be admired,' and indeed, she must, because she has become wiser than most princes, generous and beautiful in her mere fifteen years. Yet even her wise simplicity of character is insufficient preparation for the fallen world into which she is about to be introduced. Classical education has always recognized that everyone – even those of the sweetest nature – needs what it has to offer, though some refuse it.

Contemporary educators also recognize the insufficiency of innocence. They are always talking about 'street-proofing' children. By this they usually mean introducing children to the sexual habits and drug dependencies of perverts and addicts. They claim that their classes work on the principle of inoculation, injecting a little of the disease so that immunity can develop. The ways in which this view is wrong and shallow are a vast subject, best left for another day.

Prospero, at any rate, sees more deeply. Inoculation cannot help Miranda because even she already has the disease. She is not in danger only from violent external forces like Caliban, who tried to rape her when she taught him language. Prospero recognizes that she is also in danger from Ferdinand, who loves her, and even from herself. The fall is in her no less than in the man she would have for her husband. Prospero sees in the love that develops between Miranda and Ferdinand an ambiguous thing one that contains the seeds not only of joy and blessing but also of bitterness and the curse. His stern instructions to them are not fanatical fetters imposed by some Victorian prude. But they *are* standards, on which he will not compromise, as the permissive 1960s taught my generation to do. Prospero aims at the golden mean between prudery and permissiveness, which is discipline.

How little he resembles the sex educators who abound in our modern schools. He gives his daughter to Ferdinand, but with this instruction:

> If thou dost break her virgin-knot before
> All sanctimonious ceremonies may
> With full and holy rite be minister'd,
> No sweet aspersion shall the heavens let fall
> To make this contract grow; but barren hate,
> Sour-eyed disdain and discord shall bestrew
> The union of your bed with weeds so loathly
> That you shall hate it both.

Such words strike even the most traditional of us as quaint today, but 'barren hate, sour-eyed disdain and discord' make a fair description of many of the marriages of this permissive age, especially the growing number that end in divorce. Either Prospero's harsh words are cruel falsehoods, as the sexual revolution of the 1960s maintained, or they are true. And if true, they reveal another fact that has always been recognized by classical education: discipline is a universal need; innocence is not sufficient.

Submission, Not Creativity: Ferdinand

Some of today's educators would disagree with Prospero's stern admonition to Ferdinand, not because they encourage sexual licence in particular, but because they dislike whatever sounds 'repressive.' They think that children are geysers of creativity that will naturally come gushing forth if only the artificial impediments of society are removed. They would like us to accept a simple division of things: on the one hand we have free-flowing creativity; on the other, repressive social restrictions. Just remove the repressive rules, revoke the crazy commandments, they say, and the fountain of creativity will pour forth its copious gifts.

This theory is very attractive, because it is easy to understand and generous in its view of human character. But it is also very wrong. It arose in the nineteenth century along with the psychological theories of Sigmund Freud, and it utterly triumphed in educational theory in the twentieth century. To begin to see what is the matter with the theory of 'creativity,' ask yourself this question: In what other arena of life – other than school – do we find it to be true that removing disciplinary restrictions improves 'creativity'?

'Classical education knows nothing of diplomas, except in a secondary way. Real education involves acquiring an appetite for excellence, or what the ancients called "virtue," and allowing it to transform your soul.'

There is a story of a man who watched his neighbour put in a new garden all summer. When it was finished, and colour cascaded from tasteful trellises and ornaments, and every prospect gratified the eye, the neighbour remarked: 'It's a fine thing that you and Mother Nature have created.' 'I'm glad you like it,' replied the gardener dryly, 'but you should have seen it when Mother Nature had it all to herself.'

Or what about sports? Nature endows some people with astonishing gifts of speed, agility, balance, strength, and so on. And yet only those whose gifts are honed by disciplined practice go far as athletes. Those who rely on creativity alone are useful only for warming the bench.

Now why would what is true of gardening and athletics not also be true of life as a whole? One of the fundamental assumptions of classical education is that the cases are exactly parallel. And since classical education is education for life, not merely for learning, it cannot be separated from submission to rules.

Modern education, therefore, has it all wrong. We need not choose between unfettered creativity and repressive rules any more than we are forced to choose between a patch of weeds and a pesticide-drenched lawn. Our life should be neither weedy nor sterile; it should be a *garden*, a place in which weeds are repressed and flowers encouraged. But that requires discipline. A classical education guides nature without thwarting it. Submission to the rules of art, not creativity, is education's chief concern.

Rags and Riches: Stephano

The scene shifts once again in the mirror of *The Tempest*, and now the drunken butler Stephano is reflected. Having decided to be king over all the island, he puts himself in league with the monster Caliban and the clown Trinculo. Their plan is to kill Prospero and so seize power. They fail, of course, but the play explains their failure by means of an insightful image.

When Stephano and his ridiculous subordinates stumble upon a rack of royal clothing, which Prospero has cleverly left in their way, they forget their bloodthirsty errand and fall to preening and prancing and quarrelling with one another about who looks best in what. Though seeking riches, they are led astray by rags. Behind their foolishness is a lack of understanding: they seek power, but cannot tell the difference between its outer appearance and the inward reality.

In a symbolic way, their confusion points towards something fundamental: classical education aims to get beyond appearances to the underlying and often hidden reality. Stephano is content to strut about in the robes of office, not knowing that real power resides only with those who, like Prospero, possess *authority*.

Some students are like Stephano. They thunder uncomprehendingly through the corridors of schools until they at last are granted a degree. Wrapping themselves in the appearance of learning, they say goodbye to education and go forth to seek a commanding position in the world. In the children's film *The Wizard of Oz*, the scarecrow wants something no wizard can give – the power to think. So resourceful Oz gives him a diploma instead, and the scarecrow, foolish as ever, is content. Perhaps the movie should receive a 'Restricted' rating for letting slip that cynical truth about much of what calls itself education.

Classical education knows nothing of diplomas, except in a second-ary way. Real education involves acquiring an appetite for excellence, or what the ancients called 'virtue,' and allowing it to transform your soul. No degree need be attached to that achievement, and people with many degrees sometimes have not attained it. They may be what the philosopher Immanuel Kant called 'a plaster cast of a man' – people who have all the facts at their fingertips but are strangers to truth, who are long on information but short on judgment, who may know many things yet are not wise.

If we are honest, we can see ourselves in Stephano the drunken butler. We, too, rush headlong down byways looking for wealth, pres-tige, and power. And all too often we settle for even less, for trashy imitations of these things. But a classical education teaches us to have a healthy scepticism of any shortcut to wealth, prestige, or power. It makes us suspect any path that does not include the long route of moral disci-pline. Classical education knows the difference between rags and riches.

Aiming at the Long Term: Gonzalo

Look into the mirror of *The Tempest* and you see a long stretch – twelve years of dramatic time. And not just any twelve years. They are the years of Miranda's primary education. The play implicitly recognizes real education as an extended season of growth and cultivation, whose rich harvest must be patiently awaited.

'The best fruit ripens last,' said the philosopher Schopenhauer when speaking of the education of boys. Boys may be obstreperous, undisci-plined, nasty, foolish, and hopeless at school. The ancient philosopher Plato called them 'muddy streams that have not yet run pure.' Yet some of those very boys will grow up to be saints, thinkers, or poets, proving, as Schopenhauer said, that 'the best fruit ripens last.'

But the tardy development, particularly of boys, puts education at a distinct disadvantage compared to certain recent pedagogical tools such as Prozac and Ritalin, which can instantly transform rowdy stu-dents into docile learners. But here, once again, appearance gets the upper hand over reality. Classical education recognizes that we are dealing with human souls, each of which is like a docile carthorse yoked together with a plunging stallion. Drug the stallion and you extinguish the soul's energetic fire. A child requires not sedation but discipline. Each one must learn to master the horses that draw the chariot of his soul, and that process should be expected to take some time.

In *The Tempest*'s closing scene, the good old counsellor Gonzalo suddenly realizes the long lapse of time required for his own education. All the characters are assembled in front of Prospero in a scene resembling the Day of Judgment. Both good and evil deeds are now laid bare, and Prospero is merciful yet unsparing in his judgment of each man before him. Suddenly Gonzalo realizes that the entire voyage on which they had set out, though it had been conceived without any thought of Prospero's island, has found there its fulfilment. And suddenly we, the audience, are made to consider the voyage of our lives.

The old man's vision is one of the finest moments in the play:

O rejoice
Beyond a common joy! and set it down
With gold on lasting pillars: in one voyage
Did Claribel her husband find at Tunis
And Ferdinand, her brother, found a wife
Where he himself was lost, Prospero his dukedom
In a poor isle, and all of us ourselves
Where no man was his own.

Prospero's 'poor isle,' where each man finds himself, is a school.

It was Socrates who first pointed to the connection between education and self-knowledge. 'The unexamined life,' he said, 'is not worth living.' What use is a degree, a job, a paycheque, a career, an office, unless there is a real human being behind it? You might as well wish that someone else would obtain these things as to obtain them yourself and still have no personality. On the little island of school, or on some other island, sooner or later the great question must be faced: *Who am I?* That is what school is for. That is the surprise examination with which your courses end, and only those prepared to wrestle with that question ever really graduate. That is why real education aims at the long term.

Now what about this business of *graduation*? It is a sore point with educators like myself. It is the thing that students learn to do every year and teachers never. We often envy the students we send out into the world, always staying behind ourselves, like elderly invalids, looking at life through a window. But in the end, even teachers must graduate, and I turn at last to thinking about how Prospero did it.

Packing It In: Prospero's Farewell

The image of *The Tempest* is beginning to fade, the enchanted mirror will soon reflect nothing but the sky. The play is nearly at an end when Prospero comes to centre stage to take his farewell from his spellbound isle. Soon he will become an active participant in the life of Milan, and this time he will be meticulous in performing his duties, the neglect of which has caused him to be exiled on this island for many years.

Like Shakespeare himself, Prospero has grown old as an observer of life, and he now must enter into the practice of living, putting aside the magic by means of which his entry into life has been deferred. Again, like Shakespeare himself, Prospero must retire from his magical life to enter a moral one. Is it then Shakespeare the dramatist or Prospero the teacher whose retirement address *The Tempest* records? It is both, for it acknowledges the different spiritual helpers by whose magic teachers, no less than dramatists, are able to do their work:

> Ye elves of hills, brooks, standing lakes, and groves;
> And ye that on the sands with printless foot
> Do chase the ebbing Neptune; and do fly him
> When he comes back; you demi-puppets that
> By moonshine do the green sour ringlets make,
> Whereof the ewe not bites; and you whose pastime
> Is to make midnight mushrooms, that rejoice
> To hear the solemn curfew; by whose aid
> Weak masters though ye be – I have bedimmed
> The noontide sun, call'd forth the mutinous winds
> And 'twixt the green sea and the azur'd vault
> Set roaring war: to the dread rattling thunder
> Have I given fire, and rifted Jove's stout oak
> With his own bolt; the strong-based promontory
> Have I made shake, and by the spurs plucked up
> The pine and cedar: graves at my command
> Have wak'd their sleepers, op'd, and let 'em forth
> By my so potent Art.

That's what we teachers do, is it not? It is at least what we try to do. And if students think our classes are less exciting than that, don't we remind ourselves of the point about taking the long look? We hope that years from now, looking back, students will remember school as the place where the graves opened and released their dead – where they saw Alexander once again establishing his empire; where they witnessed the love of Romeo and Juliet; and where they shared in Newton's wonder as he discovered the law of universal gravitation. Each of us who loves to teach has some share of Prospero's 'potent art,' but a time approaches when we, like Prospero, must lay down the sorcerer's mantle and walk away diminished into an uncertain future. How, then, does Prospero continue? With noble resignation, he says:

> But this rough magic
> I here abjure; and when I have requir'd
> Some heavenly music – which even now I do ...
> I'll break my staff,
> Bury it certain fathoms in the earth
> And deeper than did ever plummet sound
> I'll drown my book.

The marvellous techniques we have acquired for bringing alive the past, and making vivid things that education requires us to know, are of no use in the prosaic world outside the school. They are the ladders that our students climb up, kicking them aside when they have served their purpose. And when finally we go out these doors, following so many generations of our students, we, too, must leave those faded props behind. And here I am speaking not just of our retirement, but of every afternoon. We have obligations to fulfil to family, to state, and to God. And we must go in spirit to Prospero's Milan, where, he says, 'Every third thought shall be my grave.'

The Greek language distinguishes *kairos* from *chronos*, the golden moment from mere passing time. Prospero's art taught him to calculate that moment, and then to create the tempest by which he could deliver his student Miranda to her fortune and himself to his duty. But the moment was deeply touched with sadness, and more than art was required to make him seize it: he needed courage.

Learning, of course, goes on forever. But classical education recognizes an opportune moment to begin one's formal education and another one to end it, for education that does not issue in a good life is vain. Classical education, therefore, has to teach us what Prospero learned – the difficult art of knowing when to pack it in, whether at four p.m. daily, after earning a BA or a PhD, or once in a lifetime at retirement. Even those who scribble essays must finally make an end. Prospero shows us how, in simple words, coloured by deep melancholy and spoken in front of the curtain, after the play:

> Now my charms are all o'er thrown,
> And what strength I have's mine own,
> Which is most faint: now, 'tis true,
> I must be here confined by you,
> Or sent to Naples. Let me not,
> Since I have my dukedom got,
> And pardon'd the deceiver, dwell
> In this bare island by your spell;
> But release me from my bands
> With the help of your good hands:
> Gentle breath of yours my sails
> Must fill, or else my project fails,
> Which was to please. Now I want
> Spirits to enforce, Art to enchant;
> And my ending is despair,
> Unless I be relieved by prayer,
> Which pierces so, that it assaults
> Mercy itself, and frees all faults.
> As you from crimes would pardon'd be,
> Let your indulgence set me free.

PART IV

The Contemporary World

1 Perfecting Inhumanity

DAVID GAUTHIER

I do not want to know that six million Jews were murdered by Germans. I do not want to know that my fellow human beings are capable of conceiving and executing a policy of systematically exterminating a people. I do not want to know that such a policy can be successful – that only a few will raise their voice against the ultimate inhumanity of man.

I do not want to know these things because they implicate me, not as a murderer, but as a bystander, a man whose lack of concern and imagination permits these things to happen. Knowledge condemns. But knowledge also redeems, for it is only the painful awareness of what man has done that enables man to do differently.

Rolf Hochhuth's great drama, *The Deputy*, takes as its theme the bystander. Here is the murderer, here is the victim – there can be no doubt about the identification. Now here is the bystander, unable to avoid seeing what takes place. How does he respond?

The bystander was the Roman Catholic Church in the person of its pope. Pius XII was a man of policy. No one would deny that, as a man of policy, he performed his duty to his God, his Church, and his fellow human beings as he saw that duty. But inhumanity knows no policy.

> 'Knowledge condemns. But knowledge also redeems, for it is only the painful awareness of what man has done that enables man to do differently.'

Pius XII passed by on the other side of the road. His silence – agonized, compassionate, yet silence – had a thousand reasons. But what are a thousand reasons to confront a million corpses? His response was inadequate.

In Denmark, when the Germans ordered Jews to wear the Star of David, the king also put on the star. What would the outcome have been had Pius been a man of imagination instead of a man of policy? For a pope to wear the Star of David would be a scandal – the sort of scandal in which, one gathers from the Scriptures, his master would have delighted. Such scandals move mountains.

The significance of Pius's inadequacy turns on the central place of the Roman Catholic Church in European civilization. If the institutions of civilization are unable to protest against a barbarity undreamed of by mere barbarians, then what is civilization?

Six million Jews were murdered. To alleviate our feelings of guilt, we displaced some thousands of Arabs so that the Jews might reclaim their ancestral land. Two million Israelis – each with his passage home paid for by the blood of three of his fellows.

Our world has perfected inhumanity. In the weapons of mass destruction devised since the Second World War, we have acquired the ability to exterminate impersonally, automatically. The victims need no longer be transported across Europe, to march one by one into the gas chambers.

The same failure of imagination that left Pius helpless before the Nazis threatens to leave us helpless before a less deliberate but more encompassing evil. We know what others have done, but we have only begun the painful process of recognizing what we may do, if we fail to resolve our conflicts by peaceful means.

In Hochhuth's drama, the failure of Pius's response to the murder of the Jews leads a young Jesuit to assume the Star of David, to make the response his church would not make. But the priest can only accompany the victims, to die with them. His response is all that an individual can do, but here the merest individual is inadequate.

One righteous man is better than none, but ten would have been needed to save Sodom. We cannot escape the awful burden of responsibility with the hope that so few will suffice today.

2 Society Is Only as Good as Its Apologies

JOHN RUSSELL

Visiting the sins of fathers and mothers on their children seems profoundly unjust. Children, after all, bear no direct responsibility for the actions of their parents. Why should they be punished for their parents' wrongs?

But having children apologize for the wrongful acts of their forebears is something we have come to accept and, often, to expect. In fact, apologies of this kind have become a common part of the contemporary political landscape. Take Tony Blair's apology to the Irish on behalf of the British, or the Canadian government's apology to Second World War Japanese-Canadian interns, or, more recently, its apology to aboriginal Canadians who were mistreated in residential schools. These are just a few examples of widely applauded apologies made by one generation on behalf of another.

Yet despite the approval that has greeted these actions, it may be difficult to explain why we believe they are morally appropriate. Why should apologies be required of people who are innocent of the original wrong, people who may not even have been alive when the wrong occurred? Indeed, what purpose could they serve? Isn't an apology empty unless it is expressed by the wrongdoers themselves?

Apologies of this sort need not be without merit. Indeed, they may be morally required. We can see why by examining the difference between apology and punishment. Why do we find one appropriate, and the other not, when we think of the responsibilities of later generations for past wrongs?

Suppose for a moment that current generations were actually guilty for the wrongdoings of previous generations. If this were true, we could hardly find punishment of them unacceptable. But we have rightly rejected this. It implies an idea of group or collective responsibility and guilt that is morally inappropriate and profoundly uncivilized. The children of Nazis are not themselves responsible for acts of genocide. It would be a denial of our very idea of moral responsibility – that each person is responsible for his or her own choices – to say that they share responsibility for such terrible acts.

It is profoundly uncivilized to punish later generations for the wrongs of earlier generations. But it is often a crucial step towards civilizing our relations with others, and towards advancing moral progress, to apologize for the sins of earlier generations. Why is this so?

Foremost, an apology sets the historical record straight, and this has important moral and societal implications. These are partly reflected in the idea that those who do not learn history's lessons are bound to repeat its errors. But there is also a more basic point to be made.

An apology sets the historical record straight, and this has important moral and societal implications ... Until we come to grips with historical wrongs, it is often difficult to move forward in common purpose.

Failure to acknowledge historical wrongs inevitably puts in doubt the status of victims as full-fledged members of a community. Why? Because an unacknowledged wrong continues to serve as powerful evidence that such people are not regarded with the same respect accorded others. An apology responds to this. Saying we're sorry attempts to repair a fractured moral community. It does so by publicly acknowledging a failure of respect among its members while undertaking a commitment to maintain that respect in the future. Underlying all this is an affirmation of moral responsibility for choices and actions affecting others.

This is the reason why later generations often have obligations to apologize on behalf of their forebears. It is part of a process of moral healing and reconciliation. Apologies contribute to this through their implicit recognition that we are all entitled to equal respect. Such recognition is the basis for a sense of personal dignity in relations with others. Without this recognition, there can be no true moral community.

Until we come to grips with historical wrongs, it is often difficult to move forward in common purpose. Suspicions and animosities may be left to brew. Our conception of ourselves and of our history may remain unclear. An apology responds by publicly affirming that we are civilized in ways that some of our ancestors were not. It says that we are prepared to acknowledge certain grievances as legitimate.

For this reason an apology by itself is often not enough to restore a moral community. Later generations typically need to acknowledge historical wrongs because they have benefited improperly from them. Restitution of some form therefore may be required as well.

However, acknowledging responsibility to repay benefits wrongly obtained is not the same as taking responsibility for the wrongful acts themselves. In this sense we bear a measure of moral responsibility concerning past wrongs. But we bear responsibility only to the degree to which we refuse to acknowledge and right those wrongs. For we then extend the wrongs by our complacency, even if we are not originally responsible for bringing them about.

This is the only sense in which later generations can be said to be morally responsible for the wrongs of earlier generations. Failure to acknowledge that one has benefited wrongly from injustices shows a preparedness to live with, and benefit from, unjust acts. This is also a reason why victims of injustice may legitimately doubt that they are being regarded with appropriate respect, even by those not directly responsible for past wrongs.

It follows that whenever we have benefited from past wrongs we have a special responsibility not merely to apologize. Injustice needs to be rectified whenever it is in our power to do so. This civilizes us by removing any implication that we are prepared to accept or tolerate such wrongs. Indeed, this is why we judge the sincerity of apologies by the actions that accompany them. It is a check on whether we have become better moral persons – or moral hypocrites.

The recent surge of apologies for historical wrongs is not something to be viewed with cynicism. It may be costly. It may be difficult to determine what justice requires for wrongs done long ago. But such apologies are nevertheless welcome evidence of moral progress and of increasing civility in our relations with others. Ultimately, it shows that we are on the path to treating one another with the respect that each of us deserves.

3 Three Malaises

CHARLES TAYLOR

I want to write here about some of the malaises of modernity. I mean by this features of our contemporary culture and society that people experience as a loss or a decline, even as our civilization 'develops.' Sometimes people feel that some important decline has occurred during the last years or decades – since the Second World War, or the 1950s, for instance. Sometimes the loss is felt over a much longer historical period: the whole modern era from the seventeenth century is frequently seen as the time frame of decline. Yet although the time scale can vary greatly, there is a certain convergence on the themes of decline. They are often variations around a few central melodies. I want to pick out two such central themes here, and then throw in a third that largely derives from these two. These three by no means exhaust the topic, but they do get at a great deal of what troubles and perplexes us about modern society.

The worries I will be talking about are very familiar. No one needs to be reminded of them; they are discussed, bemoaned, challenged, and argued against all the time in all sorts of media. That sounds like a reason not to talk about them further. But I believe that this great familiarity hides bewilderment, that we don't really understand these changes that worry us, that the usual run of debate about them in fact misrepresents them – and thus makes us misconceive what we can do about them. The changes defining modernity are both well known and very perplexing, and that is why it's worth talking still more about them.

The first source of worry is *individualism*. Of course, individualism also names what many people consider the finest achievement of modern civilization. We live in a world where people have a right to choose for themselves their own pattern of life, to decide in conscience what convictions to espouse, to determine the shape of their lives in a whole host of ways that their ancestors couldn't control. And these rights are generally defended by our legal systems. In principle, people are no longer sacrificed to the demands of supposedly sacred orders that transcend them.

Very few people want to go back on this achievement. Indeed, many think that it is still incomplete, that economic arrangements, or patterns of family life, or traditional notions of hierarchy still restrict too much our freedom to be ourselves. But many of us are also ambivalent. Modern freedom was won by our breaking loose from older moral horizons. People used to see themselves as part of a larger order. In some cases, this was a cosmic order, a 'great chain of Being,' in which humans figured in their proper place along with angels, heavenly bodies, and our fellow earthly creatures. This hierarchical order in the universe was reflected in the hierarchies of human society. People were often locked into a given place, a role and station that was properly theirs and from which it was almost unthinkable to deviate. Modern freedom came about through the discrediting of such orders.

'A society in which people end up as the kind of individuals who are "enclosed in their own hearts" is one where few will want to participate actively in self-government. They will prefer to stay at home and enjoy the satisfactions of private life, as long as the government of the day produces the means to these satisfactions and distributes them widely.'

But at the same time as they restricted us, these orders gave meaning to the world and to the activities of social life. The things that surround us were not just potential raw materials or instruments for our projects, they had a significance given to them by their place in the chain of being. The eagle was not just another bird, but the king of a whole domain of animal life. By the same token, the rituals and norms of society had more than merely instrumental significance. The discrediting of these orders has been called the 'disenchantment' of the world. With it, things lost some of their magic.

A vigorous debate has been going on for a couple of centuries as to whether this was an unambiguously good thing. But this is not what I want to focus on here. I want to look rather at what some have seen to be the consequences for human life and meaning.

The worry has been repeatedly expressed that the individual lost something important along with the larger social and cosmic horizons of action. Some have written of this as the loss of a heroic dimension to life. People no longer have a sense of a higher purpose, of something worth dying for. Alexis de Tocqueville sometimes talked like this in the nineteenth century, referring to the 'petits et vulgaires plaisirs' that people tend to seek in the democratic age. In another articulation, we suffer from a lack of passion. Kierkegaard saw 'the present age' in these terms. And Nietzsche's 'last men' are at the final nadir of this decline; they have no aspiration left in life but to a 'pitiable comfort.'

This loss of purpose was linked to a narrowing. People lost the broader vision because they focused on their individual lives. Democratic equality, says Tocqueville, draws the individual towards himself, 'et menace de la renfermer enfin tout entire dans la solitude de son proper coeur.' In other words, the dark side of individualism is a centring on the self, which both flattens and narrows our lives, makes them poorer in meaning, and less concerned with others or society.

This worry has recently surfaced again in concern at the fruits of a 'permissive society,' the doings of the 'me generation,' or the prevalence of 'narcissism,' to take just three of the best-known contemporary formulations. The sense that lives have been flattened and narrowed, and that this is connected to an abnormal and regrettable self-absorption, has returned in forms specific to contemporary culture. This defines the first theme I want to deal with.

The disenchantment of the world is connected with a second massively important phenomenon of the modern age, which also greatly troubles many people. We might call this the primacy of *instrumental reason*. By 'instrumental reason' I mean the kind of rationality we draw on when we calculate the most economical application of means to a given end. Maximum efficiency, the best cost–output ratio, is its measure of success.

No doubt sweeping away the old orders has immensely widened the scope of instrumental reason. Once society no longer has a sacred structure, once social arrangements and modes of action are no longer grounded in the order of things or the will of God, they are in a sense up for grabs. They can be redesigned with their consequences for the happiness and well-being of individuals as our goal. The yardstick that henceforth applies is that of instrumental reason. Similarly, once the creatures that surround us lose the significance that accrued to their place in the chain of being, they are open to being treated as raw materials or instruments for our projects.

In one way this change has been liberating. But there is also a widespread unease that instrumental reason not only has enlarged its scope but also threatens to take over our lives. The fear is that things that ought to be determined by other criteria will be decided in terms of efficiency or 'cost–benefit' analysis, that the independent ends that ought to be guiding our lives will be eclipsed by the demand to maximize output. There are lots of things one can point to that give substance to this worry: for instance, the ways the demands of economic growth are used to justify very unequal distributions of wealth and income, or the way these same demands make us insensitive to the needs of the environment, even to the point of potential disaster. Or else, we can think of the way much of our social planning, in crucial areas like risk assessment, is dominated by forms of cost–benefit analysis that involve grotesque calculations, putting dollar assessments on human lives.

The primacy of instrumental reason is also evident in the prestige and aura that surround technology, and makes us believe that we should seek technological solutions even when something very different is called for. We see this often enough in the realm of politics, as Robert Bellah and his colleagues forcefully argue in their book, *The Good Society*. But it also invades other domains, such as medicine. Patricia Benner has argued in a number of important works that the technological approach in medicine has often sidelined the kind of care that involves treating the patient as a whole person with a life story, and not as the locus of a technical problem. Society and the medical establishment frequently undervalue the contribution of nurses, who more often than not provide this humanly sensitive caring, as against that of specialists with high-tech knowledge.

The dominant place of technology is also thought to have contributed to the narrowing and flattening of our lives that I have just been discussing in connection with the first theme. People have spoken of a loss of resonance, depth, or richness in our human surroundings. Almost 150 years ago, Marx, in *The Communist Manifesto*, remarked that one of the results of capitalist development was that 'all that is solid melts in air.' The claim is that the solid, lasting, often expressive objects that served us in the past are being set aside for the quick, shoddy, replaceable commodities with which we now surround ourselves. Albert Borgman speaks of the 'device paradigm,' whereby we withdraw more and more from 'manifold engagement' with our environment and instead request and get products designed to deliver some circumscribed benefit. He contrasts what is involved in heating our homes with the contemporary central-heating furnace, with what this same function entailed in pioneer times, when the whole family had to be involved in cutting and stacking the wood and feeding the stove or fireplace. Hannah Arendt focused on the more and more ephemeral quality of modern objects of use and argued that 'the reality and reliability of the human world rest primarily on the fact that we are surrounded by things more permanent than the activity by which they are produced.' This permanence comes under threat in a world of modern commodities.

This sense of threat is increased by the knowledge that this primacy is not just a matter of a perhaps unconscious orientation, which we are prodded and tempted into by the modern age. As such it would be hard enough to combat, but at least it might yield to persuasion. But it is also clear that powerful mechanisms of social life press us in this direction. A manager in spite of her own orientation may be forced by the conditions of the market to adopt a maximizing strategy she feels is destructive. A bureaucrat, in spite of his personal insight, may be forced by the rules under which he operates to make a decision he knows to be against humanity and good sense.

Marx and Weber and other great theorists have explored these impersonal mechanisms, which Weber has designated by the evocative term 'the iron cage.' And some people have wanted to draw from these analyses the conclusion that we are utterly helpless in the face of such forces, or at least helpless unless we totally dismantle the institutional structures under which we have been operating for the last centuries – that is, the market and the state. This aspiration seems so unrealizable today that it amounts to declaring us helpless.

I want to return to this below, but I believe that these strong theories of fatality are abstract and wrong. Our degrees of freedom are not zero. There is a point to deliberating what ought to be our ends, and whether instrumental reason ought to have a lesser role in our lives than it does. But the truth in these analyses is that it is not just a matter of changing the outlook of individuals, it is not just a battle of 'hearts and minds,' important as this is. Change in this domain will have to be institutional as well, even though it cannot be as sweeping and total as the great theorists of revolution proposed.

This brings us to the political level, and to the feared *consequences for political life* of individualism and instrumental reason. One I have already introduced. It is that the institutions and structures of industrial–technological society severely restrict our choices, that they force societies as well as individuals to give a weight to instrumental reason that in serious moral deliberation we would never do, and which may even be highly destructive. A case in point is our great difficulty in tackling even vital threats to our lives from environmental disasters, like the thinning ozone layer. The society structured around instrumental reason can be seen as imposing a great loss of freedom, on both individuals and the group – because it is not just our social decisions that are shaped by these forces. An individual lifestyle is also hard to sustain against the grain. For instance, the whole design of some modern cities makes it hard to function without a car, particularly where public transport has been eroded in favour of the private automobile.

But there is another kind of loss of freedom, which has also been widely discussed, most memorably by Alexis de Tocqueville. A society in which people end up as the kind of individuals who are 'enclosed in their own hearts' is one where few will want to participate actively in self-government. They will prefer to stay at home and enjoy the satisfactions of private life, as long as the government of the day produces the means to these satisfactions and distributes them widely.

This opens the danger of a new, specifically modern form of despotism, which Tocqueville calls 'soft' despotism. It will not be a tyranny of terror and oppression as in the old days. The government will be mild and paternalistic. It may even keep democratic forms, with periodic elections. But in fact, everything will be run by an 'immense tutelary power,' over which people will have little control. The only defence against this, Tocqueville thinks, is a vigorous political culture in which participation is valued, at several levels of government and in voluntary associations as well. But the atomism of the self-absorbed individual militates against this. Once participation declines, once the lateral associations that were its vehicles wither away, the individual citizen is left alone in the face of the vast bureaucratic state and feels, correctly, powerless. This demotivates the citizen even further, and the vicious cycle of soft despotism is joined.

Perhaps something like this alienation from the public sphere and consequent loss of political control is happening in our highly centralized and bureaucratic political world. Many contemporary thinkers have seen Tocqueville's work as prophetic. If this is so, what we are in danger of losing is political control over our destiny, something we could exercise in common as citizens. This is what Tocqueville called 'political liberty.' What is threatened here is our dignity as citizens. The impersonal mechanisms mentioned above may reduce our degrees of freedom as a society, but the loss of political liberty would mean that even the choices left would no longer be made by ourselves as citizens, but by irresponsible tutelary power.

These, then, are the three malaises about modernity that I want to deal with. The first fear is about what we might call a loss of meaning, the fading of moral horizons. The second concerns the eclipse of ends, in the face of rampant instrumental reason. And the third is about a loss of freedom.

Of course, these are not uncontroversial. I have spoken about worries that are widespread and mentioned influential authors, but nothing here is agreed. Even those who share some form of these worries dispute vigorously how they should be formulated. And there are lots of people who want to dismiss them out of hand. Those who are deeply into what the critics call the 'culture of narcissism' think of the objectors as hankering for an earlier, more oppressive age. Adepts of modern technological reason think the critics of the primacy of the instrumental are reactionary and obscurantist, scheming to deny the world the benefits of science. And there are proponents of mere negative freedom who believe that the value of political liberty is overblown, and that a society in which scientific management combines with maximum independence for each individual is what we ought to aim at. Modernity has its boosters as will as its knockers.

Nothing is agreed here, and the debate continues. But in the course of this debate, the essential nature of the developments, which are here being decried, there being praised, is often misunderstood. And as a result, the real nature of the moral choices to be made is obscured. In particular, I will claim that the right path to take is neither that recommended by straight boosters nor that favoured by the outright knockers. Nor will a simple trade-off between the advantages and costs of, say, individualism, technology, and bureaucratic management provide the answer. The nature of modern culture is more subtle and complex than this. I want to claim that both boosters and knockers are right, but in a way that can't be done justice to by a simple trade-off between advantages and costs. There is in fact both much that is admirable and much that is debased and frightening in all the developments I have been describing, but to understand the relation between the two is to see that the issue is not how much of a price in bad consequences you have to pay for the positive fruits, but rather how to steer these developments towards their greatest promise and avoid the slide into the debased forms.

4 Humanism and Its Role in the Contemporary World

PETER LOPTSON

Movements and institutions often have a spirit or feel or tonality to them that is independent of their formal purposes or defining rationale. Often this stems from their history: from features of the cultural climate or of the personalities or values involved in the context of their original launching. From this perspective, humanism may be seen as a development of the eighteenth and nineteenth centuries in Western European culture, coming out of Enlightenment stances and concerns affirming individualist free thought, the values of science and scientific inquiry, and opposition to the institutionalized authoritarianism of organized religion.

That authoritarian force was very real, and without question it regimented, imprisoned, harassed, tormented, and warped many hundreds of thousands of minds subject to its control or direction in many or most human societies, up to the relatively recent past, and for some societies, to the present day. This can and should be affirmed unequivocally, even if it deserves saying as well that religion has also played a positive and creative role in human life. Many humanists would dispute that there is any such positive role. I myself do think that there is, but I certainly don't see it as obvious. I think a case has to be made that religion has done anything good at all for humanity in general. As indicated, I think that case can be made. But I personally both respect the opposing view, and can without difficulty get with enthusiasm into the spirit of several varieties of antireligion – political anticlericalism, even of a Jacobin republican stripe; moral antipuritanism, the affirmation of the absolute right to probe, and to mock, anything at all; and other forms of good-humoured or angry or principled opposition to priestcraft and its machinations, mystifications, and impositions on children and adults.

Nor do I think that all of the battles for freedom of thought, expression, and practice in the religious sphere are in the past, even in Western societies. The struggle to keep at bay ideologies that, without rational foundation, would fetter and impose conformity on groups of people is probably a never-ending one; and as in other spheres, the price of freedom is never-resting vigilance. This general fact still applies to struggles to impose, and to resist, religious ideas in the school system, and to some degree in the marketplace of cultural expression and communication. Organizations of biblical literalism continue to seek to interfere with the teaching of evolutionary biology in the school systems of the United States and Canada – with more energy as well as more success in the former than in the latter. And other topics, historical and moral, have a religiously coloured force or role in contemporary life that is independent of rational warrant. Some religious groups are seeking to turn back the clock, and could well succeed unless there is continued spirited and informed intelligent opposition.

Still, most of those battles have been fought, and won. Barring cultural catastrophes that are not now foreseeable, and (perhaps) also so long as vigilant guardians of our intellectual liberties remain at the dikes, with particular exceptions relating to local issues (usually politically tinged ones, such as birth control in some countries, marital law in Israel, and aspiration to national political office in the United States), practically all national societies of Judaeo-Christian religious heritage are now places whose citizens can lead wholly non-religious lives, publicly, without penalty, risk, or barrier to full participation and success in the social, economic, political, or cultural spheres. This

'The struggle to keep at bay ideologies that, without rational foundation, would fetter and impose conformity on groups of people is probably a never-ending one; and as in other spheres, the price of freedom is never-resting vigilance.'

was not true even seventy years ago, but it is true now. It is indeed thanks in considerable part to the endeavours of humanists (whether or not they applied this name to themselves) that this is true now. The ranks of individuals who played a role in this effort include some of the most illustrious names in the Western tradition: Voltaire, Condorcet, Tom Paine, J.S. Mill, T.H. Huxley, Emma Goldman, Bertrand Russell. These people are giants, as well as heroes, of this tradition and this struggle, as are a great many others who might be named.

The intellectual freedoms these efforts produced are part of the broad liberal heritage ignited in the European Enlightenment, and realized – by no means perfectly, anywhere, even yet – in the twentieth century. The Liberal Enlightenment tradition does face real enemies in modern life, and these are, I think, matters of important concern for humanists. I will go on to discuss some features of the contemporary struggle, as I see it.

At the present time the greatest threat from religion to the Enlightenment heritage and freedom of thought, in the Western world, does not come from *organized* religion, or at any rate from organized religious denominations or churches. Some of the latter are in fact beneficent forces in contemporary life. There is in my view nothing to fear from most varieties of liberal Protestant Christianity, or from Quakers, Unitarians, Jews, or western Buddhists. Many individual members of these religious bodies, and a number of the groups they have formed or contribute to collectively, are enlightened, principled champions of human rights and of toleration. The same is true also, I think – though with more qualifications – in the cases of individuals and structures within Catholic and Orthodox varieties of Christianity, and indeed of most non-evangelical and non-fundamentalist religious bodies in the Western world.

The main contemporary enemies are three religious constituencies. In order of their power – and hence the magnitude of the challenge they pose – they are fundamentalist Islam, the organized political Christian right, and irrationalist New Age religion. It would be easy both to exaggerate and to underestimate the danger presented by each. All are enemies of liberal values and of science, and all are fundamentally antidemocratic (though the last of the three is least so, and is often a champion of the pluralism it benefits from, though with a much greater interest in 'free speech for me than for thee,' to paraphrase Nat Hentoff's apt image). *Within* Western societies, at least as great a danger as any of these three, is the cluster of positions sometimes called postmodernism, or multiculturalism. Unlike the first three phenomena referred to, this last enemy is largely secular and this-worldly.

Some brief comments on each of these enemies of the Enlightenment. The menace of Islam is to some degree a bogeyman created by the mass media and by some political constituencies in the contemporary post-communist world – in particular, in the period following the 2001 terrorist attacks in New York and Washington. Yet there can be no mistake: the values and practices of Islam are as illiberal, as suppressive of human autonomy and free thought, and as superstitious, as any that were ever held by the major Christian churches in the darkest days of their power. And though Islam is primarily centred outside the Western world, its reach is expanding; its politicized and militant fundamentalist arms are encroaching increasingly on the Western world; and in any case, the billion human beings it subjugates morally and intellectually are our brothers and sisters, whose fate matters intrinsically, just as it will have bearing on our future. Islam is in a state of troubled contestation with modernity and with the Western world – though related, these are not quite the same thing – and there is every reason to expect continuing rough waters into the foreseeable future. Internally, this force is fuelled primarily by the fear that considerable numbers of Muslim men have of losing control over Muslim women. This puts the matter very starkly, and arguably it is an oversimplication; no doubt, there is very much more to the dynamics of these geopolitical developments than my overview can provide. But again, there is no question: Islam is a religion that denies the full adulthood of half of humanity, the female half. It also has absolutely no tolerance for *dissent*, for blasphemy or for apostasy, and has not the slightest interest in the creation or preservation of structures for such tolerance.

The reality of the irrational power of Islam in the modern world is expressed well by the case of Salman Rushdie in the 1990s, even though the Islamic decree ordering his murder came just from one particular militant Muslim society. What is most striking about his case for the point I want to make here is that although Rushdie had many defenders in the West, he had few if any *imitators*. In the modern Western world it is easy to ridicule or lampoon Christianity, and many people do. Humanist humour often consists in just such drollery – and why should it not? But ask yourself which brave soul among you, or among any of us in the Western world, would undertake to put together a play or a film whose central motif was a comic send-up, a satirical spoof on (say) the sex life of Mohammed, or a depiction of his life and career as ludicrous fraud. (A *Life of Brian* version of the foundation of Islam, say.) That such artistic enterprise or courage would be rare, and might be rash, seems well confirmed by the case of Theo van Gogh in the Netherlands; in November 2004, he was murdered because he made a film depicting the subordination of women in a Muslim society.

Right-wing Christian fundamentalism is a social and political problem chiefly in North America – in the United States and Canada – not especially in other parts of the world that are of Christian or Judaeo-Christian heritage. Since at least the seventeenth century, there have been recurrent waves of evangelical Christianity in Western societies; impassioned, intolerant would-be saviours have quite often sought the political power to force their world views, values, and priorities on their fellow men and women. There still are plenty of sincere evangelical and fundamentalist Christians knocking on doors, distributing leaflets, and by other means trying to win hearts for Christ. But as I read the contemporary scene, it is not primarily these people who are the enemy of liberal Enlightenment; or insofar as it is people of this kind, they are chiefly foot soldiers, dupes of people whom we can reasonably doubt have service to Christ as their first priority. Today's right-wing Christian fundamentalism seems to be primarily a *political* phenomenon with political and economic rather than religious aims. Some of these aims are sincerely philosophical: the people in this movement truly believe that our socio-economic order should consist chiefly of two-parent, different-sex nuclear families, with women emphasizing their domestic role as mothers and wives rather than their economic one as breadwinners. This movement also values other 'traditional' – arguably, largely *nostalgic* – conceptions of the roles of men and women; of parents and children; of the state in its relations with individuals and families. It has sharply defined views of what *majorities* – cultural majorities, for example – are entitled to; and of what communities that are not majorities are *not* entitled to within a wider national fabric. These views and values are not primarily religious ones, and many people largely or entirely without religious views share them. (I dare say some humanists may possibly share them also.) Yet these views and values are given, under the umbrella or mantle of Christianity, a religious coloration. And especially in the United States, there is quite good reason to believe that this movement is led essentially by a self-aggrandizing group of political opportunists (and *economic* ones – many of these people are, quite simply, hucksters with an eye on accumulating *loot*). That is to say, the Benny Hinns and Joyce Meyers of the current scene do not represent the power and menace of religion, though they are worrisome enough on other grounds.

To be sure, concerns legitimately felt need not stem from apprehensions of the direct coercive political power of an irrationalist constituency. The culture and values of the Enlightenment can be at risk – *are* at risk – from movements in contemporary life that may sabotage or sap that legacy in more indirect ways. Two somewhat amorphous phenomena constitute the form this attack is currently taking. One is more or less religious, the other chiefly not.

In recent years the old idea of a left–right continuum in politics and ideology – also an Enlightenment idea, stemming from the French Revolution – has been rendered complicated and opaque, if not actually antiquated. (For example, is being a very strong environmentalist to take a position on the left, or on the right, or at the centre? Is strong advocacy of what is called *reform* in Eastern Europe left-wing, right-wing, or neither?) At any rate, if this political–ideological continuum can be employed here, with all due caution, we can say that the Enlightenment tradition in general, and its rationalist humanist wing in particular, has been used historically to confront opposition to its right. Organized religion, the principal enemy, was establishmentarian, reactionary, conservative. In the cases of the two oppositional phenomena I now speak of, liberal rationalist humanism meets enemies to its left.

The Enlightenment tradition, it is argued by these foes, is Eurocentric. It is logocentric. It is androcentric, or at any rate, masculinist. It is scientistic. If not narrowly positivist and empiricist, it is at any rate naive and quite unsophisticated about science, failing to realize that science, like everything else, has a cultural and historical *location* and is just one of a great variety of *paradigms* for constructing, contending with, and – perhaps especially so in its case – *controlling* the world. This tradition, and definitely humanism (according to these opponents), makes a god of science and is selectively attentive and inattentive to its qualities. Science, according to this perspective, mostly seeks to control and manipulate the natural world. Science gave us pollution and environmental degradation. If not actually responsible for war, it made war truly dangerous – it made war *scientific*. The rise of science was and still is part of a Western European, aggressive, imperialistic, and racist expansion into the rest of the world, one that has commandeered its resources and labour and trampled on its ideas, cultures, and alternative ways of knowing and being in the world, ways that were and are just as good (maybe better, in some cases). This ruthless aggression made its earliest attack – so this critique continues – its first expropriative cultural and cognitive assault, closer to home, on women, its own women. Science is rape, and certainly it is the denial and silencing of the experience of others, including the whole female half of humanity. And the European Enlightenment, and the liberal humanist rationalist tradition that is one of its products, is complicit in this brutality, its genteel tones notwithstanding.

You see the idea, and perhaps how it may be characterized somewhat as an attempt to outflank humanism and its fellow travellers from the left.

I have called one wing of this attack more or less religious in type, and the other more or less secular. The first is also 'low culture,' the second 'high culture' – which may be just a way of saying that the second is to be found very explicitly in university settings, and the first not. At any rate, the first, religious wing of this attack is in some ways the more dangerous, but also the one whose defeat is the more certain. This is because this wing makes claims about the world, and the world – again and again, over and over – does not oblige. This cluster of popular movements includes beliefs in and attempts to practise past-life regression, astrology, Kabbalarian numerology, Wicca (or witch-craft), recovered repressed-memory syndrome, systems of antiscience, and holistic medicine. It also embraces so-called paranormal phenomena such as telepathic communication and clairvoyance. This list could be enlarged, and some adherents may be more benign than others. They have also quite varying degrees of direct engagement with liberal humanist positions, or of disaffection with Western culture.

Even the least malign of these beliefs has ill consequences. They encourage and perpetuate credulity, 'magical' and wish-fulfilling views of reality that happen to be untrue. In most cases their harm is still greater. People make important decisions on the basis of astrological data. Beliefs in widespread satanic ritual abuse cults, and beliefs in memories of childhood sexual abuse where no memory whatsoever had survived of it until 'restored' by particular forms of psychotherapy, have both led in recent years to a great deal of misery, including completely baseless convictions and prison sentences and life-destroying and equally groundless accusations by adults against their own parents. Because these are still matters of some controversy, let me state most emphatically that there is clear corroborative evidence that a great deal of genuine sexual and non-sexual abuse of children by adults, including their parents (most often fathers or stepfathers), has taken place and undoubtedly continues to take place.

What all these developments point to is the absolutely vital necessity of there continuing to be observed and applied – and therefore, of necessity, of there continuing to be *understood*, and *valued* – canons of critical empirical investigation. That is to say, these phenomena show that we need *science* – that individual and social justice and our very liberties depend on it.

I turn finally to the last of the major enemies of Enlightenment and of humanism. Over time, this enemy may not pose a very great danger to liberal rationalist humanism, since it is mostly confined to universities and is definitely contested there, if not yet with full success. Nonetheless, this movement has been formidable and continues to be so. It draws from and appeals to one set of liberal Enlightenment values – namely, pluralistic diversity and tolerance – and uses them against the central place that Western scientific and cultural paradigms have long enjoyed. The valorization of tolerance and diversity of values, styles, and norms – all liberal norms – prompts or feeds *relativistic* positions, both cultural relativist and moral relativist. These in turn prompt and feed critiques of science as simply a way of dealing with the world, one among many others that are just as valuable or plausible. To these ideas is added a Marxist or post-Marxist critique of Western colonial, imperial, and military history. A distinctive additional note completes the brew – the Marxist-inspired but not genuinely Marxist-in-fact view according to which all social and cultural phenomena are to be analysed in terms of power relations and dynamics. Foucault is a key expositor of this idea.

Part of the potency of this conjunction – the central so-called postmodern idea – is that all, or virtually all, of its ingredients have a degree of plausibility. That degree is simply exaggerated in the full combination, to quite implausible degrees; and the foundational, and shared, stresses on tolerance and pluralist diversity, act as impediments that freeze or slow or blur possibilities of resistance. After all, one does not want to be ethnocentric, or otherwise to vaunt, promote, or extol what is one's own or resides where one is; or to dismiss or denigrate other cultures, styles, or values.

There is surely a great deal of negativity to lay at the door of the West. That Western Europeans are strikingly *worse* than other people does not seem probable; but that they are particularly better, or have not done quite a lot of damage to other people, is also unconvincing. It is also reasonable to argue that 'the rise of the West' from the late 1400s on was a multifaceted phenomenon, and that the extraordinary development of science in the seventeenth century played an integral part in this. West European colonial and imperial expansion, and technology and science, have been parts of a single world-historical process; it is likely that the latter could not have occurred without the former.

Nonetheless, science and liberal democracy are the West's most important cultural gifts to the world. Not even postmodernists want to replace the second of these gifts; they want to denigrate and trivialize it by arguing that it is a mask for keeping the power of ruling elements, but they do not propose replacing it so much as revising and augmenting it. This places humanists and other defenders of Enlightenment ideals in the position of having to claim, and argue, that liberal democracy is not easy to improve upon. This *is* an inherently conserving, or conservative, stance to take; but there seems no help for it. It really doesn't seem a good idea to dismantle the idea of the value, autonomy, and equality of each adult citizen, even if the dismantling – giving some protected or weighted status on the ground that the deprecations of others do not yet enable them, or the society as a whole, to cope with autonomous adulthood – even if this dismantling is only supposed to be temporary.

As for science, my own view is that science is a much more fragile flower than people often think. Genuinely scientific thinking and methodology are *not* obvious, easy things for human beings to acquire, apply, or preserve. They require learning, example, and trial and error – like science itself. It is more natural to human beings to be impressed by a few resembling cases than to have the patience and motivation to see whether those resemblances point to a really stable pattern in the nature of things, or not. There is a danger of scientific culture evolving into a rare, elite commodity possessed mostly by cadres of specialist servants of governments and industry. The danger is not one of wicked scientists conspiring to poison the environment or foist undesired products on a hapless general public. There are genuine menaces to the environment, and many individual scientists do have much to answer for in the chronicle of applied science. If we are to meet environmental challenges, science is our only hope; but science will need to be ethical and humanistically informed, it will have to be good and indeed highly creative science. The greater danger posed by a scientifically educated elite lies in the ignorance and propensity to superstition this would leave the rest of the population in. *This* battle – for humanists and for everyone who cares about the future of the planet and of the human species – is the battle to foster and augment critical thinking and scientific rationality, and not just about immediate technical matters of service to employers, but about all facets of life.

5 All Things Being Unequal

MARK KINGWELL

There is a scene in David Mamet's play *Oleanna* where John, the terminally self-involved professor, reads out the list of charges his abused student has brought against him. 'You say I am elitist,' he says, 'which seems to be a word that simply means bad.' Indeed, as William A. Henry III notes in his book *In Defense of Elitism,* the term 'has come to rival if not outstrip "racist" as the foremost catchall pejorative of our times.'

The reason is simple. There is a basic tension in a democratic society, between the egalitarianism of 'All people are created equal' and the inescapable fact that some people are smarter, richer, more beautiful, or more talented than others. A favourite response to this tension is the forcible levelling of difference, the anti-elitist attempt to eliminate not only social inequalities but natural ones too.

So we've been told to refuse all judgments of 'quality,' to foster self-esteem instead of achievement in schools, to play down the exceptional and the extraordinary. From here it's not much of a step to the dystopian vision of Kurt Vonnegut's science fiction story of phenom Harrison Bergeron, a gifted athlete and genius who is killed by the 'U.S. Handicapper-General' after he throws off the sandbags and electronic headband designed to make him equal to everyone else.

But none of this hand-wringing about elites is really new. In the 1790s the fledgling U.S. government experimented with social levelling in the business of diplomacy. Thomas Jefferson's 'Pell Mell Etiquette' called for the obliteration of most distinctions of rank and birth. Pecking orders all abolished, visiting dignitaries would be treated just like other down-home folks. The effort was a policy disaster. It achieved only one egalitarian goal: it succeeded in giving everyone equal offence.

Democratic equality does not, and cannot, mean that everyone is the same. It's not just that systems of rank are necessary to realize some kinds of efficiency (the military, the diplomatic corps). Some people just are more gifted than others; the genetic lottery is not committed to equality. So the question isn't, are there intractable differences between people? Of course there are. The question is, what are we going to do about them?

We no longer – in theory, anyway – tolerate elites of bloodline or family connections. We do tolerate elites of physical beauty, athletic ability, and (apparently) facility in memorizing and repeating other people's words in front of a camera. But these are numerically tiny, the talents they muster evanescent – they pose no deep threat to equality. No, the really powerful elite in today's society is actually one of intelligence, an upper class of information manipulators and symbol tumblers. And what's troubling about this elite of cognitive ability is precisely that it seems to be based on merit.

In their now infamous book, *The Bell Curve: Intelligence and Class Structure in American Life*, Harvard psychologist Richard J. Herrnstein and conservative author Charles Murray offered some gloomy – and brutal – reflections on the New Elitism. The United States, they said, is now dominated by a 'cognitive elite' of high-IQ managers and professionals. These people are increasingly more powerful than, and isolated from, an intelligence-deficient underclass in which crime, poverty, and political apathy are rampant. And, oh yeah, this underclass is predominantly black.

Herrnstein and Murray say they recognize the dangers of a cognitive elite separated from the rest of society, but their policy suggestions are all about how to expand the cognitive elite rather than control it. Immigration should be limited, they say, to counter the lowering effects of population expansion. (Dumb people are getting in!) And, to avoid 'dysgenesis' or intelligence dissipation through breeding, birth control should be made more widely available to those at the low end of the bell curve. (Those dumb people breed like rabbits!) They defend these attempts to fatten the high end of the bell curve by gesturing towards economic competitiveness, but the effects are discriminatory and, on their own evidence, racially targeted.

This analysis comes gift-wrapped for antiwelfare conservatives, especially if they happen to be closet racists too. It also provides apparently irrefutable genetic support for Murray's earlier contention, in *Losing Ground*, that welfarism doesn't alleviate but rather traps people in poverty. Now we know why: quota-based affirmative action programs, welfare, most forms of social assistance, all are doomed to fail because no amount of standard-lowering or monetary gifts can alter a person's genes. Biology is not exactly destiny, but it's pretty darn close.

Good polemicists both, Herrnstein and Murray shamelessly manipulate their statistics, confuse correlation with causation, and artificially limit the notion of intelligence. Their weak palliatives about emphasizing the positive aspects of racial 'clans' (blacks are better athletes, for example) are just cheerful racist hooey. Like all statistics, these leave no room for individuality, inviting the reduction of everyone to his or her group. Nor is there any way to measure the lingering social effects of poverty, or the inferiority complexes of formerly enslaved groups. In the words of one critic, they 'substitute intelligence for moral worth.'

All true. The fact is, though, society does seem organized to reward intelligence, not moral worth. If it were not, IQ would not be such a good predictor of worldly success. What *The Bell Curve* really does is provide scientific phrasing for the uncomfortable truth that brighter people are going to succeed more than others.

Indeed, the book's argument is oddly reminiscent of the 'noble lie' of Plato's *Republic*. To preserve the caste system necessary for social harmony, Socrates suggests telling citizens a mythic story about different metals being mixed in the souls of different classes of people. Citizens won't accept a ruling class based on a claim to superior wisdom, but they will accept a divine ordinance that gives the rulers golden souls. Our own scientistic culture prefers statistical ordinance, but the impulse to sugarcoat inequality is the same. These days we soothe ourselves with the thought that, if the graphs show it, it cannot be otherwise.

'Democratic equality does not, and cannot, mean that everyone is the same. It's not just that systems of rank are necessary to realize some kinds of efficiency (the military, the diplomatic corps). Some people just are more gifted than others; the genetic lottery is not committed to equality. So the question isn't, are there intractable differences between people? Of course there are. The question is, what are we going to do about them?'

Plato was more explicit about eugenic controls, by the way. No condoms-for-the-poor rubbish for him. He said the rulers, in their wisdom, should forcibly remove children from their parents at birth and stream them into castes.

The Bell Curve's deficiencies aside, it's hard to denounce a cognitive elite. Intelligence seems not only good but honest: a difference we can respect. The problem posed by the New Elite is therefore not, as it was with bloodline elites, mere existence. The problem is, instead, one of growing social irresponsibility. As the cognitive elite has grown in power through the decades following the Second World War – the decades creating a world ruled by information – it has increasingly set itself apart from society at large.

In his recent book *The Revolt of the Elites*, American critic Christopher Lasch advances the elitism debate by noting that the cognitive elite has defected from the social role privileged classes formerly occupied precisely because it is merit-based. Like Henry and Herrnstein, Lasch is not around to expand on his views: all three analysts of elitism died while awaiting publication of their respective books. (The statistical significance of that doesn't bear thinking of.) But Lasch's book probes what *The Bell Curve* seems happy to ignore, the dark underside of an intelligence-based meritocracy.

Twenty per cent of the American population now controls more than half the country's wealth. The disparity between rich and poor is wider than at any time in the last fifty years. The upper-middle-class is now composed of 'symbolic analysts.' It is 'a "new class" only in the sense that their livelihood rests not so much on ownership of property as on manipulation of information and professional expertise.' The new elite includes bank managers and businesspeople, but also information managers like journalists and academics. It is diverse and often in conflict with itself – conflict that deflects attention from the plight of the less-gifted majority.

Bolstered by a world ruled by information, the symbolic analysts enjoy a style of life that is lavish, even decadent, and insulated. Because their colleagues and friends may hail from different social strata, they do not see just how similar their education and success has made them. United only by wealth and ability, 'they lack a common political outlook' but share a disdain for those less able. 'Simultaneously arrogant and insecure, the new elites regard the masses with mingled scorn and apprehension.'

That scorn and apprehension is returned in spades, as we know. But this mutual enmity in turn leads to defection: the revolt of the elites. The new managers of information and money – unlike the old elites of bloodline and land – feel no sense of attachment to community or devotion to such traditional virtues as prudence, obligation, charity, or loyalty. We cannot imagine them caring for indentured servants, taking part in village fetes, or collecting for jumble sales.

Worse, their vaunted meritocracy is, according to Lasch, 'a parody of democracy,' in which the privileged take refuge in abstract equality of opportunity when confronted with the less well-off. Because success is predicated on the merit of intelligence, they think justice has been served: everybody had the chance to be smart, after all. They then siphon off talent from the lower classes with, for example, minority scholarships to elite schools, leaving those classes leaderless and stagnant.

The talented thus 'retain many of the vices of aristocracy without its virtues.' The new aristocracy of brains and education – and let's be honest: if you are reading this, you're probably part of it – is increasingly isolated. Its members begin to seek shelter behind the gates of private suburbs, patrolled by private police forces, their garbage collected by private contractors. Not only do they feel no sense of attachment to the less well-off, they regard them as a positive threat.

Lasch's analysis is on the money. But his suggestions for improvement are no more helpful (though slightly more palatable) than Herrnstein and Murray's. Lasch thinks that elites will feel more attachment to society if they cultivate the values of the lower-middle-class – a holdover from his argument in *The Culture of Narcissim*. But this is romantic nonsense. No bank manager or lawyer is going to feel more commitment to the poor by going bowling or watching *Roseanne*. Lasch's rosy, family-values view of Middle America is anyway too Disneyfied, too sanguine. There is no democratic promised land in the middle of the bell curve.

The hard questions are still unanswered. How can a large and powerful cognitive elite be reconciled with the egalitarianism at the heart of democracy?

Elimination is the not the answer. Elites are not going anywhere. And, the cries of levellers aside, nor should they. John Stuart Mill, no friend to conservatives, knew that true elites (as opposed to self-styled ones) provide an important example to society and help it flourish through innovation and effort. Neither spasmodic disapproval of elitism nor the retreat of elites into self-interested enclaves of privilege is of any use to society. They are two sides of the same coin.

What we need instead is an elite that supports a culture of modified *noblesse oblige* – or, accepting that intelligence determines the new aristocracy, *intelligesse oblige*. We need a body politic in which privilege (even when meritocratic) implies obligation, where success (even when the result of hard work) demands devotion to community.

Creating such a culture of obligation will not be easy. Given the presumption of the New Elitism, that privilege accrues only to merit, it's hard to defend these commitments in terms of what elites owe their fellow citizens. The privileged won't buy it. After all, they worked hard to get where they are and everybody else can just get off their butts and get a job.

At the same time, current means of holding the privileged responsible – graduated income tax, for example – are enforced and, as a result, resented. This actually encourages the defection Lasch fears. The reason conservative writers are always careful to speak of government redistribution of wealth, as if anything gained by market efforts was one's by natural (and not social) right, is that they want the wealthy to view taxation as the enemy of promise.

Nevertheless, there is a way that social obligations can be made compelling. Along the way, we just might get the new elite to see that privilege cannot exist apart from society, that there is no wealth or success without people against whom achievements are measured – that old-fashioned virtue, minus old-fashioned condescension, is important after all.

In 1971, Harvard philosopher John Rawls published a thick book called *A Theory of Justice*, which made an elaborate argument for a very simple conclusion. The genetic lottery, Rawls argued, is just that – a roll of the dice. For that matter, so is relative wealth at birth. Fine. But now consider: What if you didn't know how the dice would roll for you, didn't know your social position and allotment of talents? What kind of principles of justice would you support then, placed behind a notional 'veil of ignorance'?

The answer, Rawls suggested, owed much to our basic intuitions about fairness in distribution. In a way, his thought experiment is analogous to an old device for solving dinner table disputes. We both want part of the remaining cake. So we agree that I will cut the cake, but you will choose the first piece. My only sensible option then is to cut the cake into equal halves. When I don't know what portion I'm going to get, equal distribution simply makes sense.

Behind the veil of ignorance, then, we would support equal liberty and access to social positions – meritocratic equality of opportunity. We could not insist on equality of outcome, given inevitable differences in ability, but we would demand that any inequalities of outcome be constrained by a crucial rule: they must make the worst-off class as well off as possible. After all, there but for the grace of the gene-gods go you.

Justice doesn't have to mean vast redistribution of wealth, or costly participation by the well off. It does have to mean we take seriously the true meaning of democratic equality: that each of us is, as a citizen, no better – no more worthy of consideration – than anyone else. Democratic justice is not opposed to success and privilege; it should not thwart effort by seeking to make everyone the same. But democratic justice tempers privilege with the thought that even the less gifted have a right to be here. Equal moral worth is the cornerstone after all.

It's not much, to demand that social success be conditioned by regard for others, but it's more than recent debates about elitism have managed to produce. It's also more than we have in the current political culture.

PART V

Authority and the Individual

1 What Is Government For?

TRUDY GOVIER

Why have governments? One short and simple answer is to maintain law and order. On this theory, the only purpose of government is to keep down violence, protect persons and property, and defend the state against invasion. With this limited government we have what's called the minimal state.

But a minimal state is utterly impractical in modern times. In fact, the functions of the minimal state lead immediately to expansions. Without support for the poor, gross inequities in material welfare threaten the social order; protection of life and property requires efforts towards social justice. And given the complexities of modern societies, protecting life and property also requires extensive regulation and the monitoring of products and institutions. Imagine having to inspect farms, meat processing plants, and supermarkets for yourself to avoid food poisoning, or perform a do-it-yourself chemical analysis of toothpaste and shampoo to escape bodily injury!

The minimal state is nothing more than an ideological fiction; it exists nowhere in the contemporary world. Contemporary governments do more than keep down crime and invasion. They provide education and health services; regulate foods, drugs, and professional qualifications; establish and maintain a communications and transportation infrastructure; and provide services and benefits to vulnerable members of society.

Until recently, most people took such functions for granted. Comfortably, we assumed without question that it was reasonable for government to regulate products; employ meat inspectors; license drivers, doctors, and therapists; set curricula for public education; maintain roads and postal service; and so on and so forth.

In the current political climate, with governments rushing to privatize and so many people assuming that private enterprise is necessarily more efficient than government, we can no longer make these mundane presumptions. What used to be prevailing wisdom has come under attack. Leaders on the right brand government as wasteful, inefficient, and not to be trusted. Private business, they believe, can do things better.

Like a snake casting off its old skin, governments in Alberta and Ontario have sought to shed their functions. Behind such initiatives is a generalized trust in business and distrust of government. This attitude is definitely open to criticism. It is based on a double standard. Inflated salaries, poor decision-making, corruption, inefficiency, and shoddy work are just as much features of some businesses as they are of some governments.

Furthermore, the idea that private businesses can and should replace government in many of its functions ignores the distinct features and role of government.

What is special about government is that it, and it alone, is charged with serving and protecting the public interest. Charities, individuals, and not-for-profit groups may seek to further the public interest, but only government has the promotion of public well-being as its official task. Government has the constitutional ability to pass laws and monitor and enforce compliance with those laws. It has a monopoly on the legitimate use of force within its area of jurisdiction. It has the ability, through taxation, to raise revenue to finance its activities. And it is accountable, through the electoral process, to citizens within its territory.

'The responsibilities, powers, and accountability of government make it very different from business. One may speak of wanting to run a government in a "businesslike manner," but to think that government should be or become a business is to make a fundamental mistake.'

In all of these ways government is unique. For these reasons it also has unique responsibilities. Public goods such as safe roads, clean air, and conserved resources cannot be established by individuals or private groups. They require regulation, coordinated action, and the support of public resources.

The responsibilities, powers, and accountability of government make it very different from business. One may speak of wanting to run a government in a 'businesslike manner,' but to think that government should be or become a business is to make a fundamental mistake.

In an essay on the federal debt, Andrew Coyne notes that 'government should only do what only government can do. If someone else, private or provincial, can do the job as well or better, let them.'

Coyne deserves applause for raising the question of the role of government and for proposing an answer. But his position is flawed for three reasons. First, because it is too negative, presuming a bias against government. Second, because it ignores the unique position of government. And third, because it avoids any explanation of what doing something 'as well or better' would amount to. (One suspects Coyne's criteria would be financial, although he doesn't say.)

The role of government is to serve and protect the public interest. The role of business is to make money. These functions are very different and they often conflict. A pertinent example is that of driver training and licensing, now privatized in Alberta. One who has a business teaching and testing drivers has an interest in having people pass the test and become satisfied customers. To maintain a successful business he needs a reputation for getting people through the examination. This interest puts a downward pressure on standards. Yet the public interest is in having rigorous standards for new drivers.

Consider too the sale of alcohol – also privatized. Someone who owns a business selling alcohol has an interest in getting more people to consume more alcohol so as to increase profits. But having more people drink more is against the public interest: it will result in increased traffic accidents, crime, alcoholism, domestic violence, work absences, and medical problems. This conflict was noted with alarm by Calgary police superintendent Gerry Baxter and Brad Zipursky of the Alberta Alcohol and Drug Abuse Commission. Both have expressed concern about discounts and proposed benefits (frequent flyer points, add-on products) for frequent customers at liquor stores – fearing an increase in crime and social problems as a result.

Such conflict will emerge in an even more acute form if the Klein administration implements its plan to privatize jails. A private business running a jail has a business interest in keeping that jail full: pay is according to beds occupied. This gives such a business a vested interest in increasing the amount of crime and the number of not-yet-rehabilitated criminals. Both are demonstrably contrary to the public interest.

Privatization is also questionable in any context involving the protection of the vulnerable – children, the elderly, the sick, the disabled, and the extremely poor. Just because these people are so vulnerable, those charged with responsibility for them must be publicly accountable.

In the area of child welfare, the Klein government is also proposing to delegate its responsibility to local and community groups, rather than to private businesses. Hopefully such a plan would avoid conflicts between financial and client interests. It might also serve to eliminate layers of cumbersome bureaucracy. But the plan raises other issues: the competency of local authorities, the assurance of minimum standards of protection and care, and the coherency of policies in varying communities.

When essential services such as health, education, the regulation of professionals, and safety standards are involved, government has to do its job. Society is sustained through its fundamental institutions, which must be maintained by the government that society supports. Matters such as social welfare, health care, and education are essential in any modern society. Of course money should not be wasted, but the criteria for how well these institutions function are not exclusively financial. The purpose of having an educational system is to educate and train future citizens, not to make money. The purpose of having a health system is to preserve the health of the citizenry, not to ring up a profit.

Any government that seeks to avoid or transfer its responsibility for furthering the public interest and sustaining the society from which it emerges fundamentally misunderstands its own role. To assume that privatization is good because business is generally better than government is simplistic in the extreme. It follows that if a government is unwilling to carry out its essential functions, it should step down and let others take on the job.

2 How to Make Governments Competitive

ANDREW IRVINE

One criticism the political left often makes of big business is that it tends towards monopoly. Small businesses compete with one another, keeping prices low and services high. But as businesses increase in size to take advantage of economies of scale, competition becomes less and less. Oversight mechanisms – anticollusion laws and review bodies of various kinds – exist to help guarantee that the public interest is served, but almost everyone agrees that these mechanisms, necessary though they may be, are not as efficient as direct competition.

Although it is often overlooked, this same point can be made about governments. Governments form the largest monopolies in the world today. Not only do they have sole control over their jurisdictions, they also have the legal right and physical force to back up their monopolies. For anyone concerned about the evils of monopolies, governments represent the ultimate challenge.

How do we limit the effects of government monopoly?

One way is by electing, not just a government, but an official opposition as well. Another is by keeping the legislative, executive, judicial, and monarchical functions of government separate from one another. Yet another is by splitting government into several separate levels: federal, provincial, and municipal.

But as Canadians know all too well, these checks and balances are all too often ineffective. The federal government now has in place an election funding law that outlaws all significant political donations from corporations. Instead, tax dollars are to be distributed to political parties in proportion to their placing in the last election, thus almost guaranteeing the winning party's political dominance into the foreseeable future. In much the same spirit, governments over the past decade at both the provincial and federal levels have attempted several times to outlaw third-party election advertising; something that makes it more and more difficult for public opposition to governments to be expressed at election time.

Power, once concentrated, always tends to further concentrate itself. This by itself should serve as a warning that governments – especially large and powerful governments – have the potential to become unrepresentative and at times corrupt.

Even more significant is that as governments have expanded their monopolies during the twentieth century, they have done so without sufficient regard for future generations. Two unwelcome consequences are especially worth noting.

The first concerns finances. By amassing huge debts and deficits, governments have placed a large and intractable tax burden on future generations. It is important to recognize that in no other case would we think it morally permissible to tax people without their permission. The slogan 'No taxation without representation' even served as the rallying cry for the American Revolution in the eighteenth century.

Against this fundamental principle of democracy is the simple fact that it is always easier to take money from those who have no voice than from those who do. By living beyond their means, large governments take money not only from people who won't directly benefit from its expenditure, but also from those who have no say in whether they are willing to be taxed or in how their tax dollars are to be spent.

'By giving tax dollars directly to our local hospitals, schools, and community groups, we would not only be cutting out government as "middleman," we would also be developing a genuine incentive for governments to "earn" our tax dollars.'

When Adam Smith wrote *The Wealth of Nations* in 1776, he identified four areas for which governments were to be responsible: defence, the judiciary and public safety, education, and public works. Today, in contrast, governments are tempted to become responsible for everything, from relieving poverty to advancing regional development, from the health of its citizens to the regulation of our news media and hockey commentators.

In response to this temptation, Canadians need to insist, not only that governments not slide back into deficits, but also that they adopt balanced-budget legislation.

The second unwelcome consequence of expanded government monopolies is that, as government jurisdictions grow, other institutions – the family, businesses, religious institutions, community charities – all become less and less significant. The growth of what Margaret Thatcher used to call 'the nanny state' means that psychologically, we and our children have become more and more dependent on government. Often we simply assume that if a task is too large or too complex for us to do it ourselves, the only option is to give it to government. Like all large businesses, large governments benefit from economies of scale; at the same time, though, they lead to greater inefficiencies and reduced individual initiative.

How can these problems be resolved? One way is to deny governments a monopoly role in health care, education, infrastructure, and the like. When private-sector firms are allowed to participate in these areas, either on their own or through public/private partnerships, the burden on government to be all things to all people is reduced.

An even more promising response would be to rework Canada's tax policies for charities, making charitable donations 100 per cent deductible against individual income tax.

By giving tax dollars directly to our local hospitals, schools, and community groups, we would not only be cutting out government as 'middleman,' we would also be developing a genuine incentive for governments to 'earn' our tax dollars. Under this plan, the amount of money being spent in the public sphere would remain constant. It's just that, as in any other competitive environment, governments would need to convince taxpayers that they can do a better job of feeding the hungry and healing the sick than can their competitors.

To guarantee the viability of those government ministries, such as defence, that really must remain the exclusive jurisdiction of government, we may want to cap the amount of discretionary taxation that any individual taxpayer can give to other sources at, say, 50 per cent. In addition, in order that services not be disrupted, this change could be phased in over many years.

For anyone concerned about government monopolies, this kind of tax change could well rid Canada of government inefficiency. For the first time, Canadians would have real power to determine exactly how and where their tax dollars were spent.

3 Where My Rights End – and Yours Begin

MARK KINGWELL

Does a motorcyclist without a helmet pose the same kind of danger to others as a cigarette smoker? Is a bridge without a high fence the equivalent of leaving a loaded gun in the house? Is obesity on a moral par with child abuse? Is my suicide a form of harm inflicted on my parents?

These questions, none of them fanciful, concern individual freedom, the right to control my body and mind – what we might call individual sovereignty or *the right to self-use*. The classic statement of this right is J.S. Mill's *On Liberty*, that impassioned argument against tyranny of the majority. There, Mill draws on a tradition of personal ownership already established by John Locke, who made the body and its labour our first legitimate possessions.

'In that part [of conduct] which merely concerns himself,' Mill writes of the free man, 'his independence is, of right, absolute. Over himself, over his own body and mind, the individual is sovereign.' There is no possible justification for infringing this power of self-use, including the alleged happiness, wisdom, or benefit to him and others. 'These are good reasons for remonstrating with him, or reasoning with him, or persuading him, or entreating him, but not for compelling him, or visiting him with any evil in case he do otherwise.'

The sole exception is what Mill calls self-protection: if the exercise of your liberty harms me, I have the right to curb it. Or, as Oliver Wendell Holmes said, 'Your right to swing your fist ends where the end of my nose begins.'

Which sounds simple. But even pure theoretical debates about self-use rapidly become a tangle of analogies and second-hand harms. You certainly have the right to kill yourself with cigarette smoke, but not to poison me with the noxious exhalations of your filthy habit. You have the right to drink yourself stupid, but not to drive afterwards and knock a teenage pedestrian to her death.

Add the real-world condition of a universal health care system and the equations immediately go quantum in complexity. Now the jerk tooling his Ducati down highway 401 without a helmet isn't just a jerk, he's a potential drain on our tax resources. Your vast consumption of

Timbits and Chicken McNuggets is suddenly my problem too, since I end up underwriting your long stays in hospital.

Now add new kinds of harms in the form of 'psychological costs' or 'social consequences': the suffering and neglect of the obese mother's children, the grief and self-recrimination of those left behind by a suicide. Finally, mix in some controversial claims about sanity or mental balance – which qualities, if we lack them, mean that our liberty is no longer our own affair – and you have a recipe for legislative disaster.

The liberal position, the one that Locke, Mill, and most Canadians favour in some form, is that you don't legislate rationality or morality – you don't lay down in law what counts as smart or good. Legislation may start off with reasonable measures to secure our rights, but pretty soon, mixing and jumbling factors, it leads us down the path to the notorious nanny state, or rule by what P.J. O'Rourke famously called 'the Safety Nazis': some dull bureaucrat's milquetoast version of good sense. We begin by mandating seatbelts (costless, sensible, hard to object to) and soon find ourselves, bizarrely, attempting to ban perfume in public places or ordering Halifax police officers to tackle Polar Bear Club members trying to get a wintry dip in the harbour.

> 'The point of liberty isn't merely that we enjoy it ... It is also that individual liberty is the only principled route to the kind of diversity of personal projects that is human life's glory.'

O'Rourke's libertarian position strikes many in this country as peculiarly American. And it is indeed a recurring theme in American culture; some disgruntled, funny, self-destructive guy – it's always a guy – launches a bitter riff against those who want to crack down on dangerous pleasures. (Denis Leary does a neat version of it in the action movie *Demolition Man* as the reluctant leader of an underground resistance movement.) Because individualism is so often defended and so deeply enshrined in American life, there is always – at least in theory – a healthy debate there about perceived state-backed encroachments on liberty.

Here in Canada, suspended somewhere between libertarian and socialist extremes in the political culture, we are more ambivalent. The received wisdom says we favour a greater degree of collectivism than our neighbours to the south. Our Charter of Rights and Freedoms, the product of a sprawling, pluralist postwar society, certainly enshrines more social nuances and communal goods than the Americans' Bill of

Rights. Yet we don't pursue social democracy consistently, or against the deep individualism of the liberal tradition.

And of course Canadians know that the wholly sovereign individual is a myth, an essential piece of fiction we use to understand, and maybe extend, the value of our lives. We all exist as part of a community, a web of care that at once sustains us and inhibits us. We are free to jump off that web, but we ought to think long and hard before doing so.

The elaborate suicide barrier along Toronto's Bloor Street Viaduct, whose metal stanchions weirdly resemble crucifixes, is a case in point. The barrier is arguably, after its fashion, a form of Mill's remonstration or entreaty. It delays the moment of decision and so possibly keeps another sovereign individual, another experimenter in living, on the web. It says, 'Of course you may go, my friend. I could not reasonably prevent you. But let's talk before you do.'

Fine. In fact, though, how voters respond to a legislated control on self-use often depends on how the issue is framed or what imaginary scenarios of disaster are constructed – those fictions that we in the philosophy business call 'intuition pumps.' If a proponent can present a catalogue of alleged potential harms, jumbling various principles and arguments, citizens may find themselves acceding to things that, in theory, they oppose: random searches without cause, for example, the basis of seasonal drunk-driving crackdowns.

More disturbing still, in the wake of terrorist attacks, otherwise liberty-loving citizens, including many formerly Jeffersonian Americans – were suddenly shrugging off racial profiling, targeted extraditions, intrusive personal searches, and even, God save us, actual *torture* of captured prisoners.

The trouble with liberty is that it can't just be for us and not them, or for now and not later. You can't fight a war defending values that our war measures themselves flout. And we should always remember that it's not such a long step from the complacent mantra of today's lengthy security lines – 'If you've done nothing wrong, you have nothing to worry about' – to the collective surveillance programs and state-rewarded snitching of Orwell's imagination.

The point of liberty isn't merely that we enjoy it, that we might just get our kicks by feeling the wind in our hair or biting down on juicy red meat. It is also that individual liberty is the only principled route to the kind of diversity of personal projects that is human life's glory. Innovation in life, like innovation of all kinds, happens at the margins. There, where people are engaged in experiments in living (altering consciousness, altering bodies, testing the limits of experience) lies the future of our species. Some of those experiments will fail, and there will always be costs that trickle down to the rest of us in some form. But there will be benefits too.

The battle over mandatory seatbelts is over, probably for the best. In the battles still to come – over new drugs, new thrills, and maybe new spills – the onus is always on the state to show why the law should ever extend to protecting us from ourselves.

4 Guns

JAN NARVESON

Do people have the right to possess firearms? Here is an argument in support of the view that they do.

What we want is a world in which nobody kills anybody – 'we' being the good folks. But we live in a world in which some people are ready to kill other people, and in which some of them do in fact kill some of those others. The question of what precisely to do about the latter – how much of what sort of punishment, say – is a vexed one, which I don't especially address in this short essay. In contrast, the question of what to do about the former – the ones who are ready to kill, or otherwise attack and assault others – is definitely the one I want to address here. I admit to being somewhat stimulated in this by the murder of a graduate student in my university department, a young woman who, if she had been armed instead of being a wholly vulnerable young woman, would almost certainly still be with us today.

A classic view about government is that, whatever else it may do, part of its job is to protect people, especially from being killed and from other attacks on their bodily integrity. (Part of the classic view is that government also has a responsibility to protect people's property. Obviously it does, and obviously it doesn't take this responsibility very seriously. I will mostly skirt this latter issue – or, as I think it, non-issue. In any case, almost nothing that follows depends on this point.)

How is government to deal with its basic responsibility to protect people?

To start, we can make a division between two general ways in which government might try to do something to honour its responsibility. One way is to protect citizens directly by placing guards in such a way that people threatened with attacks can be defended prior to actually being attacked: defended, then, in the sense that the attacks are actually headed off or prevented in one way or another. Either the would-be assailant is frightened off, or he is, say, shot dead before he manages to shoot his victim, and the person doing the threatening or shooting is a police officer.

A second way for government to honour its responsibility is to refrain from preventing its citizens from defending themselves. This means, in effect, upholding their right to defend themselves. The particular means by which this might be done (in a fairly sizable variety of likely cases) is through the possession and use of firearms, under the discretionary use of the possessor.

Let's take an analogy. Food is essential to life; no item of any economy is more basic. But food production and distribution in most places is in private hands. Governments interfere somewhat, but in the main, what food is grown and who eats what is determined almost entirely by private action. At the same time, those few countries in which governments have played a very large role in food production and distribution have been the sites of all of the world's really large-scale bouts of starvation. To say that government production and distribution of food is a 'failure' is to understate matters grotesquely: it is, in a word, a disaster. Wise students of politics don't think that governments have evaded their responsibility by letting people grow and distribute food on their own.

'It has been said innumerable times, and correctly every time, that governments, in making guns illegal or very difficult to obtain, prevent us – the good people – from protecting ourselves, but do nothing whatever for the bad ones who, after all, are in the business they are in precisely because the fact that their activities are illegal doesn't deter them from engaging in them.'

On the contrary, the ones who try to do it themselves are the irresponsible ones: Mao, Stalin, Castro, Kim Il Jong, and Robert Mugabe (to name just some of the main culprits) were and are enemies of their own people in this respect.

What about personal defence, then? The first thing to appreciate is that governments attempting to defend people in the first way have a record that, while perhaps better than that of the communists in the food department, is nevertheless frankly miserable. And that is hardly surprising. Few citizens would actually like to have policemen stationed outside their doors at all times. Or inside, for that matter – for after all, many killings are domestic. In any case, to say that the cost of doing so would be prohibitive is, again, to understate matters grotesquely.

And in fact, governments, generally speaking, almost entirely confine themselves to the role of attempting to apprehend murderers after the fact. Insofar as people, and especially property, are literally protected by anyone, they are almost entirely protected by people acting on their own, or in a fair number of cases by privately contracted agents – night watchmen, security guards, bodyguards, and so on. The number of private security agents in today's North America exceeds by many times the number of public police officers. It is they, not the police, who provide the overwhelming share of protection in these countries.

Of course, by far the most important of all protection devices is the normal moral and prudential sense of ordinary people. Virtually all of us have been taught to think that murder is wrong, and virtually all of us, on attaining adulthood, think we were taught wisely. Virtually all of us refrain from aggression, to the point that few of us would even think of killing anyone, or even, for that matter, of hauling off and punching someone, even if we were capable of doing so. This is the way it should be, and the way it must be in a working, civilized society.

But as pointed out at the beginning of this essay, 'virtually all' is not 'all' and there is the question of what to do about the rest. We want to secure ourselves from these few people if we can, and the question is how to do it. In many places, such as the street I live on, it is reasonable to take the view that there is no problem and, so, to do nothing. I do not own a firearm, and although I don't know whether any of my neighbours do, I doubt it. In any case, none of us has ever had the least occasion to resort to one in the several decades I have lived in my present home. I am one of the many fortunate people in this part of the world, in this respect. But we all know that there are many who are less fortunate. The question is what these people should do. Often the answer is this: learn how to use a firearm, equip yourself with one, and teach all those in your household about its safe use and, especially, safe storage and non-use. In many places, those who succeed in doing so may well end up appreciably safer than if they had not.

This reminds me of an academic colleague in another city, who purchased a lovely old home, made still lovelier by his efforts and those of his wife, but which was in a neighbourhood that had become the site of criminal activity over the years – indeed, to the point that every house on his block had been burglarized in the recent past, most more than once, many repeatedly. His own house, however, has a rather attractive though unobtrusive plaque by the front door explaining that the owner is a member of the local gun club and is licensed to possess a firearm. He also has an elaborate security warning system, which guests have to learn about with some attention in order to avoid embarrassment – as I found on my first visit there. His house, besides being very attractive, has the distinction of never having been burglarized in all the twenty-some years he has resided there. As we read in Robert A. Waters's *The Best Defense*, this man's story is probably replicable, at some approximation, in literally millions of cases on both sides of the border separating Canada from the United States.

On occasion, things will go wrong. One member of a family will perhaps kill another with the family firearm, or perhaps meet accidental death as a result of a mishandled gun. But of course, no records are kept of the number of murders that do not happen because the intended victim was known to be capable of defending himself. Of anecdotal evidence there is plenty, but by the nature of the case, statistics are all but impossible to collect. On the other hand, careful records are sure to be kept of all the accidents and domestic shootings. Those are what make the newspapers; the success stories, such as that of my academic colleague, do not.

Might my friend be equally safe if he had only the elaborate security system, but no guns? This is a good question, but an armed thief, who could be quite sure of encountering no serious resistance on entering, would still be able to make off with some valuable works of art and other things in the time between entering and setting off the alarm, and the arrival of any public police officer. Indeed, any citizen concerned about this would not be ready to settle for protection by the police, but would engage, at considerable cost, a private security firm, which would promise to be at his door within some specified number of minutes. But no firm that didn't actually have live-in guards could equal the dispatch with which a trained resident gun handler would be in a position to provide any miscreant with a very unwelcome set of alternatives.

It has been said innumerable times, and correctly every time, that governments, in making guns illegal or very difficult to obtain, prevent us – the good people – from protecting ourselves, but do nothing whatever for the bad ones who, after all, are in the business they are in precisely because the fact that their activities are illegal doesn't deter them from engaging in them. Such persons would, rationally, be enthusiastic proponents of harsh gun laws. Criminals in England must be jubilant at the many measures the British government has taken that are apparently designed to make life easy for thieves, assaulters, murderers, and rapists. When a citizen can be sent to jail for defending himself against an armed attacker who is let off with perhaps a mild reprimand, the classical function of government has gone severely awry.

Do we have a right to defend ourselves? Of course. Those who think otherwise must suppose that the citizen is not really a citizen at all, but merely one more servant of government and of the criminal classes whose activities are exacerbated by governments' derecognition of its citizens.

Are guns dangerous? Of course. That is their point – to be dangerous to whatever their owners take aim at. Obviously, the right to own guns is accompanied by a responsibility to use them safely when using them at all, and of course not to use them on any but those posing great and immediate dangers. This is obvious to the point of cliché, and those who would elevate it into a case for depriving citizens of this right must be operating in a rather rarefied part of the social world. But legislation must not be based on irrelevant cases. It is people who are in some genuine danger that the right to bear arms is concerned with, and those of us who live in ivory towers are not qualified to judge their cases in the light of ours.

There is one point through which a considerable measure of further security could also be achieved – namely, the manufacturer of any firearm could be held responsible to a considerable degree for any murders committed with the weapons it makes. This would encourage the manufacturer to keep track of the people to whom it sells its weapons. It would also give that firm an incentive not to sell its weapons to people it suspects, and to introduce systems for alerting people to the dangers its weapons impose. The same responsibilities, of course, could apply to all intermediate links in the chain. The man the murderer got his gun from should be subject to serious penalties, for example, just as at present we may not sell an automobile to someone if it is known to be in dangerous condition.

Such efforts to make it less likely that guns will be used to murder rather than to defend need thought and effort. But depriving citizens of what, realistically, might be their only means of effective defence is crossing the line, very decidedly, into despotism.

5 Religion Isn't on Trial

JOHN RUSSELL

How can a modern democracy keep the responsibilities of church and state separate and still be fair to religious citizens who want to participate in public life? It is exactly this question that lies at the heart of several recent Canadian court decisions.

Chamberlain v. The Surrey School Board of BC follows the now familiar pattern of weighing religious freedom against the recognition of homosexual rights under the Charter of Rights and Freedoms. The case originally arose when the Surrey school board refused to give 'recommended learning resource' status to three picture books for kindergarten and Grade 1 students that depicted children living normal lives with same-sex parents.

The request for this mainly symbolic designation (the books were not prohibited from use in classrooms)

'The basic idea of justificatory neutrality is that the state cannot act as an advocate for, or give special preference to, particular religious or secular ideals of the good life.'

created a furor among some religious parents and church leaders. They apparently persuaded the board that encouraging the use of such books would interfere with their religious freedom to inculcate their children with certain heterosexual ideals of family relations.

The teacher who sought this designation, James Chamberlain, appealed to the courts to overturn the board's decision on the grounds that it violated the province's School Act. That act requires public schools to be run on a 'strictly secular and non-sectarian basis.' Hence, it apparently prohibits using religious ideals to justify public school policies. It adds that 'the highest morality shall be inculcated, but no religious dogma or creed shall be taught.'

Thus, the main issue of law that emerged in *Chamberlain* concerned how to interpret and apply the separation of church and state contained in this legislation. This raised puzzling questions of principle.

If state and church are indeed separate, so that no state educational policies are to be based on religion, how can religious citizens participate in democratic decision-making? Are secular ideals privileged over religious ideals? If so, does this reflect a failure to recognize the dignity and equality of religious adherents within a democratic system of governance?

These questions have been with us since at least the seventeenth century, when the philosopher John Locke (a devout Christian), seeking an end to religious wars and strife, and setting the template for modern democracies, argued that the church 'is absolutely separate and distinct from the Commonwealth.' But the question remains: Does this turn religious adherents into second-class citizens?

Contemporary philosophers, from social welfare liberals like John Rawls to libertarians like Robert Nozick, have advanced what appears to be a fair solution to this problem. That solution goes by the name of 'liberal neutrality' or, sometimes (and more aptly), 'justificatory neutrality.'

The basic idea of justificatory neutrality is that the state may not act as an advocate for, or give special preference to, particular religious *or* secular ideals of the good life. Such ideals are expressed in those values and doctrines that comprise an individual's final ends and that give deepest meaning to his or her way of life. Among them, of course, are different religious and secular visions of the family and of sexual relationships.

It follows that according to justificatory neutrality, the state has no role to play in protecting or advocating any specific religious or secular models of heterosexual or same-sex parenting that are consistent with standards of fundamental justice. Neither, therefore, is the state to make policy decisions or pronouncements on the relative merits of Christianity, Islam, Buddhism, or atheism – or of baseball versus philately or hockey.

What is crucial to emphasize is that justificatory neutrality does not single out religious ideals for special exclusion. Religious citizens are not relegated to second-class status, because the use of the state to promote secular ideals of the good is equally limited by this principle.

But how can justificatory neutrality leave any role for government action, if neither religious nor secular ideals of the good can form the basis for public policy?

Government retains its neutrality, and thus its respect for citizens' diverse ways of life, by justifying its activities according to what is just in the distribution of *fundamental means* or *resources* (liberties, opportunities, income, the social bases of respect and dignity). In this respect, the fundamental freedoms – of speech, association, liberty, security of the person, and so on – that are contained in the Charter are instructive. It is no accident that a pluralist culture that originally separated church from state in order to secure stable and tolerant social relations would treat such freedoms as fundamental rights. After all, they are the all-purpose means for pursuing any ends or conception of the good, but patently fall short of constituting such ends.

Justificatory neutrality thus imposes a limited, moral neutrality on government. It prohibits or discourages activities that violate fundamental freedoms. It affirms those democratic character virtues – civility, tolerance, respect, fairness, responsible citizenship, and so on – that are required to support fundamental freedoms. It promotes our understanding of culture and religion as vehicles for promoting respect and tolerance, as long as this falls short of advocacy or special preference. Thus, justificatory neutrality explains how the 'highest morality shall be inculcated' in our public schools without relying on religious *or* secular dogma or creed.

This principle can assist courts as they attempt to resolve issues of the sort that *Chamberlain* raised. If the courts conclude that bodies such as school boards are significantly motivated by the desire to shelter or protect particular religious ideals of the family, this principle would mean that those bodies' decisions must be disallowed. Doing this reflects no disparity in treatment of religious citizens.

Regrettably, such actions may place schoolchildren at the centre of public controversy. But we have a precedent for this from the civil rights era, when such risks were taken to secure equal respect and liberty for oppressed minorities. Same-sex parents and their families deserve similar support in our time.

6 Do Children Have Rights?

THOMAS HURKA

One aim of the 1990 World Summit for Children, co-chaired by then prime minister Brian Mulroney, was to urge ratification of the United Nations Convention on the Rights of the Child. Now, children have rights, but they're not the same as the rights of adults.

Competent adults have a right of autonomy, a right to make free choices about their lives even if those choices aren't always best for them. They can choose a career that isn't best suited to their talents, or marry unwisely. It's their life, and so long as they don't harm others, they're entitled to decide freely how to live it.

Moralists disagree about how strong this right is. Some think it's absolute, so that it's always wrong to interfere with a person's private choices. Others think the right can sometimes be outweighed. If a person's actions will be very harmful to himself or herself, others have a right and even a duty to intervene.

But however strong an adult's right to autonomy, it's not shared by children. A ten-year-old boy can't decide to stop going to school just because he doesn't like it. Nor does he even have the right to decide what time he goes to bed. It wouldn't do him serious harm to watch an extra half-hour of TV, but it's not for him to make the choice.

This doesn't mean that parents should always boss around their kids. Sometimes they should let them make choices, so that they can grow up knowing responsibility. But this isn't a matter of the children's rights. It concerns their long-term good, which is still in their parents' care.

So what are children's rights? A child can feel pain just like an adult, so if torture violates an adult's right it does the same to a child. Children also have a right to autonomy: the autonomy they will exercise in the future. They have what philosopher Joel Feinberg calls the 'right to an open future,' the right to enter adulthood with a great many options open to them and a developed capacity to choose among them.

Articles 28 and 29 of the UN convention affirm the child's right to education, which must be provided free of charge. Education increases a child's future earning power and imparts intrinsically valuable knowledge, but a further important function is to prepare him or her for a life of autonomous self-direction.

Education does this partly by increasing a child's options. Even if he or she later doesn't take the highest-paying job, it's important to have had it to choose against. Education also gives the child the intellectual tools needed to evaluate options rationally and to make, in the fullest sense, a choice among them. And finally, education increases a child's awareness of possibilities. Through literature and the study of other cultures, children learn that there are other value systems and ways of living than those they're familiar with.

'A friend of mine, himself agnostic about religion, takes his children to church, because he wants them to grow up knowing enough about religion to make an informed choice about it.'

This right also imposes obligations on parents, who must likewise let their child grow up to choose freely. They act wrongly if they shield the child from exposure to beliefs and values other than their own or pressure him or her unduly into becoming, say, a lawyer.

There's some balancing needed here, for parents, too, have rights: to base a family life on their values and to try to pass those values on to their children. Perhaps the right balance is this. Parents needn't give equal time to all value systems but must at least let their child be exposed to lifestyles other than their own. They must leave options open, even if they don't encourage them all equally.

Some parents do more. A friend of mine, himself agnostic about religion, takes his children to church, because he wants them to grow up knowing enough about religion to make an informed choice about it. This is more than can be demanded as a child's right; parents who don't do it aren't wrong. But it respects the same future freedom that, at a lower level, is protected by right.

Children aren't now entitled to make choices that are bad for them, but they will be later on. This gives them an important right: to be allowed to grow into adults who can make autonomous decisions about themselves.

7 A Market Economy Makes Us Better People

THOMAS HURKA

It was a winter's night and I was walking past a restaurant I knew. The maitre d', Fernando, spotted me through the window, waved, and came out for a chat. I wasn't a frequent customer, but when I ate at the restaurant it was partly for the warm atmosphere. Here Fernando was spreading that atmosphere into the street.

I was reminded of the incident when my wife returned from a stay in communist Czechoslovakia. She described how in state-run restaurants there the waiters would say there were no places even though every table was empty. (When they learned you were a tourist, who might tip or change currency, they'd change their tune.) In a shoe store she was asked her shoe size. 'I don't know the European size, but at home it's 7½.' 'If you're that stupid, how do you expect me to serve you?'

A classical aim of socialism was to improve personal relations. The idea wasn't that capitalists didn't really love their spouses or children. But a market economy was supposed to create barriers to fellowship in the wider community.

One barrier was economic inequality, especially a system of economic classes. People from different classes would feel awkward with one another. There would be arrogance among the rich, and servility or resentment among the poor.

'There's something in a market economy that encourages altruism and that isn't found in state socialism. You may not be aware of it, but it's working behind your back to make you a better person.'

Another barrier was the competitive market structure. In business, people would try to outsell their rivals and drive them out of business. In private life, they would try to out-consume and out-possess. When the economy set people so much against one another, how could they ever come together?

Yet it was in capitalist Canada that a restaurateur risked a chill to greet an occasional customer, while in Czechoslovakia there was a surly refusal to serve. Could the free market make us kinder and gentler?

In some sectors of a market economy, including restaurants and retailing, your success depends very much on the service you give. Customers want to be treated with civility and warmth and take their business to outfits that provide them. (In a survey of Canadians shopping in the United States, 28 per cent said their main reason for crossing the border was better service.) In capitalism, there's a reward for service that doesn't exist under state socialism, where your earnings are unaffected by the number of customers you attract.

Of course, you might give service without really caring about your customers. You could wear a friendly mask that you drop the minute you're out of their sight. But I doubt many people could keep up the act that consistently, and I also suspect we'd see through it. To serve convincingly, you have to want to serve for its own sake.

A businessman at a meeting I recently attended generalized this idea. He said that making money is one of the things you can't do by trying to do it. You have to aim at something else, such as filling people's needs, and let profits come as a by-product.

If this is right, the rewards in capitalism can't influence your conscious reasoning. You can't say, 'I'll make more money if I value service as an end,' because that values service as a means. But the incentives can work indirectly.

One way is by natural selection: only those who care about serving stay in business. Fernando has been successful in his restaurants partly because of his personality; Basil Fawlty would go broke in a week.

The other way is by psychological reinforcement. When you do something nice for a customer, you get more business, and even if you don't notice the connection, this makes you more likely to be nice the next time. When you're rude, you're penalized.

And the reinforcement can spread beyond your business life. The socialist argument assumed that your work experiences can affect your attitude to people generally, and the same seems right here. What makes you want to help customers can make you helpful to all.

Of course, the picture won't be simple. Capitalism has many sides, and if some improve human relationships others make them worse. I doubt that junk bonds or beer ads did anything positive for anyone's character.

Still, there's something in a market economy that encourages altruism and that isn't found in state socialism. You may not be aware of it, but it's working behind your back to make you a better person.

8 Questions for the Census Takers

ANDREW IRVINE

Like millions of other Canadians, I fill out a census form whenever one is sent to me. During the last census our household was one of the lucky ones required by law to complete the long form. I did my civic duty, even though the form was thirty-two pages long and asked more than two hundred questions about my and my family's education, ethnic background, and income.

After completing the form, I began to wonder. Is there *anything* the government believes it doesn't have a right to know about me? Are there *any* limits it feels obliged to impose upon itself when asking questions of its citizens? In a democracy, should it simply be assumed that government has a right to ask us anything?

> *'After completing the census form, I began to wonder. Is there **anything** the government believes it doesn't have a right to know about me? Are there **any** limits it feels obliged to impose upon itself when asking questions of its citizens?'*

One worry is about the mandatory disclosure of living arrangements. Thirty years ago when the federal government decriminalized homosexual acts between consenting adults, Pierre Trudeau summed up the theory behind Canada's new legislation by saying that government had no place in the bedrooms of the nation.

It now appears that we no longer believe this. Whether they have told their friends and families or not, gay and lesbian couples are now required by law to disclose their living arrangements to the government, not only on the census form, but also when they file their income tax each year. Whether they want to or not, all law-abiding gay and lesbian couples have now been 'outed.'

Another worry concerns race. Of the fifty-seven questions involving so-called 'socio-cultural information,' several are about race, ethnicity, and ancestry. In them, a careful distinction is made between West Asian, Southeast Asian, Japanese, Korean, and Chinese sociocultural groups. Yet no similar distinctions exist for people whose ancestors originated in either Africa or Europe. Here, Black and White are the only choices. Such categories are notoriously vague and subjective; furthermore, they have no basis in scientific fact.

Defenders of these kinds of questions might argue that this information helps the government provide services to its citizens in their language of choice. But if this is the intent, earlier questions specifically about language should have been sufficient.

Instead, as we are told on the census form itself, this information 'is collected to support programs that promote equal opportunity for everyone to share in the social, cultural and economic life of Canada.'

Yet this is hardly an incentive for many people to complete these questions. Canada's so-called 'employment equity' laws long ago adopted the Orwellian practice of building lies into their very names. Instead of promoting equal opportunity, these laws provide incentives for employers to treat different groups of citizens differently. Citizens are thus placed in the position of being required by law to provide information they know to be false, thereby supporting programs they know to be harmful.

A university colleague once told me that he believed he could discover who the most powerful social groups were at any time in Canadian history. All he had to do was read the tax code. There, within a single document, is a record of every successful lobby group and, by omission, a record of every unsuccessful one as well. If farmers had more political influence than factory workers during the 1950s, this inevitably shows up in tax concessions of various kinds during that period. If film companies are today more powerful than farmers, again, this will be reflected in the tax code.

Using this same line of reasoning, a census is more than a tool for government to get information about its citizens. It is also a tool for citizens to get information about their government. Reading the census tells us who has the ear of government today and what the government's agenda will be tomorrow.

In other words, questions about unpaid housework and unpaid child minding, just like questions about race and living arrangements, are all informative. Never mind that men and women notoriously fail to agree about how many hours of unpaid work they each contribute. The mere fact that these questions are being asked, and that others are not, tells us something about the influence of the feminist lobby and about what the government's agenda will look like several years from now.

And what are we to conclude from the fact that nowhere in this year's census are we asked how often we buy a new car, or how often we have sex, or whether we do any of our banking offshore? What are we to conclude from the fact that we have not yet been asked whether we are planning to have any children in the next five years, or whether we would prefer to send our children to public or private school, or whether we have temporarily left the country to obtain a timely medical procedure that was unavailable at home?

Unless we believe that there are at least some limits on what governments have a right to know, it looks like these and a thousand other questions like them will just have to wait until next time.

9 Responsible Government

ANDREW IRVINE

One provincial government has now introduced fixed electoral terms for MLAs. Other governments and political parties are considering the idea. Fixed terms certainly simplify election planning, but is this enough to justify overturning centuries of parliamentary tradition?

In the United States, fixed terms are the norm rather than the exception. In contrast, British and Canadian parliamentary tradition has long accepted the idea that responsible government requires flexible election dates.

The reason is simple: if governments are to remain responsible to the people who elect them, elected representatives must have the power to force unpopular and corrupt governments to return to the people to obtain a fresh mandate. Should a government lose the confidence of our elected representatives, it cannot continue to govern, even if it is not yet nearing the end of its mandate. Fixed election dates would make this aspect of responsible government a thing of the past.

In Canada, the struggle for responsible government first arose during the first half of the nineteenth century. Men such as William Lyon Mackenzie and Robert Baldwin of Upper Canada, Louis-Joseph Papineau and Louis-Hyppolite LaFontaine of Lower Canada, and Joseph Howe of Nova Scotia all argued passionately and persuasively in favour of the principle that governments must be responsible to the electorate rather than to the Crown. Without the consent of our elected representatives, they argued, no government can be permitted to remain in office.

Although elected legislative assemblies existed in Canada in one form or another as early as 1758, it was not until 1848 that the principle of responsible government became accepted in practice. Prior to 1848, legislative assemblies remained responsible to the British Crown rather than to the electorate. When the Province of Canada won responsible government in 1848, LaFontaine became premier. Nova Scotia adopted many of the same principles of responsible government that same year.

Today, the idea of responsible government remains a central component of Canadian democracy. We still accept the idea that governments can govern only with the consent of our elected representatives. If

Cabinet loses the confidence of these representatives – for example, if the government is defeated on a major bill, or if the opposition is successful in passing a non-confidence motion – then according to convention, it must call an election or else resign.

Lack of confidence can occur for a variety of reasons. For example, if there is a minority government, it becomes necessary for Cabinet to obtain the support of individuals outside its own party. Should these MPs, MPPs, or MLAs become convinced that the government is no longer acting in the best interests of the electorate, they can cause that government to fall.

Similarly, it is important for ordinary MPs, MPPs, or MLAs to have the power to force a corrupt prime minister or premier to either resign or call an election. Without this option, complex impeachment procedures, such as those in the United States, would be necessary. American president Richard Nixon, for example, remained in office much longer than he should have because under that country's constitution the executive is not responsible to Congress to the same degree that Canadian premiers and prime ministers are responsible to their respective legislatures and parliaments.

The idea that a government should continue to govern for a full four or five years without the confidence of the legislature or of parliament is anathema to parliamentary tradition; and if opposition members are given the power to force a government to face the electorate, surely members of the governing party itself should be able to exercise this same power. For if MPs, MPPs, or MLAs of any party become convinced that it is important to consult the electorate, it can only be in the interest of democracy that they be given the power to do so. Should free trade, or Quebec separatism, or any of a host of other issues unexpectedly become important, why shouldn't our elected representatives be able to consult the ballot box for direction?

'If governments are to remain responsible to the people who elect them, elected representatives must have the power to force unpopular and corrupt governments to return to the people to obtain a fresh mandate.'

Of course, even with flexible election dates, many Canadians today believe that governments require greater accountability, not less. Because prime ministers and premiers have such tremendous influence over the careers of ordinary MPs, MPPs, and MLAs, backbenchers are often unwilling or unable to vote against Cabinet policy or even to voice opposition to such policy in caucus. Thus what we require is more, not less, power for elected members and for ordinary citizens. The ability of our elected representatives to vote against Cabinet on many issues without having their caucus memberships threatened becomes crucial. Similarly, the ability of ordinary citizens to recall their MPs, MPPs, and MLAs only serves to strengthen, not weaken, the practice of responsible government.

In contrast, the idea that the life of a government should for a time lie beyond the reach of both citizens and their elected representatives runs counter to many of the principles underlying democracy itself. Legislation requiring fixed terms would either permit the house or legislature to call early elections, or it would not. If it did, the result would differ little from our current system. If it did not, such legislation could in no way be said to increase government accountability.

It is also worth remembering that not all institutional change is for the better. Prior to Confederation, women were permitted to vote provided that, like men, they owned a sufficient amount of property. Following Confederation, this right disappeared for over half a century. It was not until 1918 that the Conservative prime minister Robert Borden passed legislation that once again allowed women and men to vote as equals in federal elections, and it was not until 1960 that another Conservative prime minister, John Diefenbaker, passed legislation that removed all remaining forms of racial and religious discrimination from the federal Elections Act.

Fixed election dates have some advantages. The primary one is that they make it easier for governments to govern. They give governments a fixed, predictable period of time in which to bring forward their legislative agendas. But such advantages are similar to the advantages of a blank cheque, and thus typically come at great cost. For anyone who favours reform that increases rather than decreases government accountability, the idea of fixed electoral terms will not be an attractive one.

PART VI

Free Speech

1 The Most Beautiful Thing in the World

ANDREW IRVINE

'The most beautiful thing in the world is freedom of speech.' Even though these words were first spoken over 2,300 years ago by Diogenes, the ancient Greek Cynic, they have a distinctly modern sound. After all, without free speech and other fundamental civil liberties, we would lack the basic cornerstones of contemporary democracy. The freedom of people to speak openly, without fear of government reprisal, is what allows us to raise issues that we as citizens feel to be important. Free speech, freedom of association and peaceful assembly, and the freedom to exercise our franchise are what allow us, as citizens, to exercise our sovereignty over government. As a country's civil liberties are weakened, its claim to being a democracy is correspondingly diminished.

The old Republic of South Africa provides a case in point. Whether we think of it as a democracy with an extremely limited franchise, or as a democracy in name only, by the 1980s the government there had instituted more than one hundred laws restricting the movement of ideas. In some respects these laws were remarkably powerful: newspaper and magazine articles were censored, journalists and writers were detained, editors were prosecuted, and papers were closed.

Yet even in those dark days, many of that country's censorship laws remained largely impotent. Speeches by political leaders were smuggled in and out of prisons and around the country, and it became a badge of honour to possess them, no matter how dry or boring they might be. Legal challenges to censorship were mounted, editorials against apartheid were published, and many government policies were ridiculed, until even this became illegal. When one edition of a newspaper was banned, the paper changed its masthead, publishing the same material under a new name, free from the banning order. Instead of publishing an illegal photograph of a violent police action, another paper printed a 'connect-the-dots' version, along with explicit instructions that readers were not to connect the dots.

Blank spaces were also banned, as was obliterated text. Both had been used by the *Weekly Mail* to indicate the extent of censorship; but as Anton Harber, a founder and coeditor of that paper, reports: 'The authorities realised that nothing frightened the public more than white spaces in newspapers: vivid imaginations filled the spaces with reports far worse than those that had been removed.' Hence there was the absurdity of making it illegal to print nothing.

Other policies were equally comical yet frightening. The Key Point Act made it an offence to photograph or publicize so-called 'key points' around the country. At the same time, the list of sites that had been designated by the government as 'key' remained classified. The only way for a newspaper to discover it was in possession of an illegal photograph was to publish it and then wait to see whether charges would be laid.

During this time, the amount of material censored was phenomenal. The peace sign was banned, as was the book *Black Beauty*. The film *Roots* was banned for the reason that 'a substantial number of blacks would, judged on the probabilities, substantially experience great or greater hate against the white [race] as a result of seeing this film.'

Reading this, we may feel relieved that censorship of this kind does not and cannot occur in Canada. Yet this is not so. Many cases indicate just how fragile our civil liberties remain. The removal of protest signs at the Asia-Pacific Economic Co-operation (APEC) meetings in Vancouver, the censorship of gay and lesbian reading materials, and the encroachment on the religious freedoms of teachers trained at Trinity Western University – all serve to remind us just how easy it is for governments to overstep their authority. Even worse, current law explicitly gives many Canadian governments the power to place limits on our freedom of expression, and for many of the same reasons as in the old South Africa.

Just as a South African court decided that *Roots* should be banned because failure to do so would increase the likelihood that one group in society would 'experience great or greater hate' towards another, many provincial and federal human rights codes ban some types of speech. Furthermore, they do so for exactly the same reason. For example, section 7(1)(b) of British Columbia's Human Rights Code states that 'a person must not publish, issue or display, or cause to be published, issued or displayed, any statement, publication, notice, sign, symbol, emblem or other representation that ... is likely to expose a person or a group or class of persons to hatred or contempt because of the race, colour, ancestry, place of origin, religion, marital status, family status, physical or mental disability, sex, sexual orientation or age of that person or that group or class of persons.' Thus the South African and Canadian cases differ only in the details of their application.

Perhaps it is these details of application that are important. Perhaps, unlike the old South African government, Canadian governments can be trusted to censor only that speech which deserves to be censored. Unfortunately, such trust is bound to be illusory. State agencies have a poor record with regard to censorship, and our abdicating of this responsibility to the state is equivalent to throwing away the very building blocks of democracy. Without civil liberties, citizens are no longer able to exercise their sovereignty over government. In the words of U.S. Supreme Court justice Hugo Black: 'Free speech is always the deadliest enemy of tyranny.'

But the advantages of free speech do not end here. In any society that wants to eliminate hate, it is important to know who the hate-mongers are. Before electing candidates to our local school boards, it is not just interesting to know their views on evolution and multiculturalism, and on history, immigration, and race, it is essential. Because censorship laws regularly push this type of information underground, it is not accidental that such laws

'As a country's civil liberties are weakened, its claim to being a democracy is correspondingly diminished.'

are typically accompanied by increased degrees of state surveillance. At the same time, when this information does not go underground, because it is illegal it is sometimes given even greater prominence in the media and in the public consciousness than it deserves.

Thus, censorship laws are typically inefficient in achieving their goals; that, or they tend to hamper society's need to know who the hate-mongers are, what role they play in our communities, and what type of influence they have on public policy. Given the choice between asking the state to identify these people and allowing them to identify themselves, most of us will prefer the latter.

And still there is more. Censorship laws, besides being both inefficient and contrary to the principles underlying democracy, effectively divide a country's population into first- and second-class citizens. If university professors and government appointees are allowed to debate the question of how many people died in the Holocaust, but other Canadians such as David Ahenakew, James Keegstra, and Doug Collins are not, we have effectively set up a division between citizens that no healthy democracy can long support. Free speech is something we extend to the foolish as well as the wise, the young as well as the old. Once we begin to decide who may or may not be granted the privilege of free speech, we have begun the slide towards a dictatorship of either the left or the right. Hopefully, in Canada, we will be able to reverse this trend towards censorship before it is too late.

2 The Porn Wars

JOHN DIXON

My father died without ever having read a book. On one occasion, however, he went to see a play. I remember this cultural expedition not simply because it was an anomalous family event, but because he and my mother returned home much earlier than planned. The performance of Erskine Caldwell's *Tobacco Road* had been raided by the Vancouver Police, and the audience sent away to ponder a close encounter with a danger to its morals.

Those were the days! The bad old days to be sure, in the sense that our governments moved with insolent confidence to proscribe, censor, and punish such a wide range of expression. But good old days in the sense that a civil libertarian, concerned to protect freedom of expression, had no need of subtle philosophical or political instruments in order to detect where the front line was. It was, if you will, a conventional war, and conventional wars supply not only recognizable enemies, but also (more important yet) recognizable friends. The bad guys were those who hadn't yet understood the separation of church and state and who sought to impose their moral sensibilities (exhausted from the grapple with Darwin, and not yet really exposed to Kinsey) on everybody in reach. And the good guys were just about everybody else who could read without moving their lips.

And the stuff that was censored! James Joyce, Simone de Beauvoir, D.H. Lawrence, Lenny Bruce. You didn't have to be a librarian to see that the material under attack was chockablock full of big words and *big ideas*. Sisters and brothers of the shining path linked arms and fought their way past the Hicklin rule (and its Canadian imitations) into the 1960s and the arms – if not the laps – of Hugh Hefner and *Playboy*. Hefner's genius was to surround all of those pictures with words, lots of words and ideas. The girlie magazine was out of the closet, and the girls were 'dressed up' in *Playboy*'s clever format of 'philosophy' and serious writing. It was an idea whose time had ... well ... come.

When I was an eighteen-year-old research assistant for the zoology department, I was sent to Campbell River to buy supplies for the field crew. Old Professor X, the leader of the study, instructed me to buy the customary bacon, cereal, milk, beans, eggs, butter, and mumble, mumble.

What was that, Professor? A Playmumbleboymumblemagazine. Gosh. Even the professor 'read' *Playboy*. Maybe he was into Feiffer's cartoons. Maybe.

Even Gloria Steinem's infiltration of the Bunnies and her subsequent exposé did nothing to turn back the tide. Steinem was way out in front. The rest of North America – and the world, it seemed – was back in camp catching up on its seeing. *Playboy*'s imitators crowded into the market, and the audience was soon judged (correctly) to be ready for the ultimate mysteries of the pubis. Well, perhaps that 'ultimate' was a bit premature. Those who asked where it would all end knew (as did the rest of us) that it wouldn't end until everybody's sexual imagination had been served. That is, until all heterosexual, male sexual imaginations had been served.

'Imagine a planet on which the intelligent life is possessed of an urgent, plastic, and polymorphous sexual appetite. Then imagine that these beings are, from birth, among the universe's more facile and compulsive fantasizers. That is, imagine our situation. Could anything be more likely – nay, inevitable – than that we should become prolific producers and consumers of fantastic representations of our sexuality?'

There was the rub. There was the flaw. As my generation put aside its Zig-Zag papers and beads, straightened up, and started looking for work in the 1970s, everybody seemed to notice at once. Pornography was pornography for men, and women were the subject material – or the 'object' material, as we were soon taught to realize. The wisegals started to do some very wide-awake thinking, and we were soon where we are now: patriarchal society sexually objectifies women in order to consolidate its infantization of them. In maintaining women as its 'girlies,' male power panders to its own sexual and political interest, and effectively subjugates half of the human beings on the planet ... and so on.

Thus began the time of sorrow for civil libertarians. For if, as the feminists argued, pornography was the symptom of inequality and at the same time actually productive of oppression, then the classical civil libertarian arguments against censorship were no longer relevant. And if civil libertarian arguments were irrelevant, and the civil libertarians kept on making them, then ... civil libertarians were either the conscious or unconscious tools of the exploiters. It was very soon the case that we got to be called unconscious exploiters only on our luckiest days.

We did what we could; that is, we did what we knew how to do. We wrote more stuff, painstaking explanations of our reasons and motives. We went around the province talking to the people who still had time for us. I gave my version of Nixon's 'I'm not a crook' talk: 'No, I'm not sexist. Yes, I am a feminist. No, we don't agree that the research proves that pornography causes violence against women. No, we don't think that censorship of even violent pornography will change anything – except impair the quality of free debate that is essential to a democratic community and, perhaps more tangibly, that will be needed if we are ever to form a clear account of ourselves as sexual beings. Yes, some civil libertarians are women.'

We were now involved in a very unconventional war, and old friends had become new – and in some cases, very angry – enemies. Some civil liberties groups in this country and in the United States fared poorly, and split on the subject before lapsing into silence on it. By the beginning of 1985, I was asking myself Chernyshevsky's question: 'What is to be done?' And I was starting to think that the answer was to get a whole lot more combative with some of our meanest opponents. And then Varda Burstyn and June Callwood and Sara Diamond appeared, along with several other contributors, in Burstyn's anthology, *Women against Censorship*. No encircled wagon train, on hearing the first bugles of the approaching cavalry, could have matched the relief of civil libertarians. My (almost certainly disastrous, even if cathartic) 'No more Mr Nice Guy' act was shelved before I put it on the road, and we were into a fresh situation.

What had happened? Why does Varda Burstyn's book make such an enormous difference to the porn wars? There are two reasons: Burstyn's people are all women, and they are really smart. The class warfare tone of the pornography debate had produced such an impasse that men could no longer speak to the question with any telling effect. (I am speaking in generalities now, but they are generalities that govern the political fact.) Only the voices of women could possibly make a real difference, and preferably the voices of women who spoke from outside the ranks of organized combatants.

Women against Censorship does not just supply us with a collection of women's voices raised against censorship. In it we find, to take one instance, an enormously intelligent and intelligible paper on the social scientific studies of the relationship between the use of pornography and violence against women. The author, Thelma McCormack, tells us that 'the findings with respect to sexual offenders and pornography users – do not show any pattern to support the view that pornography is the theory, rape is the practice.' And in connection with the experimental studies, McCormack raises damaging questions concerning both methodology and interpretation, adding that in any case, 'everyone agrees that experimental data cannot be the basis for social policy.' Thelma McCormack is a professor of sociology at York University and president of the Canadian Sociology and Anthropology Association.

I wondered why I had never heard of Professor McCormack's exhaustive study, since I am something of a compulsive consumer of research in this area. In her introductory note, she tells us that the monograph was originally prepared for the Metropolitan Toronto Task Force on Violence against Women. This group not only chose to disregard her report, but also consigned it to a sort of non-existence. According to McCormack, 'students, journalists, librarians, and other members of the public who have tried to procure copies of it from the Task Force receive evasive answers about its existence.'

Varda Burstyn's book has made it possible for men to talk about pornography again. What have we got to say? For my own part, I am most decidedly not saying the same old thing. I used to claim, without a lot of conviction or emphasis, that women had a kind of enlightened self-interest in opposing censorship, since they needed a free space in which they could create their own images of sexuality. Men had had a very long run at imagining their sexuality in pornography – producing some pretty hair-raising stuff along the way. How could we be sure that, if women were to set about the imaginative task of exploring their own sexual hopes and fears, it would be consistent with generally received views of decency or 'eroticism'? I believed this, but didn't think that it was likely to be made apparent until it was too late and the censors began snipping from the fantastic works of women as well as men.

Sara Diamond's 1985 conference, 'The Heat Is On,' showed me how unreliable a prognosticator I could be. Diamond's Vancouver conference of North American women writers, artists, video and film producers, and performers made it clear that many women were already well into the work of answering Freud's question: 'What does a woman want?' and that the ideas and images that were emerging were not likely to be welcome at the Miss America Pageant – or in Victoria or Ottawa. When women roll up their sleeves, or whatever, and get down to serious sexual fantasy, the products are as inconsistent with patriarchal *and* matriarchal notions of 'good sex' as when men do it.

And is that really very remarkable? Imagine a planet on which the intelligent life is possessed of an urgent, plastic, and polymorphous sexual appetite. Then imagine that these beings are, from birth, among the universe's more facile and compulsive fantasizers. That is, imagine our situation. Could anything be more likely – nay, inevitable – than that we should become prolific producers and consumers of fantastic representations of our sexuality? To console ourselves for all the real stuff that we cannot or must not really do; to explore ground that we might go on to occupy; to hum a bit of an overture before the performance ... or during it; or to engage ourselves just for the hell of it. And we will talk. We will communicate with one another, even to the point of marketing the products of hacks and virtuosos alike.

So now what? The big questions still loom over the sexual landscape. What do men and women want? And what can we afford to let one another have? No use pretending otherwise: male porn tells us that what at least a few men want is a miserable, spiteful, cruel version of sex that nobody in their right mind can regard as anything but pitiful. Good to know. But viewed with an eye to its proportionate offering of 'object' matter, pornography reveals that the vast majority of masturbating men (for masturbation is, as we all know, the first and last use of every 'girlie' magazine) are much closer to adoration than to hurting as they go to their completely undemanding, ever-compliant, eternally youthful, and absolutely unobtainable partners.

As for what women want: artists, writers, and film-makers such as participated in 'The Heat is On' conference are hard at work producing some fresh answers. They are leaning into a relentlessly resistive set of cultural and political forces, and dodging fire that ranges from the friendly to the frankly misogynist. People like Varda Burstyn and Sara Diamond are representative of what toughness and brains can do along the lines of holding an act together under impossible circumstances. Civil libertarians could not do better than to throw in with them in the fight against censorship.

For this much at least is certain: we cannot afford *not* to let one another at least imagine what we want. Because imagining what we want is the way in which human beings both discover and decide what is wanted. And if we aren't free to give expression to our figuring, we will neither know what to hope for nor what to give.

Want to go out to a play?

3 The Bessie Smith Factor

JOHN DIXON

It was once believed, by very many educated people, that listening to jazz caused impressionable women to turn to a life of sexual immoderation and drug addiction. Testimony before congressional committees of investigation in the United States indicated (and this out of the very mouths of those whose lives had been ruined by phonograph records) that the blues arrangements of Bessie Smith were particularly powerful agents of corruption, destroying the modesty and self-control of pretty much everyone who strayed within their noxious precincts. I offer this historical note to illustrate what I propose calling the 'Bessie Smith factor' – that is, to illustrate the consequences of mixing sexual paranoia with a deficient notion of the principle of causation.

The Bessie Smith factor would be a source of innocent fun were it the case that it existed only as a sort of anachronistic footnote to Western life. It continues to plague us, however, as a very unfunny rationale for censorship in the armoury of the forces of darkness. To understand the workings of the factor remains an important task for us of the shining path, and to this end I offer the following brief analysis of it.

The Bessie Smith factor is rooted, as are all deeply mischievous mistakes, in a plausible, though fallacious, account of reality. Smith's blues had real moral and cultural freight, telling, as they did, of a different set of possible sensibilities and values (that is, sexual and sensual liberation for everybody, along with a wry commentary on social justice) that was inconsistent with the received view of such things in the United States of the 1930s. Bessie Smith songs were most definitely not expressive of contemporary community sexual or sumptuary standards. And they were attractive, in that they were at once beautiful and smart ... two features of the world that are evenly alluring to human minds. When one conjoins these considerations with the amazingly resilient fallacy that whatever society does not make unlawful it (by implication) approves of, part of the case for censorship takes shape. (In connection with this remarkable sociological fetish, I cite, for the benefit of the disbelieving, Jillian Ridington of the B.C. Periodical Review Board: 'When you put it in a magazine for public consumption, it's making it public that this is a common and okay sexual act.')

But the central and driving feature of the Bessie Smith factor is, of course, sexual paranoia. In the 'original' Bessie Smith case, paranoia is evidenced in the quaint, prurient fear that women are weak vessels in which are conjoined vestal innocence and a slumbering capacity for sexual rapacity that would, if unleashed, turn the world (read 'the world as now constituted') upside down.

It is important to recognize (at the first pause in our urbane laughter) that it isn't altogether silly to be scared about this: if women really were the sort of creatures envisioned by this wet nightmare, our personal and social arrangements would be badly shaken, if not swept away.

This is true because the centrepiece of our sexual game plan as a culture is the achievement and maintenance of everyone's capacity to (in some, as yet imperfectly determined measure) control themselves. And if it is the case that one of the central offices of marriage and the family is this task of institutionalizing and domesticating lust, then anyone with a healthy appreciation of the power of sexual passion will look to the preservation of some version of the status quo with affectionate care. Whether we view expressions that evoke sexual arrangements that are (seemingly, at least) inconsistent with marriage and self-control as actually influencing such anxious-making choices, or as simply another of the consequences of what are, in fact, already changing tides of opinion and practice, it isn't foolish to be concerned by them.

It is, however, both nutty and dangerous to be scared out of our wits, and what we see in the Bessie Smith case are rather thoroughly witless dreams of womanhood menaced by sexual phantoms – dreamers that owe their power at once to yearning and fearing. Reality, of course, provided some surprises. It turned out that we could shake a few reefs out of the sails, allow women a full measure of sexual responsibility and autonomy, and keep civilization after all. America could live through the blues.

This was far from obvious to everyone in the 1930s. Then, as now, the sexual paranoia discussed above was joined with a strange view of the principle of causation that amounted to, in simple and practical terms, the confusion of 'cause' with 'influence.' It is this important confusion that we turn to now.

There can be no doubt that what we see, or read, or hear, can influence the way we think, and what we think has (I hope) something to do with what we choose and do. The story about the 'influences' that 'connect' books, magazines, songs, videos, and poetry readings with what we finally do is, I take it, the story about what we have come to call our 'minds.' Perhaps only one thing can be said with real confidence about the workings of human minds: we have made insignificant progress in our efforts to achieve a scientific (causal) understanding of them. I say this not as an enemy of science, nor as any sort of obscurantist. I am, in fact, one of those who regard science as one of our magnificent achievements, and believe that it has, at very many points, replaced pathetic and (in some instances, at least) cruel suppositions with real understanding. But one of the essential things to learn about any tool is the limitations that govern its successful use, and it is obvious that the real scientific account of the mind is going to be either a very recondite and/or complex one if causal, or of such a form as to embody a revolution in the way in which we conceive of nature.

An example may help. Imagine that I show you, in order to find out what your response will be, a picture of the Eiffel Tower. You say: 'Paris.' We might then say that I caused you to say 'Paris' by showing you the picture of the Eiffel Tower. Now, this claim can mean two very different things. On the one hand, it can mean that among the manifold of causes that we presume, in our scientific mood, to account for your actions, the showing of the picture to you proved, in this instance, to be a causal factor. This is, in a sense, the description of the world from a sort of scientific rhetorical posture, and it is fair enough. On the other and very mistaken hand, we can mean that in the showing of the picture of the Eiffel Tower, we discover the sole and exhaustive causal account of your 'Paris' response. But if we mean this, we would be making a huge mistake. Because if we did have or could have such a simple causal account of the

'It is, God knows, hard to have much respect for the minds of other people; it is hard to imagine or believe or hope that they are scenes of deliberation and choice, rather than some form of switching station in which the contents of tabloids are turned into actions that are either trivial or discreditable. But this is no more than to say that it is hard to believe in democracy.'

mind, we would be – as a feature of the possession of such an account – in a position to predict the production of effects before the operation of the cause. But anyone with the slightest experience of human beings and human minds (that is, all of us) will know that this is exactly the kind of predictability that is unavailable to us. Consider, as a confirming example of this unpredictability, what any of your best-known companions in life would be moved to respond as a consequence (in the sense of 'effect') of your showing them a picture of the Eiffel Tower. I confidently predict that you will be unable to predict what the effect of this 'expression' of yours will be. If your friends are anything like mine, responses will run the range from worried and silent gazes to: 'Five dollars if you throw in the frame,' 'You're trying to exorcize Canadian cooking?' and badly sung renditions of 'Gigi.'

This cheap experiment illustrates how silly it is to hope that one can identify simple causal relations between expressions and actions when real human minds are involved. Of course, when the soil will not yield hope, we can still prop up sprigs of pretence in it.

We have, as a species, a positive rage to know, and when we cannot satisfy this appetite with reality, we resort to our facility for making believe. Samuel Johnson spoke to the operation of this tendency in eighteenth-century medicine in his review of Lucas's *Essay on Waters*: 'It is incident to physicians, I am afraid, beyond all other men, to mistake subsequence for consequence.'

The Bessie Smith factor works, as does a lot of terrible social pseudoscience, by confounding subsequence and consequence, and by so abusing the concept of causation that it operates, as the linguist Noam Chomsky pointed out a couple of decades ago, as a mere homonym for the genuine article. Thus, if we enter into the dumb spirit of the enterprise, we can say that jazz causes the corruption of female minds. We offer anecdotal evidence for this causal relationship, in the form of people who testify that it worked that way on them – a version of getting people to 'explain' what 'caused' them to say: 'That's the Eiffel Tower' – and we're in business as 'scientists' unlocking the mysteries of the nature of social life.

What is lost in this shell game is the idiom we use to give expression to what the mind really does, as in 'thinking,' 'intending,' 'judging,' 'choosing,' and so on. And with the loss of this idiom, we confront the emergence of a vision of human beings that is devoid of the specific qualities of personhood. That is, we are invited to think of ourselves as mindless.

This would be an innocent comedy, were it not the case that it makes a difference back in the real world. But the Bessie Smith factor has acquired substantial political significance in that its currency has gone a long way towards presenting the issue of censorship to us in a way that disarms our democratic resistances. In order to understand how this works, we need to recall something of the source of our democratic sensibilities.

Consider what it is, fundamentally, that offends us when we hear of some benighted jurisdiction in which the government has suppressed the publication of 'opposition' newspapers. It is not, obviously and significantly, a simple matter of being fond of the truth. We abhor the suppression of the press, even when satisfied that it produces a lot of half-truths and outright lies. Neither is our commitment to freedom of the press grounded in a belief that the written word is an innocuous thing that can never justify the momentous fuss of state interference. No. We think that the press is a powerful player on the political scene, and are perfectly aware of the existence of rotten media that distort the truth when they stray close to it. Yet we still insist that the press must be absolutely free (barring the protections afforded private persons by libel laws, and so on) to address the minds of any and all citizens who care to attend to it, without the interposition of any filters or obstacles by the state.

The reason for this insistence on the freedom of the press is that we, out of our thoroughgoing democratic prejudices, locate the legitimate seat of sovereignty, in any nation, in its people. In our own country, our identity as self-governing citizens is made explicit by our constitution and cemented in place by a long tradition of democratic practice. The sovereign of Canada is the citizenry of Canada. We are not ruled by our representatives in the various legislative tribunals of the nation: these are but among the instruments we use in governing ourselves. And since no sovereign can submit itself to censorship without yielding up control over its own mind, democratic conviction has given rise to democratic sensibilities that hate censorship as one of the marks of the tyrannical.

Our commitment to freedom of expression is not limitless, however; we are willing to set aside our protection in the case of speech that is indistinguishable from action in its effects, as in criminal incitement. In these cases, we have teased a very limited class of expressions away from the main body as being productive of criminal results, not as a consequence of any of us being persuaded, or influenced, or led by them to so act, but rather because they operated as a cause of criminality. Thus Justice Holmes's famous instance of the person falsely crying 'Fire!' in a crowded theatre. The point, in such a case, is not that harm follows from speech, but rather that the harm that follows in such a circumstance is an effect of speech that has all of the simple force of a cause. For the darkened and crowded theatre is exactly the setting in which there can be no possibility of discussion, or deliberation, or the effective advancement of opposing views, or any of the public thinking that we identify with the activity of the democratic forum.

Turn now, with these considerations in mind, to these two propositions:

(1) Bessie Smith records may influence the imaginations and sensibilities of some of our citizens, and these attitudinal changes may, in their turn, result in the adoption of lifestyles that we fear or dislike.

(2) Bessie Smith records cause those who listen to them to do things that cause harm to themselves and others.

The first proposition, couched in good old mentalistic language, is probably true. It has its proper analogue in propositions such as: 'Allowing the works of Marx and Engels to be taught and advocated in our universities may influence some young people to become Marxists and work for the violent overthrow of our system of government.'

The force of the second proposition is that, by counterfeiting causal predictability, it presents the threat of jazz to us as one of incitement. Thus it seeks to sidestep the institutions and laws that protect freedom of expression, and that we have put in place out of our democratic respect for the freedom of human minds.

That this attempt to sidestep our constitutional freedom is undertaken out of the highest motives is, I believe, incontestable. That caring, public-minded women and men should fervently desire to have a larger and improving say in how we conduct our personal and social lives – and that they should also want to frustrate those who give currency to visions of the human scene which they find to be fearful, disgusting, immoral, and dangerous – is not simply understandable; it is really, all things being equal, commendable. The democratic truth of the matter is, however, that all these things are not equal, and that we have committed ourselves to a plan of government which gives precedence to freedom of expression as the farthest-seeing guarantee of our happiness.

In a 1985 decision in the U.S. Court of Appeals, Judge Easterbrook spoke to this characteristic of democracy in confirming the judgment of the District Court that struck down an Indianapolis ordinance making the publication of pornography a civil tort:

Under the First Amendment the government must leave to the people the evaluation of ideas. Bald or subtle, an idea is as powerful as the audience allows it to be. A belief may be pernicious – the beliefs of Nazis led to the

death of millions. A pernicious belief may prevail. Totalitarian governments today rule much of the planet, practicing suppression of billions
and spreading dogma that may enslave others. One of the things that
separates our society from theirs is our absolute right to propagate opinion that the government finds wrong or even hateful.

Quoting the Indianapolis ordinance, which details the ways in which
pornography may influence the formation of regressive attitudes towards women, Judge Easterbrook continued:

Yet this [attitudes that flow from pornography] simply demonstrates the
power of pornography as speech. All of these unhappy effects depend on
mental intermediation. Pornography affects how people see the world,
their fellows, and social relations. If pornography is what pornography
does, so is other speech ... Communism is a world-view, not simply a
Manifesto by Marx and Engels or a set of speeches. Efforts to suppress
communist speech in the United States were based on the belief that the
public acceptability of such ideas would increase the likelihood of totalitarian government.

Judge Easterbrook's point is, simply, that as a democratic community,
the United States has accorded a special role and importance to the
minds of its citizens. Management of those minds through censorship is
one way to seek to provide for the public good, but the Constitution of
the United States – and our own – gives precedence to a different plan,
one that is grounded in its national hope for, and faith in, the judgment
of its citizens.

   This is the right place for me to bring out my major premise: trying to
be a real democracy entails having respect (or at least acting – that is,
legislating – as if you do) for the minds of our fellow citizens, because it
is those minds which join in a collegial relationship as the ruling authority of our nation. The 'cash value' of that respect, the substantial direction and constraint it imposes on our institutions and laws, is that we
must forbear the management, by state censorship, of the forum in
which those minds have their public and political life. It is true that
some of us may be influenced by songs, magazines, videos, or whatever
other expressions, to choose imprudent or even criminal courses of
action; some of us always think poorly and unsteadily, and we all make
at least some mistakes. But for a community committed to democracy,
those facts do not legitimize the adoption of a censorship that bespeaks

a general lack of respect for, and faith in, the minds of our fellow citizen-rulers.

It is, God knows, hard to have much respect for the minds of other people; it is hard to imagine or believe or hope that they are sites of deliberation and choice, rather than some form of switching station in which the contents of tabloids are turned into actions that are either trivial or discreditable. But this is no more than to say that it is hard to believe in democracy; that is, it is hard to believe that it could ever be wise policy to trust the governance of our nation to the people – to place the provision of our common happiness or (gulp!) unhappiness – in their hands.

The real secret of the adherents and proponents of the Bessie Smith factor, and the deep significance of their grotesque oversimplification of the mind, is that they have effectively given up on democracy and are looking to develop a different sort of governance. And this final result and object of their program may have more to do with their popularity than has their bad science. We may really be so disaffectedly out of patience with our fellows that it is no longer possible for us to approach the common tasks of community with anything like a general respect for the human mind. We may really be, as a democracy, out of gas.

We tend not to think so down at the civil liberties office ... that is, on most days. In fact, I think that when Canadians confront instances of nickel-plated undemocratic practice, we, all of us, discover reserves of spirit tapped by our indignation. A case in point – a rather unlovely example of the Bessie Smith factor – is the Little Sister's Book and Art Emporium case, in which Canada Customs seized as prohibited material some sixty book and magazine titles that were directed to the bookstore from the United States. Among the titles seized were volumes of poetry by Allen Ginsberg, essays by Jean Genet, fifth-century BC Greek poetry, and so on, as well as 'safe sex' pamphlets that were to be used in combating the spread of the AIDS virus. The salient point to take, however, is that Little Sister's is a gay and lesbian bookstore and that the materials it sells are, generally, of special interest to homosexuals. Meaning, bluntly, that the greatest portion of the titles seized by customs were straightforwardly descriptive or depictive of homosexual acts.

Readers may be surprised to learn that descriptions or depictions of homosex (which mirror permitted descriptions or depictions of heterosex in every particular save the cherished orifice) are prohibited entry into Canada when detected by the customs authorities. Readers are to be

excused if they draw the inference from this that such expressions must
be against our laws. But that would be a false inference, since what is or
is not legally obscene in Canada is a mystery that the Criminal Code
adumbrates with an oracular obscurity. We are told there that the forbidden areas of sexual expression comprise 'any publication (of which)
a dominant characteristic is the undue exploitation of sex, or of sex and
any one or more of the following subjects, namely, crime, horror, cruelty
and violence.' No mention of anal sex, but then again, no specific
mention of any specific sexual activity whatsoever. Hence, before the
obscenity laws can be used, they must first be interpreted.

Unsatisfied, as was Oedipus, with inactivity in the face of obscure
advice, Customs decided to interpret the oracular voice of the Criminal
Code by turning to two of its favourite sources of wisdom: opinion polls
and lower prairie courtrooms. Thus, in an article in the *Vancouver Sun* in
early 1986 ('Guidelines Called a Real Porn-stopper'), concerning Customs' then new policy directives we read that

> Douglas Cruickshank, Director of Prohibitive Importation in the Depart-
> ment of National Revenue, said the guidelines were drawn up after the
> government reviewed its own polls 'and after we received a lot of corre-
> spondence from special interest groups.' He said three recent court deci-
> sions – in Alberta, Manitoba, and Ontario – influenced the drafting of the
> guidelines. Particularly useful, Cruickshank said, was the Alberta Court
> of Queen's Bench decision by Justice Mel Shannon.

Of the new guidelines, which took such a generous view of the notion
of obscenity as to extend it even to printed descriptions of sodomy
(possibly 'undue'? maybe 'horrible'?), the pro-censorship camp offered
unbuttoned praise. Hence, Ms Ridington, still of the Periodical Review
Board, enthused in the 'Porn-stoppers' article cited above:

> 'Wow, those [guidelines] are really going to keep a lot of stuff out,'
> Ridington said when told the contents of the guidelines, which were
> released Wednesday by the federal government. 'Those are tougher than
> the Attorney General's guidelines we work under. If they hold themselves
> to them, they will keep a lot of stuff out that was allowed in before,' she
> said in welcoming the guidelines. 'There won't be any need for a review
> board.'

That superior courts had supported interpretations of the obscenity
provisions that identified descriptions and depictions of anal sex as not

obscene (Supreme Court of Canada, *Towne Cinema v. Regina,* May 1985) did not impress Customs. And so we have the absolutely marvellous situation that confronts us in the present instance. An authoritative agency of the federal government, charged with administering the Criminal Code for the purposes of prohibiting entry to criminal expressions, sets about the momentous task of interpreting the law by dipping into the old mail bag and plumbing the judicial backwaters of the country.

What is really at work here is one of the more remarkable variants of the Bessie Smith factor – a homophobia that extends even to printed descriptions of gay sex. We are all of us familiar with the tedious nitwits who evidently believe that homosexuals have a sort of werewolf power to turn decent vulva-worshipping guys into raving, Nelly 'cage aux folles' characters. One stolen kiss, and BINGO! – sequins, feather boas, and all the rest. In the case of Customs picking on expressions of gay sexuality, we confront the spectacle of the administration of justice inspired by the fruity thesis that books and magazines actually incite homosexuality. Of course, it is possible that Customs may be motivated by even more discreditable and illogical considerations, but there is a limit to the fecundity of my imagination.

Here is the triple-distilled craziness at the centre of the Little Sister's case: Customs is prohibiting entry to printed descriptions of activity that is perfectly legal (that is, anal sex between consenting adults), even while it is permitting entry to filmed portrayals of activity that is perfectly criminal (such as murder mysteries). Can a healthy mind make any sense of this without appeal to the operation of the Bessie Smith factor?

This is not the place to offer a 'defence' of homosexuality, or to canvas the variety of views concerning its roots in nature or nurture. I have my own ideas about this, influenced in part by my living for some years with a lesbian aunt (who was one of the dearest and most powerfully formative influences of my adolescence), but they are, finally, of little importance. What is of central and overriding importance is that adult Canadians have a right to choose and live their own sexual lives. No matter that the sexual lives chosen by a few may resonate, for the majority of us, with all of the alien and scary power of Bessie Smith's black sex or Allen Ginsberg's queer sex. Fear of flying is no fair reason to forbid it to others, and no less is it true that being frightened of human sex – in any of its rather marvellously plastic manifestations – can never be a legitimate reason to interfere with either the doing or the talking about it by those whose desires are thus innocently engaged.

4 Words Matter

JOHN RUSSELL

Words matter.

That is the gist of the B.C. Supreme Court's 2003 decision to uphold disciplinary action against Quesnel high school counsellor Chris Kempling for expressing antihomosexual views.

Kempling was suspended for thirty days by the B.C. College of Teachers for letters he published in the local newspaper between 1997 and 2000. The letters described homosexuals in words usually reserved for those thought to have slipped past the edge of humanity. Kempling appealed to the B.C. Supreme Court last summer, arguing that the college's sanction violated his right to freedom of expression under the Charter of Rights and Freedoms, The court has now rejected that appeal.

'If a constitutional, liberal democracy is to succeed, public officers must understand and respect the boundaries of their public and private lives and duties. That citizens can usually accept such boundaries is one of the great discoveries and achievements of our culture. It is also a main cause for optimism that tolerance and respect among people of diverse beliefs and backgrounds is possible.'

The case produced country-wide debate and confusion about the nature and limits of free speech, and it continues to do so. Civil liberties organizations in particular have been criticized by religious fundamentalists and others for caving in to political correctness and failing to defend Kempling's right to express anti-homosexual views. But in a thoughtful and clarifying decision, Justice R.R. Holmes agreed with the position taken by the B.C. Civil Liberties Association that Kempling's expressions were not protected speech.

The key finding of the court was that Kempling's public statements explicitly linked his discriminatory views to his professional role as a teacher and school counsellor. Thus, Kempling did not simply criticize homosexuality as a private citizen (which the court recognized he had every right to do). He explicitly represented his remarks as the views of a public school counsellor. That link, plus the discriminatory content of his remarks, called into question his capacity to treat all students impartially according to law. By implication, the impartiality of the school system was cast in doubt. More concretely, Kempling's words created the public apprehension that he would use his professional role to contravene minority protections for homosexuals under the Charter and provincial laws.

The court's decision should be welcomed by all. It will help ensure that our public institutions can operate effectively according to the values of the Charter and the rule of law. It asserts, in effect, that no professional can use his special public status or role to announce, or otherwise create the impression, that he will use his position to violate legally mandated obligations, including minority protections, and then say he is protected from sanction as part of his right to free speech. If that were permitted by those performing public roles or responsibilities, trust and confidence in our public institutions would be impossible.

Kempling's own intentions to use his position as a schoolteacher and counsellor to discriminate against homosexuals were unequivocal. In one letter to the editor about homosexuality he stated:

> I refuse to be a false teacher saying that promiscuity is acceptable, perversion is normal, and immorality is simply cultural diversity, of which we should be proud ... To all my critics I say 2 Peter 24-19. Read it and weep.

In another letter, he added:

> Some readers may be wondering why I am putting my professional reputation on the line ... Sexual orientations can be changed and the success rate for those who seek help is high. My hope is that students who are confused over their sexual orientation will come to see me. It could save their lives.

More broadly, in a constitutional democracy like ours, those with public duties must be prepared to live up to the principles of the Charter and the law in performing their roles, whether they agree with those principles and laws or not. As a professional schoolteacher and counsellor, Kempling has a public duty to uphold homosexuals' legal rights to equal dignity, respect, and tolerance in his professional activities. That cannot be reconciled with teaching them that their lifestyle is perverted, immoral, promiscuous, and sinful.

Someone who is apparently unwilling to make the appropriate compartmentalization between his public duties and his private beliefs is incapable of fulfilling his public role and responsibilities, whether he has actually discriminated against someone or not. It is evident from Kempling's letters that he appeared unwilling to carry out that compartmentalization, at least at the time he wrote his letters. (He has since reported that he never intended to discriminate against homosexuals.) But words matter, and they speak for themselves about how Kempling saw his professional role, as the court recognized. Kempling should reflect that he is lucky still to have a job.

What is the lesson of the Kempling affair? If a constitutional, liberal democracy is to succeed, public officers must understand and respect the boundaries of their public and private lives and duties. That citizens can usually accept such boundaries is one of the great discoveries and achievements of our culture. It is also a main cause for optimism that tolerance and respect among people of diverse beliefs and backgrounds is possible. This should be more than cold comfort to Kempling and his supporters.

5 When Liberty Loses Out

Is tolerating hate speech ever beneficial?

Perhaps surprisingly, the answer is Yes. But because we are so often reminded of the many potentially harmful consequences of hate speech, we sometimes forget that allowing people to speak their minds has its benefits.

For example, although hate speech sometimes advances the goals of its advocates, it more often effectively identifies the hate-mongers. And having done so, it allows us to take issue with what they say.

Who among us would vote for hate-mongers or Holocaust deniers such as David Ahenakew or James Keegstra if they were to run for our local school board? How many of us would elect them to represent us as our MPs? Not many.

In fact, were they to run, Ahenakew and Keegstra would receive far fewer votes than the largely anonymous names and faces that we sometimes support as part of a local electoral slate, or that we support because we are dissatisfied with a current incumbent.

Simply put, we know what Ahenakew and Keegstra stand for. And it is because we, as Canadians, have allowed them to speak their minds that we recognize they don't represent either us or our values.

Outlawing hate speech means that it is harder to discover just who the hate-mongers are. It is not a coincidence that many of those who advocate stricter laws banning hate literature also advocate the increased use of surreptitious government surveillance to help law enforcement agencies root out such people once they are forced to conduct their business in secret.

But if we as a society want to know who they are, why not simply let them tell us?

Permitting hate speech also forces us to pay attention to social injustices, and to confront and address hateful stereotypes. For example, denials of the Holocaust have been a great spur to the careful historical documentation of Nazi atrocities. They have also encouraged the pursuit and prosecution of war criminals and the commitment of resources to fight racism and all manner of other prejudices against minorities.

These are no small benefits. As the great nineteenth-century defender of free speech John Stuart Mill recognized, truth lapses into complacent dogma when it faces no quarry from falsehoods, and complacency often leads to inaction.

It can also be more difficult to identify hate speech than we are sometimes led to believe. For example, several years ago a small group of University of British Columbia students was caught on videotape overturning tables and ripping up the posters of a highly publicized anti-abortion display. By way of justification, some of these students claimed that the display's controversial comparisons of abortion to the Holocaust and to lynchings of blacks by the Ku Klux Klan constituted hate speech. They believed for this reason that the display should not have been allowed on campus.

'Is tolerating hate speech ever beneficial? Perhaps surprisingly, the answer is Yes.'

But if something as central to our political culture as the debate over abortion were to be curtailed in this way, surely many other controversial presentations would also have to be classified as hate speech. Controversial comments about immigrants, or about religious groups, or about the gay and lesbian community might all end up being classified as hate speech.

Unfortunately, when it comes to tolerating the views of others, it is too easy to think that everyone deserves the right to free speech – but only provided they don't disagree with any of our own most cherished views.

How did the UBC administration react to this event? Unfortunately, instead of coming to the defence of its students' free speech rights, it decided to take a largely 'hands off' approach. In documents filed in court, UBC stated that it would take 'no position' with respect to those students who requested that an injunction be granted to protect their right to free speech while on campus.

With regard to larger issues, however, UBC has taken a position, and for anyone concerned about free speech rights on campus, it is not an encouraging one. The university not only declined to assist its own students in defending their free speech rights, but also took the position that while on campus, students have only those free speech rights that the university chooses to extend to them.

In the words of UBC's lawyers, 'UBC recognizes the Plaintiffs' contractual right to conduct presentations of this or other types pursuant to the terms of any license granted by UBC. UBC does not agree that in conducting the presentation the Plaintiffs are exercising any other contractual, common law, or constitutional rights as alleged in the Statement of Claim.'

It goes without saying that institutions such as UBC have long enjoyed the right to enforce place, time, and manner restrictions on public displays and demonstrations. Just as guarantees in favour of freedom of information don't mean that I have a right to read your private mail, guarantees in favor of free speech don't mean that you have the right to disrupt my classroom lecture, or to insist that the university allow protesters to speak whenever and however they choose. One person's right to free speech doesn't translate into another person's obligation to listen.

But neither does it follow that students have no rights to free speech, other than those licensed to them by the university. In making the claim that while on campus, students have no 'contractual, common law, or constitutional rights' other than those granted to them by UBC, the university has gone well beyond its right to enforce place, time and manner restrictions.

In taking this position, UBC runs the risk of compromising its central mandate – namely, its duty to encourage the advancement of knowledge; and because of this, the university's position can only further serve to chill expression rights at UBC and on other university campuses across the country.

6 Protesters Deserve an Apology

ANDREW IRVINE

Wouldn't it be nice if the next time you received a speeding ticket you could just say to the police officer, 'Thanks for your trouble, Constable, but I don't think I'll pursue this,' and that would be the end of it? Or if you were found guilty of obstructing justice, wouldn't it be helpful if you could just turn to the judge and say: 'With respect, your honour, I believe you've got the facts wrong,' and then you would be free to go?

This might not be how things work for you or me, but it seems to be the way things work for former prime minister Jean Chrétien.

After months of public hearings into events surrounding the 1997 Asia-Pacific Economic Co-operation (APEC) conference, and after painstakingly sifting through thousands of pages of evidence, this is what Public Complaints Commissioner Ted Hughes concluded about the involvement of the prime minister and his staff: 'I am satisfied that ... the federal government, acting through the Prime Minister's Office, improperly interfered in an RCMP security operation.' In addition, this 'improper and inappropriate' interference occurred on at least two occasions, and as a direct result security arrangements were compromised.

Was this the result of an honest mistake on the part of the prime minister's right-hand man, Jean Carle? Well, no. As Mr Hughes concludes, 'Mr Carle, in his testimony, agreed that he understood that as a consequence of [his actions], students who were peacefully protesting had to cease that protest and some of them were arrested.'

Mr Carle also testified that he understood that 'there was no security reason' that would have justified his intervention in these matters. As a result, says Mr Hughes, 'I have concluded that the removal of the protesters was an unjustifiable infringement of their rights under section 2(b) of the Charter.'

On a separate occasion, Mr Hughes reports that Mr Carle again 'vehemently opposed' RCMP security provisions in order to advance the objectives of the Prime Minister's Office. Concludes Mr Hughes, 'I am satisfied that Mr Carle demanded that the size of the "demonstration area" be reduced in order to accomplish his own agenda and I reject his explanation that the reduction was necessary to ensure the safety of the protesters.'

In other words, Mr Hughes has found that on more than one occasion members of the RCMP allowed themselves to be inappropriately influenced by members of the Prime Minister's Office and, as a direct result of this influence, at least some law-abiding Canadians were wrongfully arrested. Mr Hughes also found that Mr Carle's 'expression of concern for public safety' was 'spurious' and that in his various dealings with conference organizers he was less than honest.

These are serious findings. In fact, for Canadians who believe that it is the job of the RCMP to protect citizens' rights and enforce the law – and not to advance the political objectives of our politicians – it is hard to imagine findings more serious.

'Who knew that avoiding responsibility could be so easy? All Mr Chrétien had to do to avoid culpability was to state that, with respect, he disagreed with Mr Hughes's findings of wrongdoing.'

How did Mr Chrétien respond? Did he admit that mistakes were made? Did he clarify his role in directing Mr Carle's activities? Did he apologize or offer compensation to the protesters who were wrongly arrested? Or to the RCMP officers whose professional reputations have been compromised as a result of his office's interference?

Not exactly. Instead, he and his office responded as follows: 'With respect to the two isolated incidents, in which Mr Hughes was critical of federal officials, the Government has publicly stated that it, respectfully, disagrees with Mr Hughes.'

Who knew that avoiding responsibility could be so easy? All Mr Chrétien had to do to avoid culpability was to state that, with respect, he disagreed with Mr Hughes's findings of wrongdoing! It's too bad this kind of option isn't available to the rest of us.

During Mr Hughes's inquiry, testimony was also heard that the minister responsible for the operation of the Prime Minister's Office is the prime minister himself, and that under the Canadian parliamentary system, it is this minister who must take responsibility for the errors of his subordinates. Responsibility needs to be accepted by the relevant minister, even in cases in which there has been no direct involvement by that minister, in order to make clear the responsibilities that ministers have for managing and overseeing their departments.

It is only in this way that citizens can ensure an appropriate degree of public accountability.

If a prime minister had no advance knowledge of these interventions, then this may seem harsh. But under the Canadian constitution there needs to be strong recognition that responsibility for this type of wrong-doing lies with the minister himself. It is only by recognizing this responsibility that core democratic values are respected and upheld.

It is also important to remember that the RCMP Commission for Public Complaints was not convened primarily to investigate the actions of the then prime minister or his office. As a result, the absence of a finding specifically incriminating Mr Chrétien should not be understood as a finding of blamelessness on the part of the former prime minister. In fact, just the reverse. Given that the only significant testimony exonerating Mr Chrétien came from Mr Carle, and given that Mr Hughes specifically found Mr Carle to be an unreliable witness, there clearly remains a cloud over Mr Chrétien and his office.

When mistakes are made, it is important for individuals to take responsibility for them. In the current case, the errors were significant. Some members of the RCMP engaged in actions that were not only illegitimate but also unlawful. These unlawful acts included unjustified arrests, inappropriate strip searches, the unjustified infringement of free speech rights, excessive police violence, and the unjustified confiscation of property. These actions deprived members of the public rights guaranteed to Canadian citizens under the Charter and were, at least in part, attributable to inappropriate intervention into security arrangements by members of the Prime Minister's Office. If a politician of Mr Chrétien's standing was involved in these activities, then this matters a great deal.

For many months, Mr Chrétien repeatedly told the Canadian public that it was important to let the commission do its work. Now that it has done its work and made findings of inappropriate behaviour on the part of both the RCMP and the Prime Minister's Office, it is time for Mr Chrétien to step forward and take his fair share of responsibility. If he doesn't, what guarantee do Canadians have that these types of events will not be repeated in the future?

7 Big, Bad Ideas? No Big Deal

STAN PERSKY

What if you have not only big ideas but bad ideas? What if one of your big, bad ideas is that it's okay for adult men to have sex with adolescent males between the ages of fourteen and seventeen?

What if you also think it's okay to go around talking about being in love with boys, and to discuss in public the finer points of the matter – which boys to fall in love with, how to pursue and persuade them, and all the rest?

Or, finally, what if you rattle on about the 'beauty of boys and young men,' noting that 'the sight of them throws you and many people like you into such an ecstasy that, provided you could always enjoy the sight and company of your darlings, you would be content to go without food and drink, and to pass your whole time with them in contemplation of their beauty'?

No, the author of the above lines is not Vancouver writer–photographer Robin Sharpe, the man at the centre of the 2001 Supreme Court of Canada decision that upheld – but somewhat narrowed the scope of – the country's child pornography laws.

The author of the passage I've quoted is the Greek philosopher Plato, writing in *The Symposium*. Penned 2,400 years ago, *The Symposium* is the first explicit discussion in literature about the love of boys, and much else. And it certainly sounds as if the author is advocating or counselling some activity that, if not strictly in violation of the 'advocacy' section of Canada's child pornography law, is surely unpopular and offensive in the minds of many Canadians.

So, Plato seems to have a 'bad' idea. What should we do about it?

Nothing, said Chief Justice Beverly McLachlin in her majority decision in *R. v. Sharpe*. 'While ... Plato's *Symposium* portrays or discusses sexual activities with children,' McLachlin admits, nonetheless it 'cannot be said to advocate or counsel such conduct in the sense of actively inducing or encouraging it.'

Of course, Plato could also escape prosecution in Canadian courts by offering a defence of 'artistic merit,' given that *The Symposium* happens to be a masterpiece. Or at least he once could have. Some Canadian legislators have since noticed that possible loophole, too, and have proposed to eliminate the artistic merit defence if the material portrays people under the age of eighteen.

But I'm not as sure as Chief Justice McLachlin is even about the advocating and counselling aspect. When I first read *The Symposium*, at age fifteen or sixteen, I found it pretty persuasive. My dad, who had given me Plato to read, didn't think it was a big deal. He didn't think Plato would corrupt me; he figured I would be able to decide for myself what to do with my recently awakened erotic interests.

'My dad, who had given me Plato to read, didn't think it was a big deal. He didn't think Plato would corrupt me; he figured I would be able to decide for myself what to do with my recently awakened erotic interests.'

The Plato case is just one small example of how difficult it is to craft a child pornography law that protects children while not infringing on our rights to free speech, thought, expression and publication. When the Canadian Parliament hastily cobbled together such a law in 1993, mostly for political purposes, the result was a sloppy, vague, and overly broad statute. It was the first law in Canadian history that criminalized the mere *possession* of expressive materials. (We already had a law that made the production, distribution, and sale of child pornography illegal.)

Parliament would have been wiser to pass a law that simply said, 'Possession of photographic representations of children and young people that are produced as a result of sexual offences against actual children is a crime.' And that's all. No complicated add-ons, no creation of a net that captured all sorts of thoughts, writings, drawings, and other representations that ought to be perfectly legal.

But, alas, Parliament didn't do that, and that's why Chief Justice McLachlin and the rest of her court had to roll up the sleeves of their judicial robes a few years ago and clean up the kiddie porn law.

Whether the Supreme Court got it 100 per cent right has been debated ever since. Because sexual offences against children (including child pornography) are such a hot-button issue, it's difficult to remember that part of the debate is about free speech, something that's vital to the citizens of a democracy.

Almost everybody in Canada is against sexual offences against children and against child pornography involving the use of actual children in its production. But if you utter so much as a word about free speech, you're likely to get branded as being soft on child pornography.

This isn't a label that should be applied to the Supreme Court. After all, it upheld and clarified the law. The court said, however, that it's not a crime to have offensive thoughts and to write them down, as long as you keep them to yourself. That is, you have a right to have even bad ideas.

I think the court could have gone further and said it was all right to publish and distribute your bad ideas about sex, since we're allowed to air all our other bad ideas. The court also said it was legal to make photographic representations of the sexual activities of people under eighteen, as long as the sex was legal and the people making the photos (whether under or over eighteen) kept them to themselves. That means a sixteen-year-old boy taking a photo of his erect penis in a mirror, or a seventeen-year-old couple videotaping their honeymoon night, will not be guilty of a child pornography crime as long as they keep the images to themselves. Of course, if they show the pictures to the other kids at school, they'll be guilty of distributing kiddie porn and the kids at the lunch table will be guilty of possessing it, so the court-amended law still doesn't quite make sense. Nonetheless, the Supreme Court recognized there was something wrong with the law and tried to fix it, rather than strike it down and tell Parliament to start all over.

The solution was a compromise – a pretty clever one, in my view – but not everyone will be happy. I, for one, feel better knowing I can read Plato. More important, most parents feel better knowing there are laws to protect their children. However, a whole whack of social conservatives and their legislative representatives still think the country is on the road to perdition. They believe that a law that prevents advocating and counselling illegal sexual acts with people under eighteen does not go far enough. They want the statute to say that any 'description' of illegal sexual acts with people under eighteen also ought to be a crime, and that it does not matter whether the description is a work of art or not. If they get their way, that means goodbye to Plato, and a whole lot more.

PART VII

Reverse Discrimination

Revenue Departments

1 Why Equality Doesn't Mean Treating Everyone the Same

THOMAS HURKA

Judy Rebick raised some hackles recently. Commenting on the Constitution, the then president of the National Action Committee on the Status of Women said, 'We understand that equality doesn't mean treating everyone the same way.' There were angry letters to the *Globe and Mail* recalling George Orwell's *Animal Farm*, where 'some animals are more equal than others.'

Ms Rebick's concept of equality isn't Orwellian – it's obviously correct. Think about people with disabilities. As a society, we spend more on these people than on those without disabilities. We build special access ramps to buildings; we subsidize wheelchairs; we provide closed-captioned TV news. If equality meant treating everyone the same way, this would all be unjust. There would be Charter challenges to handicapped parking zones: they reserve the best parking spots for a limited few. But we don't take this line. We recognize that treating people with disabilities the same way as others would be unjust: it would ignore their special needs.

'Equality demands an equal chance for all. But sometimes giving that equal chance means treating people differently – levelling a playing field that would otherwise be full of bumps and hollows.'

Equality means giving everyone an equal chance to participate in social life: an equal chance to make choices, and to offer themselves for choice – as a friend or employee – by others. In an ideal world, equality could be secured by treating everyone the same, but when some face special obstacles, they need help to overcome them.

The idea isn't to produce 'equality of results,' where everyone has the same job or income. Some people, given an equal chance to participate in social life, may choose not to, preferring leisure and quiet to prestigious but high-pressure work. Others may lose in fair competition for this work, because they lack the talent for it. What equality demands is just the chance at fair competition.

The different treatment that equality requires for people with disabilities can also apply in hiring. Hence the appropriateness of some 'employment equity.'

A University of Calgary report notes that in 1990, only 22 per cent of professors hired at the university were women, even though in 1988, 30.6 per cent of Canadian PhDs went to women. This may be an accident, based on the fields the hiring was in. (There are ten times more women PhDs in English than in physics.) But often this kind of discrepancy reflects 'systemic discrimination' – not conscious bias against women, but hidden factors that work against them.

People on hiring committees may have a mental picture of a good candidate, based on their experience of successful past employees. If these employees have mostly been male, the picture will be male. A qualified woman may fit it less well than a less qualified man.

Systemic discrimination creates a disability for those who face it – not a physical disability, but a socially imposed one. And it demands steps to remove it, such as a rule requiring that a woman be hired unless a man is 'demonstrably better.'

This argument doesn't justify everything done under the name 'employment equity.' The Calgary report recommends a goal for the university of 30 per cent women professors by the year 2000. Given the expected rate of retirements, reaching this goal would require hiring roughly 40 per cent women over the next decade – more than the current proportion of PhDs. If this more ambitious goal is justified, it must be on other grounds.

Sometimes gender or race is a positive qualification for a job. A university is for education, but students don't learn only in lectures. They learn by interacting with one another, which is why some universities go for a socially diverse student body. Students also learn by interacting with their professors. A professoriate that is overwhelmingly male sends a skewed message about who can and cannot succeed; in these conditions, a woman, as a woman, can improve the university's teaching.

Or we can care about equality in the next generation: giving its young women the same encouragement and role models that young men have always had. This is another reason for preferring women professors.

In *Animal Farm*, some animals are 'more equal than others' because they want a better chance at the good things in life. This is wrong: equality demands an equal chance for all. But sometimes giving that equal chance means treating people differently – levelling a playing field that would otherwise be full of bumps and hollows.

2 Hidden Meanings

LEO GROARKE

Confucius said that the key to good government is calling things by their right names. It's a helpful thought when one tries to work one's way through the muddled arguments and the moral indignation that surround recent debates on employment equity, many of them sparked by the Ontario government's proposed employment equity legislation, Bill 79 (The Ontario Employment Equity Act).

On any straightforward reading, 'employment equity' means treating candidates for jobs equally on the basis of their qualifications. This means that the best candidate gets the job, regardless of gender, race, age, ethnic background, sexual preference, or disability (unless these are qualifications for the job at hand). So understood, equity is simply fairness. In promoting it, human rights commissions and employment equity officers promote not only tolerance, but also productivity, by ensuring that merit is the sole criterion in hiring.

Listening to the Ontario government defend Bill 79, one might well imagine that it is defending employment equity so conceived. The rhetoric is punctuated by all the right catchphrases – the goal of equal job opportunities for all, the assurance that this is not a quota system, and the promise that the new legislation will 'add tremendously to productivity.'

But something else is afoot. The crux of the government's proposals is a commitment to numerical hiring goals set on the basis of population and demographic statistics. These goals are not called 'quotas,' but all the objections to quotas (among them, those that convinced the U.S. Supreme Court that quotas were unconstitutional) apply to the case at hand.

The problem with such goals and with the ways they are implemented is seen in the recent controversy over the hiring of firefighters in Kitchener. To ensure that significant numbers of women would advance beyond the test administered as the second step of the screening process – in order to get a 'leg up' on the Ontario government's proposed equity legislation, according to Kitchener's employment equity officer – women were allowed to move on with marks of 70 per cent; men required a score of 85 per cent.

This may be right or wrong, but it cannot honestly be called equal treatment for all candidates, and it is, at the least, strange to call the program under which it operated employment 'equity.' Especially since no one has accused the test of bias, the Kitchener policy is, on all accounts, one that promotes people who are less qualified and that will lessen rather than increase the efficiency of the fire department.

The Kitchener situation is mild in comparison with the Ontario government's proposal that we should use population statistics to guide the hiring process. Women are roughly 50 per cent of the population, which means, according to its logic, that 50 per cent of Kitchener firefighters should be women. Hiring targets aimed at achieving this distribution would have to give all available jobs to women, allowing any woman who took the test to move on in the hiring process even if she scored only 30 or 40 per cent.

'The crux of the government's proposals is a commitment to numerical hiring goals set on the basis of population and demographic statistics ... In a more honest time, such policies were called 'preferential hiring.' The term was too honest to garner the support its proponents wanted, so it was replaced by the term "affirmative action."'

It need not be said that such policies have many objectionable aspects. Among other things, they suggest the demeaning and paternalistic notion that lower standards should be used in hiring people from designated groups and the still stranger notion that less qualified individuals will be good role models. They ignore the fact that a slow economy is the real cause of the slow entry of women and other minority groups into the labour force.

But such policies raise even deeper questions about the way the proponents of radical versions of employment 'equity' are using language. There is not much chance that their policies would be accepted by the public if they were called what they are: proposals to enforce hiring quotas that give jobs to individuals who are not the best qualified, and proposals to make gender, race, and other considerations irrelevant to merit a crucial part of the hiring process.

In a more honest time, such policies were called 'preferential hiring.' The term was too honest to garner the support its proponents wanted, so it was replaced by the term 'affirmative action.' How could anyone deny that 'affirmative' action was positive? But the complaint that such policies were not treating individuals equally persisted. So, in another linguistic tour de force, proponents dropped talk of 'quotas' and adopted the misleading term 'employment equity.'

Twisting language to make debatable policies more palatable is, of course, a common way for the powers that be to get their points of view accepted. When former U.S. president Ronald Reagan had difficulty obtaining funding for the MX missile, he renamed it 'the Peacekeeper.' Nuclear strategists were (in)famous for calling nuclear attacks on cities 'counter value operations' and 'surgical strikes.' The neutron bomb – which destroys only people – was called 'the clean bomb.'

The muddying of the waters of political debate by vague and misleading language is, as the employment equity debate proves, as popular as ever. But it is ironic that those who were most critical of the 'nuke-speak' of the military-industrial complex are now doing the same thing.

Perhaps they learned their tricks from the Pentagon. More likely, they just cannot resist the temptation to make language a tool for their own political agenda. Just how far they are willing to take this is seen in the large-scale education program they plan to introduce to ensure that everyone understands employment 'equity.'

No doubt some recalcitrant individuals will not be able to see how such clearly inequitable policies can be called 'equity.' But most people will be cowed by the threat of being criticized as politically incorrect. Whatever one thinks of the policies it promotes, one of the results of the proposed employment equity legislation will be the debasing of the language we use to talk about such issues.

3 Affirmative Action: More Radical Arguments

THOMAS HURKA

Affirmative action means giving preference in hiring to selected groups, such as women. Its official Canadian justification is that this will ensure the best-qualified person is hired, that 'systemic' barriers don't prevent talented women from advancing as they should.

This justification works for some affirmative action. If managers systematically undervalue women, forcing them to prefer women can improve their hiring decisions. But it doesn't justify all the affirmative action in Canada.

Many Canadian schemes involve hiring above a target percentage – say, above 50 per cent women – so that the target will be reached in a particular workforce in ten or twenty years. Such schemes clearly prefer people who are in the traditional sense less qualified – that is, who will do less well in the job on a day-to-day basis.

'Many Canadian schemes involve hiring above a target percentage – say, above 50 per cent women – so that the target will be reached in a particular workforce in ten or twenty years. Such schemes clearly prefer people who are in the traditional sense less qualified – that is, who will do less well in the job on a day-to-day basis.'

An honest justification of these schemes must recognize this. Is an honest justification possible? One defence of these schemes points to the long-term consequences of affirmative action. It admits that affirmative action has short-term costs in lost job efficiency but claims that these are outweighed by long-term social benefits.

For some, the main benefit is just achieving, as quickly as possible, a representative workforce, one in which the proportion of women in top jobs equals their proportion in the population. This is morally dubious, however. Any morally significant benefits must be benefits to individuals, not groups.

But affirmative action does benefit individuals by changing people's attitudes. If the belief that women are inferior persists in Canada, either consciously or subconsciously, it's partly because women aren't sufficiently prominent in Canadian life. Moving them quickly into important jobs can help dispel that belief and the many harms it does. Seeing women lawyers and managers can dispel sexist stereotypes.

Equally important are the changes in the attitudes of women. What you aspire to in life depends on what you think you can do, which depends in large part on what people like you have done before. Women in prominent jobs can be role models, encouraging young women to work for similar success. If the young women achieve success, this will benefit both them and society, which now wastes much of their potential.

If affirmative action has these long-term benefits, is it therefore justified? If consequences were all that matters morally, the answer would be yes. But some moralists deny this, declaring that any policy is wrong that discriminates by race or gender. Affirmative action's end may be good, but it doesn't justify discriminatory means.

The issue is tricky, however. Imagine that there's a job for which intelligence is used as a qualification, so the more intelligent are hired ahead of the less intelligent. Can the less intelligent complain of discrimination? Is hiring by IQ unjust? We want, I think, to say no – but on what basis? Why is IQ discrimination not wrong?

There seems to be just one possible argument: hiring by intelligence isn't wrong because intelligent candidates will do the job better. And that's important because society benefits when the job is done better.

This argument implies a more general one. Discrimination on any basis is wrong if its social consequences are bad, but not otherwise. Discrimination that does good is morally permitted.

Using this test, race and sex discrimination come out usually wrong. They result in the hiring of less able candidates and, when the group discriminated against is disadvantaged, they perpetuate harmful attitudes against it. But this isn't the case for discrimination in favour of the disadvantaged, as in affirmative action. This discrimination can have overall good consequences and therefore be justified.

This thinking appears in the Canadian Charter of Rights and Freedoms, whose equality clauses explicitly exempt programs aimed at 'the amelioration of conditions of disadvantaged individuals or groups.' If these programs do social good, they don't violate equality and aren't forbidden.

We thus have two possible justifications of affirmative action: that it encourages the hiring of the most qualified people, and that even when it doesn't, it has good long-term consequences. A third argument says that affirmative action is required as compensation for past injustices. If women and Native people were discriminated against in the past, they should be compensated today in the form of preferential hiring.

Though common in American discussions, this argument isn't heard as much in Canada. Despite this, the objections to it are often, irrelevantly, introduced into Canadian debate.

One objection is that affirmative action benefits only the least disadvantaged members of the selected groups, those doing well enough to apply for high-profile jobs. Another is that it places the entire burden of compensation on a few white males who are no more guilty of the injustice than anyone else. If they didn't cause the past discrimination, why should they alone make up for it?

I believe these objections can be answered. If the effects of injustice are widespread and long-lasting, they can affect all members of a group, including those doing comparatively well. (If worse-off members of the group aren't benefited by affirmative action, they should get some other compensation.) And the white males, though not specially guilty of the past injustice, may be its prime beneficiaries, competing successfully against women and Native people who would beat them given an equal chance. Since they're the big winners from the injustice, it's only fair that they give up their ill-gotten gains.

In the United States, it would be vital to evaluate these claims about compensation. But in Canada the compensation argument merely supplements two more common justifications of affirmative action – the ones relating to hiring the best people and promoting long-term social good. Honest people can disagree about how much affirmative action these justifications support, but, as our Charter recognizes, they do support some.

4 Affirmative Action, Women, and 'the 50 Per Cent Solution'

LEO GROARKE

In her book *The 50% Solution*, Anne Innis Dagg proposes that half the government's funding for the arts be reserved for women. In the wake of her suggestions, *Queen's Quarterly* – one of Canada's oldest and most respected general-interest journals – has decided to 'publish in equal numbers the work of men and women [as] a first step toward giving our readers a broader and more representative range of perspectives.' Similar initiatives have been endorsed by the federal New Democratic Party, which has passed a resolution to ensure that 50 per cent of its new candidates in the next election will be women, and by special interest groups and professional organizations.

The advantage of the 50 per cent solution to sexist hiring is its simple, straightforward nature – it provides a concrete, easily definable goal that allows relatively simple assessments of progress in its direction. It is unfortunate that the solution is also simple-minded, most significantly because it confuses a numerical with a moral notion of equality.

Consistently applied, the principle of 'rep. by pop.' implied by the 50 per cent solution suggests that men and women should be equally represented in all occupations, and that variants of the 50 per cent solution should be applied to other groups. To take an initially plausible example, if blacks are 8 per cent of Canada's population they should occupy 8 per cent of the jobs in banking, in universities, and so on. As plausible as this may seem at first glance, it entails conclusions that are dubious, absurd, and morally repugnant – among them, the conclusions that 50 per cent of midwives should be male, that Jews should not be allowed to enter any occupation in which they are currently 'over'-represented, and that there are not enough white professional football players. Such conclusions should make us think twice about a social policy based on the principle that the make-up of the population at large should determine the make-up of particular professions.

Among other things, those who propose the 50 per cent solution assume (1) that it is the logical conclusion of affirmative action policies, (2) that it creates the gender ratios one would expect in professions free of gender bias, (3) that it invigorates staid professions, and (4) that it furthers women's interests. But each of these assumptions is doubtful or insufficiently established.

The essence of affirmative action is preferential treatment for women, native people, blacks, and so on. In hiring, affirmative action policies are justified as a way of creating professions that are free of prejudice and discrimination and characterized by competition for positions unsullied by considerations of sex, race, and ethnic background. Like others, I have argued that these goals sometimes outweigh the reverse discrimination, the possible backlash, and the compromise in excellence that affirmative action might initially entail. This said, an honest appraisal of affirmative action must admit it has costs that must be taken seriously. If we really are opposed to gender bias, we cannot, for example, welcome (though we may have to accept) reverse discrimination against young white men, who solely because of their colour and their sex are less likely to get jobs.

The 50 per cent solution is extremely problematic from this perspective because it does not allow the hiring of a man (or a woman) if the quota of males or females it implies has not been met, even if he (or she) is, from the point of view of ability, vastly superior. In cases such as these, the 50 per cent solution is much more problematic than ordinary affirmative action; at the same time, its benefits are much less significant. The most important moves towards non-discriminatory attitudes are the result of the breaking of initial barriers rather than attempts to attain the numerical equality emphasized by the 50 per cent solution. For example, the hiring of women professors is a way to provide role models for women students, but such moves have the greatest significance when there are few or no women in the university community. They are, in contrast, of very debatable significance and easily outweighed by other considerations when one addresses the difference between 30 per cent, 40 per cent, and 50 per cent women faculty.

A concrete case can make this clearer. To take one with which I am myself familiar, a committee of the Canadian Philosophical Association (the CPA) has proposed that philosophy departments in Canadian universities should, as soon as possible, be made up of 50 per cent women. This goal would require that women be hired in such departments at rates very significantly above the rates of similarly qualified men. Though only 28 per cent of philosophy PhD students are women, the committee has proposed that they be awarded a good deal more than 50 per cent of the available positions. According to its own figures, 80 per cent of the women – but only 40 per cent of the men – who earn PhDs in the present decade should be awarded jobs.

In order to ensure its goals are met, the committee has recommended policies that would make avoiding men a primary goal in the hiring process. Men are, for example, to be hired only when they are *clearly and unequivocally superior* to all female candidates' or *substantially better suited for the appointment'* (my emphasis). These are, on the face of it, stringent requirements; they are even more stringent in practice. For hiring committees are usually considering candidates at the start of their careers. In such situations they must assess candidates by considering their potential – which rarely allows for unequivocal conclusions. If there are, as the committee itself claims, 'always differences that may be weighted or valued differently,' there will be no cases when the hiring of a man can be justified. Certainly there will be many cases where the candidate most reasonably judged to be the most qualified is not hired.

The CPA committee is also advising philosophy departments to change their programs to facilitate the hiring of women. Among other things, this means they should avoid hiring in subject areas 'overwhelmingly dominated by men,' keep job specifications 'as flexible as possible so as to generate a larger pool of female applicants,' and hire outside preferred areas of expertise 'if they find a first rate woman with other interests.' Special opportunities should be made available to women – but not men – who hold part-time appointments, and graduate and undergraduate programs should be re-examined

'The 50 per cent solution is extremely problematic ... because it does not allow the hiring of a man (or a woman) ... even if he (or she) is, from the point of view of ability, vastly superior.'

with a view to increasing the number of women who gain the qualifications for university appointments. If, despite all these measures, a male manages to make his way to the top of a department's list of candidates for a position (and one may wonder how this is possible), a department should 'consider deferring the appointment for a year,' perhaps by explaining to the administrators at the university in question that it wants a woman.

These measures are strong medicine. They imply levels of reverse discrimination far and above those implied by standard affirmative action, which demands only that women be given some preference in hiring policy. Given that the CPA proposals make it possible that a woman PhD student ranked in the bottom ten of one hundred female graduate students should be hired over a man ranked in the top twenty-five of one hundred male students, they raise serious concerns about compromises in quality. They make it *reasonable* to conclude that women will be hired because they are women and not because they show evidence of superior ability. For that reason they are troubling from the point of view of role modelling and more general attitudes to women. One has to imagine similar consequences across a whole range of disciplines and professions (and, if consistency is to be maintained, in those fields dominated by women), in order to appreciate the extent of these negative implications.

Originally, affirmative action policies were conceived as a way of eliminating attitudes that promote discrimination – as a way of removing impediments that were not allowing free and fair competition for jobs. This goal stands in stark contrast to the 50 per cent solution, which proposes a numerical formula that would override the role of free and fair competition. In this way, the 50 per cent solution would add to the goal of a non-discriminatory society a very specific, numerically exact conception of what that society should look like. Its proponents are not satisfied with changing attitudes – especially when they do not precipitate the society they envision – and are willing to go much further: the policies they are proposing would mandate and enforce their own conception of a society free of gender bias.

Many feminists have argued that the persistence of gender differences in most occupations is a sign of the extent to which sexual discrimination is embedded in our society. Because it is no longer easy to find laws and institutions that are blatantly discriminatory, they postulate much more subtle forces of social conditioning that convince men and women they should conform to gender-biased stereotypes. It is this that allegedly produces the gender differences that characterize various professions. The problem is that such views dogmatically *assume* rather than prove this account of gender differences. When we use this account as a principle of interpretation, it is almost always possible to *hypothesize* conditioning that explains differences in gender – the social forces at work in any circumstance are, after all, enormously complex. But such explanations beg the question, founded as they are on a prior commitment to the view that the sexes are the same – a commitment that turns the existence of gender differences into a circular proof of sexual discrimination.

In answer to such claims, it can be said that it is hard to find clear evidence of systemic discrimination against women in many of the professions for which the 50 per cent solution is proposed. Within Canadian universities, significantly more than 50 per cent of the undergraduate students are women. To support them, they have an infrastructure of women's centres, women's scholarships, employment equity coordinators, sexual harassment codes, language policies, and affirmative action programs at all levels of university life. A whole range of women's journals speak to the concerns and interests of women scholars, as do professional organizations and conferences that are closed to their male counterparts.

This infrastructure provides young women far more opportunities for professional advancement than are enjoyed by their male competitors. In view of this, it is not surprising to find Andrew Irvine concluding, in his comprehensive survey of statistics on hiring in Canadian universities (published in *Dialogue: The Canadian Philosophical Review*), that

> despite commonly stated assumptions to the contrary, the ... statistics make it clear that claims of significant, sustained, widespread discrimination in hiring against women in Canadian universities remain unsupported by the available data. If anything, the data show exactly the opposite. If discrimination has occurred over the last twenty years, it is much more likely that it has been occurring in favour of, rather than against, women.

An earlier, more limited study (published in *Atlantis: A Women's Study Journal*) that I conducted concluded that it has been the slow rate of turnover in university appointments, not discrimination in hiring, that has produced a slower rise in the number of women faculty than might otherwise be expected.

An open-minded investigation of the matter must leave open the possibility that the persistence of gender differences in some occupations is a reflection of different abilities, aptitudes, and inclinations that characterize males and females (not universally but in general). Certainly, a range of biological differences characterize men and women. There is no easy way to decide how much they should be reflected in career decisions, but the kind of cautious scepticism such a situation calls for is not at all compatible with the assumption that it always makes sense to require that jobs in particular professions be handed out in equal numbers to men and women.

The notion that every occupation should be split 50/50 between the sexes is often defended as a way to introduce a 'feminine' perspective that will allow new and better ways of doing things – ways that are, for example, more caring and less confrontational. This claim is in itself problematic, for it is very debatable whether there *is* a theoretical perspective or orientation that can be said to characterize women as a group.

There is, however, a more basic problem with the argument that we should pursue the 50 per cent solution in order to gain a feminine perspective: it blatantly contradicts the assumption that men and women have the same abilities, attitudes, and inclinations. And this assumption must be the basis of any suggestion that all occupations must be divided 50/50 between the sexes. This assumption suggests that we should not expect women's perspectives to be fundamentally at odds with those of men, and that existing differences in perspective will be a result of different social circumstances – differences the 50 per cent solution aims to eradicate. One cannot have it both ways. Either men and women are the same and we should not expect a special women's point of view or they are different and we should expect the sexes to gravitate towards different occupations. In either case, it is not possible to muster a compelling defence of the 50 per cent solution.

I want to finish by considering a more general question: whether the 50 per cent solution serves women's interests. Those who propose it take this as obvious, but this is because they assume that women's interests are homogenous. Obviously, the 50 per cent solution means that some women who would not otherwise be hired in some professions will be awarded jobs, even with lower qualifications than men who apply for the same jobs. The interests of these women are the interests of particular women, however, and not necessarily the interests of women as a whole.

Things are not so clear if one broadens one's perspective. Even in the case of professions where more women will be hired, it is questionable whether the presence of women who are hired on the basis of gender rather than superior qualifications is the best thing for women as a group. In a growing number of other professions and occupations, the 50 per cent solution suggests that women's opportunities should be curtailed. Women now earn significantly more than 50 per cent of the degrees in the humanities, the social sciences, education, fine and applied arts, and the health professions. So much so that this raises the question whether there is, in some areas, systemic discrimination against men (as one might argue that there are in legal matters of custody and the rearing of children). Proponents of the 50 per cent solution should be arguing that women's opportunities should be curtailed in these areas and professions. Instead, they selectively focus on the areas in which men outnumber women (for example, politics and the physical sciences) and turn a blind eye to those areas in which the numbers suggest that they should oppose the hiring of women.

Those who support the 50 per cent solution argue that the trade-offs this implies are trade-offs that are to the benefit of women – women will lose opportunities in low-status occupations that are traditionally female and gain them in high-status jobs traditionally reserved for men. This is a common prejudice that is open to debate (jobs in medicine education, the social sciences, social work, and the pharmaceutical profession are not low status), but there are problems with the 50 per cent solution even if this is so. For the moral issues raised by the 50 per cent solution make it an extremely objectionable way to attain this goal (especially as milder forms of affirmative action provide an alternative).

More fundamentally, the implicit value judgments such claims imply are objectionable, assuming as they do that traditional views of high- and low-status occupations are correct. If women are different from men, and if they are therefore likely to occupy more than 50 per cent of the positions in a particular profession that has a low status, their interests will be best served, not by artificial measures that forcibly move them to other careers, but by measures that improve the status of occupations they prefer – by making midwifery a recognized profession, by ensuring that women who decide to stay at home are well supported, and so on. To anyone committed to women's interests, the way in which the 50 per cent solution ingrains traditional assumptions about important and unimportant work is yet another reason for thinking it is ill-conceived.

5 'Fixing' What Ain't Broke

GRANT BROWN

Imagine a scenario in which an appointed committee is vested with the power to redistribute body parts so as to equalize opportunities among members of society. If you have two good eyes, for example, you might be required to 'donate' one of them to a blind person. The repugnance of this scenario is appreciated by everyone; yet something similar is afoot in Canadian society, and our universities are leading the way.

Next to our own bodies, nothing so intimately defines us and our place in society as our careers. Many people, especially academics, choose careers that reflect their individual abilities, their unique ambitions, and their personal ideals. Careers also provide a network of social relationships within which most of us live our daily lives.

Because of the central importance of careers, antidiscrimination laws have been in place for several decades. But current employment-equity initiatives typically go far beyond antidiscrimination laws, and indeed contradict them by imposing requirements on employers to redistribute careers according to some preconceived pattern – by, in effect, imposing handicaps on members of a particular biologically defined group. Before being embraced, coercive attempts at social engineering such as this must be scrutinized very closely.

Promoting Equality of Opportunity

'Employment equity' initiatives fall into two quite distinct categories. Policies of one type promote the status of disadvantaged people by empowering them: by providing them with opportunities to upgrade their educational qualifications, by improving their working conditions, and by eliminating whatever unfair discrimination might exist. Examples of policies of this type, in the academic context, include providing student loans and scholarships for economically disadvantaged individuals, making provision for 'stopping the tenure clock' for family-related reasons, and requiring that job searches be conducted broadly and openly. Policies of this type tend to promote equality of opportunity.

In contrast, policies of the second kind promote the (relative) status of disadvantaged people by handicapping others. Most notable among these policies is preferential hiring for members of designated groups. (Preferential hiring policies themselves vary in strength, from modest tie-breaking schemes to policies of not even entertaining applications from candidates who do not belong to a designated group.) The goal of the second type of policy is equality of outcome. Other examples of preferential policies include offering reduced teaching loads (hence greater research opportunities), special research funds, or incentive pay specifically to members of certain groups. Such policies empower members of those groups, but in ways that would be thought unfair in normal contexts.

'Employment equity' policies of the second kind are the controversial ones. The reasons for this are easy to appreciate: equal-opportunity policies broaden the pool of qualified candidates and thereby tend to improve academic quality; equal-outcome policies narrow that pool and thereby tend to degrade academic quality. Equal-opportunity policies take into account the interests of all individuals equally, and thus tend to promote mutual respect; equal-outcome policies discount the interests of certain individuals, and thus tend to be highly divisive. Saying you want to 'equalize opportunities' through preferential hiring is like saying you would give your right arm to be ambidextrous.

Since virtually nobody disputes the validity of equal-opportunity policies, we may frame the controversy over 'employment equity' summarily as follows: Are the undeniable losses in terms of academic quality and opportunity resulting from (redistributive) equal-outcome policies compensated by reasonable demands of social justice? Indeed, are they even compatible with the reasonable demands of justice? My answer is no. In explaining why, I focus on preferential hiring for women, for several reasons. First, hiring is the most salient and important form that preferential policies take. Second, women constitute by far the largest of the four usual target groups. Third, preferential policies for women are more widespread than policies for any other group. And fourth, data on the situation of women is more readily available than for any other group.

In almost all cases where preferential policies have been introduced, they have been defended – mainly, if not entirely – as a means of combating morally unjustified discrimination. Indeed, it is difficult to see how any other justification could be morally weighty enough to 'trump' such fundamental values as procedural fairness and equal rights for all members of a civilized society. Thus it behooves supporters of preferential hiring to demonstrate that systemic discrimination against women within universities is still a problem in need of correction. In fact, several careful studies of hiring practices over the past thirty years or so show that women are represented in university faculties in Canada in the proportions one would expect given their historical availability in the applicant pool. If anything, in fact, women have been hired in proportions in excess of their availability – increasingly so in recent years.

To show that systemic discrimination against women within Canadian universities is a myth, it will be sufficient to note three things: the proportions of faculty positions going to women in recent years; the hiring policies that have been adopted at many institutions in Canada; and claims about the difficulty of recruiting and retaining qualified women due to competition from other universities.

Let's begin with the University of Alberta. There, the proportion of women being hired to tenure-track positions has risen from 28 per cent in 1986 to 37 per cent in 1989 – in each year outstripping the proportion of women earning PhDs by a fair margin. From 1988 to 1990, 53 women were hired from 464 women applicants (11.4 per cent), whereas 117 men were hired from 2,019 applicants (5.8 per cent). Thus a female applicant was twice as likely to be hired as a male applicant. (Assuming that talent is not correlated with sex, the probability of 53 or more women being hired from this pool purely by chance is 1 in 30,000.) In the Faculty of Arts, 29 per cent of the applicants were women while 70 per cent of the jobs (21 out of 30) went to women. That is, women were 5.7 times as likely as men to be hired in the Faculty of Arts. (The probability of this happening by chance is 1 in 450,000.)

Similar results are found at the University of Western Ontario. There, the proportion of women hired was 49 per cent in 1990–1, and 40 per cent in 1991–2. In 1991–2, 37 of 333 female applicants were hired (11 per cent), compared to 56 of 953 male applicants (6 per cent). Again, women were about twice as likely to be hired. At the University of Windsor, approximately 70 per cent of all tenure-track positions from 1988 to 1990 went to women – two-and-a-half times what you would expect given the proportion of women earning PhDs in the relevant period. At the University of Manitoba, 'only' 26 per cent of hires were women in 1988–9, though in the previous two years the numbers were 55 per cent and 33 per cent. The University of Victoria hired 43 per cent women in 1990; the University of British Columbia, 49 per cent in 1990–1; Simon Fraser University, 35 per cent in 1990; and in 1992, 80 per cent of those hired at Concordia were women.

Of course, in many cases the extent of preferential hiring need not be inferred from statistics. Many Canadian universities have express policies that give preference to women, and in many more the practice is informally enforced by the administration even in the absence of an expressed policy. (The University of Alberta is an example of the latter.) Several departments at the University of Victoria, for example, have advertised for female candidates only. St Laurence College has recently followed suit. The Ontario College of Art, Ryerson Polytechnical Institute, and the University of Windsor have set-asides for women only, ranging from 80 to 100 per cent of retirement replacements. This is not even to mention the near-universal commitment to the 'goal' of achieving 'parity' in some ridiculously impractical period of time.

Not Enough Women to Go Around

The only thing preventing most universities in Canada from hiring an even greater disproportion of qualified women is the fact that there are not enough to go around, given the frantic scramble to hire them. (Smaller universities are experiencing an unnatural enrichment in the pool of male candidates, since qualified women tend to accept positions at more prestigious institutions. This makes hiring women especially difficult at smaller institutions.) It is so difficult to deny that women are strongly preferred in hiring these days that it is not even disguised anymore. One contributor to the *Status of Women Supplement* of the *Canadian Association of University Teachers Bulletin* (March 1991) says, 'Although some hiring is being done, departments where women have been chronically scarce are competing with universities and other employers throughout North America for qualified women applicants.' The University of British Columbia *Faculty Association Newsletter* of 1 May 1991 advises that 'applications from outstanding women should receive immediate response to avoid competition from other universities.'

Discrimination against Men

What such observations and recommendations indicate is that qualified women are not going begging for jobs; on the contrary, there are relatively few of them, and competition for them is particularly strong. This should establish once and for all that the putative 'underrepresentation' of women within Canadian universities is not a product of systemic discrimination against women. Indeed the only form of systemic discrimination that is compatible with the observations made here is systemic discrimination against men.

In order genuinely to promote justice, rather than special interests, employment policies would ideally have to identify all and only those individuals who were discriminated against in the past, and favour them in hiring over all and only those individuals who were discriminated in favour of in the past – to the same degree as each was favoured or disfavoured. Granted, we cannot expect any implemented policy completely to meet this ideal; unfortunately, 'employment equity' is such a crude and blunt instrument as to be totally incapable of performing such delicate surgery as is required. In fact, for a number of reasons – I will mention only three here – preferential hiring is bound to create more cases of injustice to individuals than it rectifies.

The first problem with 'employment equity' is that it picks out for preferential treatment groups so vast and heterogeneous that to treat all members of these groups as 'disadvantaged' is naive and simplistic. As many males as females live in poverty in Canada; and as many girls as boys are born into privileged, progressive families. In fact, one striking fact about recent high-school education in Canada is that boys have a much higher dropout rate than girls. In 1990–1, 70.2 per cent of girls in Quebec went on to CEGEP, compared to only 52.9 per cent of boys. This trend has already percolated up to the university level, where a much higher per centage of undergraduate students are women.

What is relevant to determining the success of a policy is its effects at the margin. Presumably the most qualified and most advantaged men and women would secure university teaching jobs whether preferential hiring was widespread or not. Therefore, those men who will be bumped from the job queue because of widespread preferential hiring of women will presumably be the most disadvantaged of the qualified men – those with impoverished backgrounds; homosexual men; short or unattractive men; men from a visible minority or uncommon religious denomination; men whose second language is English (or French); or men who possess whatever other characteristics might lead to disadvantage. Conversely, some of the women who will be bumping (disadvantaged) men from the job queue will be less academically qualified but more privileged women – those who are attractive, middle-class, able-bodied, Anglo-Saxon, and from 'progressive' families. (Some women who are equally capable and equally disadvantaged will also be bumping men from the job queue. The justice of this is at best debatable.) In other words, the most significant net effect of preferential hiring for women will be that relatively privileged women bump relatively underprivileged men from university jobs.

Let us suppose, for the sake of argument, that women have been and continue to be systematically disadvantaged in their pursuit of a university career; and let us suppose further that this problem can and must be addressed at the level of groups rather than individuals, even though both these assumptions are false. Even then, the prevailing means of 'correcting' this situation would not be the most sensible and fair. The disadvantage suffered by women – to the extent there is any – was not created by the current and future classes of male graduates; nor as yet have they benefited from it. Rather, the primary perpetrators and beneficiaries of past systemic discrimination within the universities must be members of that group of men who are now securely tenured. Thus a more sensible and fair policy would be to have tenured men shoulder the bulk of the burden of 'correcting' for perceived past (and present) injustices. Since many securely tenured men so enthusiastically embrace the goal of gender balance, one might suppose that they would eagerly step aside

> 'Saying you want to "equalize opportunities" through preferential hiring is like saying you would give your right arm to be ambidextrous.'

for the sake of women whose positions they evidently believe they have usurped. Alas, this possibility seems entirely to have escaped their notice. Yet it is nothing short of perverse that these men so gallantly impose the sacrifices required by preferential hiring upon young men (and their wives and children), who are not responsible for past discrimination, who have benefited least from it, and who are in the worst position to pay the price to correct for it.

Since I do not believe that the perceived problem of gender imbalance in the universities is genuine, I cannot endorse coercive measures to correct it. I can, nevertheless, recommend certain voluntary measures that tenured male advocates might consider – if they wished to be true to their cause. To begin, tenured men who endorse the goal of 'gender balance' could offer to resign or take early retirement or part-time assignments, on condition that their positions go to qualified women. They could even take one of these options without being assured of this condition, since we have seen that current hiring trends guarantee women a more than fair chance of getting the vacated positions. At the very least, tenured men could offer to open their positions up to competition from women on the same terms as they would impose on male candidates in regular job searches. Finally tenured men could establish and contribute generously to a trust fund, the disbursements from which would go to compensate young men who lose career opportunities due to preferential hiring for women. (A contribution of 10 per cent of salary would not be out of line. The money could be designated to pay off student loans incurred while training for an academic career, or to pay for future retraining, for example.)

Tenured male supporters of preferential hiring do not respond very well to these suggestions. Some have offered as an excuse for not adopting the above measures the belief they could do more good for more women over the remaining course of their careers by staying within the system than they could by giving one woman a job. But this excuse for making no personal sacrifices to achieve their ideals is utterly inadequate. A general policy requiring tenured men to open their positions to women would do more than any individual could hope to achieve by working informally for their cause.

There is a well-worn, undemocratic path to enforced political correctness within Canadian universities. After establishing an administrative office or committee whose ostensive purpose is to gather information about the status of various target groups within the university, the task quickly shifts, without further discussion, to the promotion and enforcement of predetermined partisan policies. Typically, a network of activist-insiders infiltrates key positions in the administration, faculty association, or other authoritative bodies. (This is easily achieved: most of the genuinely productive members of the academic community cannot be bothered to consume themselves with the politics of university life; often rightly, they think they have more important work to do.) The activists then develop initiatives and spring them on an unsuspecting community of academics as a *fait accompli*. Official publications and forums are deemed to be the exclusive preserve of the holders of power. Those who do manage to express opposition are shouted down as racists, sexists, and homophobes; more extreme means of intimidation are also sometimes used to silence them.

It is past time for serious academics to demand an end to the self-serving propagandizing of the special interests within the academy, to demand the dismantling of their separate fiefdoms, and to demand that they get on with the real business of the university: the pursuit of knowledge.

6 It's Affirmative Action, and It's Bad for Universities and Students

GRAEME HUNTER

Should Canadians come first in university hiring? 'Of course!' you may say. But is it really so obvious? Well, obvious or not, it's the law.

Before a university can hire a professor from another country, Citizenship and Immigration Canada requires a demonstration that no qualified Canadian is available for the position. Normally a university can satisfy this requirement only by a multistep process. First it must announce a competition for which Canadians alone are eligible. If any Canadian applicant is found adequate (they don't have to be superstars), then he or she must be hired ahead of any foreign candidate no matter how brilliant. It is only if no satisfactory Canadian is available that a new competition may be opened in which foreigners can compete as equals with Canadians. By that time, however, any attractive foreign star the university may have been hoping to snare will be happily employed elsewhere and the long-deferred second competition will be reduced to a shot in the dark. The 'Canadians first' policy therefore means that inefficiencies occur. But it also creates real injustice, not only towards foreign applicants, but also to local students and faculty, who in some cases can be stuck for decades with teachers and colleagues who were less than the best available, but who happened to be Canadian.

Are university teachers and administrators then unanimous in opposing such government intrusion on their autonomy? Apparently not. The *Ottawa Citizen* reports that teachers strongly support the 'Canadians first' rule and oppose a movement among some university administrations to change it.

Perhaps, but I try to have a better opinion of my fellow professors than that.

To me the policy appears so clearly defective, that I should be surprised if many professors support it. For one thing, putting Canadians first is a kind of 'affirmative action.' That term is a sweet name for a foul reality. What 'affirmative action' really means is giving preference to candidates based on their race or sex or, in the case here under discussion, their country of origin. These are matters that candidates can do nothing to change and that normally do not enhance their performance in the university posts for which they are being considered. To hire people on the basis of such pseudo-qualifications is thus to outrage principles of fairness and merit, to which any self-respecting university ought to be committed. But this point is so obvious in itself and has been made so frequently and well, that affirmative action is rarely given public support today, except by those people whose livelihood depends on portraying themselves and others as victims. That is why the most outspoken opponents of affirmative action come from within the very groups that affirmative action laws attempt to favour. Which ought to surprise no one.

> *'Equipped with his degree, the scholar needed no other passport in order to teach at any university in the world. Thus universities were among the first places to rise above the angry divisions of race and xenophobia and to conceive of a world in which all could be fairly treated, because all acknowledged a common standard of excellence and a common love of truth.'*

Most people wish to be taken seriously at work for what they do well, not as tokens of some race, sex, or nationality. Indeed, the single greatest moral failing of Canadian universities today is that almost all of them have formal and binding commitments to one or more kinds of affirmative action. Fortunately, many ordinary Canadians oppose affirmative action when it concerns race and sex. If they are consistent, they should also oppose its nationalistic version.

But the 'Canadians first' affirmative action law also clashes with a noble and longstanding tradition of universities, one that stretches all the way back to their origins in the Middle Ages. At that time the university's most advanced degree (now called a doctorate) was proudly and simply described as a *venia legendi*, meaning 'permission to teach.' Equipped with his degree, the scholar needed no other passport in order to teach at any university in the world. Thus universities were among the first places to rise above the angry divisions of race and xenophobia and to conceive of a world in which all could be fairly treated, because all acknowledged a common standard of excellence and a common love of truth.

To put 'Canadians first' in hiring moves in the opposite direction. We took a false step in creating this law some years ago. Now it is time to bury it and move on.

7 The Curious Case of Country C

GRANT BROWN

Injustice is ubiquitous in this world. Heaven knows there is enough of it in Canada that we do not have to look abroad to fill newspapers with alarming stories of discrimination and oppression. Still, we might learn something about how a blind eye is turned to injustice by considering the case of a relatively minor country – call it Country C – which, amazingly, ranks favourably in United Nations reports.

Country C contains two groups, the majority Xs and the minority Ys. In spite of what the UN says, the standard social indicators suggest that the Ys are an oppressed minority. Among other things, oppressed people tend to experience poorer health, more violent victimization and aggression, discrimination in the administration of justice and in employment, and disadvantage in educational attainment. The following is a brief indication how the Ys fare in these respects, relative to the Xs.

The infant-mortality rate among Ys is higher than that among Xs. Ys are also more prone to alcoholism, drug abuse, and a host of psychological problems. Adding insult to injury, a highly disproportionate amount of public health-care money is spent on Xs. About twice as much medical-research money is spent on illnesses experienced almost exclusively by Xs, than on those experienced almost exclusively by Ys. In the final analysis, the life expectancy of Xs is five years longer than that of Ys.

In Country C, Ys are a particularly brutalized group. Most violence committed by Ys is directed at Ys themselves; whereas most violence committed by Xs is also directed at Ys. Overall, Ys are twice as likely to be victims of violence and three times as likely to be murdered, compared to Xs. Yet the mainstream media of Country C devote a hugely disproportionate amount of their coverage to the violent victimization of Xs, especially by Ys. Government commissions have been set up to look into the problem of violence against Xs, but not into the much larger problem of violence against Ys.

Ys are about nine times more likely than Xs to spend time in prison. Besides the harsher social conditions that tend to make violence a part of the Y culture, this difference is due in part to the fact that the law in Country C treats violent Xs differently from violent Ys. Ys are more likely than Xs to be investigated, charged, and convicted for similar crimes on similar evidence; Xs are more likely to be believed innocent, given favourable plea bargains, and awarded probation – even when participating together in the same crime with Ys. In violent conflicts between Xs and Ys, it is standard police procedure to haul the Ys off to jail even before establishing who was at fault or who was the aggressor. Perhaps most alarmingly of all, the law of Country C recognizes several excuses for Xs to kill Ys, with no parallels for Ys who kill Xs. In a large number of cases, Xs who kill Ys serve no time at all in prison.

Although a minority of the general population, Ys account for about 85 per cent of the homeless adults in Country C. It has been estimated that as many as half of these street people have been displaced from their homes by angry or violent Xs. Public money is spent on subsidized housing and shelters for needy Xs, much of it to the exclusion of equally needy Ys. (Public housing for Ys takes the form of jail cells.)

The education system, although officially integrated, nevertheless systematically favours the Xs. Especially in the early grades, when lifelong attitudes towards scholastic achievement are formed, the distinctive needs and interests of Ys are ignored or trampled on. Few Ys have teacher training at the primary level, leaving young Ys without positive role models. As a result, the grades attained by Xs are, on average, higher than those attained by Ys throughout their school years; and Ys also have higher failure and dropout rates than Xs at every level from primary school to university. In

'Among other things, oppressed people tend to experience poorer health, more violent victimization and aggression, discrimination in the administration of justice and in employment, and disadvantage in educational attainment.'

spite of this, attempts to ameliorate the educational disadvantages of the Ys by running Y-only schools staffed by Y teachers are deemed to be unconstitutional in Country C – though X-only schools and programs are permitted and even encouraged. Many millions of dollars of public money are spent on scholarships and other inducements aimed exclusively at increasing the participation rate of Xs at the country's universities, even though the participation rate of Xs is already significantly higher than that of Ys.

One academic study reported that if current educational trends continue, Ys will be completely eliminated from the job market by the year

2050. Meanwhile, Xs continue to enjoy legislated employment preferences and benefits in Country C, ranging from giving the position or promotion to an X whenever there is an approximate tie, to excluding Ys from even applying for certain important public-sector jobs. Manual labour and high-risk jobs remain the preserve of Ys. (Over 95 per cent of occupational deaths occur to Ys.) Not surprisingly, then, Ys own a disproportionately small share of the private wealth in Country C.

X-ists, who dominate media discussions of these issues in Country C, account for this array of facts by maintaining that Xs are innately superior to Ys – physically, morally, and intellectually. X-supremacist groups, supported mainly by public funds, claim that Xs are naturally more suited to govern, in both the public and the private sector, and openly yearn for a world ruled by Xs. Ys who dare to complain about the inequities in their society are trotted out as proof of the snivelling, inferior nature of Ys. The hate-mongering laws that exist in Country C do not proscribe hate mongering directed at Ys.

Perhaps you are wondering how such a deeply racist country as this could have fooled the United Nations for so long. A very good question – except that X and Y represent chromosomes, not races.

PART VIII

Life and Death

1 Taking the Prime Minister at His Word

GRAEME HUNTER

Not all of former Prime Minister Chrétien's pronouncements were happy ones. During his time in office there were even some rumours that he was losing his grip. And yet when he was in China he said two things exactly as they needed to be said. He told the Chinese in careful but unambiguous terms that they are wrong to tread so callously on what we in the West call 'human rights.' And he responded perfectly to the predictable reply from someone who may have been a student, but who was more likely a plant. She said that they understand human rights differently in China. 'That's your right,' replied the PM. 'Just let the debate begin.' Chrétien was not being a bull in a China shop, or an ugly Canadian abroad. He was not seeking to impose his own 'values' on a sovereign country. He was after something noble: to open up the free trade in opinions, in a free market of ideas.

The prime minister made it clear how insignificant it is for a country to tolerate those with whom it agrees. Everyone does that. Toleration only becomes meaningful when it is extended to those with whom one disagrees. Anyone who has read John Stuart Mill's famous essay *On Liberty* knows that we do well to tolerate those with whom we disagree. If we are right and they are wrong, they will eventually be refuted and their ideas forgotten. If, on the other hand, they are right and we are wrong, then by not suppressing them we have given ourselves that most valuable of gifts: a corrective for our errors. Wise people pray for their country as the *Book of Common Prayer* prays for the church: where she is in error, correct her; where she is right, strengthen her.

Chrétien's exhortation in no way loses its worth and importance if it also has application at home. That is fortunate, because it does apply here. Of course, no informed person would compare the magnitude of the abuses in China with those in Canada. No Canadian could fail to rejoice in the heritage of freedom that is our legacy from past generations. But that legacy is threatened in Canada in a way that Chrétien abroad seems not even to suspect. Is there some way that identical abuses can be obvious in China but invisible here? I think exactly that can happen. Here is how.

Chrétien called on Chinese officials to tolerate even those who advocate fundamental changes to China's system of government. To our prime minister, such a request seems eminently reasonable. After all, he tolerated, without necessarily liking, the NDP to his left, the Reform to his right, and, perhaps more easily, the minuscule band of Conservatives at his elbow. Why can't the Chinese do the same? Well, the answer is that the Chinese do precisely the same. They tolerate within the party those who want to go a little faster and those who want to go a little slower on the path they are going. What they do not tolerate are those who put the path itself in question. In Canada we have a better record with real dissent, but it is not unblemished. Let me take one case in point.

'Toleration only becomes meaningful when it is extended to those with whom one disagrees ... If we are right and they are wrong, they will eventually be refuted and their ideas forgotten. If, on the other hand, they are right and we are wrong, then by not suppressing them we have given ourselves that most valuable of gifts: a corrective for our errors.'

Linda Gibbons is a harmless grandmother who nevertheless has spent the best part of the last four years in maximum-security prisons for women in Ontario. How can that be? It is because she prays. You will say that prayer is not yet an offence in Canada. But it is in some locations within this country. She prays outside the Scott Abortion Clinic in Toronto. She does not molest those who go in and out on their lawful business. She prays for them. She prays especially for the little ones who go in but do not come out. During the reign of the NDP in Ontario such actions were declared illegal, however, and a so-called 'bubble zone' was brought into existence within which every form of protest was illegal. The Conservatives, then in opposition, declared this monstrous, but they lifted not a finger to repeal or oppose the policy throughout their mandate. Still, some will say, a law is a law and if she breaks it, she can hardly complain if she is charged. As those on the wrong side of the bars put it, 'If you can't do the time, don't do the crime.'

In reality, however, although Linda Gibbons would love to be charged with the 'crime' she is committing, her accusers are always careful to charge her with something else: obstructing justice being the favourite. For if they were to charge her with the 'crime' of violating the bubble zone, the bubble zone would itself come under judicial scrutiny, and she would have the opportunity to challenge the constitutionality of the legislation. Her accusers fear their bubble might burst during such a test.

Why do we in Canada permit an unjust law to be enforced against a just person, depriving her first of the right to peaceful protest and then, by imprisonment, depriving her of all her rights at once? We permit this because Linda Gibbons, and people like her, challenge the path this country is taking far more than do any of our political parties. We are moving towards what Pope John Paul II has called a culture of death; she calls us back to a culture of life. We are rejecting the religions and traditions out of which we came; she is pleading with us not to be so hasty.

Many disagree with her. That is well and good. But we do not confront her fairly either in our media or in our courts. We hide her bodily in prison, and her views are hidden just as effectively by media silence. We are like the student-plant Chrétien confronted recently in Peking. When challenged, we think it enough to point out that we understand human rights differently. Oh that Mr Chrétien would intervene here with the fine words he used abroad: 'Well and good. Let the debate begin!'

2 Abortion and the Moral Standing of the Fetus

THOMAS HURKA

As in other countries, the abortion debate continues to rage in Canada. But it still generates little light, marked as it is by dishonesty on one side and arrogance on the other.

The central issue in the abortion debate is what philosophers call the 'moral standing' of the fetus. Does the fetus have the same moral standing as an adult? If so, is it wrong to kill it whenever it would be wrong to kill an adult? Or does it have less or no standing?

Pro-choice presentations are dishonest because they don't state or properly argue for a position on this issue. They concentrate on the right of the woman to control her body or to exercise reproductive freedom.

All can agree that women have these rights, but like others, they are limited by any stronger rights in other beings with standing. If abortion involves killing a fetus, and a fetus has full moral standing, its right to life outweighs any rights of the woman.

Equally dishonest is the argument that abortion, though a difficult issue, is one each woman must decide on her own. This would be reasonable if abortion involved only a woman herself. But if it affects another being with standing, especially if it kills that being, it is just the kind of act our laws should prohibit.

The pro-life side doesn't ignore the issue of the fetus's standing. On the contrary, it makes it the centrepiece of its position. But it is arrogant in assuming this is a simple issue to which it has a simple solution.

Most pro-lifers aren't vegetarians. They don't think it always wrong to kill an animal, and wouldn't hesitate to do so to protect an adult human from even moderate harm. Like most of us, they think adult humans have greater moral standing than animals.

Why do adult humans have greater standing than animals? It can't just be because they're humans. That would be 'speciesism,' like saying whites count more than orientals just because they're whites. If humans have more standing than animals, they must have special properties that give them this standing.

Secular moralists agree what sort of properties these are. Some cite rationality, some uniquely rich enjoyments, some free choice, but all base adult humans' greater standing in some aspect of their unique mental life.

This is relevant to the abortion debate. The simplest way to argue that fetuses have the same standing as adults is to say they actually have the properties that give adults that standing. But fetuses don't yet have rationality or rich enjoyments. If we look at their actual properties, these seem morally indistinguishable from those of animals.

In his challenge to Canada's old abortion law, Joe Borowski based his argument on the fetus's actual properties. His witnesses testified, for example, that a fetus produces its own blood and moves away from a needle. But animals too produce blood and avoid needles. How can you show that a fetus has more standing than animals by pointing to properties it shares with animals?

> 'Why do adult humans have greater standing than animals? It can't just be because they're humans. That would be "speciesism," like saying whites count more than orientals just because they're whites.'

The alternative is to argue for the fetus's standing on the basis of its potential. The fetus doesn't now have rationality or rich enjoyments, but unlike any animal, it has the potential to develop into a being that does.

This argument also has difficulties. If the fetus has the potential for special properties, why doesn't this give it just the potential for standing, rather than actual standing now? And if the fetus has the potential to develop into a being with a mental life, isn't the same true of an unfertilized sperm and egg? Yet does anyone think contraception is morally equivalent to murder?

The pro-life argument faces a dilemma. If we look at the fetus's actual properties, it seems morally indistinguishable from animals. If we look at its potential, it seems indistinguishable from unfertilized cells.

This dilemma may be partly avoidable. There may be different meanings of 'potential,' so that a twenty-eight-week fetus has the potential for mental life in a more significant sense than unfertilized cells, one that confers moral standing where the other doesn't. On reflection, this has to be so. A two-week baby doesn't, any more than a fetus, actually have rationality or rich enjoyments. Yet only an extreme view thinks it in principle permissible to kill babies. If babies have full standing, this must rest on their potential, which must differ from that of mere cells.

This seems the one route to a defensible view about the fetus. But if there are two kinds of potential, one conferring moral standing while the other doesn't, when does the first, more significant, potential appear?

The answer depends on what defines the first potential, which is a difficult philosophical (not medical) issue. But it is unlikely to appear at conception. The relevant potential is for a rich mental life, and differs from the potential of cells. This suggests that it requires the actual presence of the brain structures that will later ground a mental life. These brain structures develop during the second trimester of pregnancy but are not present before.

We seem led, then, to a moderate position on abortion, one permitting it early in pregnancy but not later on. When the Canadian government proposed legislation reflecting this position, its draft was attacked as a cynical compromise between two principled views. This assumes that to be principled, moral beliefs must be simple, which is false. If we think seriously about abortion, without dishonestly ignoring the fetus or arrogantly assuming its standing, we may be led to a principled justification of the politically most acceptable view.

3 Does Surrogate Motherhood Turn People into Commodities?

THOMAS HURKA

A young woman contracts to be a surrogate mother for an infertile couple. In return for $10,000 she'll be impregnated with the husband's sperm and, after bearing a child, will surrender it to them. Is this a perversion of the birth process that should be illegal?

Much is troubling about surrogacy as practised today. It enriches lawyers, whose fees for arranging it are often higher than the birth mother's. Many women who volunteer have troubled backgrounds; motivated by feelings of inadequacy or guilt about a past abortion, they're easy prey for exploitation. After giving birth, many surrogates want to keep their babies and, when they can't, suffer considerable grief.

Regulation could minimize these problems. Surrogacies could be arranged by a non-profit state agency that screened volunteers to ensure they made rational, autonomous choices; it could also set fair fees. The surrogacy contract could even allow women to keep their babies if they wanted. (They would then forfeit their fee.)

But these changes leave untouched what, for many, is the main objection to surrogacy: that it treats children, and women's labour in bearing them, as commodities, as things to be bought and sold in the market. As American philosopher Elizabeth Anderson says, it reduces 'children to consumer durables and women to baby factories.'

Statements of this objection often appeal to a moral principle proposed by the German philosopher Immanuel Kant: treat humanity 'always as an end and never as a means only,' or treat people always as beings owed moral respect rather than just using them for your own purposes.

Witness a British committee of inquiry that said surrogacy should be illegal because it's objectionable for some people to 'treat others as means to their own ends.' The committee was thinking mainly of the couple's treatment of the surrogate, but others argue that the mother treats the baby as a means – a means of making money.

These claims are too simple, though. What Kant's principle forbids isn't treating people as means but treating them *only* as means – that is, not also as ends in themselves.

In daily life we often treat people as means. At the bank we use tellers to cash cheques and make deposits. At the movies the ticket seller is a means to admittance. None of this is wrong if we also treat these people as ends, as beings with moral standing. This happens if they benefit from interacting with us, as they do if they're paid enough and freely choose to interact.

So the question about surrogacy must be whether it treats ends *only* as means. Let's start with the couple's treatment of the surrogate. In present conditions this can violate Kant's principle. The couple, not wanting a surrogate who will change her mind, can select a woman who will be easy to manipulate and then, through their lawyer, apply pressure on her. But with proper regulation this wouldn't happen. The couple would know, from the agency, that the woman had chosen surrogacy freely, and would allow her to keep the child if surrendering it proved traumatic.

> *'Surrogacy is different from traditional ways of giving birth, but this doesn't mean it is wrong. We have to evaluate it using our best moral principles.'*

What about the mother's treatment of the child? It's morally acceptable so long as she cares in part about the child's interests – for example, about finding it a good home. This, too, the agency can handle. By screening adoptive couples, it can ensure surrogates that their children will start life well.

Some may say that Kant's principle is too weak for the mother–child relationship; babies (though not adults) must be treated only as ends and never as means. This goes too far. In the Third World, many couples have children as an economic investment; in our culture, companionship and support in old age are common motives. They're perfectly acceptable if, once the child is born, he or she is treated as a being owed moral respect.

There are circumstances where surrogacy could be harmful. If treating mothers and babies partly as means led us, psychologically, to view them only as means, it would be best to forbid it by law. Something like this has happened with blood donation. In Canada, blood can't be sold and the level of voluntary giving is high. The United States allows a market for blood – university students can earn money by selling plasma twice a week – and giving is much less common. That blood donation can be viewed as a means to money results in fewer choosing it for itself.

But surrogacy is unlikely to have a similar effect on childbearing. Whereas the impulse to give is fragile in humans, love of children is biologically based and strong – too strong to be displaced by a small amount of surrogacy here and there in society.

Surrogacy is different from traditional ways of giving birth, but this doesn't mean it is wrong. We have to evaluate it using our best moral principles. What these show is that surrogacy isn't wrong in principle and can be (though it isn't now) acceptable in practice.

4 Are Feminists Really Pro-Choice?

THOMAS HURKA

If Canada's feminists were really pro-choice, they wouldn't be choosy about the choices they want to protect. They'd trust and respect women always, not just when they're making choices about abortions.

Most feminists assume that a fetus has no moral standing, so the only person directly affected by a decision about abortion is the woman. And they think the woman should be allowed to make this decision herself. She should be legally entitled to an abortion whatever her reason for wanting it.

One possible justification for this stand is that a woman is the best judge of her interests. She knows more about herself and her situation than any doctor or bureaucrat and can make a wiser decision. A different justification is that, even if she isn't the best judge, it's her life and she's entitled to make choices about it.

But these justifications are hard to reconcile with other feminist stands. In a brief to the Royal Commission on New Reproductive Technologies, the National Action Committee on the Status of Women (NAC) called for a moratorium on opening new in vitro fertilization clinics. It argued that in vitro fertilization is bad for women: it has a low success rate and can have dangerous side effects. But if women are wise enough or entitled to judge their own interests in abortion cases, why not also here?

Using in vitro fertilization can have far-reaching consequences, but so can a choice about abortion. A woman who has an abortion can feel remorse in later years. A young woman who does not have an abortion can drop out of high school, go on welfare, and limit her opportunities for the rest of her life. Yet NAC opposes even the mild interference with these women's freedom of requiring them to get counselling before they make their choices. (The call for counselling usually comes from pro-life groups, but there could just as well be feminist counselling.)

The brief to the Royal Commission also opposed surrogate motherhood, which NAC wants to see banned. But what if a woman freely chooses to be a surrogate, in return for a reasonable fee? If all abortion decisions are voluntary, surely this decision can sometimes be voluntary. Feminists would presumably likewise oppose any proposal to legalize polygamy. But if a woman chooses to enter a polygamous marriage, shouldn't her choice deserve respect?

Some feminists recognize these tensions and try to separate a woman's choice about abortion from these other choices. The first, they say, is genuinely private, affecting only the woman herself; the others have a larger public aspect.

This is hard to argue for in the case of in vitro fertilization, but it may be plausible for surrogate motherhood and polygamy. To legalize these practices, it may be said, is to reinforce social perceptions of women as inferior and as tied to breeding and to compound the harms these perceptions do. But this is a dangerous argument.

To believe in choice is to believe that people should be allowed to make decisions about their own lives, and this requires drawing a strict boundary around their lives. It disallows such arguments as the one that says abortion isn't a private choice because a woman having an abortion sets a bad example for other women. Nor does it allow arguments about remote or indirect effects on society. Allow these, and nothing counts as a private choice.

'To believe in choice is to believe that people should be allowed to make decisions about their own lives, and this requires drawing a strict boundary around their lives. It disallows such arguments as the one that says abortion isn't a private choice because a woman having an abortion sets a bad example for other women.'

As always, we have to ask of a feminist argument: Would its proponents accept a similar argument about abortion?

Let's go back to the young woman who drops out of high school to have a baby. She, too, sets a bad example for others – the more women who choose to limit their opportunities, the more normal their choice looks and the more women will follow their path. And she contributes to a social perception of women as tied to breeding. If effects like these are reasons for banning surrogacy and polygamy, why not also for interfering with her choice to have her baby? Or if her choice must be utterly unrestricted, why not other choices too?

Canada's feminists face their own choice: either they trust and respect women, in which case they should honour women's choices consistently; or they think women need protection and coddling at the hands of Big Sister.

5 A Rose Is a Rose, but Clones Will Differ

JOHN RUSSELL AND ANDREW IRVINE

What, if anything, should be done about human cloning? Should in vitro fertilization clinics, which are reportedly scrambling to develop new cloning technologies, be legislated out of the human cloning business? Predictably, the issue has led to much public hand-wringing and opposition. According to some, we are on the brink of a Brave New World, with armies of Deltas and Epsilons in the offing.

Although such instinctual anxieties about the nature and moral dangers of cloning are natural, they are often the product of misinformed but deeply acculturated fears about science, and about the usurping of divine prerogatives. But man has been playing God since long before he invented the plough, and there is little more to fear from the latest scientific advances concerning cloning than from in vitro fertilization itself, at least in theory. Once we remove the distorting cultural lens through which this issue is often viewed, the moral issues raised by cloning are, if anything, surprisingly ordinary and tractable.

To begin, it is a mistake to equate cloning with divine acts of creation. Unlike Adam, a clone has a real genetic mother and father, just like everyone else. It just happens that these parents are also the genetic mother and father of the donor of the genetic material, the clone's previously born twin.

Normally, this genetic twin sister or brother will function as one of a clone's parents. But there is nothing especially odd about being parented by one's older sister or brother. This happens often enough when genetic mothers and fathers die or abandon their children. And of course there is nothing morally objectionable about the mere existence of identical twins. Being parented by one's twin has a certain novelty about it. But by itself it does not challenge any deep moral or cultural norms.

What may be more problematic is that cloning permits human beings to create themselves in their own image. If not sacrilegious, such hubris on the part of man may be said to be troubling for other reasons.

Here, though, the answer is that those who aim to re-create themselves are bound to be disappointed. The very idea that they might do so rests on an error called 'the fallacy of genetic determinism.' This is the mistake of supposing that all characteristics of a living thing are fully determined by its genes. In the case of cloning, this idea is reflected in the belief that a clone's personality and physical appearance will be completely predetermined by the genetic material of the donor.

But it is an axiom of biology that the characteristics of a living thing are not determined solely by its genes. Its environment, from the non-genetic chemicals in each of its cells to the world around it, plays a fundamental role too. As a result, genetically identical beings raised under environmentally distinct conditions are bound to have many different characteristics.

A simple example proves this. All varieties of commercially reproduced roses are exact genetic copies. But we all know that the genetically identical roses in our gardens look and behave quite differently from those in Martha Stewart's garden. Such differences are due to environment. Martha, we assume, is simply a better gardener than we are. And her garden is a better place for roses. Of course, human clones will likely display even more striking differences than do roses. To see this, consider the (still) hypothetical example of baby boomers and their clones.

'Being parented by one's twin has a certain novelty about it. But by itself it does not challenge any deep moral or cultural norms.'

Boomers were raised in an environment before fast food. Their parents read Dr Spock and, as children, they had sports heroes like Gordie Howe, Bobby Orr, and Sandy Koufax. Entertainment was two channels on the TV and board games like Monopoly and Scrabble. They were also lucky enough to arrive at university post-pill but pre-AIDS.

In contrast, the boomers' clones will have to wade through the culture of McDonald's, Dennis Rodman, and Latrell Sprewell. They will have to negotiate five hundred TV channels and countless computer games. And of course their parents will have different views about raising children. They will have read Penelope Leach.

It would be a genuine miracle, then, if the boomers' clones turned out to resemble them identically in personality. Even physical appearances may differ significantly.

It must also not be forgotten that clones will have moral and legal rights. Like anyone else, they will have the right to live their lives as they see fit. And of course the choice of one's life plan nearly always has more to do with acts of fate – a chance meeting or an inspiring teacher – than with our genes.

Barely a moment of reflection, then, shows that cloning for the purpose of securing a facsimile of oneself cannot be taken seriously. A Brave New World, it seems, is a non-starter – scientifically, morally, and legally. If so, the idea affords no basis for the prohibition of cloning.

But perhaps, in a perverse way, the very misconceptions about clones warrant their suppression. For example, Tiger Woods's clone might be forced to live life with the expectation that he too will win the Masters at least four times. Or maybe Bill Clinton's clones will be presumed to be unfaithful womanizers.

These are real and potentially oppressive problems. But they are problems with which we are, in a sense, fully familiar. They again reflect society's failure to understand the fallacy of genetic determinism. Here again the proper response should primarily be one of public education. We can be optimistic, too, about its effectiveness. As we have seen, the basic fallacy is simply explained. And of course, supporting empirical evidence is bound to accrue.

More importantly, there is hardly a more repellent idea than preventing people from being born simply because they will suffer misinformed expectations or social prejudice. On this basis, we would undoubtedly have to say that until recently, blacks in the southern United States should have been prevented from having children. Indeed, the prejudicial attitudes and expectations they faced (and perhaps still face) have been more unfair and burdensome than anything a human clone would likely encounter today.

Another proposal would prohibit cloning until it has been shown that clones will not be born with serious defects. Here there is indeed appropriate room for caution. It would be foolish – to say the least – to proceed until science makes it likely that cloning could occur without significant risk. And this is something that has not yet been done.

But the state does not normally enforce such reproductive decisions on adults in other circumstances. This is so even for those who are at serious risk of producing medically defective offspring. Why should the state treat cloning differently? Given the research protocols that are already in place for scientific research concerning human subjects, and given that once cloning is available any risks associated with it are bound to diminish, there is little new in this type of objection. In the short term, such worries may rightly prove to be decisive; in theory, however, it may well be possible to overcome them.

Cloning humans eventually may have a legitimate place in the reproductive choices available to parents. When one member of a couple is infertile or carries a seriously harmful genetic trait, cloning may be a legitimate, compassionate option. This is true especially if it can be proved that its safety compares favourably with that of alternatives. To reject it outright is to give in to cultural prejudice or bad biology, or both.

Finally, it is worth noting that this defence of human cloning is morally neither novel nor revolutionary. It is itself based on a deeply rooted value. That value asserts that the primary moral issue in reproduction does not concern the origin of the genetic material of offspring. It concerns the responsibility of parents and their communities to make a loving, properly nurturing environment for their children. And there is no compelling reason to think that such an environment cannot be provided for human clones.

6 Human Stem Cell Cloning

ARTHUR SCHAFER

In 2004, legislation was proclaimed that banned all forms of human cloning in Canada. This means that the use of cloning as a reproductive technology is now a criminal offence. Unfortunately, it also means that the therapeutic cloning of human embryos for medical research or for the treatment of disease is banned.

No one is likely to lament the Canadian ban on cloning as a tool for making babies. Most advanced nations have imposed a similar legal prohibition. As a reproductive technology, cloning is so dramatically unsafe for babies (at present) that no loving parent would dream of trying to use it; and even if an infertile couple were so foolish or wrong-headed as to request it, no ethical physician would participate in the project. A regulatory prohibition would, however, have been preferable to a criminal ban. Criminal law tends to be highly inflexible and is difficult to change when circumstances (such as the safety of the technology) change over time.

'Therapeutic human embryonic stem cell cloning holds out the promise of a medical breakthrough in the treatment of many terrible degenerative diseases, including diabetes, Alzheimer's, heart disease, and stroke ... So why has Canada (along with the United States) banned these procedures?'

There is consensus, then, that human reproductive cloning is A Bad Thing, at least at present. On the other hand, therapeutic human embryonic stem cell cloning holds out the promise of a medical breakthrough in the treatment of many terrible degenerative diseases, including diabetes, Alzheimer's, heart disease, and stroke. The potential benefit to patients and to their families is immense. Canadians recognize this, and polls consistently show a 75 per cent level of support for therapeutic cloning.

Stem cell research may also, in the more distant future, enable doctors to grow a supply of transplantable organs and tissues from embryonic stem cells which have been specially tweaked so that they exactly match a patient's own immune system. This could introduce the dawn of a new kind of medicine: regenerative medicine.

Some caution and scepticism are needed. The technology may not ultimately succeed or may turn out to have dangerous side effects. The isolation and cloning of stem cells is so recent that no one can as yet be confident of its therapeutic utility. Early experimental results are promising, but potential problems lie ahead. For example, once cell growth is turned on, it may be difficult to turn it off. Cells that cannot be turned off could destroy the health or life of the patient into whose body they have been introduced. Even if the technology works, it will be many years before it is proven safe and effective.

There is also legitimate concern on the part of many feminists, who worry that the supply of human eggs required for this technology to work will place unfair burdens on women. When women volunteer to take powerful hormones that induce superovulation – an essential part of the procedure to generate an adequate supply of human ova – the volunteers are exposed to health risks. These risks include the possibility that egg donors will suffer, later in life, from higher rates of cancer. Since women in our culture are often the victims of social and family pressure, and since many are also victims of poverty, there is a danger that their 'voluntary informed consent' as egg donors may not be as voluntary, or as informed, as medical ethics requires.

Proponents of therapeutic cloning typically acknowledge these problems, but reply that it would be better to introduce stringent safeguards against the exploitation of egg donors than to lose the immense benefits to humankind that could be achieved if the technology works.

In 2004, Britain's Human Fertilisation and Embryology Authority (HFEA) gave its approval to a team of Newcastle researchers who propose to clone early human embryos. They are aiming to create insulin-producing cells that could be transplanted into diabetic patients. In February 2005, a second licence for therapeutic cloning was issued, this time to Ian Wilmut, leader of the team that created Dolly the sheep. Wilmut and his colleagues were issued a human cloning licence so that they could investigate the genetic causes of and potential cures for motor neuron disease. They plan to clone cells from patients with muscle-wasting illnesses such as Lou Gehrig's disease, harvest stem cells from the resulting embryos, make them develop into nerve cells, and then compare their defective genes with genes derived from healthy embryos.

This kind of cloning (for research and therapy), though now banned in Canada, has been made legal in Britain and a number of other countries, including Sweden, Japan, Belgium, and China. (In the United States, cloning projects are permitted so long as no federal government money is used.)

So why has Canada banned these procedures?

There is a powerful religious lobby that considers a human embryo to be the moral equivalent of a person. Since the extraction of stem cells from the cloned human embryo results in its destruction, they see this as killing a human being. Especially in the United States, anti-abortion campaigners have persuaded the federal government to withhold all federal funds from any organization conducting embryonic stem cell research. Critics argue that as a morally preferable alternative, adult stem cells should be harvested instead of embryonic stem cells.

Research is continuing on the potential benefits of employing adult stem cells, such as those present in bone marrow. If it turns out that adult stem cells work as well as embryonic stem cells, then that would be the preferred option and ethical controversy would diminish. At present, however, many scientists believe that embryonic stem cells will offer therapeutic benefits not available from adult stem cells, and they want to continue their research full steam ahead.

Proponents of embryonic stem cell research reply to their critics that stem cells are extracted from the embryo when it is nothing more than a microscopic blob. The early-stage human embryo (called a blastocyst) is not a person, they insist, since personhood requires a functioning brain and nervous system. Indeed, since the blastocyst could still divide into twins or triplets, it cannot even be said to be an individual being.

Even some opponents of embryonic stem cell research concede that it has enormous potential to benefit humankind. They tend to argue, however, that no matter how great the potential benefits may be, we ought to reject the technology because it is inherently wrong and against the will of God. As well, critics often invoke the slippery slope argument: if we develop and improve the technology of cloning human embryos for purposes of research and therapy, there will be scientists who misuse the technology for the purposes of human reproduction. That is, some evil Dr Frankenstein will take the cloned human embryos and instead of extracting stem cells from them when they are a few days old, will allow the embryos to continue their development until they can be implanted into a woman's womb, leading to the birth of a human clone.

Defenders of embryonic stem cell cloning reply that religious dogma should not be allowed to perpetuate avoidable human suffering and death. And they reject the claim that we are on a slippery slope towards cloning as a way of making babies.

Virtually all governments have now passed strong legislation prohibiting the use of cloning to make babies – because it poses completely unacceptable health risks to mothers and babies. But moral life requires that we make distinctions. There is a world of difference between putting at risk the health of mothers and babies, on the one hand, and developing a technology that has the potential to rid humankind of the scourge of diabetes and Alzheimer's, on the other.

Because the British have recognized this distinction, stem cell research is likely to flourish there, while American (and to some extent Canadian) scientists watch enviously on the sidelines.

7 Feminism, Ethics, and Cancer

SUSAN SHERWIN

In preparing to speak at the Ontario Cancer Institute, I found myself feeling unusually intimidated. After some reflection, I determined that my difficulty had to do with facing my personal fears of cancers. Because currently available data suggest that cancer will be diagnosed at some point in one of every three North American women, there is always present the barely suppressed fear that 'it' could strike at any time. If that happens, I will be dependent on medical specialists to guide me through the myriad of choices I will face and to care for me fully, whatever the outcome of my treatment. It seems especially urgent, then, that I tread carefully here, so that I will be understood despite the anger my perspective may generate and so that I maintain my convictions despite my fears of alienating a largely medical audience.

I share these feelings with you because I think they are indicative of the double-bind in which many patients and potential patients find themselves when trying to assert their own priorities concerning cancer treatment, research, and policy. I believe that these sorts of feelings are often at the heart of the ambivalent rage reported by many cancer patients, and that they can complicate patients' interactions with health professionals. I have learned from feminism to be attentive to double-binds – situations in which we feel torn between unac-

'I have learned from feminism to be attentive to double binds – situations in which we feel torn between unacceptable options – and to recognize their role in oppression.'

ceptable options – and to recognize their role in oppression. I shall therefore explore some of the ways in which cancer patients become caught up in double-binds, where their fear of offending their caregivers may leave them with no sense of control over their treatment. Feminism has taught me how fear functions to silence the oppressed and, in doing so, helps perpetuate oppression. Thus, I have learned that it is worthwhile to explore the political meaning of fear and that it is usually better to fight fear than to submit to it. My aim here is to elaborate on the significance of the complex feelings that cancer provokes and to explain some of the ways in which cancer is, among other things, a feminist issue.

Feminism Defined

Because there are many definitions and theories of feminism, I will begin by clarifying my understanding of it. Feminism involves both a recognition that women are oppressed by sexism and a commitment to end that sort of oppression. I understand oppression to be a systematic pattern of discrimination practised against a social group that has been defined on the basis of some shared characteristic, such as gender, race, class, or religion. The most extreme forms of oppression involve systematic and brutal abuses of state power in the persecution of designated minorities, such as the Nazi violations against Jews, South Africa's system of apartheid, and forms of 'ethnic cleansing' recently pursued in the former Yugoslavia. In the far more subtle forms of oppression that are endemic in our own society, members of an oppressed group are likely to have significantly less power, privilege, and opportunity than comparable individuals who do not share the relevant characteristic that defines the group.

The Politics of Cancer Prevention

The feminist approach to ethics allows us to begin each investigation of a moral issue with the assumption that women and other social groups are systematically oppressed in our society. Feminist ethics directs us to ask whether particular practices and policies deepen or help reduce that oppression. Hence, if we adopt this perspective in our consideration of current cancer policies, we might begin by asking what relation each policy has to the existing patterns of oppression. At first glance, these matters might seem unconnected to questions about oppression. After all, cancer seems to be an 'equal opportunity' disease: no one, no matter how socially privileged, is immune. Yet in many cases, specific oppressed groups are at a striking disadvantage with respect to cancer; for example, in Canada the incidence of cervical cancer is significantly higher among native women than white women, and in the United States black women die of cancer at a far higher rate than white women.

Across the North American population as a whole, we see rapidly escalating rates of cancer diagnosis for both women and men. Cancer accounted for only 4 per cent of deaths in the United States in 1900. That percentage has increased more than fivefold since then; in Canada, cancer now accounts for 24 per cent of deaths, and the death rate from cancer has risen 50 per cent just since 1971. Breast cancer alone can be expected to occur in one of every nine North American women, and the prevalence of the disease continues to rise. The parliamentary Sub-Committee on the Status of Women, investigating issues associated with breast cancer in Canada, noted that 'the incidence of breast cancer in Ontario has increased at a rate of approximately 1% per year between 1964 and the late 1980s. Although survival rates for many cancers have not improved, and cancer rates in general are increasing, women seem especially vulnerable: the incidence of cancer of the female reproductive tissues – the breast, the uterus and the ovary – is accelerating rapidly.'

What is particularly distressing about these figures is that most forms of cancer appear to be preventable, that it is within human power to reverse these trends and eliminate almost all cancers. Yet the major research emphasis continues to be on treatment, not prevention, perhaps because effective prevention would necessitate broad social and political action and would threaten entrenched and powerful special interests, whereas treatment concentrates on discrete individuals in accepted medical fashion. Also, cancer treatment is a profitable industry for many people, and there are large financial interests at stake in the current approach. The relatively few studies that explore issues of prevention focus on conditions over which patients are thought to have some degree of personal control, such as smoking, fat consumption, and participation in screening programs; these approaches also view cancer as an individual problem and responsibility. The cancer research agenda largely ignores the environmental factors widely implicated in the spread of various cancers: toxic chemicals, exposure to radiation, synthetic hormones fed to livestock, ozone depletion, and the iatrogenic (medically induced) effects of radiation treatment, drugs, and medical devices; its preventive focus concentrates overwhelmingly on individual lifestyle issues. Yet even supposedly 'individual' lifestyle behaviours vary with social and political status; for example, smoking is currently more prevalent among members of oppressed groups than among more privileged members of society, and it is promoted by powerful financial interests. Once we understand that cancer is inextricably tied to large-scale economic and political priorities, it becomes clear that its occurrence is a political issue. Nonetheless, the medical and research communities continue to investigate and treat cancer as if it were entirely a problem of distinct and unrelated individuals, each caught up in her or his own private tragedy. Cancer specialists seldom investigate or even mention the social and economic agents that bear significant responsibility for this epidemic.

The Focus on the Individual

We are now entering a more extreme version of the mindset that sees cancer prevention in terms of changing or restricting the activities of individuals but not corporations. Governments worldwide have committed huge sums of money to the Human Genome Project in the hope that, among other achievements, it will identify the specific genes that place individuals at high risk for the development of cancer. Proponents of the project presumably believe that the identified individuals will be able to take special precautions to avoid exposure to the triggering mechanisms – for example, by avoiding certain workplaces or foods. Instead of cleaning up carcinogenic environments, society seems to be hoping that this research will give specialists better guidance as to who can most safely assume particular risks. Yet, it is surely obvious that the freedom to choose a safe work environment is closely linked to an individual's class and social privilege: those who are oppressed are far less likely than more powerful individuals to be able to afford to make healthy environmental choices. The decision to pour resources into genetic and other individual-based prevention strategies is a political health-policy decision that has potentially enormous social and health consequences, yet this decision has been taken with no public discussion. Policy options must be evaluated in terms of the alternatives they replace, and the perspective of feminist ethics makes it clear that a cancer prevention policy concentrating on individual responsibility in the absence of efforts to restrict corporate sources of pollution is a product of power and influence more than of careful ethical deliberation.

Nevertheless, North American society is now committed to genetic cancer strategies. A 1993 article in the prestigious journal *Science* reported with enthusiasm that researchers would identify within a year the 'gene that predisposes women to cancer,' though the researchers had acknowledged that this gene is likely responsible for only 5 per cent of cases of breast cancer. In breathless journalistic fashion, the article reported that 'a slew of big-name gene hunters, attracted by this major prize, are now in hot pursuit of the gene.' Although the gene had not yet been precisely identified, the journal reported that screening programs based on the gene had already been established. According to this report, once a woman was identified as having the suspect gene, she would be encouraged to undergo bilateral mastectomy and removal of the ovaries as prophylactic measures. I do not want to dispute this medical advice: such radical surgery may indeed by the best medical option for a woman with a genetic predisposition to breast cancer. My point is that genes do not work in isolation: rather, their effect is a product of their DNA programming operating within particular environmental conditions, and under different conditions their effects may be different. The research emphasis continues to be on finding the gene associated with the disease in the individual, with the goal of changing the individual to eradicate or contain the gene's predicted effects. There is, however, another option: we could explore ways of preventing the gene from leading to cancer by depriving it of the conditions in which the cancer flourishes. A feminist research agenda would insist that we remember that the evidence to date suggests that most disease is, to put it conservatively, at least as much a matter of social conditions as genetic ones; indeed, in this case, 95 per cent of breast cancers are not clearly associated with the gene in question, so identifying and changing relevant social conditions should continue to be seen as the more urgent task.

Another dimension of the traditional focus on the individual is the tendency of many health care practitioners and researchers to direct their public, political energies to promoting the view that individuals can reduce their risk by accepting personal responsibility. We are told that we can avoid cancer by improving our lifestyles, monitoring our bodies for the most minimal changes and, in still too many cases, maintaining the appropriate attitude of calm and cheerfulness. The implied message is that those in whom cancer develops are somehow responsible for their fate; they must have failed to take proper care of their bodies or their minds. The rest of us can reassure ourselves that it is within our power to avoid their fate by being conscientious. Thus, while fearful, we can lull ourselves into the complacency of believing that full compliance with expert advice will protect us from incurable disease.

These public morality tales are usually offered with the best of intentions, and they may make good sense in the face of current research. Nonetheless, there is a disturbing aspect to this pattern of advice: it can be seen in the ways in which it is reminiscent of the messages women receive about the dangers of sexism. From girlhood, we are trained to be aware of the terrible violence that may be directed towards women: television, movies, and newspapers feed us terrifying stories of rape and brutality as cautionary tales. The moral, at least for white, middle-class women, is that if we behave properly – that is, if we make sure to have a (reliable) male companion on hand, make him feel good about himself and us, and avoid provocative activities – we can probably avoid such fates. Lest we be uncertain of the mechanics of 'keeping a man happy,' women's magazines, novels, and films are filled with specific advice. In this way, we are taught to read other women' s experiences of assault as evidence of their personal failings, and we learn to look for what they did to provoke the violence so that we can avoid similar repercussions in our own lives.

Discussion

Development of effective campaigns of cancer prevention will also necessitate widespread recognition that cancer is a political issue. Again, it is not necessary to seek out the 'perpetrators' or to presume some elaborate social conspiracy behind the individualist approach, which may just be the product of deeply ingrained habits of thought. Nonetheless, establishing acceptable levels of risk exposure will involve clear cases of conflict of interest, in which those whose interests are at stake have different and unequal access to power. Certain powerful segments of society benefit financially by actions that poison our collective environment, and they can be expected to resist efforts to curtail their dangerous activities. Social action is necessary to change the basic assumptions of society that encourage and subsidize carcinogen-producing industries. Social change is necessary to break the links between oppression, low self-esteem, and harmful coping behaviours such as smoking, drinking, and submission to abuse. The first step in the campaign is to understand that when we act merely as individuals, we are least able to prevent cancer. Feminist ethics reveals the importance of addressing cancer prevention at a political as well as an individual level and raises questions about the neglect of this issue as a matter of public policy and concern.

Feminists are challenging the forces that have kept women from speaking out about the politics of cancer. They observe that certain types of cancer are still regarded with shame and embarrassment, and they note the ways in which conventional medical expectations, however inadvertently, support the status quo. Audre Lorde, for example, has written of her experience with breast cancer and mastectomy and has described the strong pressure that health care workers applied to persuade her always to wear a prosthesis in public on the grounds that failure to do so was bad for morale. Lorde objected to the rationale for using a prosthesis or having reconstructive surgery on the basis that such strategies allow women who have undergone mastectomy to appear 'no different than before.' She perceived that this approach encourages women to remain silent about their experience with breast cancer, to keep it secret and private, and she challenged this aim.

If we are to translate the silence surrounding breast cancer into language and action against this scourge, the first step must be for women with mastectomies to become visible to one another, for silence and invisibility go hand in hand with powerlessness.

Lorde identified the political power of women acknowledging their experiences with cancer and condemned the ways in which our society and its agents in medical institutions that treat cancer actively discourage women from forming political alliances concerned with breast cancer. She spoke of the need to raise 'a female outcry against all preventable cancers, as well as against the secret fears that allow those cancers to flourish.' She saw that standard breast cancer treatment 'depoliticizes' disease, just as other feminists have seen that standard legal treatment depoliticizes violence against women by isolating and silencing its victims.

Another neglected area in cancer research is investigation into ways of helping patients live with incurable cancer. Many resources are poured into the search for the elusive 'cure(s),' yet little support is offered for exploring ways of improving life *with* the illness. Feminists perceive that this choice of priorities should also be seen as a political matter, in that it sacrifices the needs and interests of patients with incurable disease in the quest for 'the big prize.' Here, too, the question arises of whose interests are served by these choices and whose are harmed.

Feminists seek new models of patient–physician interactions. Furthermore, we understand that the realm of health care ethics does not end with improvements in the personal dynamics of this two-party relationship but extends far beyond. Therefore, we also focus on process, seeking innovating, egalitarian ways of defining the policies that ultimately shape health care priorities, options, and practices. To transform current patterns, it will be necessary to change not only the attitudes of individual practitioners and individual patients but also the structures that set and determine our society's approach to cancer and the sorts of care made available to its victims. Such social change will require the active cooperation of patients, health professionals, theorists, and those whose lives have been touched by cancer. Only when we learn to communicate widely about both the broad social and political issues and the deeply personal treatment decisions, will society and its institutions be able to meet the demands of feminist ethics in cancer care.

8 Cracking Down on Medical Trials

ARTHUR SCHAFER

North Americans consume a lot of pills: pills for high blood pressure, low libido, high cholesterol, acid reflux, arthritic pain, and depression. We take prodigious quantities of pills because our doctors have been persuaded and have in turn persuaded us that these pills work.

Doctors get their information about what works and what doesn't from a variety of sources, including what they were taught twenty years ago at medical school and what they were told last night by a paid consultant of some drug company after a fancy dinner. Doctors are expected, however, to base their treatment recommendations on the best scientific evidence available in the leading medical journals. We are supposed to be living in the era of 'evidence-based medicine.'

Unfortunately, when your doctor consults the medical journals she will likely discover only a thin slice of the relevant evidence – namely, the slice that makes new drugs look good. Those clinical trials which show the new drugs to be no more effective than older, cheaper drugs are seldom submitted to the journals; hence, they remain unpublished and inaccessible to your doctor.

Here's an example. Let's say that twenty studies have been done of a new class of drug for high blood pressure. Now, suppose that of those twenty studies, six are positive (favourable to the new drug) and fourteen are negative (showing that the drugs have dangerous side effects or work less well than older drugs). One might naively think that this would be the end of the story. The new class of drugs would be consigned to the scrap heap of medical research, and the hunt would continue for a better and more effective treatment.

Suppose, however, that as a direct or indirect result of drug company influence, twelve of the negative studies are not published, while every positive study is published. Physicians who then attempt conscientiously to review the literature would find six positive but only two negative studies.

Since six out of eight published studies seem to demonstrate that the new drug works well, drug company reps then spread the good word – along with quantities of free samples – to the medical community. The new drug is hailed as a medical breakthrough and rapidly becomes part of standard therapy.

This phenomenon of suppressing negative results is known formally as 'publication bias.' More colloquially, it's known as 'the file drawer effect,' because negative studies are hidden away in a company's file drawer. But if the much-touted movement towards 'evidence-based medicine' is to mean anything, physicians need unbiased data on the clinical effectiveness, toxicity, convenience, and cost of new drugs compared with available alternatives.

The pharmaceutical industry claims that when it sponsors drug trials, the resulting data become its commercial property, to publish or to suppress as it sees fit. Critics argue that it's vital for doctors and patients to know the bad as well as the good news about new drugs in order to make proper health decisions.

Happily, rescue from this alarming situation is at hand. The International Committee of Medical Journal Editors (ICMJE) has just announced that in the future it will refuse to publish the results of any clinical trial if that trial was not recorded at its outset in a publicly accessible registry. The editors hope to compel drug companies to disclose all the data from the trials they sponsor. Publication bias would thus be eliminated.

For many years, health advocates have been warning that the current state of medical research isn't proper science so much as

'When your grandmother told you "he who pays the piper calls the tune" she knew whereof she spoke. If we want public science in the public interest, we must pay for it with public funds, as we used to do before the trend towards "partnerships" with industry took hold.'

marketing through censorship or self-censorship. What seems finally to have spurred the medical journal editors into action was a lawsuit brought by New York State Attorney-General Elliot Spitzer against the British pharmaceutical company GlaxoSmithKline. The company was successfully marketing its antidepressant Paxil for use by children and young people, even though the evidence from some of the clinical trials – which it refused to make public – indicated both that Paxil was no more effective than a placebo *and* that Paxil increased the suicidal tendencies of depressed children.

GlaxoSmithKline has not admitted wrongdoing, but it has agreed to pay a multimillion-dollar settlement. It has also agreed, as have some other drug companies, that it will in future post more complete trial results on its website. The ICMJE, however, is not impressed by the companies' deathbed repentance. As one editor asks: 'Why would you put the fox in charge of the hen house?'

Perhaps it's time for governments, including Canada's, to compel companies by law to register all their results online in a not-for-profit database. The next important step will be to tackle the bias that arises from having so many of our leading hospitals, universities, and researchers sponsored by the pharmaceutical industry.

When your grandmother told you 'he who pays the piper calls the tune,' she knew whereof she spoke. If we want public science in the public interest, we must pay for it with public funds, as we used to do before the trend towards 'partnerships' with industry took hold.

9 Physicians, Limited Resources, and Liability

EIKE-HENNER W. KLUGE

Dwindling health-care resources have increasingly cast physicians in the role of gatekeepers. Some physicians see this role as fundamentally at odds with their traditional function as patient advocates. They also maintain that together with the general lack of resources, it raises the danger of legal action because they cannot provide an optimal level of service to all their patients.

Several scenarios are painted in this connection. One goes something like this: A patient with an acute cardiac condition is referred to a cardiac specialist for possible transplantation. The physician and her team evaluate the patient and decide that all other things being equal, a heart transplant would indeed be indicated. However, the patient is a heavy smoker and drinker. Furthermore, there are long waiting lists for heart transplants, and a selection has to be made. The physician and her team therefore decide that the patient does not meet all of their criteria for transplantation. Consequently they do not put the patient on the transplant waiting list. The patient dies a few weeks later. The next-of-kin take the physicians (and the hospital) to court.

A variation on this theme goes as follows: A new treatment for a particular condition has been developed. It is very expensive but at the same time very effective. However, this new treatment is not funded by the provincial health-care plan. The physician therefore does not offer the treatment to her patient but instead treats him on the basis of the modalities that are provided under the health plan. The outcome of the treatment she thus provides is not as good as it might have been if the new treatment had been used. The patient finds out about this and takes legal action against the physician for malfeasance of duty.

A third variation goes like this: For budgetary reasons, a hospital has decided not to perform a certain type of operation. Therefore the physicians who have privileges at the hospital cannot offer the operation to their patients. Another hospital, which is some distance away, does offer the operation. However, because the two hospitals are geographically quite distant from each other, the physicians from the first hospital do not have privileges at the second hospital. Consequently the patients of these physicians do not receive the operation. As a result, they do not do as well as patients who are treated at the other hospital. The patients therefore sue the physicians and the hospital for not providing appropriate and necessary health care.

These scenarios contain three separate but connected strands. One deals with *selective allocation of available resources*; another deals with the *complete absence of the relevant resources* (the treatment is available in principle but is not offered in a specific location); and the third deals with a treatment that is *offered in one location but not in another* where both are covered by the same provincial plan. These scenarios can be adjusted to fit almost any kind of situation where treatment is required but resources are limited and 'optimal' treatment is not available.

The fear is that the refusal to allocate scarce resources, or the failure to provide treatment that is available in principle but not in a particular setting, is exposing the physician and the hospital to liability. In some quarters, this fear has been elevated almost to the level of dogma.

Without a doubt, fear of legal action can influence health care decision-making; but even when it does not, it can produce severe stress. It is therefore important to be clear on what exactly resource limitation means for the ethical obligations of physicians, and what does and does not follow from their role as gatekeepers.

'Ethical conduct is the best defence against successful lawsuits. Acting ethically does not mean providing all possible health-care modalities. It means practising in the best way possible within the limits of the situation in which one is embedded.'

The first type of scenario presents neither ethical nor legal problems. Physicians have always been gatekeepers. The very concept of selective allocation of limited resources even has its own term in the medical vocabulary. It is called *triage*; and the fact that some patients experience a negative outcome because they have been triaged has never been considered a reason for saying that the responsible physician has acted unethically. Likewise, no one has ever successfully sued a physician for using appropriate triage standards. The need for triage may have been tragic. However, it is inappropriate to call someone unethical because he or she had to make such a decision.

The modern physician faced with limited resources is caught in a triage situation. The ethical reasoning that exonerates traditional triage also underwrites triage in the contemporary setting: physicians have an obligation to use the limited resources available to them in the best way possible. This means they must develop criteria of accessibility and selection. As long as these criteria are medically appropriate, and as long as they are applied consistently, the physicians who employ them are acting quite ethically. The fact that someone may suffer or even die may be tragic. However, not all tragedy translates into moral fault.

As to the second type of scenario, one of the more fundamental ethical principles is that of impossibility: no one can have a duty to do what is impossible under the circumstances that obtain. Canadian physicians practise within the limits that are set by the provincial health care plans. If these plans do not include certain treatment modalities, then they are simply not treatment choices that are open to the physicians. Physicians cannot offer treatments that are not available. Consequently they cannot be morally responsible for failing to provide the relevant treatments.

Of course, if there are treatments that are better than those covered by the provincial plan, a conscientious physician might tell her patients about them. This would give patients the option of looking around for some way of obtaining the treatments in question. However, the physician does not fail in her duty when she does not provide a treatment that is not available to her.

The third scenario also causes no ethical problems. Hospital budgets always have been and always will be limited. This is not something for which either health care administrators or physicians are responsible. In fact, no one is responsible for it. It follows from the fact that human society itself is limited and that all resources are finite. Hospital administrators have to work within the budgets they are given.

So the fact that one hospital provides a service while another does not, does not mean that the second hospital is acting irresponsibly or unethically. Hospitals serve catchment areas. Different catchment areas have different health needs, depending on the demographics and the health profiles of their client populations. (This is in part what underlies the drive for regionalization in health care.) A responsible hospital administration will use its limited funds in the most cost-effective way possible for the needs of its client population, consistent with quality of service. Therefore when resources are limited, only the services that address the major health problems of the client population in the most cost-effective way can be provided. This means that on occasion, certain kinds of services will not be available in a particular location.

However, the hospital administration need not therefore have acted unethically, even though the relevant service might be provided by another hospital in another area. Neither is a physician morally guilty for not providing treatment that is available in one setting but not in another. Different hospitals deal with the needs of different catchment areas. A hospital would be acting unethically only if it had selected its services irresponsibly – for example, if the priorities it had chosen did not accurately reflect the typical health care needs of its client population. Likewise, a physician would be acting unethically only if she did not inform the administration of the needs of her patients and did not do her best to see these needs met. But that is all she can do. The principle of impossibility comes into play once again: one cannot have a duty to do the impossible.

As to the fear of being sued: a wise old lawyer once said, 'You can be sued for anything, by anyone, at any time. The question is not whether you will be sued – because no one can prevent that – but whether you will be sued *successfully*.' Ethical conduct is the best defence against successful lawsuits. Acting ethically does not mean providing all possible health-care modalities. It means practising in the best way possible within the limits of the situation in which one is embedded.

Finally, it is sometimes argued that the Canada Health Act demands that health care consumers have the right to any of the health care services that are provided in any province. In fact, of course, the Canada Health Act entails no such thing. What it does entail is that, if a particular modality is offered by a provincial health-care provider, that modality must be available on an equitable basis to all qualified health-care consumers.

Nor does it mean that each province must ensure all possible types of treatments or that every hospital must offer every modality. It merely means that each province must take reasonable steps to ensure that all qualified residents have an equal opportunity of access, and that a hospital may not discriminate among its clients for medically inappropriate reasons. These conditions can be met by providing ambulance and transfer services. Inevitably, this will lead to negative outcomes for some patients. However, to repeat the old refrain, one cannot have a duty to do what is impossible. Resource limitation makes it necessary to make choices.

10 Children and Informed Consent

EIKE-HENNER W. KLUGE

Parents have traditionally acted as proxy decision-makers for their children below the age of majority. In consultation with the attending physicians, they have decided what health care their children should or should not receive. Of course there have been exceptions to this – for example, when the children have been made wards of the court, or when the physicians are convinced that the parents made the wrong decision and therefore challenge it. However, by and large this is how the system has worked.

This has now changed. British Columbia and New Brunswick have enacted specific legislation that entitles children to make their own health care decisions, and the other provinces have amended their general consent legislation to the same effect. The implications of these developments for medical practice are profound. To gauge their extent, it may be useful to take a brief look at what the initial reason for parents being made proxy decision-makers was, and why the situation has changed.

The reason why children below the age of majority were traditionally not allowed to make health care decisions on their own behalf was that it was assumed that they lacked maturity. That is to say, it was assumed that they could not understand the nature and implications of proposed treatments and therefore needed someone who could make the appropriate decisions for them. Parents were considered appropriate proxy decision-makers because it was assumed that they were closer than anyone else to their children and to have the best interests of their children at heart.

It was clearly recognized that the assumption of parental concern and interest might be mistaken. That is why it fell to physicians to minimize this risk. Since the physician–patient relationship held between the physician and the child rather than the physician and the parent, the primary obligation of the physician was towards the child, not the parent. Therefore, a physician who had reason to believe that a parental decision was not in the best interests of the child had the power to appeal this decision to the courts in order to ensure that the child was not harmed. In this, physicians (and the courts) followed the maxim that while parents 'may be free to become martyrs themselves ... it does not follow that they are free ... to make martyrs of their children.'

The situation began to change when the courts agreed that some children below the age of majority might nevertheless be 'mature' or 'emancipated minors.' This usually applied to self-supporting children who lived on their own. The courts allowed that such children were competent and therefore were entitled to make health care decisions on their own behalf.

A further development occurred when the courts accepted the claim that children with strong religious beliefs and 'settled dispositions' might fall into a similar category and therefore should have the right to refuse life-saving or life-sustaining treatment. Jehovah's Witness cases are particularly noteworthy in this regard.

The changes subsequently extended into the experimental setting. There was an evolving consensus that children who could not legally give consent might nevertheless be sufficiently mature to understand enough about the experimental procedures that they could reasonably refuse to give 'assent.' It was agreed that ethically, such refusal to give assent should be considered decisive, especially in non-therapeutic experimental contexts involving invasive procedures.

All of these developments placed physicians in a very difficult position. On the one hand, federal and provincial statutes (as well as professional guidelines) required that children who had not yet reached the age of majority be treated as though they were incompetent, and that the children's parents function as proxy decision-makers. On the other hand, the emerging case law and the ethics of informed consent said that what was important about the right to make health care decisions was competence, and that age was not necessarily decisive. The situation became especially difficult when girls wanted access to birth control devices or abortions without the consent or even knowledge of their parents.

The current legislative changes, therefore, are the culmination of a liberalization process that goes back some way. These changes are profound in that they do away with the presumption that, by definition, children are incapable of giving informed consent. The British Columbia statute states that 'an infant may consent to health care whether or not health care would, in the absence of consent, constitute trespass to the infant's person, and where an infant provides that consent, the consent is effective and it is not necessary to obtain consent to the health care from the infant's parent or guardian.' The only conditions the legislation attaches are that the physician must be convinced that the child understands the reasonably foreseeable risks and benefits of the health care, and that the physician must have taken reasonable steps to conclude that the care is in the child's best interests. The New Brunswick statute is similar except that two qualified medical practitioners must agree that the child is capable of understanding the nature and consequences of the treatment, and that the treatment is in the child's best interests. The changes in the other provinces' consent legislation are even more liberal in that they focus almost exclusively on competence and capacity, and leave out all reference to physicians as overseers of the children's best interests.

The new legislation is to be welcomed legally as well as ethically. Legally, because it brings statute law into line with case law and thereby removes the internal inconsistencies that used to exist. Ethically, because it captures two concepts that lie at the very heart of the notion of informed consent: first, that all people have the right to make decisions on their own behalf; and second, that what is important about informed consent is not age but the ability to understand the nature of the proposed interventions and to grasp the consequences that the various choices entail.

As the courts have found, while competence and age are correlated to a significant degree, this correlation does not hold in all cases. Most young children are not competent to make their own health care decisions; however, this does not mean that a particular child in a particular situation is incompetent. While most twelve-year-olds are not competent to make health care decisions, a particular twelve-year-old may well possess sufficient maturity and understanding to be able to make the relevant decision in a specific case. To prevent this twelve-year-old from making a decision would be to discriminate against the child solely on the basis of age. That would be unethical. It would also violate section 15 of the Charter of Rights and Freedoms.

'What is important about informed consent is not age but the ability to understand the nature of the proposed interventions and to grasp the consequences that the various choices entail.'

This is not to say that the new legislation is unproblematic. For instance, it increases the responsibility of physicians, who must now consider in each case whether the child is competent. Moreover, in British Columbia and New Brunswick, it places physicians into the unenviable position of having to decide whether the decision made by a competent child is in the child's best interests.

It also leaves the notion of best interests undefined. Does it mean what is best for the child according to medical standards? Apparently not. In a recent B.C. case, a child in acute hepatic failure who wanted to try alternative medical therapy before agreeing to a potentially life-saving liver transplant was allowed to do so – with the result that she died before she could have a transplant. Does it mean what is best according to social standards? That would be unethical, because it would punish all those children who do not share the current social values. It would also turn physicians into social monitors. Does it mean what is best for the child according to cultural standards? Finding out what that means in a multicultural society like Canada would be a hopelessly difficult task – and certainly not one that physicians are trained to do. As yet, there are no universal guidelines that would be of help.

Another problem with the legislation is that it has not yet been integrated into what for want of a better term might be called the medical decision-making culture of the provinces in which the relevant legislation has been proclaimed. Most of the consent forms and procedures in these provinces still require parents to act as proxy decision-makers for their children, irrespective of the maturity and competence of the children themselves. Likewise, most of the protocols that control access to patient records do not take these legal and ethical developments into account. This may occasion difficulties.

The changes may also raise difficulties for researchers in teaching hospitals and other settings whose activities are governed by the Tri-Council Policy Statement *Ethical Conduct for Research Involving Humans.* This policy statement, which governs all research by publicly funded researchers, agencies, and bodies in Canada, may cause serious problems when dealing with therapeutic research on children who are under the care of physicians, and where the child competently gives (or refuses) consent but the physician, guided by considerations of the best interests of the child, adopts a different perspective.

However, what is perhaps most troublesome lies not in the sphere of research but rather in that of ordinary practice. The diversity of legislation has entrenched distinct consent-rights in different provincial jurisdictions. Theoretically, it could happen that a twelve-year-old child who had made a health care decision in Ontario and expected to see it honoured could not have the same expectation if he or she was transferred to British Columbia because, unlike Ontario, British Columbia requires the agreement of the physician. Conversely, a child in New Brunswick whose health care decision had been overruled because his physician did not believe that it was in the child's best interests, could expect to see his decision honoured in Manitoba or Ontario. In an era of MEDEVAC and interprovincial consults, this may pose serious problems.

The idea that underlies recent revisions of consent laws for children is ethically defensible. Children are persons and should be treated as such. This extends to informed consent. Provided competence is present, there can be no objection to decision-making by anyone of any age. The problem for physicians is that their training has not yet attuned them to this notion. Also, the policy-making bodies of the medical profession have not kept pace with these developments, and the changes in legal recognition have not occurred in a coordinated fashion. It may be in the interest of physicians and their young patients that this situation be changed.

11 Robert and Tracy Latimer

ALISTER BROWNE

Robert Latimer and Paul Bernardo each committed acts of premeditated homicide. In the eyes of the law, there is no difference between what they did. Some think this is exactly right; others, that one must be morally blind to fail to see a difference. I will argue that certain acts of compassionate homicide ideally should not be criminally proscribed, and that, until this ideal is realized, the laws prohibiting it should not be rigidly enforced.

Let us take the need for law reform first. The Canadian Paediatric Society holds that decision makers must always act in the best interest of children; that sometimes death is preferable to life; and that when it is, life support may be terminated. All this seems right, and is in accordance with common medical practice and the law. But to draw the line of when death can be brought about here discriminates against those who are living lives that are more burdensome than beneficial and who do not require life-preserving interventions. For instance, if a child's quality of life failed to meet the Canadian Paediatric Society's criteria of a life worth living, and if the child were on a ventilator, the ventilator could be removed; if the child required surgery to preserve her life, the surgery could be withheld; but if the child did not require anything, she would have to endure. Since the need for life support is not a morally relevant difference, that is discrimination, and we thus have a case for changing the law to allow for active euthanasia.

'One may argue that there is a morally relevant difference between withholding life support, on the one hand, and injecting a lethal dose, on the other. But why one should think this is not clear.'

This suggestion immediately provokes objections. Two in particular deserve consideration. First, one may argue that there is a morally relevant difference between withholding life support, on the one hand, and injecting a lethal dose, on the other. But why one should think this is not clear. Withdrawing life support and injecting a lethal dose both cause death. The only difference is that the former does so by taking away something, the latter by putting in something, and that does not seem to be morally relevant. Withholding life-sustaining treatment is different from both in that it does not cause death. But it is not obvious why a deliberate omission should be treated as morally different from a deliberate deed when the outcomes are foreseen to be the same.

Second, one may argue that liberalizing the law opens the door to error and abuse. There will be mistakes; deaths will be brought about to relieve burdens to families rather than children; people who are disabled will be disvalued and put at risk. If opening the door to these possibilities is the worry, then the law allowing forgoing life support should likewise be found objectionable, for that poses the same risks. It is not clear why the safeguards in place to protect against wrongful forgoing of treatment would not be sufficient to protect against wrongful active euthanasia. And to rest opposition to law reform on the ground that this will adversely affect the interests of the disabled sins against the Canadian Paediatric Society's claim that we must always act in the interest of the patient. For that view entails that the interest of the patient can never be sacrificed, as the slippery slope argument sacrifices it, to the interest of a class of persons.

I now turn to the injustice of applying the current law to Mr Latimer. Let us begin by trying to see the matter as he presumably did. Tracy was a quadriplegic with cerebral palsy and the mental capacity of a four-month-old baby. Tracy enjoyed things such as music, bonfires, being with her family, and the circus. She could recognize family members, and she loved being rocked gently by her parents. On the other hand, she was believed to suffer serious and constant pain, which everyone agreed could not be left untreated. Palliation could not be achieved by way of medication because that conflicted with her antiseizure drugs, despite which she suffered five or six seizures daily. A feeding tube may have allowed for more effective medication, but surgical palliation was the chief hope. Tracy had undergone numerous surgeries in her lifetime, including two to cut stronger muscles and tendons to balance weaker ones, and another to implant rods to support her spine, all of which imposed painful recoveries. One left her in a cast from chest to toes for six months. The surgery now contemplated involved removing her upper thigh bone, which would leave her lower leg loose. The anticipated recovery time was one year; the procedure would cause pain; there was no guarantee that the surgery would succeed in controlling the chronic pain; the doctors suggested that further surgery would be required in the future to relieve the pain emanating from various joints in Tracy's body. The Latimers perceived the proposed surgeries as torture and mutilation, and Mr Latimer formed the opinion that it was not in Tracy's interest to face that future. Given this opinion, it is understandable that a loving parent would take matters firmly in his own hands rather than pursue medical treatment.

But there was no shortage of critics. Those who pointed to cases where parents persevered and disabled children flourished, or to Stephen Hawking or lesser lights who live eminently worthwhile lives, missed the point, for there is no parity between these people and Tracy Latimer. Likewise missing the mark are critics from the disability community who contend that any mercy shown Mr Latimer strikes at them. Disability was only contingently connected to the condition that rendered Tracy's life intolerable. She could have just as easily been in an unacceptable condition because of accident or disease. Exempting Mr Latimer from the full force of law gives one no more grounds for thinking less of the disabled than for thinking less of people with failing kidneys. One may suggest that people nonetheless *will* draw that conclusion. Even so, Mr Latimer and his family should not be penalized for the public's bad logic. To insist that Tracy be kept alive in an unacceptable state so that others would not be harmed would have been unfair to her, and to insist that Mr Latimer be punished is, for the same reason, unfair to him.

A more interesting line of criticism is that the decision to end Tracy's life was premature. Some physicians weighed in with suggestions of treatments they thought should have been tried; some challenged Mr Latimer's opinion of Tracy's quality of life and prospects. This criticism provokes two difficult questions. The first is: When can we say that a child's quality of life is so low as to make the life not worth preserving? One response is that life is so precious that as long as there is any possibility of a worthwhile quality of life emerging, the life must be preserved. This standard would be defensible if treatment never had adverse consequences. But treatment that may achieve the best outcome may also incur the worst, and this makes the standard implausible. A reasonable person may choose to forgo the best to avoid the worst when those outcomes are equally probable and of equal but opposite value. It could not therefore be wrong to choose this for those who cannot decide for themselves. And if, as Mr Latimer and others saw it, the odds are greatly against a good outcome, and the worst outcome is far more evil than the best is good, to try for the best is an unethical gamble.

But others disagreed with how Mr Latimer saw it, and this raises the second question: How are such disagreements over quality of life to be resolved? Sometimes logic and closer inspection of the evidence can get at the truth. But sometimes they cannot, and opinion remains divided. It is unacceptable to proceed mechanically on the most optimistic opinion, for (as we have just seen) that may be an unethical gamble. It is likewise unacceptable to act on whatever the majority thinks, for it is unfair to give everyone an equal say in a decision when not everyone will be equally acquainted with or interested in it, or equally required to bear its consequences. The answer given by the U.S. President's Commission is that when opinion is divided, the family, in recognition of its special knowledge and concern, should be allowed to make the decision. It is hard to see what answer could be better. But if we accept it, then, in the absence of a more objective resolution than the courts offered, it is Mr Latimer's judgment that should carry the day.

So there is reason to think Mr Latimer acted reasonably in an unjust legal situation. What then justifies punishing him? He does not deserve punishment or stand in need of reformation. To punish him beyond what he deserves in order to deter others is unjust. Fear of undergoing a judicial ordeal similar to Mr Latimer's is arguably as effective a deterrent as fear of imprisonment. The claim that murder must be denounced is undermined by the fact that analogous cases of euthanasia have resulted in probation or a suspended sentence. Punishment would be apt only if Mr Latimer acted negligently in forming his opinion that Tracy's life was not worth living – that is, if he did not carefully weigh the facts and options – or if he did not really believe that at all and acted from other than altruistic motives. But there is no coercive evidence in favour of either of these. Everything in the appeal court's trial transcripts points to Mr Latimer acting on the basis of a conscientiously formed belief and out of concern for Tracy. Thus, even if the facts were other than he believed, or if he erred in forming his opinion that Tracy's life was not worth living, it is hard to find a clear rationale for any punishment, let alone punishment to the full extent of the law.

One who is sympathetic to the forgoing may nonetheless argue that the law is the law, and nothing to save Mr Latimer could have been, or now can be, done. But this is not so. Prosecution is at the discretion of the attorney-general, and Mr Latimer need not have been charged; a lesser charge could have been laid, as it has been in other similar cases of euthanasia; juries have a common law right (and arguably moral duty even absent that) to bring in a not guilty verdict if they think applying the law would lead to an unjust result; a Royal Prerogative could now free Mr Latimer. These expedients seem fashioned exactly for this kind of case. But they all also call for courage and compassion, and so far the only principal who has shown those qualities is Mr Latimer.

12 Mercy Killing: The Deep Divide

JOHN RUSSELL AND ANDREW IRVINE

'I will neither give a deadly drug to anybody if asked for it, nor will I make a suggestion to this effect ... Into whatever houses I enter, I will go into them for the benefit of the sick, and will abstain from every voluntary act of mischief and corruption.'

Here, in its essentials, is the famous Oath of Hippocrates, or, as it is often summarized, 'I will serve the sick and do no harm.' It indicates that the question of euthanasia was alive even in the fifth century BCE. Prohibitions against physician-assisted suicide were in effect even then.

Recent Canadian decisions such as *Latimer* in Saskatchewan and *Rodriguez* in British Columbia force us to think carefully about the Hippocratic ideal. On the one hand, Canadian courts and legislators have refused to endorse any major changes to Hippocrates' position. The official view is still that physicians and others may not kill or abet killing, even mercifully to end a life that has become an ordeal of unspeakable pain and loss of dignity.

On the other hand, there is a fairly clear consensus, accepted by the courts, that leniency was appropriate in the sentencing of Robert Latimer. And in B.C. there was only a perfunctory investigation, with no prosecutions, in the physician-assisted death of Sue Rodriguez. This was despite the fact that her death followed a ruling by the Supreme Court that, even if carried out for reasons of mercy, euthanasia does not presently escape the murder provisions of the Criminal Code.

Clearly, Canadians and their institutions are deeply divided over this issue. This is a disturbing situation for everyone. For while Canadian institutions are not yet officially prepared to retreat from the Hippocratic ideal, neither do they seem fully committed to its enforcement.

Canadians on all sides of the debate over euthanasia can rightly fear that their institutions will act inconsistently and arbitrarily and that the equal treatment of citizens before the law will be in jeopardy. Is there any way out of the current situation?

It is possible that euthanasia experiments in Holland, Oregon, and Belgium will help resolve things one way or another. Such social experiments are often harbingers of change. But perhaps they won't prove anything either, at least not for some time.

One thing we can be certain of is that these cases require judgment, patience, and tolerance from all parties, especially from the physicians who are on the front lines and from our legal institutions. As Hippocrates also reminds us, 'Life is short, and the Art long; the occasion fleeting; experience fallacious; and judgment difficult.' In effect, Hippocrates asks physicians to cultivate patient, non-dogmatic judgment, but his lesson applies to everyone. As fallible beings we exist under conditions that necessarily impose uncertainty on our practical deliberations.

Another way of making this point is to notice that once we have the ability to exercise judgment, it is impossible to hide from this fact. Any decision to 'let nature take its course' will itself be an exercise in judgment. In practice we know this to be so: rarely do we avoid medical measures designed to lessen extreme pain and suffering, even when such measures may have the unwelcome consequence of shortening life. Once we have the ability to intervene medically, the moral responsibility of deciding whether to intervene or not is unavoidable. After eating the fruit of knowledge, it is impossible to return to the Garden of Eden to avoid the burden of judgment.

> *'Once we have the ability to intervene medically, the moral responsibility of deciding whether to intervene or not is unavoidable. After eating the fruit of knowledge, it is impossible to return to the Garden of Eden to avoid the burden of judgment.'*

What amounts to good judgment in these cases requires us to consider whether it is ever justifiable to bring about death deliberately by direct or indirect means. The basic moral question is whether there is always a moral difference between ending a patient's life by withholding treatment and bringing about death by less passive means, for example, by lethal injection.

Hippocrates and his contemporary followers think there is always a moral difference between these cases. They claim, in effect, that killing is always worse than letting die. But most contemporary philosophers doubt that there is any intrinsic moral difference between these two types of actions. They argue that most cases of killing are indeed wrong, but not all are. Once a decision has been made to withdraw or withhold treatment, then in certain circumstances the hastening of death by deliberate means for mercy's sake has already been recognized as an acceptable way of ending life. The rationale is no different in cases of bringing about death by more direct means. The basic reasoning and the intentions are the same in both cases.

Moreover, active intervention has the advantage that, once it is decided that a life of suffering is not to be endured (a decision, remember, that is also made in the case of withdrawing or withholding treatment), that life will not be prolonged any more than necessary. If this argument is correct, the Hippocratic position cannot be defended except on arbitrary grounds.

Perhaps it is this arbitrariness that is now becoming evident in recent legal decisions. As further cases appear, these and other problems with the Hippocratic position may become more evident. As Aristotle, a near contemporary of Hippocrates, put it, 'The facts harmonize with a true account, whereas the truth soon clashes with a false one.'

Hippocrates might properly caution that this remark overestimates the ease of finding answers to difficult moral questions. But over the long term, Aristotle's basic idea has been proven over and over for many issues of great and apparently intractable public controversy. There is no reason to think his words will not prove to be true again.

13 Nancy B and Nancy F

LESLIE BURKHOLDER

Many medical professionals and ordinary people still think there is generally or always a morally significant difference between passive euthanasia and active euthanasia. On the one hand, they think that it is ethically proper for a medical professional to stop treatment, at a competent patient's request, even when the foreseen result is that the patient will die. That is, they believe that passive euthanasia is sometimes – for instance, when it is fully voluntary – morally acceptable. On the other hand, they also believe that it is morally wrong for a medical professional to administer to a patient, even at that patient's competent request, anything which is intended to cause the patient's death. In other words, they think that active euthanasia isn't morally acceptable.

Many or all of those who say there is such a difference would certainly say that the following two cases are ethically quite different:

Nancy B. Nancy B had a mechanical ventilator, an artificial lung, attached to her, but outside her body. Without its continued action she would die by suffocation. She had a muscle-wasting illness; this is what had destroyed her lungs. Her medical condition would get no better and eventually would probably get worse. She saw no point in continuing to stay alive. She wanted to die by having the ventilator withdrawn or turned off. She couldn't do this by herself. Someone else, preferably a member of the staff at the hospital where she was staying, would have to do it for her.

Nancy F. Nancy F also had a muscle-wasting disease, although not the same one as Nancy B. Sooner or later, she would need a mechanical ventilator to allow her to breathe. But for now, the lungs she was born with were performing their function. Her condition would fairly rapidly worsen until eventually she died. She saw no point in continuing to stay alive until then. She wanted to die now by having someone, preferably a knowledgeable medical professional, administer a dose of morphine strong enough to stop the action of her lungs. She couldn't do this by herself. Someone else would have to do it for her.

I think there is a simple argument which says that what these people believe – at least about the cases of Nancy B and Nancy F – is false. There is no moral difference between the two cases.

Consider, not merely the Nancy B and Nancy F cases, but some intermediate imaginary cases. (The Nancy B and Nancy F cases are both based on real Canadian cases. Some details of the intermediate cases are science fiction. There are no implantable artificial lungs, for example.)

Nancy C. Nancy C had mechanical ventilators, artificial lungs, inside her body. These replaced her natural lungs, which had stopped working some time ago. Without them she would have died by suffocation. She had a muscle-wasting illness; this is what had destroyed her natural lungs. Her medical condition would get no better; eventually it would be worse. She saw no point in continuing to stay alive. She wanted to die by having the artificial lungs inside her body turned off. This could be done outside her body by remote control. She couldn't do this by herself. Someone else, preferably a staff member at the hospital where she was staying, would have to do it for her.

Nancy D. Nancy D also had mechanical ventilators, artificial lungs, inside her body. These replaced her natural lungs, which had stopped working some time ago. Without them she would have died by suffocation. She had a muscle-wasting illness; this is what had destroyed her lungs. Her medical condition would never improve and it would probably get worse. She saw no point in continuing to stay alive. She wanted to die by having the artificial lungs inside her body turned off. The easiest and least painful way to do this would be to administer a dose of a chemical agent strong enough to stop the action of her implanted artificial lungs. She couldn't do this by herself. Someone else, preferably a knowledgeable medical professional, would have to do it for her.

Nancy E. Nancy E had received cadaveric lung transplants. They replaced her natural lungs, which had stopped working some time ago. Without the lung transplants or a mechanical ventilator, she would have died by suffocation. But she had a muscle-wasting illness; this is what had destroyed her original lungs and would even eventually destroy the transplants. Her medical condition would never get better; it would only get worse. She saw no point in continuing to stay alive. She wanted to die by having someone administer a dose of morphine strong enough to stop the action of her transplanted lungs. She couldn't do this by herself. Someone else, preferable a member of the hospital staff where she was staying, would have to do it for her.

The argument or reasoning is perfectly obvious: it is a virtuous slippery slope. Suppose, to start at the top, that it is definitely not wrong for a medical professional to help Nancy B die in the way she wants. (This is what many people believe who think there is an important difference between the cases of Nancy B and Nancy F.) Then it is hard to see why it shouldn't also be acceptable to assist Nancy C. The only difference is that the artificial ventilators or lungs are inside Nancy C's body. In Nancy B's case, there was an artificial ventilator but it was outside her body. Can that make a difference? It is hard to see why. But if it is morally acceptable to help Nancy C die then it must also be morally proper for a medical professional to help Nancy D die.

'Many medical professionals and ordinary people still think there is generally or always a morally significant difference between passive euthanasia and active euthanasia ... I think there is a simple argument which says that what these people believe is false.'

Again, there is a small but plain factual difference between the cases of Nancy C and Nancy D. To make Nancy D's artificial lungs stop functioning it is necessary to administer by injection a chemical that stops them from working. Their action cannot be stopped from outside her body. This hardly seems like it could make a moral difference in the present context between the cases of Nancy C and Nancy D. But then, if it is not morally wrong to help Nancy D die then it is also not morally improper to help Nancy E die either.

The only difference between these two cases is that, in Nancy D's case, the ventilator is an artificial, mechanical device implanted in her body, replacing the lungs she was born with. In Nancy E's case the lungs are natural lungs, although not the ones she was born with. Could that make a moral difference? It is difficult to see why. So the Nancy D and Nancy E cases are morally the same, and if it is not wrong to help Nancy D, then it is not wrong to assist Nancy E.

Finally, the only difference between the case of Nancy E and the case of Nancy F concerns where her lungs came from. Nancy E hasn't the lungs or 'natural' ventilators she was born with; she has someone else's lungs. Nancy F has the lungs she was born with. If that makes no moral difference, then the Nancy E and Nancy F cases are ethically equivalent. And if it is morally not wrong to help Nancy E die, it cannot be morally wrong to help Nancy F either.

Of course, it is possible still to insist that it is morally unacceptable to help Nancy F die. But anyone who thinks this must also believe that it is improper to assist Nancy B. That's what the argument or reasoning, if it is sound, proves. The virtuous slippery slope argument establishes that the two cases are morally indistinguishable. What the argument or reasoning proves is that you cannot accept both that it is ethically acceptable to help Nancy B die and that it is unacceptable to help Nancy F die.

Again, it is possible to insist that even if these two cases are morally the same, this doesn't show that more generally, or always, active euthanasia is morally the same as passive euthanasia. This insistence is logically impeccable. On the other hand, the virtuous slippery slope argument presented here for the moral equivalence of the cases of Nancy B and Nancy F can obviously be mimicked for many other instances of active and passive euthanasia. The recipe is to start with either an instance of active or an instance of passive euthanasia, then to find or invent a similar case of the other, and then to construct appropriate intermediate cases, each case erasing a small factual difference that makes no moral difference. So, even though my argument only establishes the ethical equivalence of the Nancy B and Nancy F cases, it is easy to see how to establish that generally, for many different pairs of cases, or even always, active euthanasia is morally the same as passive euthanasia.

14 Is Death Really All That Bad for You?

THOMAS HURKA

In the movie *Annie Hall*, when Woody Allen is getting serious about Diane Keaton, he wants to talk about death. So let's talk about death. But let's start with the cheery view: that it's nothing to worry about, not bad, not a harm to you at all.

This was the view of the Greek philosopher Epicurus, today remembered mainly in the names of restaurants and cookbooks. This isn't totally misguided: Epicurus thought the only good thing is pleasure, or more precisely, freedom from pain. But he wasn't a big fan of feasting and womanizing. For him the key to a happy life was philosophy, which teaches you that death isn't bad and thereby saves you needless anxieties.

To be bad for you, Epicurus argued, something has to affect your conscious experience, and in particular, cause you pain. But death can't cause you pain, since when you're dead you don't exist. (Dying can be painful, but that's different from being dead.) Death can't hurt you because you're not around to experience it. So why fret about it?

'People who fear death, said Epicurus, are confused. They imagine that they'll somehow survive death, see the loss of the things they loved in life, and be pained by what they see. But this won't happen: death is only non-existence.'

People who fear death, said Epicurus, are confused. They imagine that they'll somehow survive death, see the loss of the things they loved in life, and be pained by what they see. But this won't happen: death is only non-existence. And non-existence won't be new to us. Before we were born we didn't exist for infinitely many years. If we don't regret this – if we don't mourn that we weren't born twenty years earlier – we shouldn't fear dying a little earlier.

When we read his arguments, we can envy Epicurus' 'philosophical' attitude to his coming death. But we also think he has to be wrong. Death is bad, often the worst thing of all. The comforting arguments must be flawed.

Let's start by agreeing that death can only be bad for you if it affects your experiences. Granted this, death can't be bad in the way pain is, for how it feels. But it can be bad for what it prevents. If life is good, it is so because of its pleasures and enjoyments, and death cuts these short. It prevents the good feelings you would have if you stayed alive. Death isn't bad considered by itself, but it is bad for what it disallows.

This point holds even more if, disagreeing with Epicurus, we think that things other than pleasure are good: understanding, achievement, family life. Death also stops you from having more of these.

If death is just a loss, not all deaths are equally bad. Someone who dies young, with a rich life ahead of him, loses more than someone who dies at ninety. And some deaths aren't bad at all. If a person's future promises only the pain of a terminal illness, dying now is merciful. But these implications seem right: our reaction to a death should depend on the alternatives to it.

The harder Epicurean argument to answer is the one about not existing before our birth. Maybe not wishing we were born earlier is irrational, and we should care more about past losses.

Maybe we find the necessary comparison impossible to make. If we had been born twenty years earlier, we would have been brought up in a different decade, with different interests and a different family. Who knows what our lives would have been like? Or maybe we are attached to things in this life that an earlier birth would take away, such as love for a particular person.

Epicurus' arguments cannot entirely stem our fear of death: death remains a loss, sometimes an enormous one. But there's some comfort to be had. If death is just a loss, it is not different in kind from other bad things: the rainstorm that interrupts your golf game, the bad luck that costs you a new job. It is a bigger loss, but not something unique. In Hollywood terms, death isn't like ending a movie hooked up with someone who will make you miserable. It's more like an ending Woody Allen should be familiar with: not being hooked up with someone who would have made you happy.

PART IX

National Unity

1 If Quebecers Say No, It Clearly Will Be Out of Fear

MICHEL SEYMOUR

The vast majority of Quebecers agree that there is, in the territory of Quebec, a Québécois nation in addition to the eleven First Nations. This nation includes a national minority of Anglo-Quebecers and different communities of allophones. But it is also true to claim that Canadians do not recognize the existence of such a nation. These simple facts, I believe, provide a fundamental reason for choosing to vote in favour of the sovereignty of Quebec.

It is important, first, to define the concept of nation that I am using. A nation may come into existence as long as a linguistic community, which constitutes a majority on a given territory, forms a political community with eventually existing national minorities and immigrant communities. A majority of people within this political community must also perceive themselves as being part of a nation. In addition, the community must be involved in a specific context of choice – that is, a specific network of cultural, moral, and political influences. These external influences are explained by geographical proximity, history, and language. Another condition is that the linguistic majority must be the largest sample that we find of a group of people sharing the same language and being involved in the same context of choice. Finally, the territory must play a role in the determination of the population that composes the nation. Less numerous communities that share the same language and context of choice, but that are outside of the territory, do not belong to the nation, while minorities with a different language on the territory may be part of the nation.

'A new political arrangement is required, one that would lead to the existence of different sovereign states in an economic and political union.'

Nations are thus determined by three main features: language, context of choice, and territory. According to this concept, Belgium, Canada, Spain, and Switzerland, for example, are multinational states. The originality of the concept is also that it is compatible with admitting 'national minorities' as integral parts of the nation. These minorities are extensions of a closely related nation existing in a different territory, and they perceive themselves in that way. According to this concept of 'national minority,' the Russians in the Baltic states, the Hungarians in Slovakia, the Arabs in Israel, the Anglo-Quebecers in Quebec, and the Franco-Canadians in Canada are all examples of national minorities.

Our sociopolitical concept of the nation must thus be distinguished from the ethnic and the exclusively civic conceptions. Ethnic nationalism leads to violence and racism, while exclusively civic forms of nationalism lead to exclusion and forced assimilation. According to the civic conception, nations are nothing more than sovereign states. But with that concept, we unfortunately are unable to say that colonized peoples, Acadians, First Nations, and Quebecers are all nations.

So Canada is a multinational state and all Canadians should perceive themselves as being part of a multinational state, but they do not. Apart from a very small minority of thinkers, the vast majority of Canadians perceive Canada as being one (civic) nation in a multicultural diversity. Some feel that we have to learn to live together with these deeply different perceptions of what Canada is all about. But in most polls, it now appears that a clear majority of Quebecers would opt for sovereignty if an economic and political partnership were possible with the rest of Canada. After trying for so many years to live with their fellow Canadians within the confines of a multinational state, Quebecers realize that this is not the way Canadians feel about the country. If they do not choose to vote Yes at this point, it clearly will be out of fear. The No campaign has systematically contended that the sovereignty of Quebec would lead to a radical *separation* from Canada with no hope of maintaining a partnership, even though there are nowadays in Europe and elsewhere sovereign countries that enter into an economic union. It is, of course, a good strategy on the No side to describe the sovereignty of Quebec as leading to such a radical separation, but it is a strategy that exploits fear and not reason. The same kinds of remarks apply to the suggestion that the sovereignty of Quebec would be *illegal* or that Quebec would not be *viable* because of the debt it would have to incur.

We should instead accept these irreconcilable differences between Quebecers and Canadians. A new political arrangement is required, one that will lead to the existence of separate sovereign states in an economic and political union. Would there be two sovereign states or would there be four? That depends on Canadians, of course, and on whether they eventually come to perceive themselves as part of a distinct nation without Quebec.

But instead of accepting these differences, Canadians have up to now chosen to force their views on Quebecers. They have ignored the historic demands of Quebec for more autonomy within the federation, and they have imposed a new, illegitimate constitutional order that has been rejected by the vast majority of the members in the National Assembly. They even rejected Meech Lake. And now they hope to crush the sovereignists in any upcoming referendum. But a majority of No votes, at this point, can only be obtained through fear and not through rational arguments, and it is for this reason that our deep problems remain unsolved.

2 Equality between Peoples

MICHEL SEYMOUR

The motives behind Quebec nationalism are not exclusively symbolic. They can also be explained, in part, by the fact that the federal government has, through many of its policies over the past forty years, favoured the economic development of the Toronto region at the expense of the rest of the country. The implications of this are especially profound because one of these regions is made up of a distinct people, which means that the federal government is violating the principle of equality between peoples.

One can certainly understand the need for economic development programs when a community is situated in a peripheral region, when the population is too small to develop itself, or when the community doesn't have a sufficient number or diversity of economic resources. This is the case, notably, in the Maritime provinces, and the only way to compensate for this unequal development is to establish a system of redistribution. But this is not the case in Quebec. The latter is a heavily populated region in an economic heartland and is rich in resources. In addition, Quebecers (except for First Nations people) constitute a people or nation, however we define these expressions. Yet Quebec is one of Canada's poorest provinces. Montreal is, at this time, the poorest city in Canada. Several factors account for this, but we cannot presume that policies put in place by the federal government over the past forty years have not had an impact.

Among the federal measures that have been detrimental to the development of the Montreal region we can name the opening of the St Lawrence Seaway, which caused considerable harm to the Port of Montreal; the National Energy Program, which killed the petrochemical industry in the eastern part of the city; the Auto Pact, which resulted in an agglomeration of businesses in the Toronto area; the federal research and development policy for science and technology, which has always placed Quebec at a disadvantage to Ontario; and federal policies for the purchase of goods and services, which have always been unequal. We could add that the federal government has made major investments in nuclear power in the Ottawa region and has generally favoured development in the Kanata industrial zone. Besides all this, it stalled for many years before imposing a twenty-year protection on pharmaceutical patents; this delay allowed Ontario's generic-drug industries the chance to develop and compete unfairly with Quebec's pharmaceutical industry. Ottawa also gave in to Toronto's powerful lobbying, preventing for a time the creation of international banking centres in Vancouver and Montreal.

This disproportionate development – the fruit of federal government policies – is the main reason why Quebec is a poor province. It must be noted that other factors have played a part in placing Montreal at a disadvantage. Political uncertainty following the election of a sovereigntist party in Quebec in 1976 resulted in the displacement of executives, corporate headquarters, and capital, which hindered Quebec's development. But the appearance of a sovereigntist movement in Quebec was first and foremost an *effect* of unequal development, not the principal cause of this inequality.

Federalists point out that Quebec derives a number of advantages from its links with the federation. These advantages include equalization payments. Even though it constitutes no more than one-quarter of the population, Quebec receives almost one-half the equalization payments that Canada distributes to the provinces. If all transfers were taken into consideration, it would be seen that Quebec receives one-third of these.

If we were to take into account all of the taxes collected from Quebec by the federal government, and the total spending carried out by the federal government within Quebec, including transfers such as equalization payments, we would have to note that in the federal budget of 1996–7 there was an outstanding balance in favour of the federal government. It is, however, normal to arrive at such an outstanding balance at the federal level. Thanks to this positive balance, the government is able to pay a part of Quebec's share of the interest on the debt. So the federalist argument runs as follows. Even if Quebec were to pay in more than it receives in the future, Quebec's contribution to total federal revenues would be only about 21 per cent because it would not be able to contribute enough to cover its own share of the interest on the debt. The figure of 21 per cent

'Quebec is one of Canada's poorest provinces ... Several factors account for this, but we cannot presume that policies put in place by the federal government over the past forty years have not had an impact.'

corresponds to Quebec's contribution to the Canadian GDP and not to the percentage of the population it represents. One can therefore state that thanks to equalization, Quebec is paying federal taxes equivalent to less than the share of the population it represents. But this federalist argument is not decisive. Quebec's fiscal contribution can be seen as fair, because it makes sense for Quebec to be taxed according to the strength of its economy, not according to its population.

As far as the profitability of federalism for Quebecers is concerned, one could believe that everything evens out in the end, but this would ignore the following facts. First, we must consider why the Canadian government is in debt. One reason is the federal spending power. The government of Quebec has always opposed the abuse of this federal power. Second, tax shelters for businesses have mainly benefited Ontario, where the Canadian economy is more and more centralized. Third, the Bank of Canada advocates high interest rates. These high rates have harmed mainly the regional economies, like that of Quebec, because their purpose is to cool Ontario's overheated economy. There are without a doubt other factors worth mentioning, but it seems that the high federal debt is mainly the result of policies that have been detrimental to Quebec.

Be that as it may, let us admit that Quebec must contribute its fair share to the service of the debt. Even so, the federal government has been reducing its transfer payments to the provinces in the name of deficit-fighting. Since 1996–7, Ottawa has cut transfer payments to the provinces by about $6 billion. As a result, Quebec has suffered a substantial decrease in transfer payments.

Would Quebec be better off with the right to equip itself with an economic infrastructure like Ontario's? Or would it benefit more from transfers and redistribution payments, the purpose of which is supposedly, to 'rebalance' the wrong suffered? The answer is obvious. Transfer payments will never amount to more than financial 'compensation' measures. But there's more.

In the context of difficult public finances, transfer payments from the federal government to the poorer provinces have been reduced more and more, while the economic effects of federal policies favouring Ontario are at risk of becoming permanent. This is why we can legitimately ask ourselves if the federal government has taken the principle of equality between peoples into account.

3 Unity Poses Questions Already Answered

JOHN RUSSELL AND ANDREW IRVINE

What is it that binds us together in such a way that makes us want to live together under a single flag?

One answer is that each nation is a homogeneous people, a people with similar history, language, and culture. This is the *pure laine* conception of nationhood offered by Gilles Duceppe and the Bloc Québécois. Under it, minorities are always outsiders. By implication, and often by law, they exist as unequal members of society unless or until they choose to conform to the customs of the majority.

In contrast, the answer most Canadians – including most Quebecers – have regularly favoured is one, not of conformity and inequality, but of tolerance and equality. It is an answer that recognizes that unity does not mean uniformity. It asserts that minorities need not conform to the language or culture of the majority in order to share a common political community.

On this view, nations are not defined by the sameness of a people. Instead, they are defined by common aspirations and by a common commitment to political institutions designed to serve all citizens, whatever their background. These institutions do not find their origin or purpose in the service or aspirations of a particular people. Rather, they aim to create a mutually beneficial context of opportunity for all, and a forum for working out common goals and ideals.

The *pure laine* conception of nationhood assumes that we can only be happy and prosperous when living among our own kind. This idea runs deep in human history but it needs to be resisted, especially in the context of nation-building. It ultimately reflects an isolationist feature of human psychology that is fundamentally at odds with the integrated yet plural reality of the modern world. Socially, economically, and morally, it is an anachronism, despite its re-emergence in recent years.

Even so, our other model of the nation-state is not without problems.

The demand of minority groups for cultural recognition is not frivolous. What room, if any, can be made in a liberal-democratic society to foster such recognition? Can such recognition be achieved without retreating into a *pure laine* version of nationalism?

While debate on this issue continues among newspaper columnists and political philosophers, in some sense we already know the answer. It is a remarkable fact that Canada has already successfully traversed this ground. At least where Quebec is concerned, Canadian federalism has undeniably succeeded in providing a secure context of choice for French-speaking Quebecers without undermining the rights of other citizens.

Thus there is little question that Canada has been realized as a nation in a manner that is consistent with the best model of nationhood available. Canada's success constitutes a vision that has bound us together in the past and that deserves to do so in the future. Even where we have sometimes failed, most notably in our relations with Native communities, this model provides the best hope for the future.

If this is correct, accepting the disintegration of the Canadian nation would be a retreat to the tribalism of the *pure laine* model. Of course, the tendency towards tribalism is not new. One need only recall the 1904 debate between Jean-Pierre Tardivel and Henri Bourassa in which Tardivel argued for an isolationist view of Quebec, Bourassa for a federalist one. In Bourassa's words, 'We are working toward the development of Canadian patriotism, which in our eyes is the best guarantee of the existence of two races and of the mutual respect they owe each other.'

Seen in this way, the current debate about the future of Canada is not really a debate between French and English. Rather it is a debate over the capacity of Canadian federalism to accommodate diversity within the liberal-democratic ideal. But in a real sense, this debate is already behind us. Our federal system has been remarkably successful in allowing minority interests to flourish within a single nation. It has also enabled Canadians from all parts of the country to obtain the benefits of living in a large, prosperous, liberal society.

It is too often forgotten that these successes were clearly sought and anticipated by the men who brought about Confederation in 1867. Not only Macdonald and Brown, but Cartier, Dorion, Langevin, and Taché all understood both the benefits and the risks of founding a nation like ours.

According to Etienne-Pascal Taché, the then Premier of Canada, each individual province was like a farmer who relied on the good will of an obliging neighbour for access to a needed highway. If Confederation did not occur, the provinces would remain minor entities, beholding to one another and without the benefits of unity.

According to George Brown, founder of the *Globe* newspaper, all

Canadians would be able to take pride in building a nation from the kind of diversity that has regularly 'plunged other countries into all the horrors of civil war.' Confederation offered the chance that all 'these great evils and hostilities may justly and amicably be swept away for ever.'

For Taché, the issue of English domination had ended on 3 September 1841, the day the British granted Canada responsible government. On this day, all Canadians 'without distinction of race or creed, were placed on a footing of equality.' Looking towards the future, Taché believed that the structure of the new federation would help guarantee that 'tolerant and liberal' feelings towards minorities would continue to remain a part of the fabric of the new nation. Canada would be able to embrace its diversity without fear that minorities would be either harmed or assimilated. Taché's words could hardly have been more prophetic, especially for French-speaking Quebecers.

'From the very beginning Canadians have self-consciously advanced a morally principled and enduring model of government, one that has achieved – where many others failed – what it set out to do.'

Such remarks expose a myth that one commonly hears, at least in English Canada. This is the myth that Canada is a mere 'accident of history,' a country artificially linked together by a national government in the face of countervailing forces of geography and culture. The implication is that Canada is not a genuine nation and so is not worth preserving.

Comments by men such as Bourassa, Brown, and Taché put the lie to this claim. From the very beginning, Canadians have self-consciously advanced a morally principled and enduring model of government, one that has achieved – where many others failed – what it set out to do.

Knowing this, many Canadians' lack of interest in further pursuing the Quebec question may not reflect hostility, apathy, or even exhaustion. It may simply reflect frustration over the failure of politicians both inside and outside Quebec to acknowledge and promote the remarkable success that Canada represents as a nation. The fact that Canadians outside Quebec do not want to change the status quo may mean only that they do not want to threaten this success, and that they already know that it affords the best available basis for nationhood.

Knowing that such a vision originally helped form Canada, and that its opponents even then were in the minority, reminds us that the ideals that supported this vision have been compelling in the past. Over time they have also proven practical. They deserve a more prominent place in the strategy for national unity in response to those who are ideologically bound to a different and more suspect conception of nationhood.

4 A Unity Referendum to End All Referendums

JOHN RUSSELL AND ANDREW IRVINE

In its current form, the national unity issue has been with us since the rise of the Parti Québécois in the 1970s. It is such a regular feature of the political landscape that many Canadians find it difficult to imagine an election campaign without it. Others believe the time has come to settle the issue once and for all.

Many, of course, would prefer some form of renewed federalism, the so-called 'Plan A' of the federalist camp. Despite this, many federalists have also begun talking about 'Plan B,' the option of clearly outlining both the procedures for, and the consequences of, separation. It is with this option in mind that the federal government asked the Supreme Court to clarify how national and international law might affect potential procedures for separation.

But there is another option that may be worth considering. Call it 'Plan C.' This is the option of having Ottawa either hold, or play a central role in overseeing, the next Quebec referendum.

Initially this idea may seem to be a non-starter. It would almost certainly be viewed by the separatists as yet one more example of Ottawa's disregard for the right of Quebecers to self-determination. But the virtues of Plan C may be compelling enough to deflect such criticism.

Plan C has the greatest potential to settle the Quebec question once and for all – something that most Canadians, including most Quebecers, would prefer. Another attraction is that it may prove fairest to both Quebecers and Canadians outside Quebec. If so, separatist objections to federal involvement in the next referendum may prove difficult to sustain.

How might Plan C work? First, federal involvement would ensure that the referendum question could be phrased in such a way that there would be absolutely no ambiguity about what voters were being asked to decide. If they were asked, for example, whether they did or did not want to remain a part of the Canadian confederation, they would not be left wondering about what might or might not happen should various attempts at negotiation between Ottawa and Quebec City succeed or fail.

Second, the referendum process could be administered by Ottawa in a way that guaranteed fairness. Scrutineers could be properly trained, and the referendum itself could be overseen by Elections Canada. United Nations or other international observers could be invited by the federal government to observe the referendum process. In addition, the kinds of restrictive rules relating to umbrella organizations and third-party advertising that have characterized past referendums could be lifted.

Third, Quebecers could be told clearly in advance that the outcome of such a referendum would be binding, not for the province as a whole, but on a constituency-by-constituency basis. Constituencies that voted to remain in Canada would do so. Constituencies that voted to leave would leave. The objection that this might lead to a balkanization of Quebec is no more compelling than the objection that Quebecers' right to self-determination might lead to a balkanization of Canada.

Plan C has none of the subtlety of current proposals for asymmetrical federalism, or of the Charlottetown or Meech Lake Accords. But it does have the virtue of allowing all Quebecers – including Quebec's northern and Native populations – to decide their future. Such a process would do the utmost to allow Quebecers to express freely their right to self-determination. And because it would be administered on a constituency-by-constituency basis, individual Quebecers themselves would be exercising this right.

There are other, more basic reasons for federal involvement in the referendum process. To begin, Quebec currently lacks any of the usual justifications for declaring unilateral independence. Quebec is not the object of some profound injustice – such as civil violence, coerced occupation, or famine – that Canada is either responsible for or incapable of protecting it against. Nor is its culture disintegrating so that there is widespread alienation and social decay. On the contrary, Quebec is one of the more desirable places in the world to live, and its culture is thriving by any measure. This is in large part due to its participation in the Canadian federation. In consequence, Quebecers' right to self-determination is a qualified one that includes a basis for federal involvement.

Liberal societies such as ours typically recognize a right to self-determination, both for individuals and for groups, as long as its exercise does not wrongfully harm others. Citizens in the rest of Canada therefore must – and almost universally do – acknowledge that Quebecers have this qualified right to self-determination.

But this qualified principle complicates the process of bringing separation about. For given Quebec's economic and social ties to the rest of Canada, separation has the potential to do significant harm to the rest of Canada, as well as to citizens inside Quebec.

For example, a poorly worded referendum question (like the most recent one) is liable to undermine the right to self-determination of all voters in Quebec by failing to indicate clearly just what choice they are being asked to make. The debate over the meaning of the most recent referendum question, the promises by separatists that they would not make an immediate unilateral declaration of independence, and later reports that Premier Parizeau did in fact plan to declare Quebec independent immediately after the last referendum, are an appropriate caution in this respect.

Just as importantly, a poorly worded question has the potential to harm the rest of Canada. This is because the threat, or occasion, of unilateral separation could be used to coerce concessions on or leave unresolved an array of economic, monetary, and social issues where it is to Quebec's advantage to do so. It is important to remember that all of these issues involve myriad agreements voluntarily undertaken between Quebec and the rest of Canada. The possibility that the separation process could be misused – that agreements could be ignored, that unfair concessions could be extracted, that favourable arrangements could be extorted – in the climate of economic and political instability that is bound to follow a separation vote is too great to overlook.

'Federal involvement would ensure that the referendum question itself could be phrased in such a way that there would be absolutely no ambiguity about what voters were being asked to decide.'

Canada has not oppressed or otherwise wronged Quebec, so it can legitimately claim an interest in preserving the right to self-determination of all its citizens, including Quebecers. It can also legitimately claim an interest in ensuring that the referendum process and its aftermath will respect the legitimate interests of all affected parties within its current legal jurisdiction. Having the federal government establish or participate in the referendum process could be the best way to meet these obligations.

By refusing to participate, the Quebec government would be casting the legitimacy of any results in doubt. But if the referendum process is genuinely fair, it may be difficult for separatists to reject. By doing so, they would risk revealing themselves as ideologues who are only giving lip service to a democratic process. This would be especially true if the federal government made reasonable efforts to enlist Quebec participation and cooperation.

For example, a referendum process might require consultation and agreement on the question and the referendum date. Both levels of government might have a role to play in scrutinizing the voting process, and so on. And of course, the Quebec government's obstruction of an obviously fair process would have clear benefits for federalists, even if it were decided that a referendum could not be run without provincial participation.

The great virtue of Plan C is that it does not insist on any particular outcome. It insists only on fairness. It insists that all the affected parties be treated fairly and that a clear process be observed. It thereby aims to establish a moral basis for all to abide by the results. It is true that Plan C cannot guarantee this. Separatists who remain in Canada after a vote may continue to promote separatism. But if the process is truly fair, then a generation can plausibly answer by saying it put its best effort into addressing this issue and that it should be put behind us. This is what most Canadians, including most Quebecers, probably want.

5 The 'Clarity' Bill in Retrospect

MICHEL SEYMOUR

In 1998 the Supreme Court of Canada released its opinion concerning the secession of Quebec. Two years later the government of Canada passed Bill C-20, described as 'an Act to give effect to the requirement for clarity as set out in the opinion of the Supreme Court of Canada in the Quebec Secession Reference.' The Supreme Court's opinion was acclaimed by almost everyone as a sophisticated and subtle piece of argument, but we cannot say the same about Bill C-20. Before commenting on C-20, I shall first provide a general outline of the Supreme Court's judgment. Then I shall try to show that Bill C-20 goes far beyond anything that was said by the Supreme Court. I shall thus argue that there is a deep discrepancy between C-20 and the Supreme Court's opinion on the secession of Quebec.

The Supreme Court's Opinion

Let me first restate the main conclusions of the Supreme Court on the secession of Quebec. The federal government had asked the Court three different questions. First, could Quebec unilaterally declare its independence in accordance with the Canadian Constitution? Second, could Quebec unilaterally secede in accordance with international law? To both questions, the Court answered No. The third question was asked in case the answers to the first two questions were different. The judges were invited to determine which of the two levels – internal or international – would supersede the other. However, since the answers to the first two questions were No, the third question was irrelevant.

The federal government immediately responded by declaring that it had won against the sovereigntists. Yet the details of the answers given by the Supreme Court were actually quite favourable to the sovereigntists. The Court said that Quebec could initiate a referendum on the question of secession. If the question was clear and the majority in favour of secession was clear enough, there would be an obligation to negotiate the terms of secession. This would be a constitutional obligation. These negotiations would have to be conducted among the Quebec government, the federal government, and the nine other provinces.

The negotiations would have to be conducted in conformity with four fundamental principles found in the Canadian Constitution: the principle of democracy, the principle of federalism, the principle of constitutionalism and the rule of law, and the principle of the protection of minorities.

A unilateral process of consultation may be initiated by a province on the issue of secession, and this will yield an obligation to negotiate, provided there is a clear majority on a clear question. This obligation follows from the principle of federalism and the principle of democracy. A unilateral secession is declared illegal and is described as a secession made without previous negotiations between Quebec and the other provinces and the federal government. If the negotiations were conducted in conformity with the principle of constitutionalism and the rule of law, there would also have to be a constitutional amendment to the Canadian Constitution. The Court does not specify which amending formula should be used. This is not yet a judicial matter. Be that as it may, it appears that a declaration of independence would be unconstitutional if it were made without an amendment to the Constitution.

However, the Court also recognizes the possibility that political actors might be reluctant to engage in a process of negotiation on secession. Quebec could then be forced to declare its own independence without the consent of the federal government and the provinces. This would be 'illegal' and 'unconstitutional,' but the international community would assess the legitimacy and the legality of the process. Quebec could indeed conduct negotiations in good faith and in accordance with the required underlying principles while the provinces or the federal government might not. Or all the political actors could act in conformity with the four principles but still reach an impasse.

If that were to happen, the legitimacy of the declaration of independence could serve as a justification for recognizing the sovereignty of Quebec. The international community could be led to such a recognition even though the declaration was 'illegal.' According to the Supreme Court, the international community would assess the legitimacy and legality issues by determining whether the political actors were acting in conformity with the four underlying principles during negotiations.

This would amount to subordinating, up to a certain point, international law to internal or Canadian constitutional law. The Court discusses the need for a clear majority on a clear question, but it leaves to the political actors some leverage on these issues.

The Clarity Bill

One may feel uncomfortable with many aspects of the Supreme Court ruling. Its greatest defect is this: the federal government *unilaterally* consulted the Supreme Court by asking three questions *unilaterally* determined by the federal government itself. These questions were submitted to nine judges who had been *unilaterally* chosen by the federal government, and all three concerned secession in its relation to the Canadian Constitution, a document that was *unilaterally* adopted without the approval of Quebec. The main question was this: 'Can Quebec *unilaterally* secede?' And the Supreme Court answered 'No'! Yet, in spite of its defects, the Court's judgment is overall well-balanced, detailed, and subtle. Unfortunately, we cannot say the same about Bill C-20. We should not confuse the two documents: C-20 and the reference case. It is not fair to suggest that those who oppose C-20 also oppose the reference. On the contrary – all those who have opposed C-20 have used the reference in their arguments.

It is indeed without precedent in the Western world that the highest court and the national parliament should both formally declare that a part of the federation may secede. But Canada is also the only long-standing democratic regime that has imposed a new constitutional order on one of its peoples without a referendum and without consultation. Even worse, it has imposed this new constitutional order against the explicit will of the vast majority of MLAs in the Quebec National Assembly. To this day, Quebec has still not signed the new constitutional order, which has been declared illegitimate by sovereigntists and federalists alike.

Also, we have very good reasons to believe that through C-20, and contrary to the Supreme Court, the federal government is not establishing as many guidelines as are possible to ease the process of secession. Quite the contrary, it is doing exactly the opposite – it is *multiplying* obstacles to complicate the process.

Indeed, C-20 has raised numerous obstacles that are not contained in the reference: interference with the National Assembly's deliberations on the wording of the referendum question; endless consultations with an indeterminate number of political actors; rejection of the rule of the absolute majority; rejection of any referendum question involving an offer of partnership; an obligation to negotiate the partition of Quebec; and so on. The Supreme Court tried to ease the process leading to sovereignty; C-20 has raised new obstacles to make it as difficult as possible.

Bill C-20 violates the principle of federalism in that it allows the House of Commons to interfere with a process conducted in the National Assembly. In effect, it allows the House of Commons to intervene during deliberations on the wording of the question – deliberations that will take place within Quebec's National Assembly. This contradicts the Supreme Court judges, who would allow the National Assembly to unilaterally initiate a process leading to a referendum.

The Clarity Bill suggests that the rule of the absolute majority is not acceptable. It stipulates that the House of Commons will 'take into account the size of the majority of valid votes in favour of the secessionist option.' The majority must therefore go beyond 50 per cent plus 1.

But nowhere do we find such a claim in the reference. When the Court speaks of a 'clear majority,' it is referring to a real absolute majority as opposed to an apparent one. The absolute majority would be apparent if there were a large number of rejected votes, or if there were an absolute majority of Yes votes to an ambiguous question, or if there were a very low participation rate.

'It is indeed without precedent in the Western world that the highest court and the national parliament should both formally declare that a part of the federation may secede.'

The Court confirms this interpretation when it explicitly states that the word 'clear' in 'clear majority' must not be interpreted in quantitative terms. It has in the context a qualitative sense. So one cannot use the Court's recommendations on the clear majority as a suggestion that the majority should be qualified. It is often said that if the Court had wanted to speak about an absolute majority, it would have done so – an indication that the words 'clear majority' cannot mean 'absolute majority.' I agree completely, and this is why I gave another interpretation of those words. But the same remark applies to the other interpretation, according to which the words 'clear majority' mean 'qualified majority.' This is not what the Court meant, for it would have used those words had it been its intention to mean a qualified majority.

It is true, however, that the Court ultimately leaves the interpretation of what is to count as a clear majority in the hands of the political actors. So let us look at the positions held by the different political actors.

Almost all political actors on the federal scene (NDP, Conservatives, Canadian Alliance, BQ), representing 62.2 per cent of the Canadian population, have explicitly repudiated the qualified-majority rule, even though some of them ultimately voted for C-20 as a whole. And we know there has been a lot of turmoil on this question even within the Liberal caucus. Also, all political parties within Quebec, representing 99 per cent of the population, agree on this issue. Moreover, all Canadian political actors in the past have accepted the 50 per cent plus 1 rule in referendums: in 1949, 1980, 1992, and 1995. The same remarks apply at the international level. The UN, the European countries, and so on have all explicitly accepted the rule. So there is an established consensus among political actors.

Here are some figures. France ratified Maastricht with 51.4 per cent of the vote in 1991. Denmark voted No with 50.7 per cent of the vote in 1992. Switzerland rejected its integration within the European Economic Community with 50.3 per cent of the vote in 1992. Sweden held a referendum favourable to its entry into Europe with 52.2 per cent of the vote in 1994. Norway voted against the European Union in 1994, also with 52.2 per cent of the vote.

Can these figures be compared with a question on secession? Well, the sovereigntists do not wish simply to secede from Canada: they want Quebec to become independent and to offer an economic and political union with Canada similar to the one now in place in Europe. So there is perhaps not such a big difference between the referendum questions of the sovereigntists and the referendum questions in Europe.

The absolute majority rule will also apply in Scotland if a referendum on sovereignty is ever held there. Both Scottish and English political leaders agree with that. The UN has applied a similar rule for East Timor, Eritrea, and Western Sahara. Whether the results of a secession vote would have to involve a large majority is not the issue. Everywhere, absolute majority has been the rule. I call that a consensus among political actors.

The federal representatives who voted for C-20 are trying to change the rules, because they are afraid they will lose the next referendum. This is clearly antidemocratic. The only exceptions to the rule of absolute majority that we can mention relate to Mikhail Gorbachev's desperate effort to prevent the Baltic states from recovering their sovereignty, and to Israel's Knesset, which voted to implement the requirement of a qualified vote to approve any agreement with Syria. However, these are perhaps not good examples to follow.

All other exceptions have involved voters that are not individuals but representatives of different regions, or an explicit qualified-majority rule in the constitution. In the United States, constitutional amendments do indeed involve a qualified majority, but such amendments concern representatives of different regions, states, and so on, not individual voters. St Kitts and Nevis does require a qualified majority for secession, but this is by an explicit agreement in that country's constitution. My argument is precisely that when the voters are individual citizens, 50 per cent plus 1 is the rule to follow, unless there is an explicit rule of qualified majority adopted in a constitution.

Of course, in a sense, an absolute majority in a referendum on sovereignty is not enough to achieve a secession. Even if the required majority is 50 per cent plus 1 in a referendum in which the participants are individual voters, we must try very hard to negotiate successfully with the federal government and the provinces so as to amend the Canadian Constitution. Of course, Quebec does not recognize the constitutional order that was imposed on it in 1982, and thus we don't accept the amending formula that was incorporated in the constitution. So we don't accept the requirements of a unanimous ratification by all the provinces within three years. Anne McLellan, when she was the federal Minister of Justice, conceded that secession is such an extraordinary event that it cannot be forced into the mold of an ordinary constitutional amendment. But some kind of agreement must be reached on a transition process that will enable Quebec to enforce a new constitutional order while Canada amends its own constitution. And all this should take place before Quebec declares its sovereignty. After a vote on secession, the federal government and the provinces will assess the results and the clarity of the question, as will the international community. So it is wrong to suggest that those who oppose C-20 want to exclude Canadians from the process.

After an absolute majority of Yes votes, we will all have an obligation to negotiate: Quebec, the federal government, and the other provinces (and Quebec will also have to negotiate directly with its eleven aboriginal peoples). These negotiations will have to be conducted in accordance with the underlying constitutional principles noted by the Supreme Court: the democratic principle, the principle of federalism, the principle of constitutionalism and of the rule of law, and the principle of protection of minorities. During the negotiations, we will have to consider the economic union as well as the interests of the provinces, Quebec, the federal government, and linguistic minorities and aboriginal peoples. All these negotiations should (if all goes well) lead to a constitutional amendment on the part of Canada.

So in a way it is true that a simple majority vote is not sufficient for sovereignty. But this does not mean that we require a qualified majority in a Quebec referendum. The only clear and admissible interpretation that we can make of the democratic principle is the rule 50 per cent plus 1, but the democratic principle is *not* the only principle we must follow in the process leading to sovereignty. And during that process, we must try to achieve an agreement with the provinces that goes far beyond the existence of a simple majority within Quebec.

The Clarity Bill also prevents the government of Quebec from asking a question that includes a reference to an offer of partnership. Of course, nowhere do we find such a recommendation in the Supreme Court reference. Worse, this aspect of C-20 goes against the very ideological roots of the sovereigntist movement, which was created initially as the 'Mouvement Souveraineté-Association.' The offer of an association or partnership with Canada was always part of the sovereigntist's ideological position, yet a negotiation with Quebec after a referendum involving a reference to an offer of partnership has now been declared illegal by C-20. According to the federal representatives, there is simply no way to formulate a clear question involving both sovereignty and an offer of partnership.

This clause also runs counter to the contemporary international scene, in which many nation-states wish to remain sovereign while at the same time accepting economic and political interdependence with other states. Canada's federal representatives are trying to reject that option. They want to force sovereigntists into a hard-line position: complete independence from Canada. They would prevent the sovereigntists from proposing a reasonable and balanced question to the population of Quebec. They are trying to force sovereigntists to ask a question relating to the creation of a traditional nation-state. This too, I suggest, is antidemocratic.

Finally, the Clarity Bill validates partition. It compels the federal government to negotiate the borders of the new state. Of course, nowhere in the Supreme Court reference do we find any sort of recommendation to redraw the borders of Quebec. Yet partition is now officially promoted and approved by the federal government. This particular aspect of C-20 is immoral and should be condemned by everyone. It runs counter to the practice of international law, which now almost universally applies the uti possidetis principle. In the recent past, all federated states have kept their borders after secession or after the dissolution of the encompassing federation: Yugoslavia, the Soviet Union, Czechoslovakia. The borders of Mali and Burkina Faso were kept intact following decolonization, after a ruling to that effect by the International Court of Justice. This ruling inspired the Badinter Commission in its recommendations for Yugoslavia. These same rulings and recommendations also influenced the report of the five international experts on international law during the hearings of the Quebec Commission on Sovereignty.

Conclusion

It should come as no surprise that moderate federalists who are concerned about Quebec are sharply critical of C-20. These moderates include the Conservative Party, the Quebec Liberal Party, the Action Démocratique du Québec, Claude Ryan, Roger Gibbins, Gordon Gibson, Guy Laforest, Christian Dufour, Senator Jean-Claude Rivest, Ken McRoberts, André Tremblay, John Conway, Judy Rebick, and Senator Pierre-Claude Nolin, not to mention a group of 160 intellectuals and ten Canadian associations led by Gary Kinsman.

In any case, C-20 has been rejected by two-thirds of the Quebec MPs in the House of Commons. It has been rejected by all three parties in the National Assembly and by 60 per cent of the Quebec population in many polls conducted after its adoption.

So I feel that the federal government should, by its very own standards, withdraw the bill. Of course, there isn't anyone in the streets of Quebec denouncing the bill. But a quiet rejection is a rejection all the same.

6 Leading the Way

PAUL GROARKE

The decision by the Supreme Court of Canada on Quebec's right to secede seems to have been applauded on all sides, without much appreciation of the legal significance of the decision.

So perhaps a primer is in order. The first thing is that much of the judgment deals with peripheral issues like the powers of the Supreme Court. It also contains a brief political history of the country.

One fact that stands out is that secessionists won eighteen of Nova Scotia's nineteen seats in Canada's first federal election; and thirty-six of thirty-eight seats in a concurrent provincial election. There may be an important lesson in the fact that this was not enough to legally secede. Nova Scotia was not permitted to leave, on the basis that it had already assumed obligations to people in other provinces.

The court also deals summarily with the argument that Quebec has a right to secede under international law. Canada has done nothing to forfeit its right of government in Quebec and is entitled to maintain its territorial integrity.

None of this really stands at the heart of the judgment, however, and the most important aspect of the legal ruling has largely been ignored. That is simply that Quebec cannot secede without an amendment to the Canadian Constitution. This raises two fundamental issues.

The first is whether the government of Quebec has the mandate to seek such an amendment. The judgment establishes that this could be obtained by a referendum, but it must be a 'clear question' supported by a 'clear majority.' This could be sticky, since the Court has left it to the political actors to determine what constitutes a clear majority; and it is not entirely clear what would happen if the two sides disagree.

Nevertheless, it is the second issue that presents the more serious difficulty. This issue is how the parties would decide the terms of the necessary amendment; and the truth is that the Court has said little in this context, other than to impose a duty on both sides to negotiate in good faith. Even so, the Court makes it clear that the difficulty is not whether Quebec or any other province can secede. No, the real difficulty lies in the specifics of an agreement. 'The devil would be in the details.'

Anyone who has seen a couple go through a messy divorce will understand the point. The theory that everyone is reasonable tends to break down rather quickly when you have to decide who owns the household goods. And there are more intractable issues in the constitutional sphere. How do we distribute the national debt? Who owns the property of the federal government for Quebec. What about minorities?

The most inflammatory issue is probably territory, and the court's judgment includes a muted warning for Quebec. 'Nobody seriously suggests that our national existence ... could be effortlessly separated along what are now the provincial boundaries of Quebec.'

Nonetheless, the court was firm that any negotiations must take place at the political level, and commentators have claimed that the judgment merely throws the whole question back to the politicians. The matter is more complicated, however, and the deeper implications of the judgment lie in the fact that the Supreme Court has said that any negotiations must respect four basic constitutional principles.

'Secessionists won eighteen of Nova Scotia's nineteen seats in Canada's first federal election; and thirty-six of thirty-eight seats in a concurrent provincial election. There may be an important lesson in the fact that this was not enough for secession to occur. Nova Scotia was not permitted to leave, on the basis that it had already assumed obligations to people in other provinces.'

What are these four principles? The first is federalism, which recognizes that neither level of government alone has the authority to determine what an amendment should contain.

The second principle is democratic. Here the court goes out of its way to emphasize that the principle of majority rule does not override other constitutional values. Democratic government is in part premised on a respect for 'dissenting voices' and the majorities in other parts of the country.

The third principle is that any exercise of political power must be in accordance with the provisions of the constitution and the rule of law. Like the fourth principle, which holds that minorities must be protected, this cuts into the rights of a seceding majority.

The real force of the judgment lies in the fact that these principles are given constitutional status by the Supreme Court. This means that a government which does not respect them is acting unconstitutionally. That raises the possibility of further litigation.

What happens if a Quebec government simply declares its independence, in complete contravention of the constitutional principles enunciated by the Supreme Court? The court's answer is simple and blunt: such an action would be tantamount to revolution and a government that acted in such a manner would be acting outside the rule of law.

After the last referendum, it should be clear to everyone that the results of another referendum might be contested by the losing side. There were improprieties in the counting of ballots, and there is a good argument that there should have been independent monitors at the polling stations. At the present time, there is no legal mechanism in place for determining whether the question posed in a referendum puts the matter fairly or whether irregularities in the campaign would invalidate the result.

This is a troubling issue, since the federal government might refuse to accept the results of a controversial referendum or question its significance. Since the referendum, we have learned that then-premier Jacques Parizeau had fully intended to declare independence if the Yes side won. This, even though the question posed in the referendum only spoke of negotiating with the federal government and could not, even at a stretch, be said to have authorized such a declaration. Those who want to leave the matter in the political realm might reflect on the fact that the Parti Québécois apparently believed that victory in the referendum would give it command of the Armed Forces stationed in Quebec.

Events move quickly, and grim questions lurk around this corner. Would the armed forces obey a government that declared its independence? What would happen if there were riots in the Eastern Townships? And what about the Securité de Quebec?

There are times when reality pushes aside the simplistic assumption that things will work out for the best: the killing of Pierre Laporte was a good example of that, as was the proclamation of the War Measures Act. It is an unsettling fact that most unilateral attempts to assert some form of political independence are usually associated with insurrection and civil war. There is a reason for that: in law, a unilateral declaration of independence is an interregnum in the rule of law, a revolutionary act that disrupts the legal order. A moment of anarchy.

It is an error to think that Canada is fundamentally different from other countries in this world. Anything could happen.

The law has its imperfections, to be sure, and there is something to the criticism that the Supreme Court is a federal bench. But Quebec is a part of Canada, at least for the present, and there is no way around that fact.

Historically, there are no legal rules here. This is the place where we enter a state of anarchy, the classical state of nature. If we ever find ourselves in such a position, only good fortune will save the country from the more predatory forces of human nature.

It is telling that the Supreme Court ultimately relies on the international order to see that the four principles which it has endorsed are respected in any negotiations. If one of the parties defaulted on its obligations, the judges reason, it would lose its 'legitimacy' in the international community. Legally, this is an important half-step towards the recognition of an enforceable moral order that transcends the normal legal or constitutional order.

Whether it has any force would probably depend on the actions of the international community. If the decision whether to recognize the independence of Quebec is made on the basis of such considerations, rather than brute politics, this is an important development that would have repercussions elsewhere.

What the Canadian decision really does is require the parties to negotiate until they reach a satisfactory legal solution. The importance of the decision on the larger international stage may simply be that it raises the possibility of a peaceful process of secession.

And make no mistake about it. If the case merely suggests that a reasonable accommodation can be found, even in situations where the most ardent political aspirations come into conflict, the world is better for it.

7 Minorities and the State

WILL KYMLICKA

The twentieth century will be remembered as a century of wars (hot and cold) between states. In contrast, the twenty-first century is likely to be a century of wars within states, in which ethnic minorities take up arms against the state. The portents are already with us, in Chechnya, East Timor, Kosovo, Sudan, Kashmir, and Rwanda, to name a few. This trend is so widespread that some commentators call it the 'Third World War.'

Canada has been fortunate to avoid the violence that has plagued other multiethnic countries. However, we've continually had to adapt and innovate to meet the challenge of accommodating diversity, while respecting individual rights and maintaining stable political institutions.

Consider immigration. Canada's approach to immigration has changed dramatically in the past thirty years. Prior to the 1960s, we expected immigrants to assimilate, and indeed tried to keep out any groups that were seen as incapable of assimilation. By assimilation, I mean that immigrants were expected not only to learn an official language and accept liberal-democratic values (as they still are), but

'Canada has been fortunate to avoid the violence that has plagued other multiethnic countries. However, we've continually had to adapt and innovate to meet the challenge of accommodating diversity, while respecting individual rights and maintaining stable political institutions.'

also to become virtually indistinguishable from native-born citizens in their style of speech, clothes, diet, housing, political views, work habits, family size, and leisure activities. It was seen as un-Canadian if immigrants were too visibly 'ethnic' in their appearance or behaviour.

This approach was repudiated in 1971, with the adoption of the federal multiculturalism policy. We now view it as natural for immigrants to cherish and express their ethnic identity, if they so desire, and to remain proud of their ethnic heritage. Moreover, public institutions, such as schools, hospitals, police, and the media, should recognize and accommodate this fact. These institutions, which historically were designed to accommodate the beliefs and practices of the British and French settlers, should now make good-faith efforts also to accommodate the beliefs and practices of immigrant groups.

Canada was the first country to adopt a multiculturalism policy (and to entrench it constitutionally), but several countries quickly followed, including Australia, New Zealand, Sweden, and the Netherlands. A government-sponsored commission in Britain just recently recommended the adoption of a Multiculturalism Act there. And while there is no official multiculturalism policy at the federal level in the United States, there are such policies at the state and local levels and within schools, the media, universities, hospitals, police forces, and even private businesses. (The eminent Harvard sociologist Nathan Glazer titled his recent book *We Are All Multiculturalists Now*).

Many commentators think that this sort of multiculturalism policy is needed to solve the problem of violence against 'foreigners' in countries like Germany (against the Turks), Spain (against the Moroccans), and the Czech Republic (against the Roma).

A second area of Canadian innovation concerns the Québécois. At various points after the French were conquered by the British, attempts were made to assimilate French-speaking Canadians into English-speaking society – for example, by removing French-speaking educational and political institutions. This was the goal of Canada's British rulers in 1840, when French-dominated Lower Canada was merged with British-dominated Upper Canada. The presence of a minority group that thought of itself as a separate 'nation' was perceived by the British as dangerous, so concerted efforts were made to deprive the French of this sense of distinct nationhood.

However, this goal was repudiated by the Confederation agreement of 1867, which recognized that the Québécois would continue to exist as a separate society, with their own language and institutions, into the indefinite future. There were various ways in which Confederation manifested this acceptance of minority nationhood, but the most important involved the decision to create a subunit – namely, the province of Quebec – in which the French would form a local majority and thereby exercise significant self-government.

This was arguably the first time in any Western democracy that a territorial sub-unit was deliberately created to enable minority self-government. Yet this idea of accommodating national minorities through territorial autonomy is now widespread. Other examples include Scotland and Wales in the United Kingdom, Puerto Rico in the United States, Catalonia and the Basque region in Spain, Flanders and Wallonia in Belgium, South Tyrol in Italy, and the Aland Islands in Finland. Many commentators think this model provides the only feasible approach for those countries in Eastern Europe, the Middle East, or the Third World that contain powerful and sometimes violent minority nationalisms, such as Georgia (for the Abkhaz and Ossetians), Turkey (for the Kurds), Nigeria (for the Ogoni), and China (for Tibet).

A third innovation concerns the treatment of Aboriginal peoples. Historically, the goal of the British colonial governors and then the Canadian state was to strip Aboriginal peoples of their lands and gradually to assimilate or 'civilize' them. This was to be achieved by eliminating all of the pre-existing legal, political, and educational institutions through which Aboriginal peoples had governed themselves, and by replacing these institutions with paternalistic rule from Ottawa. Aboriginals were considered wards of the state, incapable of governing themselves, so Ottawa decided what sorts of laws, schools, health care, and so on they should receive.

This policy was repudiated in the early 1970s. There is now a commitment, mandated by the Supreme Court and entrenched in the constitution, to uphold treaties with Aboriginals, to recognize customary law and customary property rights, to negotiate new treaties and land claims, and to restore self-government, including control over areas such as education, health care, resource development, and policing.

Canada was the first Western country to create a legislative framework for negotiating new treaties and land claims, and to recognize indigenous rights constitutionally. Similar developments have since taken place with the Aborigines in Australia, the Maori in New Zealand, the Sami in Scandinavia, and indigenous peoples throughout Latin America. The United Nations has suggested that this approach could help resolve the violent uprisings of indigenous peoples in Bangladesh, the Philippines, Mexico, and elsewhere.

It may seem surprising that these Canadian innovations have been so influential. After all, Canadians themselves do not see these policies as particularly successful. The condition of Aboriginal peoples is deplorable, Quebec almost seceded in 1995, and multiculturalism is controversial. More generally, minorities often feel they still suffer the lingering effects of older policies of assimilation and exclusion, and indeed doubt whether the larger society has really changed its attitudes. The majority of Canadians, in contrast, mostly feel that they have been very generous with minorities, and indeed have gone above and beyond the call of duty in accommodating them. Often they feel hurt that minorities are not more grateful for this generosity. To paraphrase P.G. Wodehouse, if Canadians are not actually disgruntled about these policies, they are far from gruntled.

Why, then, are these Canadian innovations adopted elsewhere? Whenever I travel abroad to discuss 'the Canadian model,' there are two aspects of our experience that other countries admire. The first concerns process. Canada has a legal framework in place for discussing issues of diversity. Policies of multiculturalism, federalism, and Aboriginal rights give the relevant groups a seat at the table, and extend constitutional legitimacy to their identities and interests. In many countries, there is simply no framework in place for majority and minorities to sit down and discuss how to live together. Our deliberations are often strained, but at least we talk to one another and develop public policies on a consensual basis.

The second concerns values. Canada has developed a political and legal culture that combines a commitment to universal values with recognition of diversity. In many countries, such as the United States and France, people are given a stark choice. They are told that citizenship must be based either on universalistic values of freedom, equality, democracy, and human rights that apply uniformly to all citizens, or on respect for particularistic identities, but that it cannot be based on both.

The Canadian experience suggests that this is a false choice. Canadian citizenship is indeed grounded in universalistic values of freedom, equality, democracy, and human rights. There is a very deep consensus on these values in Canada, one that cuts across all ethnic, linguistic, and religious lines. Polls show that we are just as committed to these values as citizens in the United States and France. We promote these values in our schools, ask immigrants to accept them as a condition of citizenship, and expect the Supreme Court to uphold them whenever they are threatened. So adherence to these values is indeed part of what it means to be Canadian.

But in the past, our implementation of these values was stained by illiberal assumptions about the inferiority of other groups and cultures. Now we are building new models of citizenship that uphold universal values of democracy and human rights while simultaneously respecting the various languages, cultures, and identities that exist in Canada. This approach is by no means uniquely Canadian, but Canada has played a significant role in developing and diffusing it.

8 The Paradox of Liberal Nationalism

WILL KYMLICKA

Nationalists are renowned for seeing plots against their national honour and national interests, and for assuming that others are insensitive to their national aspirations. Quebec nationalists are no exception to this. Lucien Bouchard has developed this paranoia into an art form, finding an insult to Quebec in virtually any statement or policy of the federal government, however innocuous on the surface.

But as the old saying goes, just because you're paranoid doesn't mean they aren't out to get you. I would not say that most English Canadians are out to 'get' Quebec, but I do believe that most English Canadians are indeed insensitive to, or uncomprehending of, Quebec nationalism. Most English Canadians do not take seriously the implications of the fact that the Québécois view themselves as a 'nation.'

This failure became clear to me, surprisingly enough, when I was working on the staff of the Royal Commission on New Reproductive Technologies. The commission received hundreds of submissions from the across the country – from professional medical organizations, women's groups, infertile couples, Catholic and pro-life groups, community health organizations, groups representing people with disabilities, and so on – and I had the task of reading through all of them.

This quickly became rather tedious, because pro-life activists say the same thing whether they come from Moncton, Toronto, or Vancouver, as do community health advocates and patients' support groups. The rhetoric, the reasoning, and the recommendations of each of these groups was utterly consistent from one end of the country to the other.

Except for Quebec. Outside of Quebec, there was a virtually unanimous desire for federal regulation of new reproductive technologies (NRTs), such as in vitro fertilization, donor insemination, and embryo experimentation. In Quebec, in contrast, most groups assumed that provincial governments should set the basic rules.

This disagreement over jurisdiction reflected an even deeper difference in attitudes towards federalism. Most groups from English Canada paid no attention to the fact that Canada is a federal system. For them, the assumption that NRTs should be regulated at the national level was not even seen as controversial. English Canadians simply took it for granted that since NRTs raise important social and ethical issues, they ought to be dealt with at the national level, rather than having each province set its own policy. Few groups made any effort to show that the federal government had any legitimate jurisdiction over this area, even though health care is in fact one of the clearest cases of provincial jurisdiction.

What this shows, I think, is that most English Canadians have no real commitment to federalism in the classic sense – that is, to a system in which provincial and federal governments are coequal, in that both have inherent sovereign powers which the other level of government cannot intervene in. In a true federal system, there are certain issues on which the federal government simply has no legitimate authority.

Yet English-Canadian groups never questioned whether the federal government had the authority to establish the sort of national licensing scheme for the providers of NRTs that already exists in Britain or France. Groups debated the merits of different regulatory schemes, but the idea that the federal government might be constitutionally prohibited from establishing such a scheme was never even considered. Of course, one might think it unreasonable for such groups to be familiar with the arcane points of federal jurisdiction. But the fact that these jurisdictional issues seem arcane to many English Canadians is itself evidence of how far the federalist ideal has receded from their political consciousness.

When most English Canadians think about federalism, they typically think of it simply as a form of decentralization. Because Canada is a large and diverse country, we have decentralized certain decisions to lower levels, including provincial governments. But this distribution of powers is largely seen as a matter of efficiency rather than entrenched principle. Moreover, decentralization may work best by giving powers to local governments rather than provincial governments. Indeed, many of those groups that favoured national standards for NRTs also favoured a radical decentralization of health care administration away from provincial bureaucracies to regional or community health councils, leaving provincial governments with little role in either establishing or administering policy.

For most English Canadians, then, powers are contingently decentralized in various ways, but the federal government is assumed to have a kind of ultimate authority over all issues, such that if something really important arises – like NRTs – it is right and proper for the federal government to intervene and establish national standards.

The Royal Commission itself, to its credit, recognized that the jurisdictional issues were more complicated. Yet it, too, endorsed a federal regulatory regime. The commission's argument involved an extraordinary interpretation of the 'peace, order and good government' clause of the old British North America Act, which allows federal intervention in provincial affairs in cases of urgent and overriding national importance. This convoluted legal argument can be seen, generously, as a bold attempt to respond to the overriding desire of Canadians (outside Quebec) to have national regulation of NRTs. But it also reflects the typical English-Canadian indifference to federalist principles. Federalism, from this point of view, is a legal formality whose anachronistic barriers can always be overcome by marshalling ingenious legal arguments.

It is this attitude towards federalism that drives Quebec nationalists up the wall. And they see this same attitude in many other areas – most notably, in the repatriation of the constitution and the adoption of the Charter of Rights in 1982 without Quebec's consent. The debate in Quebec is often described as a conflict between 'federalists' and 'nationalists.' But many Quebec nationalists argue, with some justification, that they are the only true federalists left. They argue that federalism could have provided a satisfactory form of national self-determination for Quebec, but that the English-Canadian indifference towards (true) federalism has made sovereignty the only way to ensure respect for Quebec's national aspirations.

Does this attitude among English Canadians reflect a desire to oppress Quebec, or to impose English-Canadian values on the Québécois? I don't think so. Most English Canadians assume that the Québécois share the same basic concerns and principles. Hence adopting national standards, even in areas of provincial jurisdiction, is seen as promoting shared values, not as imposing one group's values on another.

> 'Here we get to the paradox that is at the heart of the Quebec–Canada relationship. Quebec nationalists have become more and more preoccupied with maintaining and enhancing their provincial jurisdiction even as they have become more and more similar to other Canadians in their basic values. They have become more and more insistent on recognition as a "distinct society," even as they in fact become less and less distinct.'

And in a sense, English Canadians are correct to make this assumption. For example, there was no evidence whatsoever in the commission's public consultations that Quebecers differed from other Canadians in their attitudes towards NRTs. Fifty years ago, one would have expected Quebec to adopt a distinctive attitude towards reproductive technologies, based on Catholic teaching regarding the evils of contraception, abortion, and donor insemination.

But not today. And indeed, none of the Quebec groups that favoured provincial jurisdiction did so in the name of cultural differences. If Quebec were to adopt its own regulatory regime regarding NRTs, there is every reason to think it would be based on the same norms and principles as in English Canada. How then can a single national regulatory regime be seen as oppressive to Quebec, rather than as uniting all Canadians through the promotion of shared values?

Here we get to the paradox that is at the heart of the Quebec–Canada relationship. Quebec nationalists have become more and more preoccupied with maintaining and enhancing their provincial jurisdiction even as they have become more and more similar to other Canadians in their basic values. They have become more and more insistent on recognition as a 'distinct society,' even as they in fact become less and less distinct.

Quebecers now live in the same secularized, liberal-democratic, pluralist, urbanized, consumerist culture as English Canadians, worshipping the same ideals of individual liberty and democratic equality. Public opinion polls have repeatedly shown that there are no statistically significant differences between Quebecers and other Canadians in basic political values. How then can national policies based on these shared values – whether relating to NRTs or to the Charter – be seen as oppressive or insulting to Quebec?

It is this 'paradox' that explains, at least in part, the impasse in Canada–Quebec relations. Apart from a few bigots, the overwhelming majority of English Canadians have no desire to 'get' Quebec, or to insult Quebecers. But they simply do not understand why Quebecers would feel insulted by the adoption of a common national NRT policy – or a common Charter – so long as these are based on shared values.

And indeed there is something deeply paradoxical about this. Faced with this paradox, two responses are possible. One is to avoid the paradox by assuming that Quebec nationalism must, after all, be illiberal. On this view, the apparent shift in Quebec political culture towards secular liberal pluralism is simply skin-deep, and the demand for greater provincial autonomy reveals a deeper, covert desire to retreat from modernity and recreate a more closely knit and intense communal life based on shared ethnicity, history, and religion. This view denies that a truly liberal nationalism is possible – the desire for national recognition and autonomy by Quebec proves that Quebecers do not in fact share the liberal values of other Canadians.

The other response is to accept that the paradox of liberal nationalism is real and that it will not go away. This response accepts the view that Quebec nationalism is fundamentally driven by a forward-looking conception of Quebec as a pluralistic, liberal, modern society, rather than by a backward-looking communitarian or conservative ideology.

The claim that modern Quebec nationalism is a fundamentally liberal movement is hardly novel. But it is this claim that may serve as a key to resolving the paradox of liberal nationalism. Given their shared values with the rest of Canada, it may seem puzzling that Quebecers have such a strong sense of political identity. But given these same shared values, similar puzzles arise with regard to English Canada.

Why, for example, are English Canadians so keen to have national standards relating to NRTs? The answer can't be that they share common political values, since that doesn't in fact explain why they prefer federal over provincial regulation. Provinces can act on these shared values just as easily as the federal government can.

Instead, the answer surely is that English Canadians have over time developed their own strong sense of forming a (pan-Canadian) political community. And so they want to act collectively as a political community, not simply as separate provinces. They want to deliberate together, and to make collective decisions, and to create and uphold collective institutions. That is, they too want to act as a nation.

Of course, the national identity that English Canadians have developed is pan-Canadian, including Quebec. Few English Canadians would describe their nation as being 'English Canada.' And this is why English Canadians view federal legislation as pivotal to expressing their national identity. Federal regulation of NRTs would allow English Canadians to express their collective political identity, and to fulfil their deeply felt sense of collective responsibility for one another and for their shared society.

The problem, of course, is that (true) federalism places serious limits on the extent to which English Canadians can act on this national identity. The only way for English Canadians to act collectively in an area like NRTs is to undermine the federal principles that have made it possible for Quebecers to act collectively.

In other words, the impasse in Quebec–Canada relationships is not simply that Quebecers have developed a strong sense of political identity that is straining the bonds of federalism. The problem is also that Canadians outside Quebec have developed a strong sense of pan-Canadian political identity that strains the boundaries of federalism.

Moreover, both of these political identities are complex and deeply rooted psychological phenomena, grounded in history, territory, and social interactions. There is a popular myth among many liberals that whereas Quebec's political identity is grounded in irrational factors such as language and history, English Canada's political identity is grounded in a rational commitment to principles of freedom and democracy. But the fact that the English Canadians share a commitment to freedom and democracy does not explain their deeply felt desire to act as a single pan-Canadian collectivity, rather than as separate provinces. This too is a contingent and affective desire rooted in a shared sense of belonging and membership that has transcended provincial boundaries.

This suggests that if we are to unravel the paradoxes of Quebec's national identity, we need to look more honestly at the development of English Canada's political identity. For both of these identities are now straining the bonds of federalism. It also suggests that if we are to find a lasting settlement to our constitutional predicament, we need to find a political arrangement that accommodates both of these political identities. We need to find a form of federalism that allows Quebec to act on its sense of national political identity, without preventing English Canadians from acting on their equally deeply felt desire to act collectively, and not simply as discrete provinces.

9 Canadian Nationalism and the Distinctiveness Fetish

THOMAS HURKA

Canadians care about medicare; it's a source of national pride, and central to our attachment to Canada. Some Canadians care especially about medicare because they think it's distinctive of Canada, at least when compared to the United States. But it's an odd idea, that we should care most about what's distinctively Canadian. Would medicare matter less if the United States had it too?

It isn't hard to imagine. John F. Kennedy might not have been assassinated in 1963; Hubert Humphrey might have been elected president in 1968. Either might have instituted full medicare in the United States. And if so, our own medicare would be less distinctive. To think that Canadian nationalism must focus on what's distinctively Canadian is to think that Canadian medicare would then be less important. But this is to misunderstand the basis of healthy national feelings.

Nationalism is a form of partiality, of caring more about some people than about others. A Canadian nationalist cares more about relieving poverty among his fellow Canadians than among foreigners; he wants immigration policy decided mainly by its effects on people now in Canada. In this respect, nationalism is like other forms of partiality, such as caring more about your spouse or children than about strangers, and can be understood by analogy with them.

If you care especially about your spouse, it's partly for some of his or her qualities: his or her intelligence, trustworthiness, and so on. But you know these qualities aren't unique. Other people have them, some even to a higher degree. What attaches you especially to your spouse is something that isn't a quality in the normal sense. It's their having participated with you in a shared history. No one else, no matter how intelligent or trustworthy, could be the very person you fell in love with that summer, who helped you through that depression and who did all those other things with you.

Nationalism has a similar basis. A Canadian nationalist thinks that Canada has good qualities, such as a commitment to tolerance and equality. But he needn't think Canada is the best country in the world.

What ties him especially to his fellow Canadians is something historical: that they grew up with him here, experiencing the same weather
and TV shows, electing and then despising the same politicians.

That's why it wouldn't matter if the United States had medicare too.
Canadian medicare would still be a good thing about Canada, and it
would still be part of our history. It would be something we developed,
from Tommy Douglas and Emmett Hall through to the Canada Health
Act. It would be something we've all participated in, both as users of
medicare and as contributors to it. American medicare might be similar,
but it wouldn't be the system we've lived with here.

So it's a mistake to tie Canadian nationalism to distinctively Canadian qualities, and it isn't a harmless mistake: it has resulted in several
beliefs destructive to Canadian national life.

First, it's led many Canadians to embrace false beliefs about their
country. It's often said that Canada is, distinctively, a country of diverse
regions, not just Quebec compared to English Canada, but every province compared to the others. But do we really believe that, say, Nova
Scotia is more different from Alberta than Scotland is from England, or
than northern India is from southern India? Reverting to medicare, do
we think we're the only country in the world with social programs?

Some nationalists recognize that in the world as a whole, Canada is a
fairly average industrial democracy. But they say the point isn't to be
distinctive in the world. It's to be distinctive in North America, to be an
egalitarian or sharing society in the same region as the United States.
That's because the United States isn't just another country. It's our
immensely powerful neighbour and the source of our constant existential question: Why aren't we a part of them? Only as distinct from the
behemoth to the south does Canada have a reason to exist.

But there's no such existential question. Canadians have no interest
in joining the United States, as they show repeatedly in opinion polls.
And it's not because of any bogus idea about distinctiveness. They root
for Canadian sprinters at the Olympics without wondering whether
they sprint in a distinctively Canadian way.

Think again about your spouse and children. Do you face a constant
question about whether to join the family next door, just because they
have a bigger house or more money? Of course not. You're attached to
your family by a history your neighbours don't share, and that's attachment enough.

Second, the distinctiveness fetish has corrupted Canadian politics,
offering an all-purpose counter to any proposal: 'That will lead to the

Americanization of Canada.' This counter is used by the left to oppose privatization and deficit cutting and by the right to oppose employment equity and the Charter. But if something American is bad, it has to be bad for some reason other than that it's American. So let's hear that other reason. And may some American things not be good?

Consider Jean Chrétien's remark that Canada without Quebec is unthinkable. It assumes that Canada is thinkable only if it's distinct from the United States, and that it will be less distinct without Quebec. But the assumption, again, is false. Canada without Quebec would be a smaller Canada; it would lack, tragically, many people who participated in our history. But it would have no more reason to break up than a family would after one of its members runs away.

'Canadian nationalism hasn't always been based on issues about distinctiveness. Think of the nationalism of the years following the Second World War ... Canadians of the late 1940s didn't think they had fought in a war no one else had fought, or even fought in a distinctive way. It was enough that they – people with a common history – had fought alongside other nations and fought well.'

Also corrupted is commentary on the arts, which often assumes that the main point of Canadian art is to express what's distinctively Canadian. This view is hard to apply to arts like music. How does a classical violinist play Beethoven in a distinctively Canadian way? And it's even constricting when applied to literature. There are uniquely Canadian experiences, and literature that captures them can be as great as any literature anywhere. But there are also universal experiences, such as falling in love, aging, and death. Writing about exploring those experiences can likewise be great; and if it's by a Canadian, that makes it ours.

Canadian nationalism hasn't always been based on issues about distinctiveness. Think of the nationalism of the years following the Second World War, based on Canada's participation in that war. Canadians of the late 1940s didn't think they had fought in a war no one else had fought, or even fought in a distinctive way. It was enough that they – people with a common history – had fought alongside other nations and fought well.

This older nationalism was healthier than any current version based on distinctiveness. To care that your nation's good qualities be distinctive is to care both that your nation have them and that other nations do not. (The second, by the logic of distinctiveness, is just as important as the first.) But isn't it nasty to want other nations not to share your own nation's good qualities? Isn't this a kind of malice?

Distinctiveness-nationalists should ask themselves whether they aren't prone to just this malice. Do they take a kind of comfort from the violence and inequality of the United States, just because they make Canada different? Are they partly pleased when Newt Gingrich and Pat Buchanan have political successes in the United States, just because they wouldn't have them here? If so, their ill wishing only works through the nasty logic of distinctiveness.

But Canadian nationalism needn't be nasty. We can, while recognizing Canada's weaknesses, treasure its good qualities and hope other nations share them. We can want all nations to respect human rights and practice tolerance; we can hope the United States becomes less violent and even institutes medicare. If it does, Canada will be less distinctive. But that won't matter to Canadians freed of fraudulent ideas about distinctiveness and attached to one another, as to their families, by the solid bond of a common history.

PART X

9/11 and After

1 Being True to Ourselves in Times of Crisis

ANDREW IRVINE

So where do we go from here?

A tragedy of catastrophic proportions has struck. Thousands are dead and thousands more have had their lives altered forever by acts of unspeakable brutality.

Those directly affected by the events of September 11, 2001, must mourn the loss of their loved ones and struggle to piece together their shattered lives. Those of us not directly affected will want to express our condolences and sympathy to those who have lost so much. We will also want to extend a helping hand to friends in need. As modest as these actions are, we hope they will be of some comfort to those whose lives are now in turmoil.

But in the days ahead, what can we do to make the world a better, safer place for our children?

First, we need to redouble our efforts in the fight against terrorism, not just in North America, but around the world. Not only is it right to hold individual terrorists accountable for their actions, it is also right to take a harder line with governments that sponsor terrorist activity. If it turns out, once the facts are in, that this means working in concert with our allies to initiate military action against the governments of countries such as Afghanistan, Iraq, Iran, Libya, Sudan, Syria, Saudi Arabia, and North Korea, then this option will need to be pursued.

Now that the dust has begun to settle in New York and Washington, it would also be the height of negligence to refuse to consider the possibility that the worst is yet to come. What reason do we have to think that these attacks were not just the first of many? What reason do we have to think that, if ignored, terrorism will simply disappear of its own accord?

Next, we in the West need to begin taking the kind of international political action that we have been putting off for far too long. We need to recognize that terrorist threats do not exist within a political vacuum, and that a business-as-usual attitude towards governments that have little respect for human life and individual liberty can no longer be tolerated. We need to tell some countries that the issue of sanctions is going to be revisited. We need to tell China that our attendance at the Olympics will be directly linked to improvements in its human rights record over the next few years.

Far from being isolationist, these types of changes to foreign policy would require that we engage, rather than ignore, a world culture that is often hostile to the very existence of democracy.

Closer to home, we need to make it easier for suspected foreign criminals and terrorists to be deported. Together with the United States, we need to harmonize our immigration laws and look more closely at a continental energy policy and a continental security perimeter.

In Canada, we need to recognize that we have neglected our military for far too long. Decades of cuts to military spending have meant that too often, Canadians have had to rely on the generosity of our friends and neighbours in protecting our borders. The only alternative to increasing our own military spending is a Pax Americana in which Canadian interests will get little or no hearing.

How can Canadians feel safe at home when we are unwilling to spend even modest amounts on essential military hardware? How can we continue to place such heavy burdens on our men and women in uniform overseas when we continue to close our military colleges and cut back on education generally?

'The inevitable calls to abandon fundamental democratic values during times of crisis are not only unproductive. They indicate that we have misunderstood the very things that give our society the strength it needs to fight these kinds of unprovoked, brutal attacks.'

Without new submarines and helicopters, how can we defend our coastlines and oilfields? Without training in foreign languages and world history, how can Canadian peacekeepers be expected to respond to complex political and military situations abroad? Without being able to recruit the best mathematicians and computer scientists, how can we defend ourselves against computer viruses designed to destroy civilian and military infrastructure without firing a shot?

We also need to remember that terrorist attacks, such as those in New York and Washington, are not intended as attacks on individual citizens. Nor are they intended as attacks on an individual nation, as important as the United States may be.

Instead, they are intended as attacks on the democratic way of life itself. For this reason, we must refuse to allow these attacks to destroy the very features of our society that distinguish us as a democracy. Especially during times of crisis, it is important that we remain true to our most central values.

This means taking action to protect our families and our nation from unwarranted attack, but it also means speaking out against ethnic hatred and in favour of traditional democratic values. Tolerating ethnic hatred not only harms individual citizens, it also harms the very society we want to protect.

The inevitable calls to abandon fundamental democratic values during times of crisis are unproductive. Furthermore, they indicate that we have misunderstood the very things that give our society the strength it needs to fight these kinds of unprovoked, brutal attacks. At times of crisis it is sometimes tempting to think that unless we begin placing restrictions on individual privacy, travel, or the press, we will somehow be placing ourselves at a disadvantage. Yet nothing could be further from the truth.

Calls to restrict freedom of speech and the flow of information make it harder for us to trust our governments and our neighbours. Restrictions on movement and trade make our societies poorer and more isolationist. The blanket electronic surveillance of all law-abiding citizens means that fewer resources are being devoted to the kinds of focused human-intelligence gathering that is essential for fighting terrorism. The introduction of identity cards for law-abiding Canadians in Flin Flon, Manitoba, would be expensive, bureaucratic, and time-consuming. It would also give us a false sense of security and would divert our attention from the real causes of terrorism.

The simple fact is that restrictions on civil liberties, like the internment of Japanese Canadians during the Second World War, are almost never as effective as targeted military action designed to root out the problem of terrorism at its source.

Thus, far from bringing about the end of the open society, recent events could well mark the beginning of its resurgence. Only if we begin to abandon our most fundamental democratic values will the terrorists have won.

2 Vulnerability

TRUDY GOVIER

Terrorist acts bring violence to ordinary people who are not normally central to a political conflict. And this, indeed, is usually their point: to intimidate by spreading shock, alarm, and fear. Before September 11, 2001, terrorism by foreign operatives was barely known on the North American continent. That its victims were people who had long assumed themselves safe made the impact all the greater because such death and destruction were not supposed to happen here. Commenting on the shock felt by North Americans, Archbishop Desmond Tutu alluded to a sense of bewilderment. North Americans were used to the idea that battles were waged thousands of miles away; so-called smart bombs were the weapons of choice, and other people's countries were the recipients. If 'you've always been the top dog,' you suddenly discover your vulnerability, and profound shock is the result, Tutu said. It's as though you're thinking, 'Hey, I'm just like any other human being. We are like any other human society. We're vulnerable. Vulnerable.'

So far as mundane safety goes, North Americans have been a privileged group. Terrible events such as political bombings, amputations, and disappearances happened in countries far away. Even the nuclear threat felt remote and unreal to most people most of the time. These things weren't supposed to happen, not at all, and they certainly weren't supposed to happen *here*.

The events of September 11 have inspired a special kind of fear because the victims were proceeding with their everyday work lives. We feel a sense of acute vulnerability: it could happen to anyone. Even you. Even me. The perpetrators of this terror are fearful men who will go to their own deaths to attack Western culture. If you set off on a journey to attend a wedding or market a product, you could board a vehicle that somebody turns into a weapon of mass destruction. What was supposed to be a pleasant little trip could make you part of somebody else's suicidal attack. If you work in a tall building, retrieving a document from your office or preparing your hair salon for the next shampoo could be your last action before you leap from a window to escape raging fires and plunge a hundred stories to your death.

In the aftermath of September 11, travel is no longer fun to contemplate. It's a stressful prospect. We no longer just hear planes; the noise of a plane recalls images of fire and terror. Tall buildings look vulnerable and remind us of calamity. Box cutters are frightful objects. The needles of a diabetic, even paper clips or eyebrow tweezers, could become tools that help turn an airplane into a weapon of mass destruction. Artificial sweetener and baby powder might contain anthrax spores. Hand-addressed mail, once an object of interest, has become a potential hazard to be approached with care. For some, every Arabic name, even every brown face, poses a threat. Our position in the world has been upset because what was mundane is no longer so. Airplanes flying into buildings are not the only form that terrorism could take: you could breathe in toxic fumes, consume poisoned food or medications, or drink water that has been deliberately contaminated by your enemies. These aren't pleasant thoughts.

Security can be stepped up by hiring more people and by staging even more thorough inspections in a host of contexts, but it's an illusion to think that every hole can be plugged. Developing this theme, analyst David Carr commented that the United States offers especially tempting prospects for terrorists. Fifty of the world's hundred tallest buildings, the Mall of America in Minneapolis, and the Indianapolis Motor Speedway (which can seat more than 250,000 people) are just some of the targets Carr cites.

Terrorism threatens us deeply because it brings into question our ordinary lives and the trust we need to conduct them. Our vulnerability stems from our interdependence; we are linked together profoundly in our need for the basic items of life. Nearly all the trivial objects of our lives have come into contact with thousands of other people. If someone wants to alter a vehicle, poison the water, alter a pharmaceutical formula, spray crops with toxins, destroy a bridge, or plant explosives in his shoes – well, how can we stop him? Especially if he is willing to give up his own life in the process? For many North Americans, the fundamental change since September 11 is that fear has spread. What was mundane can no longer be so; what we took for granted for so many years, we can take for granted no longer.

The interdependence of human beings in complex modern societies is nothing new; there was plenty of interdependence before September 11. Human beings have long depended on one another for food, shelter, and clothing. For love and intimacy, friendship, collegiality, and neighbourly assistance. For communications, information, expertise, and advice. At deeper levels, we depend on one other for our understanding of the world, for basic knowledge, and ultimately for language and reasoning itself. In leading our own lives, we need and depend on other people. In our daily lives, we implicitly trust other people – far more people than we realize, most of them strangers. We have deep and unconscious expectations that mundane objects are reliable; we don't, for instance, expect people to poison the mail, set fire to their shoes, contaminate the water, or turn themselves into bombs. Our social trust works for us because most people act reasonably well most of the time. They do their jobs with a fair degree of conscientiousness and competence, in moderate pursuit of their own interests, while giving due consideration to others. And when things go on as expected, we don't notice our vulnerability. The reliable and good – the ordinary day at the office, the flight that arrives on time, the grilled cheese sandwich that tastes pretty good, the mail that is opened without effect – are normal and unremarked. It's the surprising and damaging events that make the news.

'We have always been vulnerable. The difference terrorism makes is that we have become aware of our vulnerability.'

The range of social trust extends far beyond the obvious because so many of the mundane *things* we take for granted are artifacts produced by human beings. Fundamentally, it is people who are the objects of our trust; when we rely on things in the normal way, we implicitly are trusting the people who provided them. This means trusting other people for their competence; we presume these people know what they are doing and how to do it. It also means trusting their motivations; we presume they are not trying to maim or kill us – and that is the presumption that terrorists make us question. Social trust is fundamental in life, and it's the upheaval of social trust that makes terrorist attacks so profoundly disturbing. They provide such appallingly clear evidence that things are not all right with our world. Sociologists sometimes say that trust is the glue that holds society together. An almost invisible web of confident reliance underlies mundane life – a web that in normal times tends to go unnoticed. We become aware of that reliance and our casual confidence only when things begin to go wrong. You could say that terrorism weakens the social glue, by inspiring fear that it just won't stick any longer. When you stop to think about it, terrorists could operate nearly anywhere. A taxi? Didn't one of those hijackers work for a while as a taxi driver? Your cup of tea? Who had access to the water used to make it? That polite young man at the Xerox machine? He might be making false documents to support somebody who wants to launch another attack.

We have always been vulnerable, and terrorism makes us become aware of our vulnerability. People who seek to destroy us could do so in thousands of ways; and many thousands of people hate us and want to destroy what they hate. Our old presumptions of confidence and security are gone, and that is why the world seems so different now.

And yet people have an extraordinary drive and capacity to continue with ordinary life. During the long and vicious civil war in Lebanon in the 1980s, television news broadcasts showed scenes of ordinary Lebanese people carrying on with their lives – somehow. I was always moved by the scenes of laundry hanging out to dry because they provided such a homely background to the smoke and gunfire. Bombs, killings, terror, mayhem, and madness; and yet someone had done the family laundry. People *lived* in Beirut. They cooked supper and washed the dishes, and no doubt many went to their jobs as usual, to support themselves and their families during the bitter civil war. Life goes on. In Sarajevo in the mid-1990s, snipers on the hillsides made every excursion risky. Even so, the beleaguered people of Sarajevo went about their lives in the middle of all this. They shopped for bread, met in cafes, read stories to their children, went shopping, kept diaries, and made love.

Surely, North Americans are no less resilient and determined than other people. Like others around the world, we crave life and have a tremendous ability to go on with it. We find ways to accept our vulnerability, reconcile confidence and vigilance, and construct a new sense of the normal.

As I thought about people who cope in turbulent times, my mind turned to the later Stoics, who lived under the depraved and mad emperor Nero in the first century. Nero should probably get some credit for later Stoicism: the terrors of his rule must have added considerably to the appeal of the doctrine. Stoic philosophy proposes a solution to the problems of vulnerability and fear. You could think of Stoic works almost as 'how to' books for surival in a dangerous world. Under the tyranny of the corrupt and erratic Roman emperors, people could be subjected to dungeons, torture, exile, and sudden execution. Epictetus the Stoic was a slave who somehow received an education and won his personal freedom. After philosophers were expelled from Rome in 89 CE, he began teaching at Nicopolis.

The central idea of the Stoics was that we need to distinguish clearly what is in our power from what is not. In our power, they said, are opinions, beliefs, attitudes, desires, aversions, and our own acts. Not in our power are the body, parts of the body, parents, brothers, sisters, children, property, status, reputation, and the acts of other people – especially the rulers of society. The secret to human happiness is to care only about those things which are within our power. 'Who then is invincible? It is he whom none of the things disturbs which are independent of the will,' Epictetus said. We cannot control our perceptions and impressions, or our original impulsive emotions. But we *can* control our responses to them. The Stoics saw human beings as creatures of will, and they counselled the need for a strong, steady purpose. We have freedom of choice about how we reflect and act, and we can discipline ourselves to limit our vulnerability. The Stoics counselled that we could achieve tranquility by using our reason and by defining the good in terms of things that depend on the will. Desires should be carefully reined in. If you've got an expensive new car, replace it with a slightly battered old one; then you'll be less vulnerable to car theft. Your car won't tempt many thieves, but if anyone were to steal it, your loss would be modest and you'd be less affected by it. Epictetus said, 'I must die. Must I then die lamenting? I must be put in chains. Must I then also lament?' Death and misfortune are inevitable, but lamenting is not – that was his point. There is no country in which he could live, Epictetus said, where death would not someday befall him. But he could control his feelings and attitudes about his death, and that's something worth doing. We can learn to discipline our desires and exercise our will, Epictetus advised. And philosophy will be our teacher.

Difficulties arise when we consider the fundamental Stoic distinction between what is within our power and what is not; for the Stoics it was all a question of control. It's a tempting model, especially when we're feeling vulnerable, because control would indeed be a wonderful thing to have. But thinking about control or non-control is an oversimplification. There is also such a thing as influence. For all that we cannot control our children, surely we influence them in many ways. In Western societies, people have at least some chance of influencing political leaders and officials. The belief that either things are subject to our control or they are not ignores certain realities; in the end, it's a discouraging dichotomy because it omits the idea that we might exert influence in contexts where we don't have full control.

The Stoics believed that nature would provide the ultimate ethical guide for men and women. Nature is reasonable; we can study it and grasp its laws, and having done so, we can uncover the ethical principles we need to guide us. The nature that grounded late Stoicism was fatalistic. What was going to be was going to be; it was terrible; people had to adjust to it and cope. They could determine their own attitudes and emotions because those, and those alone, were within the power of will and reason. As for everything else, the idea was to train yourself not to care. You couldn't do anything about your physical vulnerability, but you could make yourself emotionally invulnerable. The Stoics coped with their frightening world by trying to organize their emotions so that they cared only about the few things that were within their control. Western readers, few of whom adopt a fatalistic stance on the world, are likely to find problems with such conceptions. Faced with vulnerability, we would prefer to limit it rather than accept it as an inevitable fact of modern life.

If Epictetus and his colleagues had written a 'how to' book for the aftermath of September 11, they would have advised us to organize our lives so as to understand what fate holds for us; we would then be able to correct our emotions according to our beliefs and cope calmly with the inevitable. Such a book would have been a hard sell. 'Que Sera Sera' was a popular song in the 1950s, but few Westerners would accept the refrain that 'whatever will be will be.' Fatalism is profoundly un-modern – and modernism is profoundly unfatalistic.

Modern Judaeo-Christian frameworks incorporate some version of free will, which theologians seek to reconcile with the Creation and the power of God. The understanding represented by scientific theory shows gaps in explanation and arguably in causation itself. Political and social realities seem less predictable than physical reality, and physical reality itself has unpredictable dimensions. Surprises can happen, and some surprises are catastrophes. Yet other surprises offer unexpected opportunities and provide a basis for hope.

I found Stoic writings a delightful distraction in the weeks following the attacks of September 11. But if we're looking for a complete philosophical answer to our questions about fear and vulnerability, the Stoics can't provide it because their thinking is too fatalistic to fit our own. Even so, I think that Epictetus stated some simple but useful truths. Our attitudes are our own, and so are our feelings. We can amend these feelings according to reason, and we can improve our reason by paying close attention to what's happening – even when the information is unpleasant. Our feelings and values can be altered on reflection. Not everything is worth caring about. Many luxuries are dispensable.

Most significantly, the story of Epictetus is just one among thousands that show people in other times and places coping with chaos and vulnerability, while conducting meaningful lives in their worlds of terrifying confusion.

3 A Repeat of the McCarthy Era Would Imperil Democracy

JOHN DIXON

Many commentators say Americans are grappling with two 'firsts' – the first time in modernity they've been made to feel vulnerable on their own soil, and the first time they must do battle with faceless enemies who hide in shadows.

These claims neglect recent history. During the 'Haunted Fifties,' America struggled with the threat of a fifth column of Communist cells. And the stakes were nothing less than a credible threat of nuclear annihilation.

This was the McCarthy era, named after the senator who ran the inquisitorial House Un-American Activities Committee (HUAC). McCarthy's committee became infamous for trampling civil rights – the presumptions of innocence and privacy and the freedoms of conscience, association, and speech.

The archives of the former Soviet Union underscore the truth that even paranoids have real enemies. There were, in fact, many Communist spies in the U.S. government during the McCarthy era.

So would more rather than less McCarthyism have yielded a counter-espionage victory? That's a live question because the crucial weapon against terror is the same one required for effective counter-espionage: intelligence. Who and where are the enemy, and when and how will they strike?

History has shown that the real achievement of McCarthyism was to place an enduring scar on the body politic of the United States. To the extent that spies were actually uncovered, it tended to be the result of conventional police work.

In the wake of September 11, the then American Secretary of State Colin Powell called for 'an intelligence war' to fight terrorism, and Canada was urged to join it. But even warfare places limits on civilized participants. There is always a balance to be struck between principle and need, a balance that depends on both the importance of the principle and the likelihood that some sacrifice of it will yield significant results. For instance, according to some the torture of suspects can be an enormously productive source of intelligence, but it offends such important civil and human rights principles that its official use in the West is out of the question.

What is most decidedly not out of the question now are proposals for extraordinary limitations on privacy rights. The technology exists for both general and targeted surveillance of practically all telephone and Internet communication. Transmissions can be intercepted, temporarily stored, and screened by computers for the presence of words, phrases, or even specific voices associated with terrorist activity.

In Canada, the Communications Security Establishment (CSE) of the Department of National Defence has been involved in this kind of signals intelligence (SIGINT) work for years. The CSE shares its product with members of the ECHELON surveillance system, which includes the United States, the United Kingdom, Australia, and New Zealand.

'A democratic people do not simply **consent** *to be governed: a democratic people reserves ultimate political authority to* **govern itself.** **Thus the closely related civil rights of privacy and freedom of conscience and speech are not claimed on some abstract, general principle. They are claimed as the tools a free people require for their own work as rulers.'**

We can now expect the rationale for full deployment of this technology to be vigorously advanced. There have already been reports of CIA agents installing special surveillance systems on American Internet providers such as AOL. Should we regard the recent terrorist attacks as a good reason to legalize and perhaps widen the CSE's domestic activities by blending them with those of the Canadian Security and Intelligence Service (CSIS)? What is the correct balance now?

A good place to begin an examination of the principles involved is with the words of Alexander Meiklejohn during the McCarthy era. Meiklejohn was a constitutional scholar who dared to petition the U.S. Congress to testify against the excesses of the HUAC. 'Americans,' he said, 'did not fight for the right to advocate revolution in 1776; they fought for the right to advocate revolution forevermore.'

This refers to what Meiklejohn identified as the essential feature of democracy – the sovereignty of the citizenry. A democratic people do not simply *consent* to be governed: a democratic people reserves ultimate political authority to *govern itself*. Thus the closely related civil rights of privacy and freedom of conscience and speech are not claimed on some abstract, general principle. They are claimed as the tools a free people require for their own work as rulers.

This means that privacy and freedom of conscience and expression are not 'second order' democratic rights. Any limitation of them must be balanced against very substantial intelligence gains.

But such gains are doubtful when general SIGINT surveillance is domestically deployed. As soon as prospective terrorists know of it, they can neutralize its effectiveness by changing their communication practices. Instead of saying 'the bomb' has arrived, they could simply say 'the flowers' have arrived.

Furthermore, a computer screening system generates many 'false positives.' CSE, for example, has identified a person as a terrorist threat on the basis of an intercepted conversation in which he stated that his party was 'a bomb.'

The military part of the war against terrorism will have to be fought with judgment and extraordinary discipline if it is not to fail or even backfire. Similarly, the intelligence component of the fight must be carefully scrutinized to ensure that we do not limit or abandon vital civil rights for illusory gains.

This isn't fighting 'with one hand tied behind our backs.' It's fighting as hard as we can with an unclouded view of the resources of our enemies, and of what would count as a genuine victory.

These rudiments of strategy were forgotten in the McCarthy era, and we need to avoid living that era again, as either tragedy or farce.

4 Evil's Back – Now Let's Recover True and False

GRAEME HUNTER

If Osama Bin Laden can be credited with anything, it is with putting the word *evil* back in circulation. We're all saying it now. We no longer have to put it in quotation marks; no one pretends that it is just a relic of the bad old days before speech was sanitized by political correctness. What Osama did was evil. He is evil. That's all there is to it. On that matter almost everyone seems to be agreed.

Without a concrete example of evil before our eyes, we modern men and women find the term difficult to remember and almost impossible to use. That is because the social order of the past century or more has been built around the denial of evil. Instead of exhorting children from their earliest years to shun evil and pursue good, as was done in the past, we now think we can harness people's private vices and make them pay public dividends. Thus, instead of continuing to depict gambling (or prostitution, or drugs, or almost anything else) as evil, we describe them using the sanitary term 'lifestyle.' That is how we can justify licensing, regulating, and taxing them and so turning them to public profit.

'Our illness is not political at all, but linguistic. The word evil *may have got a toehold in our politically correct speech. But although we can now recognize it, we still lack the means to discuss it intelligently.'*

Only monumentally antisocial acts such as the deeds of September 11, acts that can never be turned to any good, call forth the use of the archaic term evil. Since the Second World War, Adolf Hitler has been our standard example. Winston Churchill called him simply 'that evil man.' But a generation has now arisen that did not know the Nazi horror and that knows no one who experienced it. For them, even Holocaust denial seems rational. That is why Osama Bin Laden has slipped so neatly into Hitler's still warm niche.

That is also why it is so uncool to say anything positive about Osama Bin Laden. T-shirts sporting the mug of Che Guevara or Chairman Mao may still be socially acceptable, but few will flaunt Bin Laden. Even tough guys are not tattooing his name or face on their bulging biceps or teeny foreheads. We have all agreed to talk about him only in the negative. The strange thing is how many different things that negative can be made to mean.

Atheists think the source of his evil lies in taking religion seriously. Believers accuse him of taking the wrong religion seriously, or of distorting his own. Postmodernists denounce him for taking anything seriously. Racists hate him for being an Arab, socialists for being rich. Some of these opinions are undoubtedly false, but it is hard to say so publicly without seeming to stand up for him.

Journalists such as Matthew Rothschild and George Monbiot have begun to write of a 'New McCarthyism.' They see an analogy between the anti-Communist fervour awakened in 1950s America by Senator Joseph McCarthy and the sudden chilling of all exchanges of opinion on the subject of Bin Laden. 'Were the founding fathers to congregate today to discuss the principles enshrined in their Declaration of Independence, they would be denounced as "anti-American" and investigated as potential terrorists,' writes Monbiot.

The problem, however, is not political repression. Our illness is not political at all, but linguistic. The word *evil* has got a toehold in our politically correct speech. But although we can now recognize it, we still lack the means to discuss it intelligently. As a first step towards finding our tongues, we need to relearn another pair of terms. To have an informed opinion about Bin Laden or any other subject, we have to recover the use of the politically incorrect words *true* and *false*. For discussion to be possible, we must be able to say that while Bin Laden himself is an evil man, not every opinion about his evil is true.

Free discussion of any topic becomes possible when people realize that, while men may be dangerous or evil, opinions can only be true or false. To speak of dangerous opinions is as silly as speaking of erroneous men. True opinions are never dangerous. False opinions are called dangerous because they are false and, being false, might lead those who believe them to do dangerous things. The reason free societies have always valued public discussion is that it permits false opinions to be detected and true ones to be made more widely known.

Before the age of newspeak we all believed the truth would make us free. The chill will come off public discussion when we recover that belief. To do so will have at least two advantages. It will raise the level of public debate, and it will bury political correctness. A great good may yet come out of the evil of September 11.

5 Freedom, Not Security, Is Fundamental

MARK KINGWELL

My buddy Todd, a criminal lawyer, got married not long ago, and the other night he and his wife had a party for their friends in Toronto. During the speeches, one of the guests remarked that Todd likes to tell people who find his job distasteful that it amounts to 'quality control on the state' – defending those whose guilt has been unofficially assumed or bad character pre-decided. Yes, some of his clients are unsavoury types; and yes, some of them eventually go down to conviction for theft, assault, or even murder. The point is that they all deserve an able defence.

The same guest, also a lawyer (there were a lot of lawyers there), went on to say this job has a special relevance now that the government is poised to deliver the legislative equivalent of the Chevy Corvair – though the Ford Pinto might provide a more apt comparison. The sweeping new security bill, C-36, under the scrutiny of a Special Senate Committee, is an example of what happens when the state makes laws in reactive mode. In Canada's peculiar form of cozy oligarchy, where the doctrine of parliamentary supremacy is really just another way of saying the Liberals can do whatever they want, quality control is more necessary than ever.

Personally, and I may just be giving in to cynicism here, I don't look to the Senate to provide it. Among other things, its review of Bill C-36 is supposed to confirm the government's claim that the bill has been 'Charter-proofed' – that is, worded so it won't violate the guarantees laid down in the Charter of Rights and Freedoms. The government doesn't want to be fighting a lot of expensive legal cases arising from C-36. But really – being cynical again, sorry – neither the senators nor the government's inside Charter 'experts' inspire a lot of confidence about the wisdom of this bill.

The commonplace has it that the recent terrorist attacks have forced us to reconsider the implicit commitments of our way of life. Like many commonplaces, that is both true and false. Yes, we've been thrown back on ourselves and forced to consider what matters to us most. But, as so often, it has become easy to lose focus and descend into a haze of sentiment and flag-waving and talking tough. The really important commitments are to much more abstract things, things it's hard to get emotional about but that nevertheless provide the basic structure of our lives.

I mean things such as the rule of law, the idea of an open society, and the ongoing, fractious nature of genuine democracy. And, somewhere in there, the special status of civil liberties.

It's a persistent problem in liberal societies that people have trouble distinguishing Hobbes from Locke. (I realize they may not put it to themselves that way.) It's easy to see why. Both philosophers offered state-of-nature thought experiments, the founding myths of the liberal state in the West. Both considered contracting individuals the basic building blocks of a society. But nevertheless, writing less than forty years apart and with England's Glorious Revolution in between, they defined the opposite poles of political justification in the early modern period. And their ghosts are with us still. Hobbes's *Leviathan* (1651) offers a terrifying pic-

> 'All law is a tightrope walk, a contingent and revisable attempt to hold in balance various kinds of goals: freedom, security, equality, justice.'

ture of a natural state where, famously, human life is 'solitary, poor, nasty, brutish and short.' The only solution to the perpetual war of all against all, Hobbes suggests, is the creation of a sovereign monarchical power with absolute authority; only through a sacrifice of complete (but self-defeating) liberty will we secure the conditions of peaceful coexistence. Or, to put it in the terms offered recently by one of my students, security trumps freedom.

Locke, in contrast, begins his *Second Treatise of Government* (1690) with a picture of the state of nature that is less stark but no less untenable: individuals in this natural condition have powerful reasons to want to move out of it, not least to secure private property. The main difference is that the resulting social order is founded on an agreement that, as with all true contracts, can be rescinded at any time if the terms are broken. Unlike the absolutism of Hobbes's monarch, Locke's democracy is subject to constant vigilance by citizens and the possibility of revolution, should the state exceed its justified limits. Here freedom, not security, is the foundation of a well-ordered society.

In times of trial, when the Hobbesian state of nature seems to threaten, we need to remember this relationship of priority. In reality, there is no such thing as the state of nature, nor a natural right to property; there are only the more or less successful attempts of human beings to arrange their political affairs as best they can. But a liberal society that puts freedom second – even for a moment, let alone three years – is one in danger of self-contradiction.

All law is a tightrope walk, a contingent and revisable attempt to hold in balance various kinds of goals: freedom, security, equality, justice. It is never perfect and it will never extend as far as we wish it to. The kernel of truth in the Hobbesian vision – a point made powerfully in the last century by thinkers such as Carl Schmitt and E.M. Cioran – is that politics is always about conflict. Sometimes we manage that conflict, sometimes we avoid it, and sometimes, most rarely, we resolve it. But it never goes away for good.

Freedom entails many associated risks. First among them is the possibility that elements both inside and outside the liberal state will find reasons (or, as we know, motives beyond reason) to resort to violence. We must protect ourselves from those threats – and liberalism, as the McGill University philosopher Charles Taylor has insisted, is 'a fighting creed' – but not at the cost of the one piece of moral authority liberals can claim for themselves – namely, that they still put freedom first.

Right now, the Liberals are not being liberals. It's time for all of us to insist they get back to their own – our own – first principles.

6 Zap! You're a Terrorist

JOHN RUSSELL

How many terrorists are there in Canada?

A lot. More than anyone ever imagined. And they may be in the most unlikely places. At least, this will be true if the federal government's controversial antiterrorism bill (C-36) gets past the Senate unamended and is thereby effectively passed into law.

How could this be so?

Bill C-36's most fundamental problem has been its capacious definition of terrorism. Many civil-libertarian critics of the bill have warned, correctly, that C-36 could, in principle, target as terrorist even utterly familiar and unremarkable instances of protest and dissent, such as non-violent civil disobedience and illegal work stoppages. In response, modest amendments have been introduced that are intended to address these concerns.

But in a way, debate about this aspect of the bill has been a diversion from more real and pressing dangers. For it would have been a quick path to political and Charter-imposed self-destruction to use antiterrorism measures against ordinary non-violent dissenters. Regrettably, the debate about protecting non-violent dissent has effectively finessed discussion away from the more pressing and difficult problem of distinguishing terrorism from other forms of political violence.

Suppose, for example, that at some not too distant time gays take to the streets in anger in Vancouver or Toronto to demonstrate against police mistreatment, or to protest violence directed at their community. This is hardly difficult to imagine. Nor is it too difficult to imagine a scenario in which the community's frustration produces enraged and even violent confrontations with police and others. A police cruiser may be set on fire, police or straight civilians may be hurt, perhaps seriously, and there may be significant property damage. Or imagine a situation where police have reasonable grounds to believe that such events are being planned. By threatening or causing serious bodily harm or property damage in order to pursue a political objective (such as promoting awareness of the gay community's frustration and demands for support), these violent activities fall within the current definition of terrorism. They would therefore invite the use of preventive detention, investigative hearings, expanded surveillance powers, and other extraordinary law enforcement measures permitted under C-36.

But of course such activities are hardly the actions of terrorists, even though they are clearly criminal and need to be prohibited. And it is not just the gay community that could be targeted.

Should antiterrorism measures be used against protesters who riot in places like Seattle and Genoa? Should such measures be applied against so-called 'eco-terrorists' who spike trees and threaten serious injury to forestry workers? Should animal rights activists be treated as terrorists for poisoning Christmas turkeys?

Again, by threatening serious bodily harm in order to achieve political, ideological, or religious objectives, these activities all fall within the current definition of terrorism. Moreover, unlike the cases of nonviolent protest and dissent, there will be powerful political and law enforcement incentives to use special measures to deal with them. But such applications of extraordinary antiterrorism powers must be resisted. Such acts are certainly heinous and criminal and not to be tolerated. But it is a perilous exaggeration to describe them as terrorist, and thus on a par with the terrorist activities to which this legislation is a direct response.

Indeed, counting as terrorists some of the more radical environmentalists, animal rights activists, anti-abortionists, anarchist hoodlums, or violent gay protestors, would needlessly multiply the number of terrorists on the ground in Canada. It would divert efforts to detect and bring to justice the real terrorists. More powerful investigative tools, including more generous electronic surveillance powers, will inevitably place a multitude of legitimate protesters under closer and more extended government scrutiny than is already permitted by the Criminal Code. This is likely to

'Counting as terrorists some of the more radical environmentalists, animal rights activists, anti-abortionists, anarchist hoodlums – or violent gay protestors – would needlessly multiply the number of terrorists on the ground in Canada.'

have a chilling effect on the political activities of many Canadians and raise doubts about the legitimacy of the campaign against terror. Finally, militant extremists may be pushed towards real terrorism, thus adding to our current problems.

We must remember that no one called for amendments to existing

Criminal Code measures to deal with violent demonstrators and other criminal militants. Using C-36 against such individuals is therefore not a proportionate response to their threat.

Moreover, there are ways in which such violent political actions are often qualitatively different from terrorism. A violent political demonstration or riot is usually a one-time event – a discrete expression of rage typically brought on by a transitory event. It does not typically aim to terrorize a whole community.

Tree spikers and radical animal rights activists are different, too. They typically issue warnings to ensure that harm is effectively prevented, not caused.

Clearly, then, we need a debate on these issues to see if we can draw more careful distinctions between terrorism and other types of violent political activity. The relevant distinction needs to be drawn between 'terrorism' and 'criminal militancy.' However, drawing this distinction will be difficult. No legislation exists anywhere that has done it completely satisfactorily. This makes it even more essential that we have a proper debate on this issue to inform public officials about their responsibility to limit the application of an overbroad definition of terrorism. Unfortunately, we have not had that debate, in Parliament or elsewhere, because all efforts have been focused on protecting non-violent dissent and protest. In effect, we have been wasting our time on a moral and constitutional no-brainer. The difficulties of satisfactorily drawing these boundaries clearly demonstrate the ongoing threat such legislation poses to a free society. Thus, such a debate should persuade the public and the government of the need for a general sunset clause for C-36.

Time is short. It is hardly clear that the Senate will recognize these unaddressed issues concerning the definition of terrorism, let alone take time to pursue them. Yet without addressing these issues, we run the real risk, in C-36, of adopting a cure that is just as bad as the disease.

7 A Slogan for Our Times

JOHN RUSSELL

Things have changed.

This is undoubtedly the signature slogan of our post-9/11 age. All the evidence so far indicates that it is not wearing well.

Ask Maher Arar. He knows that things have changed. So do the twenty-two Ontario Muslims detained under Canadian immigration law for allegedly planning terrorist attacks. So do others who have been detained for up to two years without charge both here and in the United States.

It must be a bad sign when a historical slogan can be stated in ironic opposition to its original meaning. But that seems to be where we are today.

No one should be surprised. However, it is important to be clear just how some things have changed in the wake of 9/11. At first, the things-have-changed mantra was the ideological grounding for newly minted antiterrorism laws and for closing down legislative debates around them. But it is emerging that these legislative enactments do not represent the main elements of official responses to 9/11.

In fact, the more significant changes may be more subtle and difficult to pin down. They may have to do with shifts in the culture and attitudes of government and law enforcement after 9/11. The 'new normal,' as it chillingly has been called, appears to operate significantly beyond normal law and regulation. That is one thing, among many, that is truly frightening about what has changed post-9/11.

Maher Arar is a case in point. It appears that Canadian police and security-intelligence officials may have conspired – or at least knowingly sat by – and permitted a Canadian to be abducted and sent to another country to be tortured in an attempt to obtain information about terrorism.

That is an amazing allegation. Unfortunately, it is also disturbingly credible. Such measures were never contemplated even by our own much-criticized antiterrorism legislation. If it happened, how did it happen? And what else is going on outside the law?

The real lesson here is that politicians, bureaucrats, and law enforcement personnel seem prepared to avoid normal, intended processes of law to address perceived terrorist security threats. Indeed, the concern that antiterrorism laws could lead to a weakening of the rule of law may have been well founded, but for the wrong reasons. For it may not have been the antiterrorism laws that were the greatest threat, but the political signal they sent about a new mandate: things have changed. The normal rules of a free and democratic society no longer constrain the work of fighting evil in our midst.

Another case in point is that of the Ontario Muslim men who were suspected of planning terrorist activities and who were detained on immigration warrants. The government has now given up its attempts to link them to terrorist activities. Most are being deported for immigration violations. Not one has had a chance to clear his name publicly. All will live under suspicion for the rest of their lives.

'The real lesson here is that politicians, bureaucrats, and law enforcement personnel seem prepared to avoid normal, intended processes of law to address perceived terrorist security threats.'

Ironically, some are seeking refugee status in Canada for fear of what their governments will do to them in light of these allegations.

There are troubling parallels in these cases. Evidently, going through the process of producing evidence to justify criminal code charges or to compel testimony or detention under antiterrorism legislation is too demanding and awkward – and potentially embarrassing – to take chances with. No matter. Use immigration law, or pass off the file to another country – say, the United States or Syria.

It is difficult to believe that anyone could have gotten away with this before 9/11. But things have changed. Pretty clearly, they need changing again. And while it is relatively easy to change laws, it may prove harder to identify and change what appears to have gone wrong here and to establish new mechanisms for accountability.

This is, in part, why a public inquiry into the Arar case is so essential. Aside from the fundamental merits of Arar's call for a public inquiry, it may be our best bet to uncover how the culture of law enforcement and security intelligence has altered post-9/11. The RCMP Complaint Commissioner cannot investigate these matters. Neither will internal reviews by federal ministries.

It is said that history repeats itself, first as tragedy, then as farce.

Perhaps there is a corollary about history's slogans repeating them-selves – first as irony, then as jest. Quite possibly, other Maher Arars will emerge as victims. If so, we will be firmly in the tragedy/irony stage of this process. A public inquiry into the Arar case may be the only way to stop this descent. More importantly, we all need to learn more about how things have changed post-9/11.

8 The Democratic Challenge

JOHN DIXON

There is a lot of talk just now of enemies of freedom and democracy. But there have been far more potent enemies of democracy and individual freedom than the Al Qaeda network, and they have had no need of terror or weapons of mass destruction to do their work. Socrates – along with his remarkable student Plato – remains a powerful danger to democracy, *not* because he threatens our physical safety, but because his ideas continue to mock our complacent certainty that democracy is not simply the best form of government, but the only legitimate form of government. Here is Socrates' argument, as handed down to us by Plato.

People are different in their abilities and talents, and although something can be done about this, it remains the case that some are simply going to be more intelligent, energetic, and courageous than others. Society has a lot of different jobs to do, and people are most fruitfully and happily employed at a job that fits their abilities and temperaments. Of all of the functions and vocations in a society, none approaches the importance of the ruling function. Its excellence or lack of excellence has an impact on everybody's life. Only the most fit – the brightest, most energetic, and most courageous – may be permitted to rule, and even then they must be prepared carefully for their role if we are to produce wise servants for the entire community.

'Democracy says that though it is true that everyone is not the same, it is nevertheless true that everyone is **worth** *the same. It also says that this equal worth of people must mean that no one can be excluded from participation in their own governance.'*

Now, this argument poses a tremendous threat to democracy, but not because of some terrible deception that is being perpetrated by Socrates and Plato. It proceeds from the simple fact that every single one of their premises is sound.

So what can democracy say in its own defence? Democracy says that though it is true that everyone is not the same, it is nevertheless true that everyone is *worth* the same. It also says that this equal worth of people must mean that no one can be excluded from participation in their own governance.

It is hard to pinpoint where this belief or faith in the equal worth and dignity of people came from. It is peculiar to democracy, and it is peculiar to the West. But it clearly got a boost with Christ's egalitarian interest in companions so low that they would undoubtedly scandalize British Columbia's Surrey School Board. Then, after a long history of the submersion of Christianity in the procrustean embrace of the Roman, Byzantine, and Medieval churches, Luther burst forth with his Reformation idea that each and every one of us is competent to come to God on her or his own terms.

But this equality stuff does not solve democracy's problem. It just restates it. The challenge remains: if we are to have a government of all, instead of a government of the best, then we will have a government that is less than the best, and we must suffer the considerable consequences.

So now I come to my modest point. Democracy does not – cannot sensibly – dispense with Socrates' unassailable contention that only the best should rule. What democracy can do is move the line between the best and the rest.

With Socrates, the crucial dividing line exists in the external world, where it separates the few who should rule from the very many who must be subject. We take that line out of the world, where it is obnoxious to our democratic faith, and internalize it in every citizen, where it ennobles us all.

We are to be ruled not by the best *among* us, but by the best *within* us. Each of us is to bring a self-disciplined contribution to the shared task of ruling ourselves.

This democratic leap requires an incredible act of faith. Not passive hope, but active faith. And by active faith I insist that the realization of democracy – or even its survival in some diminished form – depends utterly upon our determination to conduct our public lives with real civic virtue. If we fail in this, there will be no need for terrorists to steal our freedom from us; we shall have already turned our backs on it.

9 Kindness

TRUDY GOVIER

Good can come of tragedy. On September 11, more than fifty planes landed in Gander, Newfoundland. Gander used to be a major refuelling centre for travel between North America and Europe, but now it is a small airport where few flights land on a normal day. On September 11, things were different. The town of 10,000 people was suddenly faced with the challenge of finding beds and food for some 6,500 guests. People from churches, service clubs, shops, and medical centres acted immediately to host their unexpected and slightly bewildered visitors. There was a mass collection of food, some driven in from even smaller and more remote centres. Local inhabitants provided toothbrushes, soap, and other supplies, along with showers and, for many, guest bedrooms.

The small town of Lewisporte, some forty-five kilometers from Gander, hosted some 213 passengers from Delta Flight 15. Lewisporte is a small fishing village, and just about the whole town got involved in volunteering. The townspeople treated the anxious travellers as special guests, taking them on boat tours of the harbour and hikes in the woods. When the travellers were ready to leave three days later, they were so grateful many were in tears. Shirley Boothe-Jones was one of them. She and a fellow passenger wanted to 'do something to thank these people.' They decided to start a scholarship fund, and by the time their flight back to Cincinnati landed, they had already collected some $14,000. In January, a television show about the project reported that $35,000 had been collected. The passengers on Delta 15 felt a powerful impulse to do something in return, to give back for what they had received, to reciprocate. The scholarship fund was a wonderful demonstration of the gratitude and affection they felt towards their generous hosts for the hospitality spontaneously offered in a crisis. It's a tale worth the telling.

September 11 was the kind of day that makes people feel pessimistic about human nature. But killing and brutality were not the only things that happened that day. There were acts of striking courage and dedication on the part of rescue workers and others. And there were acts of generosity and kindness – people responding with energy and sympathy to strangers simply because they were people needing help. These were powerful testimonies to the human desire to help others. The other person does not have to be a relative, a friend, an acquaintance, or even a fellow countryman.

As a Canadian, I might try to claim some vicarious credit for the generosity of these Newfoundlanders who are my fellow citizens. In the *New York Times*, one columnist said that the kindness and generosity arose from small-town values that don't exist elsewhere in Canada. I wondered how she knew: had she carefully surveyed the rest of the country? But that's not the point, really. I don't think it's a question of contrasting small towns with big cities, or of contrasting Newfoundland with the rest of Canada, or Canada with the United States or some other country. This story is about human beings helping one another in a time of need.

> '*September 11 was the kind of day that makes people feel pessimistic about human nature. But killing and brutality were not the only things that happened that day. There were acts of striking courage and dedication on the part of rescue workers and others. And there were acts of generosity and kindness – people responding with energy and sympathy to strangers simply because they were people needing help.*'

If I'm going to take vicarious credit for the energetic generosity of the folks in Lewisporte, I'd better do it on the grounds that I'm a human being. We human beings do things like this; there are countless tales about people showing kindness to strangers, and many of these instances occur in circumstances far more difficult than those of the Newfoundlanders on September 11. Another *New York Times* article told of the 'startling kindness' experienced by the writer when he was travelling in Afghanistan in the year 2000. A struggling man living in a brick hut offered the writer the family's last piece of bread, begging him to take it. The gesture was made from a sense of deeply felt obligation to extend hospitality to a stranger. Many cultures and peoples place enormous emphasis on values of hospitality and duties to offer food and drink to guests – even uninvited ones who come from afar.

Call it the ethic of hospitality. This ethic expresses a human impulse to sustain another human being in need. It is strong in many cultures, and I suspect it indicates feelings that are profoundly basic and important in human beings. I like to think that kind and generous acts arise from the sympathetic impulses we have because we are interdependent creatures. We have survived and continue to survive by cooperating with one another.

Writing in the eighteenth century, Adam Smith began his *Theory of the Moral Sentiments* with an account of the compassion human beings naturally feel for one another. Seeing suffering or pain, we imagine ourselves in the other's place and feel awful. Capitalists, take note: this is the same Adam Smith who has long been acclaimed for his theory of free market economics and for constructing the metaphor of the invisible hand. The invisible hand is a kind of underlying coordination that makes individual transactions, motivated by self-interest under conditions of market competition, work for the betterment of the whole of society. It's remarkable, to say the least, that the grand old man of market economics began his career as a moral philosopher who emphasized sentiments of compassion and sympathy. Speaking of human sympathy, Adam Smith said, 'The greatest ruffian, the most hardened violator of the laws of society is not altogether without it.' You might say that the invisible hand can operate only if it's wearing a moral glove, presumably also invisible. Adam Smith never stopped being a moral philosopher: he remained convinced that market economies require a moral foundation of honesty, promise keeping, trust, and reliable law. Without that basis, the pursuit of profit wouldn't provide an invisible hand; the result would be powerful thieves and the capitalism of brigands. Adam Smith believed that human nature makes ethics possible: human beings can work within a moral framework because they naturally care what happens to one another – as the story of kindness in Lewisporte so powerfully illustrates.

Adam Smith's ideas were developed further by another Scottish philosopher of his time, David Hume. Hume put the point beautifully when he said, 'Our minds are mirrors to one another.' Being around a cheerful person tends to make us cheerful, but being around a depressed person tends to make us depressed. Citing these facts, Hume argued that the moods of other people affect us through the mechanism of sympathy. Because of our capacity for sympathy, we actually come to feel what others feel. Hume was an empiricist who believed that all our ideas come from sense experience. When we see another person sad or in trouble, we form an idea of this feeling and that idea becomes so powerful that it produces in us the very feeling itself. The modern expression 'I feel for you' would have struck Hume as entirely apt;

that's what he meant by sympathy. The impression of the other's suffering gives us such a vivid idea of feeling awful that we begin to suffer ourselves. Through our capacity for sympathy, we care what happens to other people; if we didn't care at all, customs and laws would count for nothing and we wouldn't bother to distinguish between useful practices and counterproductive ones. The other human being is a human being like us; we know that because we can feel it. If the other human being is a stranger, that makes no difference. The tendency to feel such sympathy is a fundamental part of our human constitution and a powerful element in what we feel and believe.

Hume and Smith would have praised the people of Lewisporte – and everyone who extends hospitality to strangers and kindness to fellow human beings in need. But I don't think they would have been surprised by this heartfelt generosity. Both of them would have said that human nature is like that. It's a cheering thought in troubled times.

To act morally, we have to respect the interests and needs of other people. We can do this most easily if we are motivated to care what happens to other people. According to Hume and Adam Smith, our natural capacity for sympathy supports this motivation. It's important not to get this story backwards. Hume wasn't saying that we assist other people because we feel their pain and selfishly want to get rid of our own discomfort. That's not quite it. We want to make other people feel better because we care about them. That's what human sympathy is, and it's a ground-level fact of human life; we human beings really do care about one another. Dare I say it, we *naturally* care about one another.

A cynical observer might hypothesize hidden agendas among the good people of Newfoundland. Perhaps they assumed that many of the travellers they helped would be rich Americans and anticipated receiving something back from them: reputation, good connections, or money, for instance. A cynical interpreter can make any good news story look bleak. No real evidence is needed; he can just hypothesize a hidden agenda. Cynics can analyse everything from a negative point of view and make other people pretty depressed while they're at it. (This phenomenon confirms Hume's claim that depressed people tend to make others feel depressed.) But when cynical interpretations are based only on hypotheses and not on evidence, there's no good reason to take them seriously. The people who received this generous help in Newfoundland don't seem to have seen their generous hosts as self-serving, and strong friendships were formed in those few days after September 11.

My sense is, it's good news; take it at face value, and don't let yourself be talked into believing that it has to mean something else. There are such things as human kindness and generosity, and believing in these things doesn't make you naive or unsophisticated.

Not being cynically inclined myself, I return to the notion that human beings have a fundamental capacity for sympathy and that's why the suffering of other people affects us in the first place. I tend to agree with Hume and Adam Smith. Acts of generosity, heroism, and kindness have a source in our basic human make-up. That's why they can be found among people in all nations and cultures.

It was Alfred, Lord Tennyson who wrote of 'nature red in tooth and claw.' As I understand the reference, Tennyson was referring to non-human animals in wild nature and to the killing that characterizes their struggle for life. Teeth, we've got, but human beings don't have claws: Tennyson wasn't saying that human nature was 'red in tooth and claw.' In any event, if he had claimed that human nature was basically cruel, he would have been wrong. Kindness and generosity do not constitute evidence that some people successfully resist their real human impulses, those that would lead them to rape, pillage, and kill. For most of us, most of the time, such impulses don't have to be resisted. They don't exist.

Human nature has to provide for cooperation. If it didn't, our species never would have survived in the first place. It's an idea left unemphasized by theorists who write about the survival of the fittest and the selfish gene; but it is taken seriously by some anthropologists who argue that the deepest human need is for social bonding. One such account is offered by Mary E. Clark, who begins her argument by pointing out that human beings have large brains in proportion to the rest of their bodies. That means that human infants are born with relatively large heads and relatively helpless bodies, which in turn means that they need care over a long period of time. To provide that care, adults have to cooperate. Clark argues that the earliest human beings must have been creatures 'programmed' to seek out and enjoy the company of their own kind; we are biologically constructed to trust one another and become members of intimate groups. As Clark would tell the human story, we are deeply social animals. Our struggle to survive involves interdependence, trust, and cooperation.

Is this too unscientific? Too simple and beautiful to be true? 'Something's wrong with this picture,' a cynic would say. And such is our exposure to deep and pervasive cynicism that we may readily follow the cynic's lead. What about the human penchant for brutality? Our notorious egoism? Our selfish nastiness? Our willingness to kill and maim one another in pursuit of our own goals? These aspects of human nature really exist and pose enormous problems. But they aren't the whole of human nature.

Acts of generosity and kindness are underrepresented in the news because they rarely pose problems. There's relatively little drama here: no scandal, no jeopardized careers, no blood and gore.

Which isn't to say that human nature is entirely good and wonderful. Nastiness persists in human beings too. It's an undeniable fact that we can be deeply greedy and selfish, envious, despicable, and resentful. There are human beings who engage in killing on a grand scale, some showing hardly a twinge of conscience, a few even taking malicious delight. If we reflect on this, it makes for a bleak picture – as journalists and theorists frequently remind us.

Yes, human beings want power. But even power requires relationships with other people, and besides, it's not the only thing we want. We also seek such things as knowledge, a sense of worth and achievement, and happiness – all of which require decent relationships with other people. We care about other people – how they are faring and how they respond to us. Our own happiness depends on theirs; and theirs depends on ours. We want to connect with them and have them want to connect with us. Moving stories about care for strangers illustrate these basic facts about human nature. The people in Gander and Lewisporte, Newfoundland, behaved with energy and generosity, and they were wonderful in a crisis, which is good news, and we should appreciate good news when we hear it. But there's even better news: these capacities for sympathy and kindness are shared by human beings everywhere.

10 Normal Behaviour

JOHN RALSTON SAUL

What is the expression of our humanness, if not to live our lives, struggling with the dynamic of an impossible balance. This is something which lies within each of us and therefore within our societies. To know, imagine, sense, think, to some extent even to understand, this constant dynamic is to express civilization's essential nature.

What is normal behaviour? Is it not to seek equilibrium?

I don't mean by that the pursuit of the Holy Grail. We are not on a line between a point of departure and one of arrival. No linear concept of progress is suggested.

To seek equilibrium is to engage in a dynamic of constant movement, constant tension, yet also to remain in the same place – the place of our real life and real society.

The tension of seeking is normal. To expect or demand resolution is to slip into ideology – a form of death. Life on a force field of qualities attracted and repulsed by each other is normal. The tension is, in and of itself, a dynamic equilibrium.

I am not describing the privileged domain of an élite which, thanks to more education and more money, has been freed to act normally, freed to use its qualities. Normalcy is not a privilege. The obligation or opportunity to use our qualities is not a reward for utilitarian success.

The many who believe that it is a reward are expressing the persistent inheritance of Plato. What is that? A frightened and self-serving conviction that society is a pyramidal structure, in terms both of power and of our capacity to use our qualities. This is marginalized individualism. False individualism. It reflects a strange combination of highly structured corporatism and self-indulgent individualism. This is the old pessimistic view of us – of each of us and all of us, together in our societies.

Reality is quite different. In scientific terms – to use John Polanyi's phrase – it is equilibrium which makes life possible. We are part of that scientific reality. What is true for an atom or a force field is true for all of us. We express this through our desire for life, for life with others, through our engagement with the non-linear nature of progress.

I was interrupted as I finished those words by the news that a hijacked Boeing 767 had been flown into the World Trade Center. From what at first sounded like a bizarre accident, a wave of explosions and accidents and deaths spread through the day, at the end of which a rather fragile, awkward man appeared on television to read a speech from a tele-prompter to reassure Americans, indeed the world. He read with his eyes glued to the scrolling words. There had been little time for the speechwriters and you could distinguish quite different styles mixed together, some talented, some not.

The essential was elsewhere, as it had been all day. Thousands of individuals were denied a choice in their destiny as their lives were pulverized. Others, in three airplanes, had not been able to find the elements in their situation to change their reality. On a fourth plane, the passengers were able to sense the swirling uncertainty of events. They seized their moment and, though they died, in effect changed their reality by saving the lives of others. In the buildings struck, thousands more were able to make choices and to act. Some were terrible choices, but acts of human will all the same – to leap to their deaths rather than be consumed by an inferno racing towards them. Moments before, they had been at their desks, calmly settling into a day of predictable behaviour, a day which had begun with the turning of a door-handle and the ventur-ing out across a section of their society.

> "The Athenian idea of citizenship – flawed and limited though it was – put public service, civic education, democracy and restraint ahead of wealth, economics, self-interest and emotion ... They were addicted to the Periclean argument that 'words are no barrier to deeds; but rather harm comes from not taking instruction from discussion before the time has come for action."

Many found ways to save themselves or help others. No doubt there were also scenes of panic, of individuals acting for themselves. But what was remarkable was that, like the future leader of the French Resistance, Jean Moulin, isolated in 1940 in Chartres, thousands were acting with an ethical sense of themselves, using their shared knowl-edge to make the best of impossible situations, imagining and intuiting their way through the rubble of civilization, thinking their way into dealing with the immediate reality of this disorder. They passed in moments from the superficial existential minutiae of an ordinary day to the deepest caverns of suffering. Some passed right through those caverns, others could not, while we, not far away, sat buttering our toast, "eating or opening a window or walking dully along" as W.H Auden put it.

All of these events were illustrations of technology as a "double-edged sword." We were reminded that this machinery is not progress in any linear, optimistic sense. It cannot lead. It is mere technology and it can be used by different humans for whatever purposes suit them. Like a paving stone in a nineteenth-century street, it is dumb and inert, waiting to be driven over by someone in a carriage, walked upon by someone grateful to be raised above the mud, or picked up by a rioter and thrown at someone else. A passenger jet may indifferently deliver you to a beach holiday or become a deadly missile. An exacto knife may cut a piece of paper or a throat.

The day was also littered by the incapacity of technology and information-dominated structures to deal with the future in a balanced or effective way. This was true from the security systems at the airports to the enormous mechanisms of national security services. It was a day on which *instrumental reason* showed itself not to be rational, but to be dependent, like all utilitarian activity, on the leadership of complex humanism.

When the news of the Boeing 767 penetrating the World Trade Center interrupted me, as it did people around the globe, I had been about to discount Vico's argument of 1744 that "philosophy considers man as he should be and so can be of service to but very few, those who wish to live in the Republic of Plato and not fall back into the dregs of Romulus." On September 11, 2001, those *few* were unable to use their positions of leadership to prevent what happened.

Once the events had taken place, individuals – among the many and the few – reacted as best they could to the demands of reality. Most acted with great effectiveness, many with courage.

Vico was wrong. Philosophy is a commentary on the nature of our existence and so on the qualities all of us share in some way. How useful is that? Well, that nature and those qualities exist whether we recognize them or not. What remains in our power is how conscious we are willing to be of our humanness. By conscious, I mean how much we wish to exercise our qualities and to do so, one in concert with the *other*. To be conscious of them is to be more confident in our use of them.

What was disturbing on that day and in the days that followed was how many of Plato's few concentrated exclusively on a narrow, linear approach towards terrorism. They talked of eradication, punishment, in effect, of revenge.

We have some 130 years of experience with modern terrorism. Concrete action is always necessary. Guilty individuals must be dealt with appropriately. We know that there will always be a minute percentage among us ready to kill others for a variety of reasons. We also know that part of the problem is not so much generated as made possible by instability, disquiet, confusion somewhere. The soft terrain from which terrorism has always operated can range from generalized poverty and suffering to directionless comfort and self-indulgence. Conscious civilizations – those which use their qualities in concert – know that they must deal with the causes of that instability and loss of direction in order to shrink that context from which terrorism feeds.

To use our qualities is to be conscious of our actions. A dynamic equilibrium implies an integrated sense of reality's complexity. For forty years now the West has led a rush to balance its trade figures by aggressively selling its armaments abroad. The world is awash in weaponry. You can trace the parallel rising lines of unstable areas slipping into violence as the quantity of weapons on the market increases. To act as if our actions do not have consequences is to pretend that we are without qualities and are naturally passive factors when faced by the actions of others. It is to reduce ourselves to forms of reaction.

"What about love?" Is not the willingness to kill yourself for your cause – taking others with you who would see themselves as innocent by-standers – a form of love? I personally might call it fanaticism or hatred. But the terrorist would no doubt see it as love – love for his cause or his own group or people. Love is always a limited vision of who the *other* might be.

That's why love is a force or a characteristic, but not a quality. In order for a society to function with a certain tension – a dynamic equilibrium – the states of being it must avoid at all costs are love and hatred, all consuming and therefore all destructive.

You might say, love doesn't have to be that way. What way then? A letter to Jane:

I am Tarzan of the Apes. I want you. I am yours. You are mine. We will live together always in my house. I will bring you the best fruits, the tenderest deer, the finest meats that roam the jungle. I will hunt for you. I am the greatest of the jungle hunters. I will fight for you. I am the mightiest of the jungle fighters. When you see this you will know that it is for you and that Tarzan of the Apes loves you.

This is as good a summary of the love argument as you can get. And it is perhaps irresistible on a personal level. You might want to adjust it slightly for urban couples, two-job families, same-sex couples, and so on, but the elements are there. This is a personal program. It isn't a social program. The related social program is laid out by Tristan and Isolde, consumed by a love potion:

"From this world, oh set us free!"
"Extinguished in the twilight's streaming
all our doubting
all our dreaming
all our memories
all our fancies."

Note that love eliminates social responsibility, doubt, imagination and memory. Common sense, ethics and reason need not even be mentioned in order to be eliminated. Tristan, as he later lies dying, sets the ground rules for his loyal servant Kuvenal:

Those whom I hate
thou hates too
those whom I love
thou lovest too.

Saint Francis believed that love might allow you to escape self-interest and hatred. He wanted "to see with the eye of the heart, hear with the ear of the heart." But he never faced the impossibility for any society to function at that level. How could everyone differentiate on a stable, ongoing basis between his high pure love, the pure carnal love of others and the love which is the hatred of others, to take just three varieties? The use of Christian love to hate non-Christians over the centuries is our primary memory of this impossibility. Indeed individuals and groups have used every major religion at different times to engage in this game of love and hate.

Francis was no sooner dead than his formalized movement of love – the Franciscans – was given responsibility by Rome for elements of the

Inquisition and the eradication of heresy. Yet he and they had withdrawn from all involvement with property and ambition. His example had brought other human strengths to the fore as he embraced the world of the poor and of nature. Ethics blossomed, a form of common sense, of intuition. It was a very great revolution which caused the power structures of Europe to tremble for a few decades. And then he died and the whole movement was recuperated overnight by those who had opposed him.

You cannot run society with such hopes if citizens do not have a solid sense of their own equilibrium. The very best intention can swing in a second from unambitious devotion or love to the pursuit of others who do not love in your way.

The great Islamic spiritualist Abd El-Kader explained carefully that love could only be a reflection of God's love for humans. "You say that you love Me?" the Koran relates. "If that is the case, you must know that your love for Me is only a consequence of My love for you."

This, of course, is precisely the Christian position. "Beloved, let us love one another for God is love."

In the Western tradition, love has never belonged to us. It has always been a godly attribute – a force which we cannot shape or control. That is why, when we have it, it overwhelms us for better or worse.

Note: I am not denigrating, minimizing, discounting or attacking love. It may well be the essential within us. After all, why wouldn't our characteristics reflect our essential nature? But if we cannot shape such a force we must in some way be passive before it. Taken beyond our personal lives, it can only become an ideology.

The same could be said of a dozen other human characteristics. To be *happy* in the modern sense: where does it leave us? "We are happy." Beckett mocks, "What do we do now, now that we are happy?" "For God's sake," the great nineteenth-century Italian leader Mazzini wrote to a friend, "do not teach your son any Benthamite theory about happiness either individual or collective. A creed of individual happiness would make him an egotist: a creed of collective happiness will reach the same result soon or late."

It is with our qualities that we make something of ourselves.

I do not mean that we face a choice between the personal and the public, but between two kinds of personal. The one – that of love and happiness and other characteristics – involves a state of being which may be a gift of the gods, whether religious or mythological. Or it may be the expression of amorphous forces within us. In either of these cases, this is the personal self which does not link you to me – to the *other* – the *other* of the world outside our personal self. If we love the *other*, to take a single example, why did we do nothing to stop the murder of the Rwandans?

The second kind of personal life is the expression of ourselves through our qualities. It ties us to a partially conscious sense of ourselves, to others, to society. When we use these qualities, even if we are alone like Jean Moulin, we are part of the humanist reverberation. Vico said in his memoirs that the one thing he feared was "to be the only one to know; a situation which always seemed to me to be the most dangerous, because it exposes us either as a god or someone demented."

With common sense we are neither gods nor demented. We have our shared knowledge. Given our stretching and contracting qualities we have the ability to live with myriad tensions – "a tension of loyalties," as Northrop Frye put it, because "there are no uncritical loyalties." And so we can embrace the idea of criticism as a positive strength; that criticism which, Octavio Paz said, could "unfold the possibility of freedom and is thus an invitation to action."

These are the elements which help us to make our way across our society every day, both in a personal and a civic way. Personal consciousness, civic consciousness; personal virtue, civic virtue. This may sound unrealistic, even boring, in its self-declared goodness.

So think instead of the idea of tension – uncertain, creative tension. This is an uncomfortable pleasure. It runs throughout our celebration of the unresolved. There is a certain eroticism in the idea of a playfully permanent state of uncertainty. There is a certain necessary boring endlessness in the idea that civilization is in permanent construction on the ever-thickening foundation of our memory.

We were taught at school about the heroic nature of Pericles and his demanding, optimistic humanist message. And then the Spartans destroyed Athens and his citizen-based experiment. When I was a student I felt that there was a certain masochistic self-satisfaction in the way this failure was presented. Now I might call it a Platonist or Hobbesian self-satisfaction. What we were rarely taught was that, despite the uncertainty and costs and complexity of this experimental society, Athens' citizens did not abandon it. The Spartans managed to hold on for a few years. Then, under the leadership of Thrasybulus, a moderate and a product of Athenian civic education, the citizens drove the utilitarian dictatorship out. In the days following their victory, they were careful not to slip into revenge. They amnestied most of those who had collaborated with the dictatorship.

What is the point of this story? That the Athenian idea of citizenship – flawed and limited though it was – put public service, civic education, democracy and restraint ahead of wealth, economics, self-interest and emotion. And that this idea had been built up, layer upon layer, from Solon through to Pericles. When the disaster came, individuals had a resilient enough memory of the public good to hold on until they could choose to go back to the inefficient, costly system of citizen-based democracy. To reject that of authoritarian efficiency and profit. They were addicted to the Periclean argument that "words are no barrier to deeds; but rather harm comes from not taking instruction from discussion before the time has come for action."

The Athenian argument always sounds grand. We lay aside our knowledge of how flawed and contradictory it was because it is the clearest example we have in our memory of individuals attempting somehow to live conscious lives. And this attempt was made through an idea of qualities and characteristics which in different ways they attempted to balance.

We use this memory as we should – not as a promise of some Utopia to come, but as a first Western context for struggling with how to live our lives and how to shape our public good.

In 1787, the aged Benjamin Franklin – struggling through all the constraints of a man who knew his history – tried to make up his mind about the proposed American constitution. On 17 September, too weak to do it himself, he had his written opinion read to the Convention by someone else. His words were filled with ethical doubts, attempts to imagine the future, rational analysis. "I confess that there are several parts of this Constitution which I do not at present approve, but I am not sure that I shall never approve them ... the older I grow, the more apt I am to doubt my own judgement ... I agree to this Constitution with all its faults, if they are such, because I think a general Government necessary ... When you assemble a number of men to have the advantage of their joint wisdom, you inevitably assemble with those men, all their prejudices, their passions, their errors of opinion, their local interests and their selfishness." At last, in an attempt to marry his common sense with an intuitive seizing of reality, he gave "consent to this Constitution because I expect no better, and because I am not sure it is not the best ..."

Given his stature, Franklin sealed the course of events, perhaps even set in place the course of modern Western civilization. We know now that he was profoundly right and profoundly wrong. The constitutional system was a good one for the half-continent which would go on to lead the world. It still permits a remarkably complex society to function without losing its necessary internal differences. But it was also catastrophic for the citizenry, because by normalizing slavery it normalized racism in a utilitarian, rational manner unprecedented in world history.

That normalization of the abnormal made it impossible for society to embrace its real intent. These institutionalized contradictions led not only to a massive civil war, but to a great wound which continues to suppurate in ways which we still cannot predict or control, altering realities at home and abroad. This was a flaw which could not work its way out.

All of our societies contain within them the contradictions which may one day incapacitate or destroy us. In this, most schools of philosophy and religions are agreed. In accepting the idea of uncertainty and opposing forces, they assume that of suffering. The great American judge Learned Hand put it that "suffering is permanent, obscure and dark. And shares the nature of infinity." The suffering of societies is simply a magnified reality of that dealt with by the thousands of individuals in those two towers who faced in some way their deaths and managed to survive or did not. Looked at as a human reality – our inability to master our contradictions as we would like – this is another way of seeing our struggle with the possibility of equilibrium.

The path through this conundrum lies less with constitutions and laws – although they have their essential roles to play – than with the individual's sense of a personal dynamic equilibrium. That is a state of being that we might call responsible individualism. It contains the tools to alter our situations in ways which can allow our societies to function.

Today's dominant rhetoric of power is designed to marginalize this reality of responsible individualism and to replace it with abstract and technological forces beyond our control. I cannot help feeling that it is precisely the opposite which will happen, because it needs to happen.

The rhetoric of global forces, whether economic, technological or military, leaves us as individuals with the demeaning and irrelevant pleasures of self-fulfilment, providing we can afford them. I sense little satisfaction among people with this enforced holiday from the ability to shape their own destinies and the shared destiny of their society. In fact, I sense growing discomfort and anger. They see their lives, their families, their streets, let us say their friendships, as reality. And this reality is the basis from which larger realities must be shaped.

Used in this way, the word *friendship* has myriad implications. It can be to society what the jury is to democracy. These are the relationships we choose. These few people are our personal engagement with the *other*. In the classical sense, friendship has always been a proof of our ability to free ourselves from the exclusivity of love and the narrowing passivity of self-interest.

So this is not friendship as love. And not a relationship of the sort which would corrupt the public good for personal advantage. This is not friendship as a version of the extended family.

Here friendship is the ability to imagine the *other*. It is not easy. It is the beginnings of tolerance. It is, as Conrad said, "more difficult for some than heroism. More difficult than compassion." Friendship is a relationship filled with uncertainty. It is the primary territory upon which we test our dynamic equilibrium – our use of our interwoven qualities.

This assumes a certain honesty within our conscious imagining of ourselves. This is not a romantic or abstract or grandiose proposition. Think over the last years. The upper-middle classes of the West – the literate, informed, influential upper-middle classes – have asserted or passively accepted a theory according to which a rising tide of income for them will raise the little boats and rafts of the poor. Protected by this romantic delusion, they allow themselves to ignore the reality of a good fifth of their fellow-citizens, stagnating or sinking economically, while all numbers show the top fifth enjoying healthy growth. And yet poverty is the one form of suffering over which societies can exercise a great deal of control.

This is the reality of human consciousness or denial. This is the reality of our lives as we open our doors and walk out into our societies. There is a tiny possibility that we may be swept up from our real minutiae into a terrible reality of violence and heightened existential choice. There is also the normal possibility that our actions and choices of the day – however small – may give comfort to a denial of our individual consciousness and the existence of the *other*. We may deny those who are the friends of *others* and live their lives somewhere out of our immediate sight. There is a certain easy comfort in such denial. We may even deny our friends, though with less ease.

I do not sense that we seek that comfort or the false freedom of denial. We understand the truer comfort of a permanent psychic discomfort in which we seek to identify reality. And we deal with reality through the creative tensions with which we attempt to balance our qualities. This is our eternal movement towards equilibrium.

PART XI

Happiness and Morality

1 Should Morality Be a Struggle?

THOMAS HURKA

Imagine that two accountants do similar jobs for different companies. One day they make the same discovery: with almost no chance of getting caught, they can embezzle a large sum from their employers. They can both use the money to pay off debts or buy a new car.

The first accountant right away says to himself, 'It's wrong to steal,' and never considers the matter again. But the second accountant is torn. She, too, knows that stealing is wrong, but she's tempted and at first decides to go ahead. Then she decides she won't, and then that she will. Finally, after weeks of agonizing, she decides not to embezzle. Who is the morally better person?

My fellow students and I were asked this at the start of an undergraduate seminar on Aristotle. The point wasn't that there was a single right answer we had to give; it was to highlight differences between ancient and modern views of ethics.

Aristotle and most other Greek philosophers would have said the first accountant is better, because he has a harmonious personality. He has correct beliefs about what's right and no appetites or impulses that conflict with them. He's integrated, stable, at one with his moral convictions.

Aristotle thought this kind of harmony was essential to true virtue. The virtuous person would, for example, be moderate about sensual pleasures, but he wouldn't find this difficult. He would dislike the taste of rich or unhealthy foods; he'd get no enjoyment from adultery even if he happened to try it.

'The Greeks valued inner harmony because they assumed that morality and self-interest go hand in hand ... What's really in your interest is leading the best life, which is a life of virtue.'

The Greeks valued inner harmony because they assumed that morality and self-interest go hand in hand. The second accountant is tempted to embezzle the money because she thinks this will benefit her. But Aristotle would say this is a mistake. What's really in your interest is leading the best life, which is a life of virtue and excludes stealing. To be tempted is to be confused.

Modern ethics is more sympathetic to the second accountant. We doubt whether virtue in Aristotle's sense is attainable; we think of morality as a struggle against evil or selfish impulses that we can't get rid of but can only restrain. (Think of dieting as portrayed in the *Cathy* comic strip. It's a battle against cravings for chocolate, ice cream, and the like. Wrongdoing strikes us as similarly delicious.)

This modern picture has partly religious origins. The doctrine of original sin says that after the fall in the Garden of Eden, all humans are corrupted. We have within us tendencies to evil that cannot be eliminated ('the old Adam') and against which we must constantly struggle. As St Paul said, 'The flesh lusteth against the spirit,' and the best we can do is lust back against it.

But there are secular versions of the same idea. Our twentieth-century psychologies teach us that we have inborn tendencies – the products now of biology rather than divinity – to pleasure, aggression, or dominance. They're the nasty, uncivilized part of our nature, and though they can be diverted, sublimated, or restrained, they can't be eliminated. The moral life, again, is a struggle against oneself.

Like the Greek picture, this modern one is tied to beliefs about morality and self-interest. But where the Greeks assume that doing what's right is the same as benefiting yourself, we think the two clash. Morality involves a sacrifice of your interests for other people's, and that's what makes it hard.

This makes us suspicious of the first accountant. Doesn't his easy virtue look like a mindless following of rules whose costs he doesn't really understand? Morality does require giving up your interests, and the second accountant's struggle reflects this. But the first accountant seems to ignore this, or to be missing some basic drives.

Our modern picture of morality is grim, in contrast with the light, harmonious picture Aristotle paints. But sometimes reality is more hard than beautiful. The German philosopher G.W.F. Hegel said that Greek civilization expressed a beautiful naivety, treating as in simple harmony what we see as opposed. You can see this in Greek ethics. There virtue is effortless because it's good for you – but we find it a struggle.

2 Why God Is Irrelevant to Morality

THOMAS HURKA

'If God is dead, everything is permitted.' That's what Ivan says in Dostoevsky's *The Brothers Karamazov* and what many people believe: without religion there's no basis for morality. I believe the opposite: that moral issues can be discussed in a purely secular way. It's an age-old issue in philosophy.

At first sight, morality and religion seem easy to separate. Many atheists have moral principles and act on them conscientiously. Some even accept the principles of religious morality non-religiously. They believe that Jesus, for example, was a great moral teacher but insist he was a human teacher, not divine.

Those who tie ethics to religion don't deny these obvious facts. They claim instead that morality without religion, though possible, is irrational – something you might go for if naive or deluded, but not if you saw clearly what the 'death of God' implies.

One argument for this is that we need God to reward virtue and punish vice in the afterlife. Otherwise, being moral is not in our long-term self-interest and is therefore irrational.

This argument assumes that we're always motivated by self-interest – which we're not. We can care directly about other people

> *'Imagine that God gives us certain commands, for example to love our neighbours as ourselves. Why, Socrates asks, does God give these commands and not others? Is it because they're morally right, or for some other reason? Either answer lands religious ethics in a pickle.'*

just as, when angry, we can want to hurt them regardless of the effect on us. We can also be moved just by the thought that something is right. If we are, and we act on this motive, we're perfectly rational.

In any case, pursuing self-interest in the suggested way won't work. In most religions, whether you're saved depends on your motives: you have to act from love or from a desire to do your duty. If your goal is only heaven for yourself, you won't get there.

The more serious argument tying ethics to religion concerns, not the motive for morality, but its possibility. If God exists, it's said, then moral principles have reality as his commands or the decrees of his will. If he doesn't they're phantoms, will-o'-the-wisps, nothing. This is the core idea of religious ethics: something's being right just is its being commanded by God. So without God, rightness is impossible.

This idea was refuted 2,500 years ago by Socrates. In a dialogue of Plato's called the *Euthyphro*, he shows decisively why religion is not only unnecessary for, but also irrelevant to, morality.

Imagine that God gives us certain commands, for example to love our neighbours as ourselves. Why, Socrates asks, does God give these commands and not others? Is it because they're morally right, or for some other reason? Either answer lands religious ethics in a pickle.

If God commands acts because they're right, then the acts are right apart from his will, and morality is real independently of God. But if he doesn't command acts because they're right, we have no moral reason to obey him. God has impressive qualities: he's all-powerful, all-knowing, creator of the universe. But these qualities are compatible with moral evil. Unless we know independently that his commands are right, obeying him is just blind submission to authority.

We can rationally follow God's commands, Socrates shows, but only after using our own moral judgment. Our reasoning can't be, 'He's God, therefore what he says is right.' It must be, 'What he says is right, therefore he is, or may be, God.'

A defender of religious ethics may object that this ignores a crucial fact: God's infinite goodness. The gods Socrates knew, the petty, squabbling gods of Olympus, weren't good and there was no reason to obey them. But the Christian god is perfectly virtuous.

This addition doesn't change the argument. We have to ask whether God's goodness constrains him, so there are things he couldn't command and still be good, or does not. If it does constrain him, God couldn't command hating one's neighbour and still be good. But this means that hating one's neighbour is wrong in itself, that is, that morality exists apart from God. If God's goodness does not constrain him, he could command anything – but then we have no moral reason to obey him. Doing so is again just blind loyalty, closer to Nuremberg than to Nazareth.

Socrates' argument doesn't deny that religion can be important psychologically, in forming an attachment to morality. Many children first come to respect morality by associating it with an all-powerful authority figure. An adult's moral resolve can be strengthened by thoughts of a divine commander and his rewards and punishments.

But let's be clear. If we rely on these religious props – and pessimists say we need them to avoid sliding into moral laxness – it's only because we're irrational. It's because we can't act morally for the one good reason for doing so, namely, that it's right to so act regardless of anyone's commandments. If God exists, he can't make things right that aren't already so. If he doesn't exist, this doesn't morally make a difference.

3 The Prime Directive

ALISTER BROWNE

The Starlight Lounge is a home-away-from-home for members of Starfleet Command. There, in an atmosphere of conviviality unmatched in the galaxy, Cadets, Admirals, secretaries, and bureaucrats democratically gather to seek refuge and refreshment. Cadet Rostov paused as he entered, waiting for his eyes to adjust to the subdued light. From the corner, someone called his name.

'Over here,' the voice said, 'join us.' The speaker was Captain Kirk, sitting at the table that, by custom born of deference, was reserved for the Most Famous Members of Starfleet. Rostov walked towards the table of now retired living legends. He had been warned, as all new members were, not to pass within earshot of the table unless one had little to do. Having long since exhausted all they had to say to one another, and now with nothing to occupy themselves except talk, these ancient mariners were always on the lookout for fresh conversationalists to catch with their glittering reputations.

'I understand you are writing your officer qualifying examinations,' began Kirk, as Rostov sat down and ordered a Mind-Melder with a twist. 'Tell us about them. I remember my exams as if they were yesterday. Still have nightmares.'

'The examinations have gone very well,' answered Rostov. 'Seven-dimensional differential topography, the astrophysics of time-reversing worm holes, transcendental critical thinking, comparative constitutional law of possible worlds – all the usual officer-breakers – gave me no problems. Nor did simulated hand-to-hand combat with a Gorgon, or the classic test – which I believe you were the first to pass – of playing tic-tac-toe against a computer. There's only one more to go, ethics. But that *is* giving me problems. I don't know where to begin on the questions they set. And it's an important test. The word among the cadets is that how we do in ethics determines whether we are on the bridge or in the engine room.'

'Let's hear the questions,' said Captain Picard as he continued, under the disapproving eyes of his companions, to extract the cashews from the nibbles dish. 'I've always been fascinated by ethics. And I know Starfleet Education encourages you to discuss such questions with others. They say it carries on a tradition begun by someone called "Socrates," though his last name escapes me.' Picard winked at his colleagues. 'Or his first, if that is his last. Maybe we can help.'

'It's a problem from the Old Days on Earth,' replied Rostov, 'and involves something called "female circumcision." Apparently it was a procedure that used to be obligatory for women in some Earth cultures, and took many forms.' Cadet Rostov pushed a button on his Cranberry Mark XLMII, and a metallic voice spoke:

> ... the most severe form of the practice is infibulation, or 'Pharonic' circumcision, where virtually all of the external female genitalia are removed. With this type of circumcision, a dramatic excision is performed ... (A. Slack, 'Female Circumcision: A Critical Appraisal,' *Human Rights Quarterly* 10, 1988, 441–2)

The impersonal voice described the operation in excruciating and horrific detail, while the huddle of veterans grimaced and, in Picard's case, turned a delicate shade of green.

'We were asked to imagine that we came across a tribe that had this as part of their culture, and to ponder – those are the Educator's favourite words, "imagine" and "ponder" – two scenarios. In the first, a young girl is about to undergo it. She screams for help. Should we intercede? In the second, the chieftain asks a physician to perform the procedure. Should the physician do it?

'Cadet Pulver spoke for many of us,' Rostov continued, 'when he said that the questions were no-brainers. Of course we should interfere, and of course no physician should do it. But the Educator, who is a philosopher, says we have to think more. Said we have to think about things that seem simple until they puzzle us, and then work through them until they are simple again. That's philosophic progress, he said. I don't see the point, really, or what the puzzle is, but I don't want to spend my career in the engine room.'

'Starfleet Education sometimes gets carried away,' replied Kirk. 'The philosophers can be particularly goofy. I remember how they tried to get us to think about how we knew the sun would rise tomorrow, or whether all life is a dream, and suchlike. But this time they have given you a real question. When I handed over command of the *Enterprise* to Captain Picard, I gave him some advice that you may find helpful.

'"Picard," I said, "you are going to see some mighty strange things out there. New worlds, new civilizations. You will quickly see that their ways are not always our ways, and some of their ways will horrify you. When you go to Xenon, you will meet the troglodytes. They have been forced for centuries to work in the mines underground. The miners labour in hard conditions, contract green lung disease, and die young. They will appeal to you to help get them out of the mines, and to prevent their children from being forced into them. You will also find that the universe is filled with planets inhabited by beautiful women, often scantily clad and looking surprisingly like Earth women, who are under the domination of cruel masters with bad haberdashers. They, too, will ask for your help. It will be hard," I continued, but you must say "No." For we are governed by the Prime Directive, and this tells us that we must never interfere with another culture." That's what I told Picard, and that holds the key to your questions. You cannot interfere with what other cultures do. But you do not have to help them do it. Pulver is only half right in his answer.'

'The rules of ethics are not discovered, like the laws of physics. They are invented, like the rules of the road. Each society makes up its own moral code. Each moral code reflects the values of the society. One society cannot be said to be better than another, and so neither can one moral code. There simply is no single overall standard of right and wrong.'

'I have thought long and hard about the Prime Directive,' said Picard. 'I didn't like it when you lectured me about it, Kirk, and after all these years in the service I like it even less. It's all very well for Starfleet Command to prattle on about the Prime Directive, but why should anyone accept it? What is its moral basis? The problem I have with the Prime Directive is –'

'I used to worry about it too,' interrupted Kirk, 'so much so that I once went to see Starflight's top ethicist. "Kirk," he said to me, "you're a young fella. Full of idealistic ideas, ready to change the universe. But you have to understand something about ethics. The rules of ethics are not discovered, like the laws of physics. They are invented, like the rules of the road. Each society makes up its own moral code. Each moral code reflects the values of the society. One society cannot be said to be better than another, and so neither can one moral code. There simply is no single overall standard of right and wrong. You are entitled to your own views, Kirk," he said, "but you have no reason to think that they are better than those held by other cultures. That's why you have to obey the Prime Directive." Those comments stuck with me, and remembering them enabled me to stay the course and be faithful to the Prime Directive, though God knows it wasn't always easy. There are a lot of good-looking women in the universe.'

'The problem I have with the Prime Directive,' carried on Picard, who was used to being interrupted by Kirk, 'is that it conflicts with something else to which Starfleet Command professes allegiance: human rights. These are things that everyone has just in virtue of being human. And not only humans have them. Your Mr Spock has them; my Mr Data has them; the troglodytes have them. It isn't easy to give a determinate list of what these rights are. But there is no question that forcing troglodyte children into the mines, and performing female circumcision on helpless girls against their will, violate them. And these rights impose strict duties on others. There is, of course, a duty not to violate those rights. But more, there is also a duty to try to prevent others from violating them. If it is within your power to prevent something wrong from happening, and you do not prevent it, you are responsible for its happening. Acknowledging human rights thus conflicts with the Prime Directive – one forbidding any interference with different cultures, the other enjoining some. Kirk can choose the Prime Directive, but my allegiance is to human rights. So full marks to Pulver: one should not do wrong things or let them happen.'

Mr Spock pressed his hands together, laid them on the table, and spoke in his characteristic measured tones. 'I believe that what we have here, gentlemen, is a failure of logic. It is true that the doctrine of human rights and the Prime Directive cannot both be true. But, to put it in terminology familiar to the smallest schoolchildren on Vulcan, they are not related to each other as contradictories, but as contraries. While both cannot be true, it is not the case that if one is true the other must be false. Both can be false. And it seems to me that this is the case.

'I fail to see why one should respect the rules or customs of any culture where these things exploit or maltreat its members, and it is plain to me that we should prevent such misuse if we can. We do not do any good or keep our hands clean if we turn our backs. Picard is right about that, and so right to reject the Prime Directive. But I also fail to see why one should say that there are things that it is always wrong, everywhere, and for anyone to do, as the doctrine of human rights has it. It is always possible to think of circumstances in which the failure to do things that are generally wrong would have such bad consequences that doing them could not be wrong in those circumstances.

'We should forget about absolutist views of *never* interfering with other cultures, and *never* doing certain things, as illogical. To decide what to do, we should scan the alternatives, determine the good and bad that each does, taking into account all their consequences, near and remote, and do what will have the best consequences, all things considered. It would be wrong to help a girl who does not want to be circumcised if that will only worsen her situation – say, by making her a social outcast in the culture in which she is destined to live – or have overwhelmingly bad consequences for others such as her family, or those who try to help. But it cannot be wrong when there is every reason to think that she will be better off and that no countervailing evils will result. Similarly, it would be wrong to perform the surgery if your refusal would enable the girl to avoid the surgery. But if the girl is going to be circumcised anyway, and the choice is between your doing it with anesthetic and sterile surgical instruments, or someone else doing it without anesthetic and with unsterile, crude implements, you should do it. Pulver is entirely wrong.'

'It is now my turn to point out a failure in your logic,' said Picard, allowing himself a small smile. 'Even if we agree that consequences are the sole relevant moral considerations, it does not follow that we cannot have an absolutist position according to which certain things are always obligatory or always wrong. Sometimes the best consequences can be obtained by setting aside general rules, but that requires good judgment. Kirk, perhaps, could be trusted to make such judgments. But can you imagine what it would be like if Dr McCoy were allowed to? And there are many more McCoys in Starfleet than Kirks. If individuals were allowed to act on their own discretion, we would get some good consequences, but many more bad ones, and so there should be some rigid rules specifying that some things can never be done. The justification for such rules is that they will produce the best consequences, not in every circumstance, but on the whole.'

'All of which seems to support the views I began with,' said Kirk, sitting back in his chair, a confident tone coming into his voice. 'We should never interfere with other cultures, as the Prime Directive has it, for allowing discretion would be predictably bad on the whole. And we should never do things that conflict with human rights, for that too would be bad on the whole. Thus we must not interfere with the circumcision, but must not help with it either. I didn't have these grounds in mind at the beginning, but I've never fussed too much about how I got to an answer as long as the answer is right.'

Spock straightened his back, a sign that he was about to speak, and addressed Picard and Kirk. 'Once you admit, gentlemen, that everything rests on consequences, I do not see how either of you can defend your positions. What reason can you have, Picard, for saying that we will get the best consequences from allowing individuals discretion to set aside the Prime Directive but not human rights? And what reason can you have, my captain, for saying that we will get the best consequences from not allowing any discretion at all? Absent any such reasons, there are no grounds for the rigid rules you both in different ways want, and absent such rules –'

'This is not helping! This is not helping!' cried Rostov, obviously agitated. 'Three people, three opinions. And that's just what they seem to be, mere opinions. The more I think of it, the more it appears that there are no right or wrong answers in ethics.'

'That's what Scotty told the examiners,' replied Kirk. 'So if you think that too, you'd better keep it to yourself.'

'And thinking that would be premature in any case,' added Spock. 'You cannot conclude that there is no right or wrong answer to a question merely from the fact that people disagree over it. Questions about rocket science have got right and wrong answers. But it is hard enough to get agreement on what the right answers are in rocket science, and ethics is not just rocket science. My advice to you is –'

But when he turned to look Rostov in the eye, to impress the advice on him, he found the chair empty.

4 Monstrous Acts Distort Reality

GRAEME HUNTER

On 6 December 1989, a young man named Marc Lepine walked into a classroom at École Polytechnique in Montreal and shot to death fourteen women. Then he shot himself. He associated these women with feminism and feminism with his own failure to get ahead in life. In his twisted mind, he seemed to be saying to himself, 'What else can I do?'

Among the families and friends of his victims, the anniversary will always be remembered as tragedy. But the murders are also commemorated each year by many who were not personally affected by them, but who see in the brutal act of Marc Lepine an allegory of the sufferings of all women everywhere at the hands of men.

To be sure, the violence of Marc Lepine reached the outer limit, but for some that very ferocity makes it all the more suitable for raising our consciousness. Through remembering 6 December, they hope to make everyone see what appears to them to be man's habitual cruelty to woman. But consider another story.

Exactly eighty-eight years before the Montreal Massacre, on 6 December 1901, another young man, Henry Albert Harper, threw himself into the Ottawa River in an attempt to save Bessy Blair from drowning. Blair had skated too close to a thin patch of ice and fallen into swift, deadly waters. Harper's friends attempted to restrain him but he rushed forward, calling back what turned out to be his last words: 'What else can I do?' He and Bessy Blair drowned together.

'We do ourselves no credit and no good if we lift base things above what is great and ennobling.'

Like Lepine, Henry Harper was not forgotten. On 18 May 1905, a statue of 'Sir Galahad' was unveiled in his honour on Wellington Street, in front of the Parliament Buildings, where it stands to this day. One of Canada's greatest poets, Wilfred Campbell, remembered his death in verse. He said of Harper,

In the common round
Of life's slow action, stumbling on
The brink

Of sudden opportunity, he chose
The only noble, godlike, splendid
Way.
And made his exit, as earth's great have gone
By that vast doorway looking out on death.

Lepine and Harper. Harper and Lepine. The questions that 6 December brings to my mind concern these two men, the women among whom they died, and the significance of those different deaths. In particular I wonder which of the two men, the hero or the anti-hero, gives a truer picture of man's relationship to woman. In our day, with the extreme politicization of the battle of the sexes, perhaps we are precluded from giving unbiased answers. Perhaps the poet saw more clearly than we do. (Don't poets always see more clearly?) Campbell wrote that Harper was not a 'hero of a hundred victories,'

But simple, unrecorded in his days,
Unostentatious, like the average man
Of average duty, walked the common earth,
And when fate flung her challenge in his face
Took all his spirit in his blinded eyes,
And showed in action why God made
the world.

I am grateful for that phrase 'like the average man.' That is the poet's answer to my question. It is men like Harper, not Lepine, who should be uppermost in our memories of what men have done and in our expectations of what they will do. Of course, we do not turn a blind eye to our tragedies, we bear in mind the massacre. But we do ourselves no credit and no good if we lift base things above what is great and ennobling. Both Lepine's massacre and Harper's self-sacrifice occurred at the outset of the Advent season and they illustrate both the depravity that makes our world a needy place and the redemptive suffering that alone can answer that need.

5 Tsunami Ethics: Jillian's Choice

ARTHUR SCHAFER

It's not as if she had scads of time to contemplate the philosophical niceties of her predicament.

One moment, Jillian Searle was breakfasting with her two young boys. The next moment, they were assaulted by the massive tsunami that washed over their hotel in Phuket, Thailand. As the three of them were swept up in the relentless wall of water, baby Blake was in her arms while she gripped five-year-old Lachlan by the hand. Trying to keep hold of both boys seemed to promise death for all three of them. Her decision was made in an instant. She clutched the baby and released Lachlan.

Choosing which of your children shall live, and which perish, must rank as just about the cruellest dilemma imaginable. Thousands of Canadian parents who saw or listened to the interview with Ms Searle must have asked themselves, as I asked myself: 'What would I have done in her place?' The truth is, of course, that none of us really has a clue. In real life, we have never faced a choice even remotely similar to the choice facing Ms Searle.

We may, however, have read William Styron's book, *Sophie's Choice*, or seen the Hollywood adaptation, starring Meryl Streep, in which a mother is compelled by a sadistic Nazi official to choose one of her children for immediate execution or else witness the execution of both. Some applauded while others condemned the mother, Sophie, for selecting one of her children to die in order that the other might live. But who could truly say that they know what they would themselves do in such an extraordinary and terrifying situation?

My personal fear is that in Jillian Searle's place I might become paralysed with anxiety, thereby condemning both children to death. (I am one of those people marked out by nature as a 'sinker' rather than a 'floater,' and share Lachlan's fear of water.) Or perhaps I would resolutely hang on to both children, accepting death for the children and myself instead of 'playing God' by choosing which shall live and which shall die.

This much seems clear: even those commentators who believe Ms Searle made the morally wrong choice are being unreasonably harsh when they condemn her moral character. She was compelled to react instantaneously. People who do their best in an emergency deserve to have some slack cut for them by those of us who judge from the safety and comfort of our living rooms. Or so I believe.

It is also worth mentioning that Jillian now claims that when she released her grip on Lachlan she attempted to transfer his hand to that of a nearby stranger. Some suspect that this version of events was merely an attempt to palliate the hurt feelings which Lachlan might otherwise have experienced. In any event, by sheer luck, Lachlan managed to grab hold of some floating debris, which saved his life. Thus, against the odds, mother and both children survived, though it won't quite do to declare that 'all's well that ends well.'

> *'Choosing which of your children shall live, and which perish, must rank as just about the cruellest dilemma imaginable.'*

The classic legal case involving decision-making in extremis is the English case of *The Queen v. Dudley and Stephens* (1884). Dudley and Stephens were shipwrecked sailors who saved their own lives by killing and eating the flesh of the moribund cabin boy. They pleaded not guilty to the charge of murder, arguing that since they faced imminent death from dehydration and starvation, the extremity of their circumstances justified what would otherwise have been a crime.

Chief Justice Lord Coleridge, in delivering his guilty verdict, was not unmindful of the 'terrible temptation' faced by the sailors and their 'awful suffering.' He acknowledged, also, how difficult it would be for anyone deprived of food and water for many days 'to keep the judgement straight and the conduct pure.' Coleridge even went so far as to admit that 'we are often compelled to set up standards we cannot reach ourselves, and to lay down rules which we could not ourselves satisfy.'

Having admitted that he could not vouch for his own conduct in a situation as dire as that faced by the accused, Lord Coleridge nevertheless sentenced both sailors to death, declaring, 'A man has no right to declare temptation to be an excuse, though he might himself have yielded to it, nor allow compassion for the criminal to change or weaken in any manner the legal definition of the crime.'

Interestingly, the sentence given to both sailors was subsequently commuted by the Crown to six months' imprisonment. The law sometimes needs to be tempered by mercy.

Now, of course, Jillian Searle committed no crime whatsoever, except perhaps the 'moral crime,' as some would see it, of favouring her more vulnerable younger son over her almost as vulnerable older son. If one has to make a life-or-death choice, then choosing to protect the more vulnerable seems on the face of it to be a reasonable criterion.

Some philosophers have argued, however, that it is always wrong to make such a choice. They claim that when the value of human life is at stake, it is 'inherently' wrong for any human being to engage in a selection process. If all cannot live, then rather than 'play God,' we should allow all to die.

I have put this proposition to my bioethics students over a period of many years, and to conferences of transplant physicians and surgeons. I can report to you that I have never yet encountered anyone who actually thinks that when a life-saving resource is in short supply – whether a kidney for transplant or a mother's hand for rescue – we should refuse to make a selection, thereby condemning all to death.

From the foregoing remarks you will have concluded, correctly, that I think Jillian Searle made an ethically defensible choice – indeed, the morally right choice. But even if I am mistaken in this belief, I would still want to insist that it would be wrong to label her a morally bad person or a morally inadequate mother simply because she may have made the wrong choice.

6 Is There Such a Thing as Moral Luck?

THOMAS HURKA

I was bicycling down the main street in Oxford and getting ready to turn right. (This was England, where a right turn is a left turn.) In a hurry, I gave only a quick look back before pulling away from the curb. I didn't see the cyclist behind me, crashed into him, and sent him sprawling into the roadway.

The cyclist was lucky. If there had been a car coming he would have been killed, but there wasn't. He brushed off his clothes, accepted my apology, and continued down the street.

I, too, was lucky. If there had been a car coming I would have been guilty of carelessly killing someone, a serious moral wrong. As it was, I had been only harmlessly negligent – nothing to be proud of, but no great sin. But how could luck have the second, excusing effect? How could fortune affect the wrongness of what I did?

A long Western tradition limits moral evaluation to things inside a person's soul, to things he or she controls. It's reflected in Christian attitudes to money. If a rich and a poor person both give to charity, the rich person may give more and do more good. But if the poor person's motives are the same, Christianity says the act is just as worthy.

The same thinking appears in judgments about responsibility. Primitive moralities blame people for things they couldn't prevent, but modern ethics insists on voluntariness. If people couldn't help what they did – if it was a physical spasm or they were forced – we absolve them of blame.

This tradition expresses a profound moral egalitarianism. Whatever is true of worldly success – of fame, fortune, or happiness – the moral life is something at which everyone has an equal chance. The moral life is a matter of inner states that outside factors, including luck, can't affect.

Although it's inspiring, this tradition isn't one we consistently follow. I learned this on Oxford High Street. If there had been a car coming, I – like anyone in that situation – would have felt terribly guilty. As it was, I shuddered briefly at what might have been and forgot the incident. But why this difference in attitude? In both circumstances my inner states, those things I controlled, were the same.

Or consider a feature of our legal system: it punishes attempted crimes, such as attempted murder, less severely than successful ones. This might make sense if the law's purpose were just to prevent future crimes. Stiffer penalties for successful crimes dissuade people who've already tried a crime unsuccessfully from trying it again. But if punishment is a response to guilt, the law is puzzling: why should a gunman be thought less guilty if his victim wore a bullet-proof vest?

We seem to believe in 'moral luck,' in luck that affects not only what happens but also the moral quality of what we do. In the bicycle example, this luck came after my act and determined what its effect would be. But there can also be moral luck in the circumstances and temptations we face.

Imagine that two husbands have equally weak characters and are equally likely to deceive their wives should the opportunity arise. For one the opportunity does arise and he commits adultery; for the other, through no merit of his, it does not. We judge these husbands differently, and so would their wives, for only one has actually deceived. But how fair is this when the other's character is no different, when his more honest behaviour is only the result of moral luck?

'A long Western tradition limits moral evaluation to things inside a person's soul, to things he or she controls. ... This tradition expresses a profound moral egalitarianism.'

There are more chilling examples. In the 1930s, German citizens should have understood Nazism and fought against it. That they didn't means they failed in ways that we in comfortable Canada have not. But can we say honestly that, in those circumstances, we would have acted better? If we can't, can we feel morally superior?

There are different explanations of our belief in moral luck, but the true one is probably cowardice. We haven't the courage to think through moral ideas that imply we can be just as morally flawed when we don't kill or deceive as when we do.

In a great 1960s folk song, Phil Ochs called for this courage: 'Show me a prisoner,' or a hobo or a drunkard, he sang,

And I'll show you a young man,
With so many reasons why,
There but for fortune may go you or I.

The song doesn't deny that what the prisoner did was wrong. It only says that if we haven't done something similar, it's because of the luck of our social position.

Like many reformers, Mr Ochs was calling for a return to old moral ideas, in this case the Greek and Christian idea that morality is a matter of the inner life, of states of our soul that we control. It's an idea we'd do well to remember when feeling smug that we've never actually killed, deceived, or connived with Nazis.

7 Why Animals Deserve Rights

KATHARINE BROWNE AND ALISTER BROWNE

In our society, animals are treated remarkably differently from human beings. We hunt, fish, eat, skin, and do fatal and painful experiments on animals, whereas we would not dream of treating human beings in any of these ways. What, if anything, justifies this difference in treatment? We will argue that the answer is 'nothing.' Both of us underwent transforming experiences when we first encountered the argument for this conclusion. In what follows we want to describe this argument and say why we think it is important.

Let us begin with an uncontroversial view. Blood sports such as dog- and cock-fighting, bear baiting, and fox hunting are wrong. The principle that makes them wrong is not far to seek: it is wrong to inflict nontrivial pain on animals for trivial ends. But if these things are wrong for that reason, it must likewise be wrong to raise animals in factory farms, or to use them for painful tests to ensure the safety of cosmetics. For, since no one needs to eat meat or use cosmetics, animals are being mistreated for human pleasure just as they are in blood sports.

If factory farming or cosmetic testing that causes non-trivial pain to animals is wrong, then subsidizing those practices by buying their products must likewise be wrong. It thus, surprisingly, turns out that shopping may be morally worse than hunting. From an animal's point of view, a natural life ended with a quick death seems preferable to life and death in an animal industry. If so, a practice that deals in the former seems better than one that supports the latter.

As misuses of animals are becoming better known, people are becoming more conscientious consumers. But granting animals full equality is still a long way off. Many hold that it is not wrong to cause animals non-trivial pain for non-trivial ends, as in burn and fracture experiments or drug testing that will lead to the diminishing of significant human suffering. Many others hold that non-trivial ends can be sought as long as no pain is caused to animals, as in experiments done under anesthetic where the animal is killed before it regains consciousness. Still others say that even trivial ends can be sought as long as no pain is caused, as do conditional vegetarians who maintain that if animals are given a happy life and dispatched humanely it is not wrong to eat them.

But we should pause before accepting these common views. In such cases we would not consider substituting human beings for animals, and this raises the question of how we can justify doing such things to animals. The principle of equality tells us that all beings should be treated in the same way unless there is a morally relevant difference between them. That is why we cannot treat men better than women, or people of one race better than those of another. Is there, then, any morally relevant difference that would justify treating animals in ways we would not treat human beings?

The first that comes to mind is simple difference in species; they are 'just animals.' But difference in species seems no more relevant than difference in sex or race. Why should a tail, body hair, or four legs be any more morally relevant than the placement of sexual organs or skin colour? To differentiate solely on the basis of species is thus an analogue of sexism and racism. It is, to use an ugly but useful word coined to underline the similarity, 'speciesism.'

It is more hopeful to seek the difference in other characteristics such as rationality, the ability to use moral concepts, creativity, and so forth. Since (so the argument would run) human beings typically have such features but animals do not, we can treat animals in ways we cannot treat human beings. But the problem is that not all human beings possess these characteristics. There are human beings who, by reason of misfortune of birth, disease, or accident, lack those characteristics as much as animals. The logic of the argument thus leads us to the view that animals and some human beings are in the same moral boat. If we can use animals for our advantage because they lack such characteristics, we must also be able to use some human beings for the same reason. If it is unthinkable to use human beings in this way then it must also be unthinkable to use animals.

'The principle of equality tells us that all beings should be treated in the same way unless there is a morally relevant difference between them ... Is there, then, any morally relevant difference that would justify treating animals in ways we would not treat human beings?'

Nor do ordinary human beings escape being morally bracketed with animals. To be sure, ordinary human beings have cognitive and emotional characteristics that animals do not. But these cannot be used to bestow superior moral standing on us as long as mentally challenged human beings are not to be regarded as second-class citizens. Insofar as these characteristics and abilities do not make a morally relevant difference between human beings, they cannot make a morally relevant difference in cross-species comparisons.

Schopenhauer once commented that principles cannot be treated like taxicabs, to be dismissed once they take us to our destination. If we take this comment seriously, the principles that lead us to condemn dog fighting, racism, and the exploitation of the handicapped should also lead us to radically revise our attitudes towards non-human animals.

8 Do Animals Have Rights?

JAN NARVESON

Animals around the world and down through history have been used by people for many purposes: for food, as a source of warm clothing, as sources of labour, for entertainment (with horse racing at one end of the violence scale and bull fighting and cock fighting at the other), for medical experimentation and, occasionally, for more or less unvarnished sadism. Are these, as some hold, morally objectionable across the board? Or are some of these actions acceptable and others not?

The view that they are immoral from start to finish is held by a considerable number of people nowadays. Do they have a point? The use of people for any of these purposes, unless specifically authorized by the person in question, would indeed be immoral. So if we are to believe that any of them are legitimate with regard to animals, evidently some generic distinction has to be made between people and animals. That there is such a relevant distinction is denied by a number of philosophers of recent times – Peter Singer and Tom Reagan come to mind, but there are others as well. Do they have a point?

'Whether you or any other person likes eating hamburgers, or enjoys the thought of animals living free from injuries at the hands of humans, is not what is at issue. What is at issue is whether those who do not share such sentiments are to be compelled to act as though they did.'

There is indeed such a distinction, but it isn't quite what many might expect. To appreciate it, we need to have a sound general appreciation of what morality is all about. Morality is about reaching agreements between thinking, practical beings who see the world differently, and then living up to them. Of course, this will be regarded as highly controversial by many people – perhaps by most. But that this should be so is itself suspicious.

It is controversial whether any particular religion is true. But by now it is happily close to being uncontroversial that, whatever the truth may be on such matters, people have a right to believe what they want in that regard, and to practise it so long as their practice does not involve secularly appraised injuries to others – such as murdering them.

Yet the same is obviously untrue of morals in general. You do *not* have a right to entertain, seriously, the 'view' that murdering people is perfectly okay. We do not have to settle the question of which religion is correct, so far as the maintenance of human society is concerned. We just have to contain the controversies. But containing them is a moral matter, not a religious one. Containing moral disagreement is an issue about small, containable, practical matters, not about major and fundamental philosophical ones.

The same is true about animals. Many people have sentimental attachments to some or many or, in a few cases, all animals. That is their right. But a theory of morals isn't founded on sentiment. Whether you or any other person likes eating hamburgers, or enjoys the thought of animals living free from injuries at the hands of humans, is not what is at issue. What is at issue is whether those who do not share such sentiments are to be compelled to act as though they did.

Morality has to do with the general direction of human behaviour in relation to our fellow human beings. When we say that this or that action is right or wrong, we address all those capable of understanding the subject – of comprehending such a claim and of deciding whether or not to accept it. Human beings are generically capable of doing such things, while animals, virtually without exception, are not. Some human beings of mature age, and all humans of less than a couple of years of age, are not thus capable – but almost all, in due course, will become or have been so. Some tiny number of animals, perhaps, may approach the capability to do such a thing, but this doesn't affect the generic issue.

Human beings are 'in on' the subject of morals in a way that no animals are, and this is essential. Since morality is about forming and living up to sensible rules for the good of all of us thinking, practical beings, this makes it a two-way street. People care, usually, about pain to themselves in a way that they may well not care about pain to others. What makes this pertinent to morals is that their actions in relation to one another reflect these concerns. My pleasures and pains (as with my other interests) need not matter to you in any direct way. Instead, they matter to you, insofar as they do, only because, like you, I am a fellow human being capable of, and intent on, carrying out plans of action in response to those things, actions that will often affect you, and vice versa. Developing 'social software' (in the form of general prohibitions, requirements, and recommendations regarding various kinds of behaviour that matter to us) is what is called for in the face of these obvious points about people.

The same simply is not true of animals. You will not get tigers to stop eating your children by addressing moral imperatives to them; for this, stout fences, bows and arrows, and firearms are needed. And we do not need to worry about the behaviour of most animals, especially those capable of domestication, in that regard. We hitch them to the plough and they do their thing, without serious complaint.

Animals are extremely useful to a great many people in all sorts of ways, and those animals are in no position to make much of a to-do about being so used. Their 'views' about the matter do not much count, and scarcely need to be consulted in most cases. Is this a hard-hearted view? Perhaps. But is it a rational view? Yes, and that is what counts here. No human is subordinate to any other, so far as his or her inherent character is concerned. The vegetarians among us act rightly; that is, they act within their rights. But so too do the carnivores, no more and no less; and so there is no case for making the latter subordinate to the former, or vice versa.

The case for animal rights has the significant demerit that it begs the question, as does the fashionable term 'speciesism.' Yes, animals can feel pain and perhaps some recognizable emotions. But it has to be shown that that fact *matters*. That the purposes for which this woman uses animals – to decorate herself, say – are 'trivial' is not something the critic is entitled to employ as a premise. Ms High-Fashion may reply that the complainer on this point can just mind his own business, thank you very much. There are people out there willing to make the fur hat, or whatever, that she wants, and she is ready to pay the price. No injury is thereby done to any of her fellow humans, and there is appreciable benefit to some of them, though it may offend some of them too. But we do not have a right to non-offence at the hands of our fellows – a point that we already should have learned in the course of some thousands of years of coexistence. We do, on the other hand, have a right against all others to live our lives as we please, and that is something the sentimental need to appreciate, along with the rest of us.

Cruelty for its own sake is a trait not to be promoted among humans, and when exercised against animals, if unchecked, it readily lends itself to thoughtless injuries to other people. For that matter, many of our relations to animals have side effects of serious concern to people. That scientists are often inhibited in their work with animals for the sake of improving medical knowledge – say, by offended enthusiasts for animal rights – is a matter for public concern. Ecological concerns, public health concerns, and many others affect particular issues regarding animals. But the concern that animals count in themselves, that they have the same sort of moral standing as the rest of us, is not supportable.

9 On a Pedestal

LEO GROARKE

Whatever else can be said, the Nagano Olympics, like most Olympic Games, highlighted the extent to which athletes are our heroes, and especially the heroes of our youth.

In the aftermath of the brouhaha over Ross Rebagliati's positive test for marijuana, some have questioned the exalted status of our athletes. It is easy to sympathize with such concerns, especially when one cringes at sports heroes such as NBA star Dennis Rodman – a man who makes millions bragging that he is as 'bad as I wanna be.'

This kind of concern has dogged the Olympics from their beginnings in ancient Greece, when Olympic victors were venerated as much as they are now, and possibly even more. The popularity of athletes was already a source of consternation for the famous playwright Euripides, who complained that 'of the thousands of evils which exist in Greece, there is no greater evil than the race of athletes.'

Instead of crowning Olympic athletes, Euripides proposed that we honour and reward citizens who are good, wise, reasonable, just, and committed to civic causes – 'things that benefit every state.' As admirable a proposal as this is, the International Olympic Committee (IOC) has shown little interest in Euripides' suggestion.

In the absence of utopian measures, do we need a way to discipline athletes who fail to meet our expectations in the world of moral, as opposed to athletic, prowess? In the wake of the publicity surrounding the Rebagliati affair (and jokes like the admittedly hilarious rendition of 'O Cannabis' aired on an American radio program), is it time to disqualify athletes who do not abide by reasonable standards of behaviour?

The IOC looks to be moving in this direction. Shortly after Rebagliati won his appeal, it established a committee to make recommendations on the marijuana issue. Dick Pound, the Canadian member of the IOC who abstained in a vote to strip Rebagliati of his medal, is one of the committee's five members.

Needless to say, the IOC's marijuana committee is not motivated by the concern that marijuana gives athletes an unfair advantage over their competitors (no one can explain how a drug that slows reaction times can help athletes flying 90 mph down a mountain on a snowboard).

Rather, the IOC is motivated by the suggestion that this may be an opportunity to send a message to the youth of the world. The message? That drugs are bad and using them has dire consequences.

However laudable this message may be, the IOC should reconsider its ill-considered attempt to turn the Olympics into a platform for something other than athletic excellence. Any move in this direction would, if it were consistently applied, be a first step towards regulations that could make a mockery of the Olympics.

'Instead of crowning Olympic athletes, Euripides proposed that we honour and reward citizens who are good, wise, reasonable, just, and committed to civic causes – "things that benefit every state."'

Above all else, fairness and consistency demand that different athletes be treated similarly. This makes it difficult to justify the present Olympic policy, which treats marijuana as a banned substance in some sports but not others. Why should it be permissible for hockey players, but not snowboarders, to have been exposed to marijuana?

One might solve this problem by banning marijuana across the board. But this is only the beginning of what consistency demands. If having seventeen billionths of a gram of marijuana in one's urine merits the loss of a gold medal, then fairness demands that similar sanctions be instituted against athletes who are guilty of an innumerable number of other, equally wrong, human failings, many of them with much greater potential for catastrophe.

How can one fairly take a medal away from someone who has a tiny trace of marijuana his system, but not from athletes guilty of drunk driving, cheating on their taxes, failing to pay their debts, criminal offences, inveterate speeding, and so on and so forth? Such activities are more than reprehensible. They are illegal (having billionths of a gram of marijuana in one's urine is not).

If the IOC is to set up a committee to penalize athletes who act in inappropriate ways away from the playing field, why has no one suggested that these illegal actions be cause for Olympic sanctions? Why not suggest that Donovan Bailey or Carl Lewis be stripped of their gold medals for the 100 meters if they are convicted of drunk driving?

A consistent IOC would need to go even further. The role that second-hand smoke plays in positive marijuana findings remains unclear and controversial; thus, the IOC has shown that it is prepared to strip someone of a medal even if its tests prove only that he or she associated with marijuana users.

Extending this reasoning further, the IOC should be prepared to take a medal away from an athlete found associating with a driver guilty of reckless driving. This is, of course, absurd. But it would be the logical conclusion of any attempt to decide who gets Olympic medals by judging character rather than athletic prowess.

In the end, a consistent IOC that takes sanctions against marijuana users is – unless it wants to be blatantly inconsistent – taking the first step down a road that would turn the IOC regulations into a quasi-legal system. This system would have to extend far beyond those cases of cheating which are its appropriate concern (cases which it could address better than it does). Such a system would have to set broad standards of behaviour, test and investigate athletes, try alleged violators, and punish them accordingly.

It need not be said that this is serious business, especially as the IOC would, in the process, deprive individual athletes of their greatest accomplishments. One may be excused for wondering whether the hand-picked cronies who are appointed to the IOC by a leader who has a dubious past are in a position to deal fairly with the complex legal and moral issues that this raises.

However much the behaviour of our athletes may be a source of frustration, the attempt to establish IOC sanctions for misbehaviour outside of the arena is no solution to such problems. We will do better to admire athletes for the phenomenal skills and dedication they possess, but to recognize the obvious – that there is no necessary connection between athletic prowess and a virtuous character. Given the extent to which material success sometimes spoils rather than improves character, the tendency may go the other way.

In the end, we are ourselves to blame for putting athletes on a pedestal. It is unfortunate enough that we seem determined to make Olympic athletes moral as well as athletic heroes. Let's not go one step further and let an arbitrary sports organization like the IOC decide what our morals are.

10 We Yearn for a Sense of Order, but ...

JOHN RUSSELL

It hardly needs saying that the metaphors between baseball and life are irresistible. A game with no clock where time is invisible and seamless. A season whose end can barely be seen from its beginning. A game where the pursuit of excellence must be steeled against the certainty of failure, for the finest teams will lose sixty games, the greatest batters will fail seven of ten times, and the most dominant pitchers will rarely win half their starts.

But we also project onto baseball and other games a yearning for how we would like things to be. We see rule-governed institutions that have been designed to be especially orderly and predictable. We assume that in games, perhaps uniquely, the rules that are laid down settle definitively the terms for cooperation and competition. They settle fully, and in advance, what conduct is permissible and what is not.

'It didn't seem right to take away Brett's home run because of a little pine tar, but rules are rules. Rules are all an umpire has to work with.'

This is a deeply cherished view of games and, because of it, games represent a refuge from the distressing uncertainty and greyness of the institutions that govern our real lives and real choices. But this is only a hopeful illusion. It obscures the inherent untidiness of rules and institutions, whether in games or in life.

Perhaps the most famous rule dispute in baseball occurred in New York in 1983. In baseball lore it is now known simply as 'the Pine Tar Incident.' On 25 July, Kansas City Royals third baseman George Brett hit a two-run home run with two out in the top of the ninth inning. Brett's home run gave the Royals a chance to win the game by putting them ahead of the Yankees 5–4.

But while Brett was celebrating his home run, Yankee manager Billy Martin was in deep discussion with the umpires. He pointed out that Brett had pine tar smeared over more than the bottom eighteen inches of his bat, and that his run therefore should not have been allowed because he had broken Rule 1.10(b), a highly obscure, seldom-enforced rule.

Another rule seemed to say that any ball hit with a bat not in conformity with the rules was an illegally batted ball. Yet another rule stated that an illegally batted ball was an automatic out.

Martin's logic appeared inescapable. Brett was out. The game was over. The Yankees had beaten the Royals 4–3. There followed a lengthy discussion among the umpires, who reluctantly, but finally, agreed with Martin.

Brett and the Royals disagreed, arguing that the extra pine tar had conferred no advantage. If anything, sticky stuff high on the barrel of a bat would be a hindrance to hitting home runs. It was, therefore, simply unfair to disallow Brett's home run.

The umpires agreed that it was unjust, but felt they had to follow the letter of the law. As crew chief Joe Brinkman put it: 'It didn't seem right to take away Brett's home run because of a little pine tar, but rules are rules. Rules are all an umpire has to work with.'

Did the umpires make the right decision? The case still divides baseball fans, players and umpires. But once we understand some things about the nature and limitations of rules, Brett's and the Royals' position looks pretty compelling.

The purpose of rules is to guide conduct, but there are several limitations to rules. First, language is an imprecise instrument. So, what rules mean and how they should be applied inevitably leads to some degree of uncertainty.

Second, those who frame rules cannot foresee all the contexts in which they may apply. This means that rules may sometimes be applied to circumstances for which they were never intended.

Third, we might try to resolve the previous ambiguities by referring to the intentions of the authors of the rules, but these too are often vague, unknown, or inconsistent.

Rules are beset by indeterminacy of meaning, scope, and intention, so it is hardly straightforward to apply them 'to the letter.'

In the pine tar case, the intent behind Rule 1.10(b) was basically unknown. It has been suggested that it may have been written in the early days of baseball as a means of keeping balls clean and in play longer as a cost-saving measure.

Because the intent was unclear, no one could or did say that the rule was written with the current application in mind. Another way of reading 1.10(b) was that bats extravagantly smeared with sticky stuff were to be removed from games with no further consequences.

What this seems to show is that wherever they are found, rules are imperfect vehicles for assuring order, predictability, or justice. A narrow-minded application of rules overlooks these issues by prejudging cases about which we are simply ignorant on mainly arbitrary grounds.

American League president Lee MacPhail implicitly acknowledged that argument. A few days after the dispute, he reinstated Brett's home run and ordered the game to be played from that point on. He acknowledged that there was a limited sense in which the umpire's decision was 'technically defensible.' But he also held that the umpire's ruling had not been in keeping with the 'intent or spirit' of the game itself, declaring that 'games should be won and lost on the playing field – not through technicalities of the rules.'

In other words, common sense could and should prevail to preserve the integrity of a game or practice. Good judgment and the exercise of discretion cannot be avoided in any complex, rule-governed human practice. Even in games there is no refuge from the need to exercise wise discretion.

The Royals subsequently beat the Yankees 5–4 on Brett's reinstated home run. In one sense, perhaps the umpire got it right: maybe rules are all an umpire has to work with. But perhaps in baseball, as in life, the ultimate rule is always to try to do the right thing.

11 Pleasure Alone Won't Make You Happy

THOMAS HURKA

Some people think that human beings want only pleasure. Some think we *should* want only pleasure. These people would love the experience machine.

The experience machine is a philosopher's machine, which means it doesn't exist. (It was invented by American philosopher Robert Nozick.) By neural stimulation it can give you any experience or inner feeling you like – of writing a great novel, of scoring a Stanley Cup–winning goal, of deep and passionate love.

You decide in advance what experiences you'd like to have (there's a menu if you're unimaginative), electrodes are attached to your brain, and you then have all the thoughts and feelings associated with your chosen activity. It's exactly as if you were writing that novel or scoring that goal.

Imagine that the experience machine is available and you can go on it for the rest of your life. (Although philosophers' machines don't exist, you have to pretend they do.) Do you want to go on the machine? Will it make your life best to go on it?

If pleasure is all that matters, the answer should be yes, since the machine gives you all the pleasure you can want. It gives you physical pleasure, and if more refined pleasures go with activities like novel writing, it gives you those too.

Yet most of us wouldn't go on the machine. This isn't just a matter of taste, like not liking Chinese food. We think that if we did want to go on the machine we'd be wrong, we'd be wanting what isn't in fact the best life.

Some minor reasons for this should be set aside. We may think that going on the machine would be immoral, because it would mean neglecting our duties to others. So imagine that others don't need us, being already well off. Or we may worry that we'll program the machine badly and get stuck in some juvenile fantasy of sex on a desert island. So imagine that we come off the machine every few years to reprogram it. (When we plug back in we forget the reprogramming and become absorbed in our new fantasy.)

Even with these changes, most of us wouldn't go on the machine. This shows something deep about our values.

What exactly is missing on the experience machine? People who plug in are detached from reality. They lack connections to the world around them, in two vital respects.

First, they lack knowledge of their surroundings. When you have knowledge, the way you think the world is corresponds to the way it really is. There's a relation of matching between the thoughts in your mind and the world outside it, and this matching is missing on the experience machine. People think they're writing a novel or playing hockey, but they're not.

Second, people on the machine don't achieve anything. In successful action, you form a goal and transfer it to reality, so that the world comes to match an idea in your mind. This, too, is missing on the machine. People intend to write novels or score goals, but their aims are never realized.

As the experience machine shows, we don't care just about pleasure or the quality of our inner experience. We want that experience connected to something outside it. There are real-life illustrations of this.

If you believe your spouse is faithful when he or she isn't, you can have the same feelings as if your spouse were faithful; thus, you can have the same pleasure. But surely being mistaken about such a vital aspect of your life is bad. Or you may die in the contented belief that you've achieved some important goal. If pleasure were all that matters, the fact that you haven't achieved this goal – yours isn't the cure for cancer – wouldn't harm you. But surely it's a loss.

'As the experience machine shows, we don't care just about pleasure or the quality of our inner experience. We want that experience connected to something outside it.'

This doesn't mean that pleasure has no value. Although not the only good thing, it can still be one good thing among others. If we had the experience machine, it might be nice to plug in for five or ten minutes a night. (TV may be a poor person's experience machine.) What wouldn't be good for a whole life can be good for bits of it.

More important, pleasure is a valuable addition to other good things. Knowledge or achievement plus pleasure in them is better than knowledge or achievement alone.

Imagine that a scientist with a profound knowledge of nature takes no pleasure in that knowledge, feeling no excitement about it. We'd think there's something wrong with this scientist. If he doesn't respond positively to his knowledge, his life has less value than it might. Likewise, if we learned that Margaret Atwood gets no pleasure from her novels or Wayne Gretzky doesn't like hockey – he plays just as a job – we'd be troubled. To have its full value, achievement must be joined by a proper pleasure in it.

Pleasure on its own, as on the experience machine, has little value. But when added to other good things, it makes them better. In Aristotle's words, pleasure is like 'the bloom of youth on those in the flower of their age.' Or as we might say, it's the icing on the cake.

12 Love Is All You Need to Understand Christmas

JOHN RUSSELL

Very many of us, regardless of our cultural or religious affiliations, are vigorously participating in the Christmas holiday season. Non-Christians and Christians alike often find this slightly discomfiting. What accounts for the easy attachment of non-Christians to a Christian religious festival? Love of a party? Of getting presents?

While some may point to the festival's pagan roots, others to the commercial enticements of the season, and still others to Christianity's hegemony over our cultural institutions, the best explanation comes from Christian religion itself – Christmas is love, and love is one of the closest things we have to a universal value. Indeed, almost all humans value their loved ones and friends – their intimates – above all else. Nothing beats intimate human companionship for making a life go well, and a life without it is typically tragic, miserable, and agonizingly boring.

If so, we can see how the celebration of love at Christmas can easily be extended beyond divine love to human love. Indeed, Christianity itself encourages this extension. For to love others as oneself – to create a human community based on love – is what ultimately fulfils divine law (Romans 13:8-10).

But if we can explain the wide appeal of Christmas in this way, we must surely want to know just what love is. What sorts of relations genuinely embody it? Why does it exert such a hold over us? Can it be extended as far as Christians and others propose, to express peace and good will to all?

Such questions are often overlooked, perhaps because they require a tolerance for philosophical reflection that is at odds with the warmth and frenzy of the season. But they demand our serious attention nonetheless.

Plato provides the first systematic philosophical treatment of love. He argues that love reflects an impulse to propagate oneself physically and spiritually in the world, permitting mortals to seek a measure of immortality.

The highest expression of Plato's love exists where a person of wisdom and virtue engenders within the soul of another that which is good and fine in himself. So, for Plato, loving relations are concerned with the promotion of the good of the beloved, which reflects the best sort of concern for another. Since this also benefits the lover, Platonic love is a way of resolving the conflict between self-love and altruism that is part of the human condition.

But Plato's position seems to make the scope of love too limited and the position of the beloved entirely too passive. For Plato, the highest form of love exists only between a mentor and a protégé. It is fundamentally a relation between unequals. Most important, it is not yet clear that the lover has sufficient concern for the beloved for his own sake. Love on this view seems too selfish – a sort of colonizing of the beloved's psyche for the lover's benefit.

Aristotle later addresses some of these problems. For him, perfect friendship or love occurs between virtuous equals who wish good upon each other for the other's sake. Like Plato, Aristotle regards a friend as 'another self,' but he is less a psychic imperialist. My beloved is 'another self' in that he or she has a similarly virtuous nature. I can see my own interests and values extended in my friend's character and projects, since they embody and promote my own values and interests. True friends help each other make wise choices, promoting their own interests in the bargain.

'It is through the injection of mystery that modern love differs from classical love. Love's object is largely undefinable. It is also unconditional.'

Aristotle's account of love and friendship is the most influential in classical antiquity, but it is repudiated by more modern, Christian-influenced views. In his *Diary of Adam and Eve*, Mark Twain succinctly portrays the modern view. After the fall, Eve contemplates her love for Adam. She avers that he is neither bright, nor considerate, nor educated, nor industrious. He is not even chivalrous (he told on her, after all). Why does she love him then? Eve concludes that 'this kind of love ... just comes – none knows whence – and cannot explain itself. And doesn't need to.'

It is through the injection of mystery that modern love differs from classical love. Love's object is largely undefinable. It is also unconditional. Eve loves Adam merely for who he is. She would love him even if he failed to contribute anything to her well-being, indeed even if he undermined it.

To some, Eve's love will appear too optimistic and unstable beside the classical accounts. But it is an obvious fact about humans that they sometimes love others for their own sake with no expectation of returns or any requirement that the person be good. To many, including Christians, this has seemed the most noble form of human love. Though it remains unclear whether it can bear the weight of universal love, it remains a challenge to more classical views.

Despite their problems, each of these accounts seems to say something that is true and important. The best evidence of this is that each of the types of love is clearly, and probably unalterably, reflected in our love for our children. For we do clearly love them most unconditionally. We want to pass along what is fine to them. Eventually, we want to extend our projects with them in lively and creative partnership. If so, it shouldn't be surprising that besides being a time for celebration of love, Christmas is also especially a time for children, for our love may be most completely expressed in our affection for them.

These accounts also explain why Christmas is a painfully difficult time for many. If love's arrow hasn't struck, or if you have lost or turned away one of your other selves, a celebration of love and friendship may only bring realization that something deep and important is missing. Love is a great human good, maybe the greatest, but it also makes us vulnerable to much sorrow and pain. Its celebration must be balanced with compassion and the knowledge that we may not be able to give or receive as much comfort as we'd like.

But we can't give it up, nor should we want to. We know enough of the value and importance of love not to turn away from it. Indeed, to quote a wisely bittersweet secular Christmas song, 'the secret of Christmas is not the things you do at Christmas time but the Christmas things you do all year through.' In a word, the cultivation of loving human relations.

PART XII

The Changing University

1 Town, Gown, and the Long Way Down

GRAEME HUNTER

Bishop's University lies in the lush and rolling foothills of the Green Mountains, just thirty miles from the border of Vermont, in the Eastern Townships of Quebec. When I first went there as a freshman in September 1970, it arguably offered the finest liberal education in Canada. That argument could still be made today. Not that Bishop's has avoided the precipitous decline in educational standards of recent years; only that it has not lost its relative standing in the process. And because it is compact and single-minded, Bishop's is a better place than many that have suffered more drastic decline to observe and understand the educational quagmire of our time.

In 1970, university was a brave new world to me. Like an immigrant meeting a foreign culture, I could at first not distinguish between the traditional and the innovative or between the innovative and the rash. It is hardly surprising, then, that most of what seemed significant to me at the time has proven to be ephemeral, while a few matters that almost escaped my notice then, now loom large as the keys to the period.

> *'The tradition of the gown long outlasted the era of knights and tournaments. ... Thus, even if the gown had been merely an insignificant fashion, it still ought to have amazed me that I should witness the passing of even a minor tradition of seven hundred years standing.'*

The first minor incident that, at the time, I could not appreciate was the vote taken in my year on the wearing of the academic gown. The only reason I remember it at all is that I was threatened with having to spend about forty dollars to acquire one, and was convinced that I could find better things to do with the money. The ideological debate surrounding the issue, if there was one, affected me very little. When I went to vote against the gown, I was voting as one bent on economy and with my mind on more important things.

As it turned out, however, even those who already had gowns were eager not to wear them, and the dress code of Bishop's changed at a stroke forever. My forty dollars were quickly spent on other things, and the issue was soon forgotten. Many years would pass before the significance of the vote struck me.

One of the earliest universities grew up in Paris around 1200. A number of qualities set it off from the rest of the city. For one thing, it was in its own quarter on the left bank of the Seine. For another, the inhabitants of the quarter spoke a language different from the French around them: they spoke Latin. That is why the university area is still called 'the Latin Quarter' today. In the third place, they dressed differently from the townsmen, wearing the plain gown of their academic guild, the Universitas. The gown was a sign of the community to which they belonged. It was not a badge of wealth or power, but nevertheless one of pride, because it set apart those engaged in pursuits often thought nobler than wealth or power.

The tradition of the gown long outlasted the era of knights and tournaments. At Bishop's, founded in the middle of the nineteenth century, it endured until September 1970. Thus, even if the gown had been merely an insignificant fashion, it still ought to have amazed me that I should witness the passing of even a minor tradition of seven hundred years standing. Being unaware of most history, however, I was not amazed. And of course I was also unconscious of the fact that more was changing here than a mere academic fashion.

Consider for a moment the symbolism of the gown. Plain though it is, it makes one of the few really effective fashion statements: it declares to the world that the simplest clothing is good enough for the scholar. It proclaims the scholar's disregard for the pursuit of status and rank that characterizes public life. It quietly announces the scholar's loyalty to the genteel community of the learned and to the satisfactions of study and conversation.

But suddenly across North America the tradition of the gown began to seem ridiculous to university students. It was as if they had fallen asleep after a wild party and awakened to find themselves dressed in some comical, antiquated costume whose significance they could no longer recall. Hastily and sheepishly, they laid it aside and put on the habitual clothing of their time and place. Outstripping Rip Van Winkle, these students appeared to themselves to have been asleep these seven hundred years, and they looked at their clothing in shame, as Adam beheld his nakedness. They seemed to say to themselves, 'There is no difference between us and the people of the town. Why then should we dress as if there were?'

To me, a callow freshman in 1970, the reasoning of my fellow students seemed impeccable. It did not occur to me then that we might have had a different and better thought. We could have said, 'These gowns set us off from the pursuits and passions of the town. What must we do to be worthy of them?' But to us they were mere relics of the age of armour – and like armour they were cumbersome, useless, the dead weight of the past.

Nor was the gown the only change in 1970. That was also the year they closed the Faculty of Theology, originally the raison d'être of Bishop's University, and replaced it with the Department of Religion. This was no mere relabelling: Theology proclaims the truths of Christianity; Religious Studies studies religions. They have nothing in common. Few students realized this at the time. The significance of the change eluded us as well.

Theology had been lodged in a graceful villa called Divinity House, in dreamy seclusion on a treed corner of the campus, beside the river. After the eviction of its faculty, Divinity House became a boisterous residence. The chapel, now deconsecrated, was converted to a common room. All this I took to be a matter of course as I moved into 'Divinity.' But there was one event in this transformation that would have tickled the fancy of Marshall McLuhan or Neil Postman, and that was so incongruous as to strike even ignorant students like myself. Onto the place where the altar had been, in the chapel now turned student lounge, a new idol was hoisted: the television. Worship picked up noticeably.

Among the many things I did not notice in 1970 was that the events I have narrated were connected. I did not realize then that the university was hoping to be carried to new glory in the strong breeze of secularism then blowing. Because I was a freshman, I had no expectations of how a university ought to bear itself, and therefore I did not observe my alma mater's ridiculous posture: bent over like a hoop and sawing frantically at her roots, fearful only that the winds of fashion would blow over her and leave her behind.

But Canadian universities got their wish. They sawed through their roots in time and were swept, like Dorothy and Toto, into a land of Oz. There they lie today, rootless hulks, ungainly presences upon the land, their huge, bare branches languishing – a riddle, an expense, and byword to their communities.

What hope is there for them? The answer is that different ones have different hopes. It is not rash to predict that in several decades many that we now know will be gone. The public does not want to pay for them, and they offer nothing that students would pay for either, if the product were not highly subsidized at public expense. So some undoubtedly will disappear. Others will become officially the technical colleges they already are in fact, continuing what they now do well – giving instruction in the place of education and information in the place of knowledge.

But I hope that some may send their roots down again into the ground from which they grew, becoming once more communities of study, nestled in the shadow of the Church. For my own alma mater, Bishop's University, this is the best outcome I could wish.

2 Are University Faculty Unnecessary?

ANDREW IRVINE

In his science fiction story, 'Mutability,' Thomas Disch begins with a quote from the 2097 edition of Baedecker's *The German States*. Towards the end of the quotation we learn that the Faculty of History in the Free University in Tübingen had been the first 'to abolish voluntarily, in 2019, the increasingly meaningless distinction between the teaching staff and the body of graduate students.'

It now looks as if one of Canada's major universities will soon be able to boast that it has successfully anticipated this action by almost two decades. If a proposal currently under discussion to introduce 'student-directed seminars' is implemented, not only will the distinction between teaching staff and graduate students be diminished, but so also will be the main difference between professors and undergraduates.

Once the proposal is implemented, even undergraduate students will be allowed to 'initiate and coordinate' university-level courses. They will be permitted to design courses, and then coordinate the teaching and evaluation of other undergraduate students, and they will obtain academic credit for doing so.

Those who are concerned about academic standards are assured that student coordinators will be required to participate in a 'preparatory workshop on facilitation skills and course planning' in lieu of the PhD normally required to teach courses at universities in Canada. In addition, a volunteer 'faculty sponsor' will be made available to offer 'guidance' to student coordinators on 'course content, class activities, and evaluation of participants.'

However, unpaid faculty sponsors will not be required to be involved in the day-to-day teaching and evaluation of the students enrolled in these courses; furthermore, student participants (in addition to the student coordinators) will themselves be 'involved in determining class work and evaluation criteria.' In addition, the 'facilitation of class meetings may rotate among participants.'

Admittedly, the terminology becomes rather confusing. 'Student participants' will be those undergraduates who are *taking* the course for academic credit, but who will also be involved in the 'facilitation' of meetings and the evaluation of other students. 'Student coordinators' will be those undergraduates who are *organizing* the course for the same academic credit but who will no doubt learn as much from the student participants as the student participants learn from them.

In other words, nobly recognizing that they alone do not have a monopoly on the knowledge required to offer a university-level course, student coordinators will share their duties with the other students involved, who presumably will be distinguished only by the fact that they have not attended the required preparatory workshop that would allow them to be designated 'coordinators.' This makes the distinction between student coordinators and student participants a little blurry, but perhaps this is of small matter once the normal distinction between students and faculty is itself deemed unimportant.

'If a proposal currently under discussion to introduce "student-directed seminars" is implemented, not only will the distinction between teaching staff and graduate students be diminished, but so also will be the main difference between professors and undergraduates.'

It also makes it difficult for faculty to look senior graduate students directly in the eye and say, 'Now that you have almost finished your PhD, we know you need teaching experience to help you find a university-level job. But we've decided to let our undergraduates teach themselves about the topic you've devoted years of your life to researching. Buck up, though. With any luck, and if the enrolments are high enough, perhaps we will be able to hire you as a teaching assistant to the undergraduate coordinator conducting the course.'

What could be the motivation for such a bizarre proposal? Perhaps it is that the university offers some 'boilerplate' courses, courses that are designed to cover very basic material and that can be taught without the many years of graduate training normally required of university instructors? Likely not.

Far from being basic, entry-level courses, the courses being proposed under this new program are meant to focus primarily on topics not currently taught. Thus student coordinators will not even have taken and passed the course they are 'facilitating,' let alone done the extensive research normally expected of university instructors. In the words of the proposal, student-directed seminars will be designed to 'promote interaction between the academic interests of students and research activities of faculty members.' This, of course, is not a bad way of describing regular graduate and senior undergraduate research seminars, but with those seminars the university normally has the foresight to ensure that faculty members are involved in more than a merely advisory capacity.

Explained in this way, perhaps the objective of these seminars will be to equip students with the skills necessary to undertake independent research. This is no doubt an admirable goal, and one not foreign to the modern university. But once again, most universities recognize that compared to traditional lecture courses, courses devoted to developing such skills regularly require an increase, rather than a reduction, in the amount of faculty supervision. Learning how to research intellectually challenging topics is no more a solitary activity than learning to pilot a 747. Students in both types of activity are *students* (surely it isn't necessary to say this) precisely because, by definition, they are not qualified to act as instructors, if even to themselves.

What alternative explanations remain? The more cynically minded might hazard the guess that this proposal is simply a cost-cutting mechanism designed to help reduce class sizes in some of Canada's already overcrowded classrooms. If so, they will hardly be reassured by the fact that the first of these courses has already been introduced as a pilot project without faculty approval and without having passed through normal academic channels.

In any event, university administrators in our more 'progressive' universities will no doubt find it comforting to have students 'facilitating' other students now that we've reached that other major milestone of science fiction, the new millennium.

3 The PC Tyranny

LOU MARINOFF

I've been invited to write about political correctness and philosophy in the North American academy. What qualifies me? I'm a refugee from political correctness. I emigrated from Canada to the United States because of an insidious quota system, euphemistically called 'employment equity,' which decrees that there are too many white, male philosophers in Canadian universities. The Nuremburg Laws excluded Jews from Nazified German universities because we were 'non-Aryan'; Jews are now excluded from Canadian universities because we are 'white.' This is a compelling irony. It compelled me to get out.

Before quitting Canada in 1994, I penned a satire on political correctness, called *Fair New World*. Libertarian lawyer Karen Selick called it 'the most politically incorrect work of art I have ever seen. It's also hilariously funny and scathingly insightful.' Since no Canadian publisher had the courage to bring it out, I founded my own press, Backlash Books, and published it myself. *Fair New World* continues to be taught in colleges and universities, by politically incorrect professors, all of whom have received Backlash Books' highest award: 'Offender of the Faith.' So much for my political credentials.

I am currently tenured at the City College of New York, which graduated eight eventual Nobel laureates during its halcyon years but where, thanks to a generation of open admissions, Great Books have been replaced by Comic Books. What kind of refuge is this? I offer two stock answers. To the cognoscenti, I reply that I have Bertrand Russell's job. Russell's appointment at CCNY was infamously denied by the New York Supreme Court, which convicted him – much as Athens convicted Socrates – of moral corruption. Instead of putting Russell to death, the court merely denied him employment. This is called 'social progress.' To the incognoscenti, I reply that I was hired by CCNY to fill a quota system: New York City was running short of Jews, so they imported me.

By now you should be persuaded that I am politically incorrect enough to write this piece. Now let me unpack the *Webster* definition. First, to which 'political sensibilities' does it allude? These generally entail a Rousseauesque-cum-Marxist vision of the world, which perceives humanity as an innocent and well-meaning horde of erstwhile noble savages, inequitably differentiated by race, class, and gender by an evil conspiracy of white male heterosexual patriarchal hegemonists, who use logic, mathematics, science, classics, capitalism, democracy, and testosterone to disenfranchise politically and deprive socio-economically the rest of the world, who are the 'victims of oppression.'

While Marx's putative 'remedy' was partly predicated on his slogan 'from each according to his ability, to each according to his need,' current political correctness is incomparably more surreal: it has no truck at all with ability, which it finds intolerably offensive and therefore among the first things slated for elimination. For example, many primary schools now give ribbons to all children who run in field-day races, because they are terrified of 'offending' and therefore also (by the puerile etiology that informs their world view) of *traumatizing* the children who do not win or place in the contest. Thus they have confused fleetness of foot with moral worthiness. This has two serious consequences.

First, at the grassroots level, political correctness fails to teach children that sportsmanship and self-development are the lasting lessons of competition. Win or lose, one is morally worthy if one runs the race and does one's best. If Jane is a better runner than Sally, there is nothing wrong (that is, 'offensive') about rewarding Jane for fleetness of foot. If Jane wins a gold medal and Sally finishes out of the medals, it means that Jane is a *better runner than* Sally: it does not mean that Jane is *better than* Sally. But a politically correct race is socially engineered: all runners

'political correctness (noun): conformity to a belief that language and practices which could offend political sensibilities should be eliminated.'

Merriam Webster's Collegiate Dictionary

must finish together, or all must receive identical ribbons regardless of place. This is an offence against fleetness of foot. It is typical of a pervasive unwillingness to acknowledge natural and acquired differences among human beings, which in turn devalues individual excellence and obliterates moral worthiness. That is an offence against humanity.

The second consequence marks a death threat to American democracy. Tocqueville presciently observed that Americans must choose between liberty and equality. Any undeluded person knows that equality of opportunity leads inevitably to inequality of outcomes. However, the inability of political correctness to tolerate unequal outcomes in the wake of equal opportunities, and its dogmatic commitment to a neo-Marxist doctrine that equates justice and fairness with a levelling of outcomes, have contorted the North American academy into a sublime estate in which equal outcomes in higher education are guaranteed by pervasive illiteracy, innumeracy, and aculturality. The academy has become a neo-Procrustean Inn, one whose former halls of learning have been converted into dormitories of indoctrination, and whose patrons (the students) have had their heads chopped off instead of their legs so that all fit equally into its deconstructed cots.

The 'language and practices' that offend the deepest sensibilities of political correctness are the same ones that form the very foundations of Western civilization: the languages of logic, mathematics, classics, philosophy – along with the language of Shakespeare, too – and the practices of science, capitalism, democracy, and due legal process, along with the inescapably allied and respective notions of reliable method, generation of wealth, government by consent of the governed, and protection of inalienable individual rights. By metastasizing like an opportunistic cancer throughout the mind-politic of the academy, political correctness has proceeded, true to the *Webster* definition, to eliminate the language and practices of Western civilization itself, and therefore to kill the very body-politic on which it parasitically feeds. Lest you deem my accusations implausible or exaggerated, I will regale you with a few examples.

Grade inflation is rampant in American universities, to the extent that undergraduate degrees are increasingly worthless pieces of paper. From the Ivy to the Poison Ivy leagues, institutions have capitulated to 'egalitarian' demands that students receive A's for attendance. They graduate hapless victims of victimology, who can neither read with comprehension nor write grammatically correct sentences. When such students receive Ds or Fs in my upper-level philosophy electives, they complain that they are 'straight-A' majors in psychology, or education, or in some other department that subscribes to the barker's slogan 'Everybody plays, everybody wins.' One very bright and hard-working student, who happened to be a black female, asked me if she had really 'earned' the A she received in my course. When I assured her that she merited the grade based on her performance and nothing else, she actually wept with gratitude – at having been allowed to display her merit. In contrast, politically correct ideology systematically deprives excellent students of opportunities to excel, so as not to 'offend' mediocrity and worse.

Political correctness eradicates individual liberties as well as merit. Princeton University's Office of Student Life annually prints a handbook lauding 'tolerance' and extolling the 'virtues' of cultural diversity. The office also compels attendance at freshman orientation films, one of which illustrates methods of contraception and abortion. When a Roman Catholic student tried to exit the cinema, asserting that she had no need watch these practices because her religion forbade them, she was physically prevented from leaving. She was coerced – in the name of tolerance and diversity! – to watch the entire film. This is another face of political correctness: rank hypocrisy.

Freedom of speech was an early casualty. In denial, Katherine Whitehorn wrote in the London *Observer*: 'The thing has been blown up out of all proportion. PC language is not enjoined on one and all – there are a lot more places where you can say "spic" and "bitch" with impunity than places where you can smoke a cigarette.' She should have been at a Canadian university in 1994, when a professor of political science remarked jocularly to a teaching assistant noted for her stern grading: 'I'll bet the students think you're a real black bitch.' The president of that university promptly shut down the graduate studies program in political science and launched a far-ranging investigation. This catapulted UBC onto the national news until eventually the university felt obligated to apologize to the department for the harm the investigation did to its reputation. Stand-up comedy proliferates precisely because the comics remain at liberty to say what – thanks to political correctness – their audiences are increasingly afraid to think.

Around the same time, Yale University was busily refusing a gift of $20 million, offered by a Texas oilman and patron of high culture. He wanted the money spent on a humanities program that celebrated Great Books of Western Civilization. Unfortunately, Yale was long since committed to the politically correct doctrine that there are no great books, that the idea of great books is a pernicious myth used to oppress illiterate and innumerate savages, to keep women barefoot and pregnant, to exploit the developing world, and to glorify dead white European males who apparently plagiarized Western civilization from an unidentified tribe of transvestites. Thus Yale could not possibly accept $20 million to teach so-called 'Great Books,' either because 'greatness' is entirely arbitrary, or because recognizing a few 'Great Books' would be offensive to a great many inconsequential ones.

PC hiring practices are utterly Orwellian. In a Canadian university, a male and a female candidate were finalists for a tenurable position in philosophy. The male was demonstrably better qualified, but the female was offered the position owing to an alleged 'gender imbalance.' Two members of the selection committee were willing to testify to the province's Human Rights Commission that the female's appointment had been politically orchestrated. But when the male finalist formally asked the province's HRC to investigate, his request was summarily denied. He was informed by the HRC that since he was a white male, it was impossible for anyone to discriminate against him.

The siege engines of political correctness have been dragged to the very walls of MIT, where cries of 'gender imbalance' herald the administrative reallocation of scientific funding to satisfy arbitrary gender quotas. Copious evidence on sex difference – much of it accumulated by female researchers themselves – shows that males are, on average and by nature, more adept than females at mathematical and spatiotemporal reasoning. But any fact that offends regnant political sensibility is dismissed as a 'social construct' and ignored by wishful thinking. The politically correct explanation for the dearth of female Newtons and Einsteins is that female geniuses have been 'oppressed' by the usual conspiracy of white males, and by the very institution of civilization itself.

And what is philosophy's explicit role in all this? It varies across a continuum. Insofar as academic philosophers are political animals, prey to the edicts of a brain-dead academy, they either resist political correctness, or pay lip service to it, or embrace it according to their respective lights or darknesses. But those who fail to resist its fatuous tyranny, or who revel in its egregious self-righteousness, become apologists for the deconstruction of the very intellectual culture that makes philosophy possible, and accomplices to the sapping of the principles that sustain that culture itself. Thus North American philosophers who champion group rights and trample on individual liberties (epitomized by proponents of quota-based hiring), who hysterically demonize reason, and who absurdly deny Hume's distinction between fact and value on the alleged grounds that all ideas are 'social constructs,' excepting this idea itself – which they take as brute fact (epitomized by Richard Rorty's flagrant antirealism) – these are not lovers of wisdom, but high priests and handmaidens of hubris.

To philosophy students who can yet read, I recommend J.S. Mill's *On Liberty*. His enlightened conception entails 'liberty of tastes and pursuits, of framing the plan of our life to suit our own character, of doing as we like, without impediment from our fellow creatures, so long as what we do does not harm them, even though they should think our conduct foolish, perverse, or wrong.'

Mill's salient distinction is between offence and harm; its implications for political correctness are pellucid. People who are offended by others' language and practices should not have the liberty to eliminate them, as long as such words and deeds are not harmful. But once this critical distinction between offence and harm is blurred – as it daily and extravagantly is by the politically correct – those who blur it arrogate to themselves the supremely illegitimate authority to proscribe whatever conduct they deem 'offensive' (for example, affairs between professors and graduate students, and ideologically unpopular research), to silence whatever speech they deem 'offensive' (such as ethnic humour and sexual innuendo), and to censor whatever ideas they deem 'offensive' (for example, that there are biologically based human differences that may not be eradicable by social engineering, and that equal opportunity virtually guarantees unequal outcomes). The near-ubiquitous conflation of offence with harm has sanctioned a thirty-year reign of political terror in North American universities, whose degenerate administrative ideologues daily micromanage the minutiae of thought, speech, and deed.

In such a totalitarian climate, philosophers who fail to draw and defend Mill's distinction between offence and harm are not only professionally derelict, but also party to the catastrophe that has ensued from its blurring.

The 'dark side' of philosophy is compassed both by what it has failed to do in defence and preservation of its own mission – the love of wisdom – and by what this failure has permitted the enemies of open and reasoned inquiry to entrench in its place – the worship of folly.

4 Privatizing the University: The New Tragedy of the Commons

JAMES ROBERT BROWN

In recent years, we have all watched the increasing commercialization of the campus. The numerous advertising posters and the golden arches of fast food outlets may be an affront to our aesthetic sensibilities, but they are, arguably, no worse than ugly. Some of the other new features of commercialized campus life do, however, constitute a serious threat to things we rightly revere. 'Privatization' and the 'business model' are the potential menace.

What do these notions mean? To me, they involve an increased dependence on industry and philanthropy for operating the university; an increased amount of our resources being directed to applied or so-called practical subjects, both in teaching and in research; a proprietary treatment of research results, with the commercial interest in secrecy overriding the public's interest in free, shared knowledge; and an attempt to run the university more like a business that treats industry and students as clients and ourselves as service providers with something to sell. We pay increasing attention to the immediate needs and demands of our 'customers,' and as the old saw goes, 'the customer is always right.'

Privatization is particularly frightening from the point of view of public well-being. A researcher employed by a university-affiliated hospital in Canada, working under contract with a pharmaceutical company, made public her findings that a particular drug was harmful. This violated the terms of her contract, and so she was fired. Her dismissal caused a scandal, and she was subsequently reinstated. The university and hospital in question are now working out something akin to tenure for hospital-based researchers and guidelines for contracts, so that more public disclosure of privately funded research will become possible. This is a rare victory and a small step in the right direction, but the general trend is the other way. Thanks to profit-driven private funding, researchers are forced to keep valuable information secret and are often contractually obliged to keep discovered dangers to public health under wraps. Of course, we must not be too naive about this. Governments, too, can unwisely insist on secrecy, as did the British Ministry of Agriculture, Fisheries, and Food in the work they funded in connection with the bovine spongiform encephalopathy epidemic (mad cow disease). This prevented others from reviewing the relevant data and from pointing out that the problems were more serious than government was letting on.

A recent study found that more than one-third of recently published articles produced by University of Massachusetts scientists had one or more authors who stood to make money from the results they were reporting. That is, they were patent holders, or had some relationship – for example, as board members – to a company that would exploit the results. The financial interests of these authors were not mentioned in the publications. If patents are needed to protect public knowledge from private claims, then simply have the publicly funded patent holders put their patents in the public domain or charge no fee for use.

In another case, financial institutions donated a very large sum to a Canadian university economics department to study 'the effects of high taxation on productivity.' The results may influence government policy. In such cases, the public and its political decision-makers get information only of a certain kind, because there is no private, well-funded foundation called the Consortium of Single Mothers on Welfare that bestows similar massive funding to discover the effects of poverty on the development of children. Public policy decisions should be based on a variety of sources of information, but the privatization of research means that one point of view – guess whose? – will tend to prevail. Publicly funded science, though far from perfectly serving all interests, has at least a chance of serving more.

'The question is to whom academics should be accountable – to use a favourite term of privatizers. The answer is simple: the public. We owe it to them to keep knowledge free for all.'

Even philanthropic groups can and sometimes do skew research and teaching. The Templeton Foundation, for example, offers awards to those who offer courses on science and religion. I teach such a course myself and feel the temptation to seek one of their awards. It seems innocent enough; after all, I am already teaching the course and they are not telling me what I have to believe. Moreover, they will put $5,000 in my pocket and give another $5,000 to my chronically underfunded department. Everybody wins, so why say no?

There are several reasons. First, it skews the curriculum. A department might well offer a Templeton-type course because it needs the money, when what its students need is a regular philosophy of religion or philosophy of science course (perhaps offering both in alternate years).

Second, although the Templeton Foundation does not prohibit atheists from winning its awards, it does insist that a certain type of literature be covered – namely, literature that sympathetically explores the science–religion connection. Top scientists are overwhelmingly nonbelievers, yet the material in a typical Templeton course gives the students the misleading impression that science and religion are in nearly perfect harmony and that disagreements are merely over details. Sound pedagogy is sacrificed, thanks to privately controlled funding.

Third, it is a degrading step down a slippery slope. If religious foundations can fund science and religion courses, then why can racist foundations not fund race and IQ courses? (They already fund racist research.) Even if they do not tell us what the course content must be, their courses give respectability and credence to views that merit neither. (It is a naive educator who believes that students may be presented with rival views and then be left to make up their own minds.) Philanthropy without strings is an unqualified blessing. But when it comes with its own axe to grind, then we had better say no.

To raise funds, many universities have instituted a system of matching grants. If an endowed chair costs, say, $2 million to fund, a donor perhaps need only give $1 million, and the university will provide the rest. But where do these matching funds come from? Usually every university department loses a bit of its budget in order to build up a pool. Do they get it back in the form of an endowed chair? Some do and some do not. The relatively applied and the headline-grabbing fields do rather well by this scheme, but the so-called pure sciences and especially the humanities are being decimated. A matching-funds scheme takes decision-making out of the hands of academics and gives it to donors. We may think that our limited resources should go to, say, Byzantine history or evolutionary biology, but applied research is more likely to be popular with donors, who are now empowered by the matching grants procedure to redirect our limited funds.

We are also asked to prepare our students more directly with the skills needed in the business world. Training in the pure sciences and humanities is taken to be obviously impractical. The government of Ontario, for instance, surveyed recent university graduates with an eye to 'skills matching.' The survey asked to what extent one's education provided the skills used and needed on the job. Dentists reported a 98 per cent match, computer scientists reported 95 per cent, and engineers reported 91 per cent, whereas those in the humanities reported that their education matched the needed job skills only to 55 per cent. I suppose an intimate knowledge of Aristotle's *Metaphysics* does not help decision-making in investment banking. But if we look for specific skills, we miss the real utility of a liberal arts education: the development of general analytic and writing abilities. It is these general skills that make those educated in the liberal arts so valuable to industry, to government, and to the larger community. It is a very short-sighted society that would eliminate this in favour of more applied education.

When Derek Bok was president of Harvard, he warned that strong leadership would be needed to protect our research goals from the eroding effects of commercial concerns. He was right to sound the alarm, but it will take a great deal more than strong leadership in the university. It will require massive government protection and promotion of public knowledge. Patent laws, for instance, must not allow the privatization of the public good. University research must be funded overwhelmingly from the public purse. And the public – rather than corporations or individual scientists (or even secretive governments) – must own the results.

To achieve this, regular academics must take up the cudgels. If they make an organized and concerted effort, academics could bring the current trend to a crashing halt. What can we do?

At the individual level, we can refuse to do contract research that requires non-disclosure and insist on keeping knowledge public. At the university level, we can put pressure on our leading administrators (who will sometimes welcome the support, since they, too, are deeply concerned) to take decision-making power out of the hands of private interests, be they corporate or philanthropic. At the political level, we can pressure government leaders to keep research and education as part of the public good.

It is easy to fall into ideological debate on this issue, with one side upholding public knowledge for the sake of social justice and the other insisting on the value of private initiative and the need to financially reward it. However, there is a better way to view this cluster of issues – namely, in terms of efficiency. The United States is unique among industrialized countries in not having a national health system. Health care is overwhelmingly private and largely in the hands of insurance companies. The cost is approaching 15 per cent of the American gross domestic product, and more than one-quarter of the population is not covered. In contrast, Canada (like most other industrialized countries) has universal coverage at a cost of under 9 per cent of GDP. Aside from the cost, it is hard to compare the relative quality of the health care systems, but one statistic is revealing: cancer patients in Canada live an average of fourteen months longer from the time of detection than those in the United States.

The superiority of public health care is manifestly obvious; it is vastly more efficient, at least when properly funded, which it is currently not in Britain. Although there are disanalogies with research and education, a public health-care system can nevertheless serve as a model for how best to proceed. Why pay royalties to pharmaceutical companies when public research is more efficient? It's cheaper, safer, and better in every way.

Profit-driven medical research in the United States is top notch. Is it the huge profits that make it so? Pure mathematical research in the United States is also top notch, but publicly funded. No one could make a penny from Wiles's proof of Fermat's Last Theorem. Scientists need good salaries and the necessary resources, and they need to have their efforts appreciated. That is more than enough motivation for brilliant, effective science.

I do not for a moment believe we should be living in an ivory tower, indifferent to the world outside. The question is to whom academics should be accountable – to use a favourite term of privatizers. The answer is simple: the public. We owe it to them to keep knowledge free for all.

5 The Factory Model Has No Place on Campus

ANDREW IRVINE

Now that George Bush Sr has received his honorary doctorate from the University of Toronto, is the debate over the corporatization of Canadian universities about to subside? Likely not.

As today's universities face continued government cutbacks, they are being forced to seek alternative sources of funding. This inevitably leads to the corporate sponsorship of everything from library collections to classrooms and this, in turn, leads to debates about academic freedom.

Many believe that donations made to universities, such as those by Barrick Gold Corporation, where Mr Bush serves as an advisor, are no different from the sponsorship of tennis tournaments by tobacco companies: no matter how good the tennis, we know that it is not simply the love of sport that has prompted the donor's generosity. Academic freedom is thus inevitably threatened whenever the objectives of a donor conflict with those of the recipient.

What critics of increased corporate sponsorship fail to recognize is that these same concerns also apply to the current funding of universities by governments. Short of raising endowments large enough to make our universities truly independent, the only real method for guaranteeing academic freedom is to increase the diversification of funding sources. By breaking the funding monopoly, universities become free to decline money from any particular source, whether public or private.

The pressure that a company such as Barrick Gold can exert on a university is insignificant compared to that of government. Having a hundred, or a thousand, such funding sources makes it easier to say No to any one of them.

Universities, by their nature, are pluralistic places. They are populated by a diverse group of characters with a wide variety of opinions. They are where many of us get our first, modest introduction to the breadth of the human condition and to the give and take of ideas. Inevitably, they are the focus of controversy. For all of these reasons and more, they are where many of us choose to devote much of our professional lives.

As the old saying goes, universities have as their purpose the production, promotion, and preservation of knowledge. That is, they are in large measure responsible for society's research, teaching, and archiving. But as the philosopher Alfred North Whitehead observed, 'So far as the mere imparting of information is concerned, no university has had any justification for existence since the popularization of printing in the fifteenth century.' Thus it is the first of these three tasks, the *production* of knowledge, which typically separates universities from other institutions such as schools and libraries.

If the metaphor must be used, universities are society's knowledge factories. For raw materials they depend on the free exchange of often controversial ideas. Hence the fuss that academics typically make about the importance of free speech and academic freedom.

But on this model the modern university is also sometimes seen to be, not just a factory, but a corporation as well. There is a 'CEO' (a university president), who gathers together an 'upper management' (a team of VPs) to set policy. There is a 'middle management' (the deans and department heads), whose job it is to implement this policy. And there are the 'factory men' (the members of faculty), the men and women employed to do the grunt work. Members of the university senate, like the shareholders of most corporations, do little except sit on the sidelines hoping that their stock will go up.

'Short of raising endowments large enough to make our universities truly independent, the only real method for guaranteeing academic freedom is to increase the diversification of funding sources. By breaking the funding monopoly, universities become free to decline money from any particular source, whether public or private.'

Despite its prominence and influence, this model of the university is fundamentally mistaken. If correct, it would mean that students were customers. It would also mean that since collusion between management and consumer makes good business sense, it would make good academic sense as well. Yet this is simply not true.

If we want to preserve the university as a meritocratic institution in which the best ideas of the past three thousand years continue to inform discourse about the central problems of our time, we need to reject the idea that universities are simply factories manufacturing and selling products designed to satisfy whatever the current consumer happens to want. Some model of the university other than that of the corporation is needed.

Even so, rejecting the corporate model of university governance is not a reason to reject corporate funding. For, luckily, there is a second model that is more faithful to the origins of the modern university. On this second model, universities are better understood as arising through an agreement between two communities. On the one hand, there is a community of scholars, the university faculty. On the other, there is society itself, the community at large. Both communities believe they have something of value to offer each other, and in fact this is true. On this view, universities are no more corporations than corporations are universities.

On this model, even with large-scale corporate funding, 'middle and upper management' need not replace the faculty or the citizenry when it comes to setting the university's agenda. Whether the paymasters are public or private, it will be the administration's job only to see that the university has adequate resources, to see that the chalk is in the classroom.

This is not to deny that the issue of academic authority within the modern university is linked to that of funding. But neither is it to accept the view that diversified funding is the problem rather than the solution when it comes to the encouragement of independent thought within our universities.

Congratulations on your new degree, Dr Bush.

6 Civil Liberties, Representative Democracy, Globalization, and Education

STEVEN DAVIS

Globalization comes in many forms. Usually, it is economic and cultural globalization that people have in mind when they discuss with alarm Coca-Cola, General Motors, and Hollywood. But there is also a political form of globalization that appears to be sweeping the globe, a change that should be seen in a positive light. More and more countries are adopting representative democracy as their form of government. Countries without democratic forms of government are now the exception. Education is closely connected to democracy, since it is not possible to have a well-functioning democracy without a politically educated citizenry. Thus the question is, what sort of education should this be? I think an education that teaches students about democracy is necessary, but it is not sufficient, and perhaps it is not the most important part of a democratic education. A just society need not only be democratic, but must also promote and protect civil liberties.

It might seem that representative democracy and civil liberties go hand in hand. However, there is nothing in the nature of representative democracies that guarantees they will protect civil liberties. In a representative democracy, citizens have a limited range of democratic rights. They have the right to vote for representatives – that is, legislators – who are empowered to legislate for the political unit. In some forms of representative democracy, citizens also vote for the chief executive (France and the United States, for example), and for the judiciary (some of the states in the United States – Texas for example). In addition, many representative democracies, like France, Canada, and the United States, have referendums in which citizens can vote directly on what becomes law. In most representative democracies, then, citizens have the following democratic rights: the right to vote in elections and in referendums,

'Part of education in a liberal representative democracy should be civic education ... But knowledge is not enough. Citizens need to develop liberal democratic virtues.'

the right to assemble and to speak on political issues, and (in some jurisdictions) the right to vote for the executive and the judiciary. But nothing in this range of democratic rights entails that a democratic government cannot curtail the rights and freedoms of its citizens. In fact, Western representative governments historically have limited even these democratic rights, especially the right to vote. At different periods and in various countries, women, slaves, Catholics, and Jews have all been excluded from the right to vote. More importantly, there is nothing in the nature of democracy that guarantees citizens their civil liberties, other than the rather limited range of democratic rights listed above. Some democracies have curtailed citizens' civil liberties and continue to do so. In fact, built into democracy is the possibility of the voting majority restricting the rights of a minority – the tyranny of the majority, as it is called.

What then are civil liberties, and how do they differ from democratic rights? Civil liberties, as the name implies, are freedoms that citizens have to speech, movement, privacy, religion, political affiliation, sexual orientation, and so on. But most civil liberties are not intrinsic to representative democracies. There is some confusion about this, since some civil liberties, such as freedom of speech, are regularly recognized as fundamental democratic rights. But freedom of speech as a democratic right is not the same as freedom of speech as a civil liberty. The latter is much broader than the former. Freedom of speech as a democratic right is limited to political speech, whereas freedom of speech as a civil liberty gives citizens the right to express unpopular views on anything from sex to religion.

One way to see the difference between democratic rights and civil liberties is to consider the election of judges. This might seem to be highly democratic. But electing judges puts their selection in the hands of the majority. One of the main tasks of judges is to interpret and uphold the law, including the laws that protect civil liberties and, thus, the rights of minorities. If the majority happens to be opposed to protecting the civil liberties of some minority – for example, homosexuals – they could elect judges who share their prejudices.

In a liberal representative democracy, civil liberties are added to democratic rights, usually as a bill or charter of rights, as in the American, French, and Canadian constitutions. It is, of course, possible for a representative democracy that has such a charter to change or limit citizens' civil liberties by voting to change the constitution, but it is politically very difficult to do so. Amending formulas for constitutions require much more than the simple majority necessary to pass a bill into law. The purpose of constitutionalizing civil liberties is thus to insulate them from the tyranny of the majority, and thus to constrain citizens' democratic right to vote. It puts certain issues beyond the will of the majority. In addition, since governments have an obligation to uphold the constitution of their country, entrenching civil rights in constitutions places an obligation on governments to protect citizens in their exercise of these rights against the interference of others and, more importantly, against the power of government itself.

This now brings us to education. Part of education in a liberal representative democracy should be civic education. Citizens should be given the means to participate politically in liberal democratic societies. To achieve this end, citizens should know about the nature of civil and democratic rights and about the democratic institutions that protect such values. But knowledge is not enough. Citizens need to develop liberal democratic virtues. This means they must value their own civil liberties and democratic rights and, just as importantly, come to respect the rights and liberties of others. Such virtues are not passive. The goal is to form citizens who have a disposition to act to protect both civil liberties and democratic rights.

What does this have to do with globalization? I suggest that as liberal representative democracies become more widespread, the probability of conflict among states will decline. The reason is that as citizens internalize democratic and liberal values, they come to respect the rights and liberties of others, including the rights and liberties of others across national frontiers. This might seem to be obviously false, since both France and Great Britain, while they were liberal representative democracies, built and maintained vast colonial empires – not something that exactly exhibits respect for the rights of others across national borders. But both empires unravelled after the Second World War, in part because the colonized peoples fought heroic wars of independence, but also in part because of the actions of French and British citizens who saw the inconsistency between France and Great Britain having vast empires and their being liberal representative democracies. As Raymond Aaron recognized early in France's conflict with Algeria, France could not hold on to Algeria and at the same time maintain its liberal democratic values. In the United States, during the Vietnam conflict, a great deal of opposition to the war came from American citizens applying their understanding of American civil and democratic rights to Vietnam. Part of the reasoning among the protestors was that if

Americans had the right to choose their own government, so too did the Vietnamese.

Does what I have said here call for a new educational contract? It does. Often civic education consists of dry instruction in the nature of democratic institutions. Although this is necessary, it is not enough. I believe that civil liberties should be at the centre of civic education. As I have pointed out, civic education must develop in citizens a set of liberal democratic values. In addition, a new contract must be forged between the long-established liberal representative democracies and the emerging democracies throughout the world to help the latter introduce liberal and democratic values into their educational institutions. This, I believe, is already under way in many countries – in Eastern Europe, for example, spear-headed by the work of groups such as the Soros Foundation. But much needs to be done in this regard so that men and women throughout the world can live in societies where they are treated with respect for their civil and democratic rights and, thus, live in freedom and security.

Sources and Credits

I. Science and the Environment

Paul M. Churchland, 'Expanding Our Perspective,' *Matter and Consciousness*, rev. ed. (Cambridge, MA: MIT Press, 1988), 167–77 (copyright © Massachusetts Institute of Technology, 1988); Andrew Irvine, 'Is It Time for a New Space Race?' (new for this volume); Thomas Hurka, 'Should We Implant Life on Mars?' *Globe and Mail*, 4 December 1990; Jan Zwicky, 'Wilderness and Agriculture,' in Sean Virgo, ed., *The Eye in the Thicket* (Saskatoon: Thistledown, 2002), 187–97; Trudy Govier, 'Murdering Trees?' (new for this volume); Jeffrey Foss, 'The Environmentalist Faith,' *The Ring* (University of Victoria), 21 January 2000, 5, and 'Do Environmentalists Ever Go Too Far?' CBC Radio-Canada Commentary, 29 March 2000 (abridged); Ian Hacking, *Representing and Intervening* (Cambridge: Cambridge University Press, 1983), 150, 220, 229–30 (abridged; reprinted with the permission of Cambridge University Press); James Robert Brown, 'Afterword,' *Who Rules in Science?* (Cambridge, Mass.: Harvard University Press, 2001), 207–12 (abridged; reprinted by permission of the publisher from *Who Rules in Science? An Opinionated Guide to the Wars* by James Robert Brown, 207–12, Cambridge, Mass.: Harvard University Press, copyright © 2001 by the President and Fellows of Harvard College); Andrew Irvine, 'Is Scientific Progress Inevitable?' (new for this volume).

II. Mind, Intelligence, and the New Technologies

Patricia Smith Churchland, 'From Descartes to Neural Networks,' *Scientific American*, July 1989, 118 (reprinted with permission, copyright © 1989 by Scientific American, Inc.; all rights reserved); Patricia Smith Churchland, 'How Do Neurons Know?' *Daedalus* 133, no. 1 (winter, 2004), 42–50 (abridged;

III. Education and Culture

IV. The Contemporary World

V. Authority and the Individual

Trudy Govier, 'What Is Government For?' (new for this volume); Andrew Irvine, 'Making Governments Compete for Our Dollars,' *Victoria Times Colonist*, 14 July 2003, A7; Mark Kingwell, 'Where My Rights End – and Yours Begin,' *National Post*, 27 November 2002, A18; Jan Narveson, 'Guns' (new for this volume); John Russell, 'Religion Isn't on Trial,' *Globe and Mail*, 14 June 2002, A17; Thomas Hurka, 'Do Children Have Rights?' *Globe and Mail*, 23 October 1990; Thomas Hurka, 'A Market Economy Makes Us Better People,' *Globe and Mail*, 16 July 1991; Andrew Irvine, 'Questions for the Census Takers,' *Victoria Times Colonist*, 28 May 2001, A6; Andrew Irvine, 'A Four-Year Elected Dictatorship,' *National Post*, 07 November 2000, A19.

VI. Free Speech

Andrew Irvine, 'President's Message,' *Democratic Commitment* 32, no. 4 (March 1999), 7–9; John Dixon, 'The Porn Wars,' in John Russell, ed., *Liberties* (Vancouver: New Star Books, 1989), 24–9, reprinted from *Democratic Commitment* 20, no 1, March 1986, 1–4; John Dixon, 'The Bessie Smith Factor,' in John Russell, ed., *Liberties* (Vancouver: New Star Books, 1989), 13–23, reprinted from *Democratic Commitment* 21, no. 2, March 1987, 1–6; John Russell, 'Words Matter' (new for this volume); Andrew Irvine, 'When Liberty Loses Out,' *Vancouver Sun*, 2 March 2000, A19 (abridged); Andrew Irvine, 'PM Should Apologize to Protesters,' *Toronto Star*, 15 August 2001, A21, and 'It's Time for the Prime Minister to Take Some Responsibility,' *Democratic Commitment* 35, no. 2, November 2001, 7–8 (abridged); Stan Persky, 'Big, Bad Ideas? No Big Deal,' *Vancouver Sun*, 3 February 2001, E21 (revised).

VII. Reverse Discrimination

Thomas Hurka, 'Why Equality Doesn't Mean Treating Everyone the Same,' *Globe and Mail*, 3 December 1991; Leo Groarke, 'Hidden Meanings: Employment Equity Arguments Are Cloaked in Doublespeak,' *Kitchener-Waterloo Record*, 24 July 1992, A7; Thomas Hurka, 'Affirmative Action: More Radical Arguments,' *Globe and Mail*, 30 January 1990; Leo Groarke, 'Affirmative Action, Women and "the 50% Solution,"' *Policy Options* 14, no. 4 (May 1993), 31–4; Grant Brown, '"Fixing" What Ain't Broken,' *Policy Options* 14, no. 2 (March 1993), 8–13 (abridged); Graeme Hunter, 'It's Affirmative Action and It's Bad for Universities and Students,' *Ottawa Citizen*, 28 February 2001, A17; Grant Brown, 'The Curious Case of Country C' (new for this volume).

VIII. Life and Death

Graeme Hunter, 'Taking the Prime Minister at His Word,' *Catholic Challenge*, February 1999, 23; Thomas Hurka, 'Abortion and the Moral Standing of the Fetus,' *Globe and Mail*, 31 October 1989; Thomas Hurka, 'Does Surrogate Motherhood Treat Babies and Women Like Commodities?' *Globe and Mail*, 27 March 1990; Thomas Hurka, 'If Feminists Are Pro-Choice, Why Don't They Honour Women's Choices Consistently?' *Globe and Mail*, 14 May 1991; John Russell and Andrew Irvine, 'A Rose Is a Rose, but Clones Will Differ,' *Vancouver Sun*, 4 March 1998, A13; Arthur Schafer, 'Human Stem Cell Cloning: How Slippery Is the Slippery Slope,' *Winnipeg Free Press*, 15 August 2004, B4; Susan Sherwin, 'Feminism, Ethics and Cancer,' *Humane Medicine* 10, no. 4 (October 1994), 282–90 (abridged); Arthur Schafer, 'Cracking Down on Medical Trials,' *Toronto Star*, 27 September 2004, A21; Eike-Henner W. Kluge, 'Physicians, Limited Resources, and Liability,' *Canadian Medical Association Journal*, 155 (1996), 778–9 (reprinted from *CMAJ* with permission of the publisher, © 1996 Canadian Medical Association); Eike-Henner W. Kluge, 'Informed Consent by Children: The New Reality,' *Canadian Medical Association Journal* 152 (1995), 1495–7 (reprinted from *CMAJ* with permission of the publisher, © 1995 Canadian Medical Association); Alister Browne, 'Robert and Tracy Latimer,' *Health Ethics Today* 12, no. 1 (2001), 12–13; John Russell and Andrew Irvine, 'Mercy Killing: The Deep Divide,' *Vancouver Sun*, 11 December 1997, A21; Leslie Burkholder, 'Nancy B and Nancy F,' *Journal of Applied Philosophy* 18, no. 2 (2001), 193–6; Thomas Hurka, 'Is Death Really All That Bad for You?' *Globe and Mail*, 7 May 1991.

IX. National Unity

Michel Seymour, 'If Quebecers Say No, It Will Be Clearly Out of Fear,' *Montreal Gazette*, 21 October 1995; Michel Seymour, 'La souveraineté du Québec: un objectif légitime,' *L'action nationale*, May 1997 (translated and abridged); John Russell and Andrew Irvine, 'Unity Poses Questions Already Answered,' *Vancouver Sun*, 6 January 1998, A11; John Russell and Andrew Irvine, 'A Unity Referendum to End All Referendums,' *Vancouver Sun*, 25 February 1998, A15; Michel Seymour, 'The "Clarity" Bill in Retrospect' (new for this volume); Paul Groarke, 'Looking for a Legal Solution,' *Kitchener-Waterloo Record*, 28 March 1998, and 'Leading the Way,' *Kitchener-Waterloo Record*, 4 September 1998 (abridged); Will Kymlicka, 'An Ethnic Stitch in Time: Minorities and the State,' *Globe and Mail*, 27 December 2000, A15;

Will Kymlicka, 'The Paradox of Liberal Nationalism,' *Literary Review of Canada* 4, no. 10 (November 1995), 13–15 (abridged); Thomas Hurka, 'Canadian Nationalism and the Distinctiveness Fetish,' *Globe and Mail*, 11 May 1996.

X. 9/11 and After

Andrew Irvine, 'Being True to Ourselves in Times of Crisis,' *Victoria Times Colonist*, 17 September 2001, A9; Trudy Govier, 'Vulnerability,' in *A Delicate Balance: What Philosophy Can Teach Us about Terrorism* (Boulder, CO: Westview Press, 2002), 1–9 (abridged); John Dixon, 'Repeat of McCarthy Era Would Imperil Democracy,' *Vancouver Sun*, 27 September 2001, A15; Graeme Hunter, 'Evil's Back – Now Let's Recover True and False' (new for this volume); Mark Kingwell, 'Freedom, Not Security, Is Fundamental,' *National Post*, 24 October 2001, A12; John Russell, 'Zap! You're a Terrorist,' *Xtra West* 217, 13 December 2001, 14; John Russell, 'A Slogan for Our Times,' *Vancouver Sun*, 25 November 2003; John Dixon, 'President's Report,' *Democratic Commitment* 36, no. 3 (March 2003), 4; Trudy Govier, 'Kindness,' in *A Delicate Balance: What Philosophy Can Teach Us about Terrorism* (Boulder, CO: Westview Press, 2002), 103–10; John Ralston Saul, 'Normal Behaviour,' *On Equilibrium* (Toronto: Penguin/ Viking, 2001), 317–29 (from *On Equilibrium* by John Ralston Saul, copyright © John Ralston Saul, 2001 reprinted by permission of Penguin Group [Canada]).

XI. Happiness and Morality

Thomas Hurka, 'Should Morality Be a Struggle? Ancient vs Modern Ideas about Ethics,' *Globe and Mail*, 11 June 1990; Thomas Hurka, 'Why God Is Irrelevant to Morality,' *Globe and Mail*, 20 March 1990; Alister Browne, 'The Prime Directive,' *Philosophy Now* 39, December 2002–January 2003, 52–54; Graeme Hunter, 'Monstrous Acts Distort Reality,' *Ottawa Citizen*, 6 December 1995, A13; Arthur Schafer, 'Tsunami Ethics: Jillian's Choice,' *Globe and Mail*, 8 January 2005, F2; Thomas Hurka, 'Is There Such a Thing as Moral Luck?' *Globe and Mail*, 10 April 1990; Katharine Browne and Alister Browne, 'Why Animals Deserve Rights,' *Animal Writes: Vancouver Humane Society Newsletter* 29 (Summer 2004), 10; Jan Narveson, 'Do Animals Have Rights?' (new for this volume); Leo Groarke, 'On a Pedestal,' *Kitchener-Waterloo Record*, 18 February 1998, A9; John Russell, 'We Yearn for a Sense of Order, but ...,' *Vancouver Sun*, 1 April 1998, A13; Thomas Hurka, 'Pleasure Alone Won't Make You Happy,' *Globe and Mail*, 13 February 1990; John Russell, 'Love Is all You Need to Understand Christmas,' *Vancouver Sun*, 23 December 1998, A13.

XII. The Changing University

Graeme Hunter, 'Town, Gown, and the Long Way Down,' *Gravitas* 4, no. 1 (spring 1997), 9–10; Andrew Irvine, 'Are University Faculty Unnecessary?' (new for this volume); Lou Marinoff, 'The PC Tyranny,' *Philosophers' Magazine* 14, Spring 2001, 47–9 (www.philosophers.co.uk) (reprinted by permission of *The Philosophers' Magazine*); James Robert Brown, 'Privatizing the University: The New Tragedy of the Commons,' *Science* 290, no. 5497 (1 December 2000), 1701–2 (reprinted with permission from *Science*; copyright © 2000 AAAS); Andrew Irvine, 'Factory Model Has No Place on Campus,' Ottawa Citizen, 9 December 1997, A13; Steven Davis, 'Libertés civiques, démocratie répresentative, mondialisation et éducation,' *Le défi de l'education mondial: Actes du collouque de Paris* (Paris: Les Canadiens en Europe, 2001), vol. 2, 110–13 (in translation).

Name Index